Cruising the
Mediterranean
A Guide to the Ports of Call

Larry H. Ludmer

HUNTER

HUNTER PUBLISHING, INC,
130 Campus Drive, Edison, NJ 08818
☎ 732-225-1900; ☎ 800-255-0343; Fax 732-417-1744
www.hunterpublishing.com
comments@hunterpublishing.com

4176 Saint-Denis
Montréal, Québec, Canada
☎ 514-843-9447

The Boundary, Wheatley Road, Garsington
Oxford, OX44 9EJ England
☎ 01865-361122; Fax 01865-361133

ISBN 1-58843-285-8
© 2002 Larry H. Ludmer

Cover photo: Mykonos at Sunset, Cyclades, Greece
© Vladpans / eStock Photo

Maps by Kim André © 2002 Hunter Publishing, Inc.

1 2 3 4

www.hunterpublishing.com

Hunter's full range of guides to all corners of the globe is featured on our exciting website. You'll find guidebooks to suit every type of traveler, no matter what their budget, lifestyle, or idea of fun.

Adventure Guides – There are now over 40 titles in this series, covering destinations from Costa Rica and the Yucatán to Tampa Bay & Florida's West Coast, Puerto Rico and the Alaska Highway. They offer complete information on what to do, as well as where to stay and eat. *Adventure Guides* are tailor-made for the active traveler, with a focus on hiking, biking, canoeing, horseback riding, trekking, skiing, watersports, and every other kind of fun.

Alive Guides – This ever-popular line of books takes a unique look at the best each destination offers: fine dining, jazz clubs, first-class class hotels and resorts. In-margin icons direct the reader at a glance. Top-sellers include: *The Cayman Islands, St. Martin & St. Barts,* and *Aruba, Bonaire & Curaçao.*

Our *Romantic Weekends* guidebooks provide a series of escapes for couples of all ages and lifestyles. Unlike most "romantic" travel books, ours cover more than charming hotels and delightful restaurants, with a host of activities that you and your partner will remember forever.

One-of-a-kind travel books available from Hunter include *Best Dives of the Western Hemisphere; The Artichoke Trail; Golf Resorts; The Jewish Travel Guide* and many more.

Full descriptions are given for each book on our website, along with reviewers' comments and a cover image. Books may be purchased on-line via our secure transaction facility.

e-books

Hunter travel guides are also available as e-books in a variety of digital formats through our on-line partners, including Amazon.com, BarnesandNoble.com and eBooks.com.

Acknowledgments

No author can write a travel guide without the assistance of others. The sheer volume of facts that must be amassed requires that other people get involved. Many of the ship facts (including itinerary information) were provided by the media relations staff of the cruise lines. I am grateful for the special help provided by (in alphabetic order) Desia Bacon, Royal Caribbean Cruises; Margie Benzigek, Star Clippers; Katy Gewartowski, Silversea; Sara Johnston, Windstar; Karen Kopta, First European Cruises; Darren Oster and Lorraine Sorrentino, Costa Cruises; Rosie Perri, Royal Olympic Cruise Line; and Denise Seomin, Princess Cruises. Their role in providing information in no way affects what I have to say about a particular ship, its itineraries or a cruise line in general. Opinions expressed here are based on information gathered from a variety of objective sources and, most importantly, by firsthand experience.

Just as you will most likely obtain valuable information from an experienced travel agent, so did I. Therefore, a large thanks also goes to Jeffrey Pressner and the entire staff of CruiseAholics, a Las Vegas-based cruise-only travel agency who provided special assistance.

Contents

Preface

This book is intended to serve as an information source for planning as well as a cruise companion to the many Mediterranean-bound travelers ready to discover the best of what this historic and beautiful region has to offer. It will enable both first-time and experienced cruise travelers to determine the particular cruise that's right for them and, once the cruising has begun, to get the most enjoyment from their time on board and ashore.

Experienced travelers rarely get their information from one source, and I wouldn't expect that you would so limit yourself. If a particular destination is of great interest to you, do further research and perhaps buy a guidebook to that destination only. As you peruse this book you'll learn that a host of cruise lines serve the Mediterranean. I encourage everyone to visit their local travel agent and grab a stack of brochures from the cruise lines. In combination with the information in this book, they will further help you decide which ship is right for you. Always remember, however, that glossy brochures are carefully designed to get your business. Be a thoughtful consumer.

Enjoy your Mediterranean vacation!

The World of Mediterranean Cruising

Cruise Popularity

The popularity of cruising has increased dramatically in the last couple of decades, and especially during the last 10 years. New cruise ships are launched into service each year – there were 80 new liners during the 1990s and it is anticipated that another 50 will be introduced over the next five years. Ships that are less than 10 years old now represent a higher proportion of all the cruise ships in service than at any time in the past. The great majority of these vessels are in the luxurious "mega-liner" category. They're bigger (capacities of more than 3,000 passengers per ship will soon be common) and even more spectacular than anything that has come before them. These new ships are built in response to an increased interest in cruise vacations and they also stimulate even more interest. If you've been on a cruise, you already understand their appeal. If you're planning your first cruise vacation, you've got a lot to look forward to!

Cruising has many advantages, especially for foreign travel. Virtually everything is planned for you by experts. You could, with minimal research, purchase a cruise tour and have a marvelous time. That's great for the many travelers who don't feel comfortable doing their own planning. Yet, as you'll see in the pages of this book, there is plenty of opportunity for those who want to be more involved in the decision-making process.

The cost of a cruise vacation may seem especially high at first. But you'll soon see that your fare includes the overwhelming proportion of expenses that will be encountered during your trip, making your vacation surprisingly affordable.

Cruises combine the best aspects of a land-based vacation – sightseeing, interesting destinations, entertainment, etc. – with the luxurious atmosphere, fine dining and numerous recreational facilities of a cruise liner. It is little wonder that cruise popularity continues to reach all-time highs year after year.

Over six million Americans now take a cruise each year.

Almost 12% of all cruise passengers travel on lines that are members of the **Cruise Lines International Association (CLIA)** and choose the Mediterranean as their destination. That includes about three-quarters of a million Americans. The "Med" is now the second-largest cruising destination after the long-established Caribbean market. The region has many attractions. The countries bordering the Mediterranean Sea have the lure of sunny beaches and a pleasant climate. The lively cities and resorts here are among the most famous in the world. Plus, countless historic treasures that span the time-line of Western civilization are open for visits.

A Survey of the Mediterranean

*T*he Mediterranean region encompasses the area covered by the Mediterranean Sea and all (or at least part of) the nations that surround it.

Geographically Speaking

The Mediterranean Sea stretches for nearly 2,400 miles from the ancient Pillars of Hercules between modern day Gibraltar and Morocco in the west to the shores of Israel in the east. At its widest point, it measures about 1,000 miles, although it is more commonly just 400 to 600 miles across. Covering approximately 970,000 square miles, the Mediterranean is the seventh-largest body of water in the world. The only bigger fish ponds are the four oceans, the South China Sea and the Caribbean Sea. The latter is only about 2,300 square miles larger than the Mediterranean. The name Mediterranean comes from Latin and means "the middle land." Given its location between three continents (Europe, Africa and Asia), that is a most appropriate title.

The Mediterranean is almost entirely landlocked. The narrow Strait of Gibraltar that defines its western-most limits allows access to the Atlantic Ocean. At the other end, the Mediterranean is connected to the Black Sea by a nearly 200-mile-long waterway through Turkey comprised of the Dardanelles, the Sea of Marmara and the Bosporus. Geographically, the Black and Mediterranean seas are hard to separate. Many people, including some scholars, consider the Black Sea to be a part of the Mediterranean. But true geographers scoff at that view. Besides the Strait of Gibraltar there is only one other outlet to the ocean, the man-made Suez Canal, which crosses the Isthmus of Suez and provides access to the Indian Ocean via the Red Sea.

The Mediterranean has several "arms" that go by other names and that are large enough to be called seas in their own right. These are the **Tyrrhennian Sea**, the **Adriatic Sea**, the **Aegean Sea** and the **Ionian Sea**. These are shown on the map on page 17. Two other seas in the region are the **Ligurian Sea** (bordered by the French and Italian Rivieras) and the **Balearic Sea** (between Spain and the Balearic Islands). Amid these seas are hundreds of islands; Sicily, Sardinia, Corsica and Cyprus are the largest.

The Mediterranean has an average depth of just 4,900 feet. However, off the coast of Greece is an area that measures 16,000 feet. Interestingly, the sea is notably saltier than the adjacent Atlantic Ocean. This is due mainly to the warm and relatively dry climate, which causes accelerated evaporation.

The Mediterranean was created by the action of plate tectonics – specifically, the movement of the adjacent Eurasian and African plates. To this day, it is still a hotbed of geological activity and earthquakes are a constant potential threat. In addition, there are also quite a few active or dormant volcanos, the greatest concentration of which is found in southern Italy and the island of Sicily.

Man & the Mediterranean

The history of this region *is*, in many ways, the history of Western civilization. Successive powerful empires and states rose and fell here, shaping the destiny of the world as we know it. The four most important were Egypt, Greece, Phoenicia and Rome. The Roman name for the Mediterranean was *Mare Nostrum*, meaning "our sea," and the entire region was under their rule for centuries. Indeed, historians refer to the Mediterranean as a "Roman lake," implying total control by the Romans. Since the fall of the Roman Empire the region has been comprised of many different nations, some world powers, others mere pawns in the chess game of world diplomacy and conflict.

The 21st-century map is far more complicated, with no fewer than 15 nations bordering the waters of the Mediterranean. (That figure doesn't include countries bordering the Black Sea, or the sovereign Mediterranean island states of Malta and Cyprus, or even adjacent countries like Portugal, which is often a port of call.) Here's the lineup. The north shore (Europe) has Spain, France, Italy, Croatia, Montenegro, Serbia, Albania and Greece. In Asia are Turkey, Syria, Lebanon and Israel; while the North African states are Egypt, Libya,

Tunisia and Morocco. Fortunately, most of the Mediterranean is more peaceful than it has been since the *Pax Romana* (Roman Peace of ancient times), but one look at the Middle East and you know that the Mediterranean still has its danger zones.

The Mediterranean has been fought over by nations for thousands of years. Ethnic and religious differences are only part of the story. Since ancient times the sea has been a vital lifeline for trade and commerce, and whoever dominated the sea links through the Mediterranean was a world power. Although the consequences of this ongoing battle were often tragic, it makes a visit to today's Mediterranean a living history lesson.

The Way to See the Mediterranean

Unless you have a year to roam, it's impossible to fully explore the wonders of the Mediterranean nations on one trip. Wise travelers pick what interests them most and figure out the best way to see those sights. The Mediterranean Sea provides access to much of the region, so a cruise vacation is a wonderful way to explore, even if the cruise experience *per se* is not what you're looking for. Of course, you can enjoy the ship and its luxuries too.

I don't work for the cruise lines, so while the brochures from those lines may present an idyllic look at the world of Mediterranean cruising, I'll present you with a more objective and balanced picture. There are advantages and disadvantages, and I intend to assist in your decisions as you plan your trip.

Advantages of Mediterranean Cruising

A cruise is essentially a complete package vacation, with an allowance for you do your own thing at ports of call, as well as before and after the cruise. It's great if you don't like to plan all the details of a comprehensive vacation, especially an overseas vacation, which generally requires more work than to a US destination. As long as you sail with a cruise line catering primarily to Americans (or at least English-speaking travelers, which is what this book will focus on), then you needn't worry about language problems, foreign food that might not agree with you, or having to get around on your own in strange surroundings. Of course, you will encounter some of those issues while in port, but the potential pitfalls will be minimized. By opting for the cruise line's pre-arranged excursions, your Mediterranean trip should be free of such uncomfortable situations.

Cruise lines like to boast that they actually save you money over land vacations because you don't have separate additional costs for hotels, food and so on. This is only partially true. If you like to stay at very expensive hotels and dine in the finest restaurants, then you may consider a cruise an absolute bargain. But although there are a variety of cruise price categories, there aren't any "budget" cruises.

Disadvantages of Mediterranean Cruising

If you have determined that a cruise is within your means, you should next consider the major shortcomings of seeing the Mediterranean by sea. Cruising is slow (even though cruise ships have the advantage of usually traveling during the night), and a two-week cruise, for example, simply cannot cover much ground. This restriction may be acceptable if you want to see only a few places during your trip. Which leads to the next major shortcoming – time allowed on shore.

Cruise liners stay between five and 12 hours at most ports of call. If they stay longer, the extra hours are either in the evening or very early in the morning, when attractions are not open. This limited time allotment is fine for small towns and other "specialized" ports of call, such as ancient historic sites or resort islands, but it can present a problem when visiting larger cities that are frequently on the cruise itinerary. In rare cases, you'll stay 1½ to two days in port, but this is the exception. One way to solve this problem is to find a cruise that begins and/or ends in a large city. You can then add days at either or both ends of your cruise.

Types of Cruises

Most Mediterranean cruises have common features (and common ports of call), but the available variety may come as a big surprise. Mediterranean cruises can be as short as three or four days and range up to two weeks or longer in some cases. However, the majority last between seven and 10 days (a seven-day cruise is the most common). Every cruise line gives a different name to each of their cruises (or category of cruises), but these generally fall into two basic types – trips that aim to travel the entire Mediterranean region and those that concentrate on a specific area.

Grand Mediterranean Cruises

These cruises try to cover the most territory possible. They are at least a week long and often extend from 10 days to as much as 18 days, a time frame necessary to traverse the entire length of the Mediterranean Sea. Most often, they stop at what the cruise line considers to be the most important ports. The list of ports in Grand Mediterranean cruises varies a great deal from one line to another, and from ship to ship depending on departure date. If you are considering this type of cruise, view the list and choose an itinerary that covers those destinations.

Because of the large distances covered, Grand cruises include some days spent entirely at sea; you don't stop at any port. If you love to be on the ocean, this can be an advantage. But if you're primarily interested in exploring points of interest on land, days at sea may be hard to appreciate. This type of cruise is a good introduction to the region and may be especially well suited to those who want to see the variety of countries, or one who expects to do this only once. Repeat cruisers may want to take in as much possible on their first cruise, with an eye to returning in order to explore specific areas.

In general, Grand Mediterranean cruises are more commonly offered on the larger, more luxurious ships. However, if you look around, you can find smaller ships doing virtually the same thing.

Area Cruises

The biggest number of cruises, especially those lasting only around a week, concentrate on a particular region. They generally spend a much higher percentage of time in port and do the majority of their port-to-port sailing overnight. For those who want to maximize shore time, these cruises are definitely better. The smaller the ship, the more likely that it will cover a more limited geographic itinerary. This is especially true in the case of sailing ships and luxury yachts. Area cruises can often be divided into two or three major sub-categories.

⚓ WESTERN MEDITERRANEAN: Covers Spain's coast and Mediterranean islands or the French Riviera, or a combination of both. May also include some North African ports in Morocco and some of the islands off the North African coast that are part of Spain or Portugal. The central Mediterranean is generally covered too, including the west coast of the Italian peninsula and the islands of

Sicily, Sardinia and Malta. The eastern Italian coast incorporates Venice, and many cruises will also stop at some ports on the Adriatic, such as Dubrovnik.

⚓ EASTERN MEDITERRANEAN: The most popular itineraries cover Greece, the Greek Islands and the Aegean portion of Turkey, including Istanbul. Extensions go into the Black Sea. Alternative eastern Mediterranean destinations will include Israel, Egypt and parts of North Africa. Many of the longer eastern area cruises combine different sections of this sub-region, especially the Adriatic.

⚓ CENTRAL MEDITERRANEAN: While western and eastern Mediterranean are terms that the cruise lines frequently use, you will also occasionally see *Central Mediterranean* itineraries. The central area definitely overlaps with these categories above, and generally covers both coasts of Italy, the central islands of Malta and Sicily and North Africa around Tunisia.

These borders are general, designed to give you an idea of coverage. Even shorter regional cruises can, depending upon their departure and ending ports, go into more than one of the regions as I have defined them. Regardless of area covered, the ship *itineraries* will also fall into one of three basic categories. The first includes those ships that have a different itinerary on almost every sailing. Another group of ships travels the same itinerary, offering east-to-west or west-to-east sailings. The final category piggy-backs two or more trips. That is, a cruise from Port A to Port B is followed by a cruise from Port B to Port C. Only Port B is common to the two trips. This is ideal if you want to combine two week-long sailings into a longer voyage. All itineraries are subject to change.

Setting Priorities

The Best Ship vs. the Best Itinerary

Deciding which ship meets your needs will be based on a number of factors.

Cruise Lines

You may feel that one or more cruise lines are better than the others based on previous cruising experience or comments from other travelers. It has been my experience that all of the major lines do an excellent job. It is their styles that vary, and that can make a big difference on a personal level.

Itineraries

Consider the length of the cruise and the ports of call. For the true explorer (as opposed to those who are primarily interested in taking a cruise), this is the most important decision. This book gives you details about the attractions/sights offered on each cruise. Shore excursions should also be included as part of the itinerary (these are discussed on page 135).

The Ship

People expect to be able to say, without a doubt, that their ship was gorgeous. The look and feel of a ship is of paramount importance to experienced cruisers and even most first-timers. In the pages that follow you'll find detailed information about each ship. As you choose your vessel, you'll soon discover that many factors come into play, including such things as the nature of the cuisine, dining formality, special accommodations for the disabled, activities for children, to name just a few. Larger ships generally offer more activities and facilities than smaller ships. On longer cruises, they may alleviate the feeling of being stuck in a small area. But unless large ships are well designed and managed, you may experience long lines for meals and for getting ashore. Large ships are sometimes too large to dock and guests often have to be run into port by tender. This can be fun, initially, but a combination of long lines and an often bouncy tender ride can become tiresome. For those with some physical disability, tender rides can be difficult.

Also, tender service may be necessary no matter what size ship you are on. Limited port facilities, the amount of port traffic, and the weather all affect port access.

Cost

How much you pay for a cruise is determined largely by the three factors listed above. For many people, getting the best buy is the other most important consideration.

Cruise Lines Serving the Mediterranean

*M*ore than 30 companies operate various types of Mediterranean cruises, the vast majority of which are traditional cruise lines that feature motorized cruise ships. Their vessels range from mid-sized or smaller (mostly older vessels) to the increasingly large luxury mega-liner category. Most of these cruise companies are American- or European-owned, and we've included only ships on which the average American traveler will feel comfortable. The European ships profiled in this book commonly carry American passengers and have crews that speak good English, even if it might be a second language. I have deliberately excluded the few lines that cater to specific nationalities (other than American and English). I've also profiled some lines (such as Costa or Mediterranean Shipping Cruises) that have a large percentage of European passengers, with the knowledge that Americans will not feel out of place on their vessels.

See *More Cruising Choices*, page 14, concerning those cruise lines whose ships and itineraries will not be evaluated.

Ships in the **luxury yacht line** category carry fewer than 400 passengers and have a style that is more in keeping with a yacht than a traditional cruise ship.

Sailing ships make a small, unique group. The hallmark of vessels in this last category is highly personalized service. These ships are quite a bit more expensive than the regular cruise ships, even though they are significantly slower.

A number of **tour operators** can book you directly onto a specific yacht in the Mediterranean. This is particularly common to trips in the Aegean islands and along the Turquoise Coast of Turkey. The ships they use are much smaller than the traditional cruise ships and luxury yachts I profile in this book, and I have opted not to include them because they offer an entirely different type of experience.

Another option here is **port-to-port** travel, which has been a fixture of this region's transportation system for centuries. Although not as common as it once was, you can still make your way from port to port by local ferry services. Trips take anywhere from a few hours to overnight. The ships are not luxury standard by any means (some are downright bad) and schedules are often erratic. Even when the service is reliable, the frequency is such that you'll generally find yourself wasting a lot of valuable time waiting. The most extensive ferry system connects Athens' port of Piraeus with the Greek islands and is a viable alternative for the budget traveler. Among other ferries that can be used for this mini-cruise approach are services that connect many of the major Mediterranean islands (including Corsica, Sardinia, and the Spanish Balearic Islands) with the mainland.

Traditional Cruise Lines

Almost every major cruise line familiar to American travelers is well represented in the Mediterranean cruise sector. The only significant exception is Carnival Cruises, although they may also enter the scene in the future.

Celebrity Cruises

Celebrity's nine-ship fleet has some of the most awesome new mega-liners. The level of luxury and variety of facilities they offer is staggering. Their Mediterranean itineraries are run by several ships which visit a dozen different ports. Celebrity is a subsidiary of Royal Caribbean, although the two operations are treated very much as separate entities. Savvy world travelers generally consider Celebrity a notch or two higher than Royal Caribbean in all aspects, especially service.

Costa Cruises

"Cruising Italian style" is more than a simple advertising slogan at Costa, one of the most popular European-operated lines and also one of the oldest. Costa has a fleet of eight ships in a variety of styles. A few of the older and smaller ships aren't quite up to the luxury standards found in most of today's mega-liners, but the newer vessels certainly don't take a back seat. Costa's sizable fleet serves more than 30 ports in the Mediterranean. Its clientele is primarily European, but there are plenty of Americans too. The popular *Costa Allegra* will not be in the Mediterranean for the 2002 season.

Crystal Cruises

A consistent award-winner among the large cruise lines, Crystal has a fine reputation for its fabulous ships and outstanding service. However, it's currently offering only one ship (out of its two-ship fleet) in the Mediterranean. A new vessel is under construction and should be in service by early summer 2003. Whether that ship will be assigned to the Mediterranean has yet to be decided.

Cunard

This famous luxury British line has operated some of the best known vessels in the history of cruising. It still caters to the upscale traveler and is noted for its fine service and British feel. Surprisingly, Cunard's Mediterranean service is somewhat limited in terms of both ships and itineraries. Right now, it has only two ships here, with another coming in 2003.

First European Cruises

This line is little-known in American cruising circles, but it has a good reputation in Europe for well-designed tours at reasonable prices. Although the company goes by the name "First European" in the States, it is known in Europe as **Festival Cruises**. Until recently, most of the fleet was older, smaller and less luxurious, but general upgrades are being made that will bring the ships up to par with the rest of the cruise world. First European introduced stunning new ships in 1999 and 2001, and an additional ship will go into service in 2002. More ships are planned for the near future. The best ships are characterized as "Premium" vessels, while all the others have been designated as "Discovery" ships. The *Bolero*, one of the older ships, is currently on charter service, but it may yet be put back into regular cruise service. It is a small ship that is quite similar to the *Azur*, which is profiled in detail in the following section.

Fred. Olsen Cruise Lines

This is a Norwegian company (the "Fred." is short for Frederik), but the style is as British – and maybe even more British – as you would find on Cunard. Americans will feel comfortable. The ships of Fred. Olsen aren't particularly large, and some travelers prefer the more intimate atmosphere this creates. Unfortunately, Olsen's ships offer a lower level of luxury than most competing vessels listed here. This is especially true of their original two ships, *Black Prince* and *Black Watch*. They have recently acquired a better ship, *Braemar*.

Holland America Line

HAL is one of the world's largest and oldest cruise lines, with plenty of experience in the field. Although it has four ships in European service, only three are currently plying the waters of the Mediterranean. Holland America has a loyal following and is known for a high level of service. Even its newest ships tend to have classic lines. Although modernizations and upgrades have been accommodated by HAL, many people are attracted by what they consider traditional ship travel.

Mediterranean Shipping Cruises

This Italian-run company has three ships of varying sizes, all smaller than most ships in use by the major lines. The vessels are somewhat older and, although nice, don't offer the same high level of luxury as the new mega-liners. MSC has been in business for a long time and knows the cruise business. Passenger manifests sport names from around the globe and it actively seeks American travelers.

Norwegian Cruise Line

NCL has a reputation for providing an affordable first-class cruise. Although definitely not near the top level of luxury, its cruises compare favorably with some of the more upscale lines. NCL currently has two beautiful and thoroughly modern vessels serving the Mediterranean cruise market.

Orient Cruise Line

This company is a subsidiary of Norwegian Cruise Lines and its three-ship fleet focuses on destination-oriented cruises. It isn't a big or even well-known line, but Orient has received consistently high marks from a number of credible sources for providing quality vacation experiences at moderate prices.

Princess Cruises

The original "Love Boat" line, Princess is the second-largest cruise ship company in the world (and will be the largest if its proposed merger with Royal Caribbean goes through). Its spectacular fleet – which is still growing rapidly – consists almost entirely of new mega-liners. Its "Grand Class" cruising features some of the largest ships afloat, along with a host of amenities and special services as part of the "Personal Choice" cruising program. Princess has never been well represented in the Mediterranean and, until recently, its selection of ships here was not the best of the fleet. Bigger and newer ships are now being introduced to the Mediterranean.

Renaissance Cruises

This line filed for bankruptcy in late 2001, although it is conceivable that it will re-emerge with new funding. Check their website (www. renaissancecruises.com or call ☎ 877-549-1124 for the current status. When in operation, the 10 ships of this luxury cruise line all carried fewer than 700 passengers and were favored by cruisers who enjoy the intimate setting. Two of their ships were in the luxury yacht category. Renaissance vessels provided a fairly high level of luxury for a reasonable price.

Royal Caribbean International

Don't go by the name – Royal Caribbean is by no means limited to sailing the Caribbean. It's one of the largest cruise lines in the world, offering a fairly wide choice of Mediterranean itineraries and ports of call. Many of RCCL's vessels are among the largest and most extravagant afloat and the two ships currently serving the Mediterranean market are definitely among them.

Royal Olympic

The Greek-owned and -operated Royal Olympic line has a lot of American and English passengers. The majority of vessels in its fairly large fleet are older and smaller than most of those in service in the Mediterranean. In fact, three or four don't offer what I would consider a luxury cruise experience, with cramped cabins and public areas. This is a good choice for budget travelers. Some new and better vessels have been introduced, but the overall quality of the fleet is still below the standard that the American cruising public expects. Even newer ships are small when compared with others in the field. Some travelers prefer this, enjoying the combination of luxury-class amenities and smaller crowds.

Luxury Yacht Lines

Radisson Seven Seas

This is one of the most luxurious cruise lines in the business and most of its fleet features all-suite ships, three of which are on Mediterranean routes for a good part of the year. Prices on these ships are high; if you're working on a tight budget, look elsewhere.

Seabourn Cruise Line

Although I've referred to several of the above cruise lines as being in the luxury class, few reach the level that Seabourn achieves. Seabourn vessels are almost in a class by themselves, with prices to match and a more formal experience all round. Perfect for the sophisticated traveler who doesn't have to worry about price. Its fleet consists of five yacht-like ships, each carrying 200 passengers or fewer.

Silversea Cruises

All four ships in the Silversea fleet are of high quality and three are based in the Mediterranean for at least part of the year. Everything that was said about Seabourn also applies to Silversea. This line is clearly for the discriminating traveler who demands the best and is willing to pay for it. It offers small, intimate ships.

Sailing Ship Lines

Star Clippers

The three wonderful ships of this line evoke images of a different era that, up to now, you've seen only in the movies. Besides the personalized luxury of small sailing ships, Star Clipper vessels have more than 30 different Mediterranean ports of call, including several that aren't visited by any other line.

Windstar Cruises

The luxury yacht feeling of Windstar vessels will definitely appeal to the upscale traveler who has a big budget. The company does an outstanding job in all aspects of the cruise experience. Windstar is a subsidiary of Holland America Line and is probably the best-known of the major lines operating sailing vessels in the Mediterranean. It is also the largest, with four different ships.

More Cruising Choices

As noted above, I have excluded some cruise lines from my research because they cater mainly to non-English speaking travelers. In addition, there are numerous reasons why I have deemed some other lines unsuitable for this book. However, you may be interested in taking one of these cruises or at least doing your own research to see if they could possibly meet your needs.

Here's a list of some other cruise lines operating in the Mediterranean. Websites are given where available so you can learn more online.

AIDA CRUISES: A German company with mostly German-speaking passengers. Has a good range of Mediterranean itineraries at moderate prices. Their two ships are average. www.aida.de.

AIRTOURS SUN CRUISES: A subsidiary of a British charter air carrier, Sun Cruises has four ships varying from hum-drum to quite nice. Mostly British passengers looking for a value cruise. Varied itineraries. www.airtours.com.

GOLDEN SUN CRUISES: This Greek company has two modest ships offering Aegean cruises only. Almost exclusively European clientele and not a luxury experience. www.goldensuncruises.com.

HAPAG-LLOYD LINE: The four ships of this longstanding German travel conglomerate range from excellent to among the best in the world. German language is used throughout by guests and crew, with some English spoken. Limited selection of Mediterranean itineraries. www.hapag-lloyd.com.

KRISTINA CRUISES: Kristina, operated by a Finnish family, runs some smaller and older ships. The company focuses on Northern Europe, but always has one ship offering a variety of Mediterranean itineraries, usually concentrating on a particular section. www.kristinacruises.com.

LOUIS CRUISE LINES: Based in Cyprus, this line operates nine different ships, primarily in the Eastern Mediterranean (including the Holy Land). There's a definite English influence in the style of their cruises. The ships range from old and extremely modest all the way up to quite modern, although none qualify as super-luxurious. www.louiscruises.com.

P&O CRUISES: Once the parent company of Princess (which was spun off as a separate corporate entity), P&O is still a large operation. It has five nice ships, some of which are older while others are spanking new. The passenger roster is primarily British. I've chosen not to include P&O in this book because their Mediterranean itineraries are too limited, restricted to the Iberian Peninsula. www.pocruises.com.

ROYAL HISPANIA CRUISES: This is an old, budget operation with just one ship. Avoid it.

Ferries

Unless you have your own boat or plan to rent one, there are just two other means of getting around the Mediterranean on the water. The first is by freighter, but this is not suitable for most travelers. A more popular way to explore the Mediterranean is by scheduled ferry service. I cannot offer details regarding these lines or their ships, but it is safe to say that none of these vessels offers the same luxury as any of the traditional cruise lines. Frequency of service varies a great deal from one route to another. For example, many of the inter-island Greek ferries have several departures each day, but longer trips are usually limited to one sailing per day or even one to three times a week. Some lines operate only during the summer months, while many others have year-round service.

Consult the *Addendum* for a listing of the major ferry lines. If you do plan to travel by ferry, do some research on the Internet or with a travel agent to gather more information on schedules and prices.

The remainder of the discussion in this section will break down ferry travel into international and local services.

International Routes

For your convenience, I have listed here some of the more important and popular routes. This information will allow you to determine if it is feasible to reach your intended destination by ferry. A listing of websites for many of the major international ferry lines can be found in the Addendum.

⚓ Spain (Algeciras and Cadiz) to Morocco (Tangier). There is also service from Gibraltar.

⚓ France (Sète) to Morocco (Tangier and Nador).

⚓ France (Marseille) to Tunisia (Tunis).

⚓ Italy (Genoa and Trapani, Sicily) to Tunisia (Tunis).

⚓ Greece (Athens/Piraeus) to Israel (Haifa) via Cyprus (Lemesos). The northern or Turkish part of Cyprus also has service to Turkey (Mersin and Tasucu) from Famagusta and Kyrenia.

⚓ Italy (Ancona, Bari, Brindisi, Trieste and Venice) to Greece (Patras via Corfu and Igoumenitsa).

⚓ Italy (Ancona, Bari, Trieste and Venice) to Croatia (Split, Hvar and Korcula islands, Rovinj and Zadar). From these, Croatian coastal services connect to Dubrovnik.

⚓ Italy (Venice) to Egypt (Alexandria).

⚓ Several Greek Islands (those near the Turkish coast) to the Turkish cities of Bodrum and Marmaris, as well as some other towns.

⚓ The island nation of Malta has ferry service to four cities in Sicily along with Genoa and Livorno on the Italian mainland and to Tunisia in North Africa.

⚓ The Black Sea Shipping Company (Chernomorsky Parokhodstvo) is a Ukrainian firm operating out of its home port in Odessa. It serves most of the major ports in the eastern Mediterranean (east of the Adriatic), including Lebanon and Syria. It also has less frequent departures to a few western Mediterranean ports as far as Barcelona.

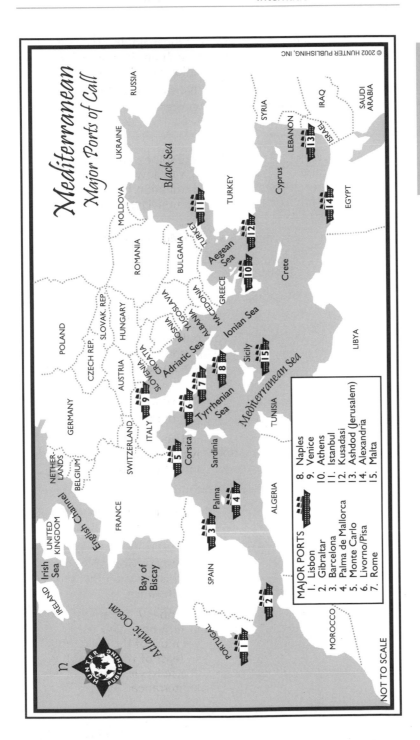

Mediterranean
Major Ports of Call

© 2002 HUNTER PUBLISHING, INC

MAJOR PORTS
1. Lisbon
2. Gibraltar
3. Barcelona
4. Palma de Mallorca
5. Monte Carlo
6. Livorno/Pisa
7. Rome
8. Naples
9. Venice
10. Athens
11. Istanbul
12. Kusadasi
13. Ashdod (Jerusalem)
14. Alexandria
15. Malta

NOT TO SCALE

PRONUNCIATION

On your travels throughout the Mediterranean region, you'll be exposed to many different languages. Although I can't offer a language lesson here, you'll find it useful to know the pronunciation of at least the major port towns and attractions.

Alicante	alee-CAN-tee
Antalya	an-TAL-ya
Çanakkale	Cha-nak-kah-lay
Cannes	Kahn
Cephalonia	Seh-feh-low-nyeh
Ceuta	SOO-tah
Civitavecchia	CHEE-vee-tah-VEK-kyah
Ephesus	EF-feh-siss
Fethiye	FEH-tee-ye
Hvar	Hvahr (an awkward word in any language!)
Ibiza	ee-bee-thah
Ischia	ISH-KEY-ah
Korcula	Koor-CHew-lah
Kusadasi	ku-shah-DAH-si
Mallorca	Ma-york-ah
Marseille	Mar-say
Nauplion	NO-plee-on
Nice	Nees
Port Said	Port SAY-eed
Sète	Set
Thessaloniki	Tess-ah-loh-nee-kee
Villefranche	Veel-fronsh

In addition to these, I have offered pronunciations of any hard-to-fathom words throughout the text.

Local Services

It's not possible for me to include the seemingly endless list of local ferry services. Most people traveling by ferry will likely use a combination of the popular routes that are outlined here. In **Spain**, frequent service runs between the mainland (primarily from Barcelona or Valencia) and the Balearic Island resorts. There are also many inter-island services. Ferries also connect Malaga, Almeria and Algeciras with the North African Spanish enclaves of Ceuta (Soo-tah) and Melilla.

In **Italy**, the mainland cities of Genoa and Livorno are boarding points for ferry service to Sardinia and the French island of Corsica. In the southern part of the country you can use Naples as the departure point for short ferry or hydrofoil service to Capri and other nearby islands. Several cities on the island of Sicily can be reached from Naples, Livorno and Genoa. There is also service from Sicily to some of the smaller surrounding islands. Many other Italian islands, such as Elba, are served from nearby mainland cities. Additionally, service runs between several different ports on the two islands. Returning to **France** for a moment, you can also travel to Corsica from Marseille, Toulon or Nice.

Not surprisingly, **Greece** has the most extensive ferry system in the region, although it isn't always the most reliable. It connects Athens' port of Piraeus with virtually every Greek Island, large or small, close by or remote. There is also extensive service between the islands, which means you can island-hop with ease. You may have to take more than one ferry and stop at an island en route since direct service is limited to the major islands. Frequency of service depends upon traffic, with the most popular destinations having at least daily service.

In **Turkey**, a Turkish Maritime Lines ferry runs between Istanbul and Izmir. There is also ferry service in the Adriatic Sea between several ports along the coast of Croatia.

The Ships

*I*f you've been thinking about a cruise vacation, chances are you've probably browsed through cruise line brochures where every ship is presented as being the best, most luxurious or most beautiful. Well, we all know that can't be the case. Logic dictates that some have to be better than others.

In this section you will find information on more than 60 different ships, broken down into two sections – one for motorized cruise ships and the other for sailing ships. The first category will be further split into traditional cruise ships and luxury yachts. More and more ships cruise here each year and most of them – especially many of the newest ones – are getting bigger and bigger. The competition is fierce and, while it can make the choices somewhat confusing, it has kept prices more affordable. Read the capsule ship descriptions and pick out your favorites. In the next section you can examine their itineraries.

Every large cruise ship offers three full meals a day, a late-night buffet, plus snacks (that can often be a meal in themselves) throughout the day. Attractive shops and chic boutiques, a casino, health club or gymnasium (often with a sauna), bars, lounges and a nightclub with entertainment are also a certainty on larger ships. Facilities are less extensive on smaller vessels. In my descriptions below, I sometimes omit these details in order to avoid redundancy, but outstanding examples (or ones that I don't like for some reason) will always be mentioned. The same is true for activities – a full slate is offered each and every day on most ships. All staterooms have a private bath, sometimes with a tub instead of just a shower. Rooms are commonly equipped with all of the amenities you would expect to find in a fine hotel.

The information given in this section is based on data available at press time, but cruise lines generally make plans far in advance so there is always the possibility of a last-minute change in ship, itinerary or price. Ships listed here were all scheduled to be sailing in Mediterranean waters in 2002. Most of the informational categories you see here are self-explanatory, but a few require some explanation.

Placed in Service: This is the year of the ship's maiden voyage. The year of the most recent major refurbishment will be listed, if applicable, in parentheses. Keep in mind that unless I indicate "major" changes/upgrades, an "old" ship is still old.

Passengers: This is the normal maximum capacity of the ship based on double occupancy. Almost all ships are allowed to have more (some staterooms can accommodate three or four persons) and that is why you will sometimes see my passenger count differing from what is shown in brochures or other sources of information.

Staterooms: There will be three numbers separated by slashes, i.e., 380/140/170. The first number indicates non-suite outside staterooms, the second is for inside staterooms, and the third is the number of suites (which are always located on the outside). Some cabins are reserved for single occupants.

Stateroom Size: This is the range of sizes for all cabins in square feet. There is usually a very fine line between the best (and usually the largest) "regular" staterooms and the lowest priced (and usually the smallest) suites. In some instances, the so-called "suites" are not much different from the better category of regular staterooms. Of course, suites generally come with additional amenities. The least expensive rooms are not always the smallest; location is also an important pricing factor. Some ships, and this is generally more true in the newer mega-liners, have a relatively small range of sizes in the regular staterooms. Note that the square footage shown here does *not* include the veranda, balcony or other outside area. As you do more research, you'll come across books and Internet sites that give a "space ratio per passenger" for each ship. This is the total area of the ship divided by the number of passengers, a statistic I feel is grossly over-rated in its importance. If you're sitting at a table in the dining room with eight people, what significance is it that the ship may have a space ratio of 30 and another has 40? You won't be able to translate these numbers into practical terms.

Meal Arrangements: All ships have two seatings (early and late) in the main dining room unless indicated otherwise. You are assigned a table for the entire cruise unless "open seating" is indicated. The open policy means that you can dine when you want, at whichever table you want. Room service is standard, so I have not included it in my descriptions. Also, just about every ship has an "afternoon tea" or similar service and a "midnight" buffet (called different things by each line), so this aspect will not be mentioned under the Meal Arrangements heading. This section only states what meals can be taken in each dining facility. Details and comments on the overall dining experience are contained in the general ship write-up.

Cruise Style: This is an indication of how formal the cruise is. It will show either the number of nights where dress is formal, informal or casual; or a general indication of the ship's policy regarding attire. A complete discussion of what each category means can be found on page 141.

Price Range: This shows the brochure rate for the lowest and highest priced staterooms and suites. The rates are for the cruise only, which means that airfares and land tours are additional. Port charges are generally included, although some additional government fees and taxes may be tacked on. These do not usually amount to anything significant. It is extremely important to note that the rates do *not* reflect any discounts offered either by the cruise line or travel agents, especially the ever-popular early booking discounts that are universally available. You can realistically expect to pay less than the prices shown. In fact, there is no good reason why you should ever pay the full brochure rate. But brochure rates are valuable as a means of comparison. See the section on discounts, page 146, for more information about how to get a better fare.

The descriptions that follow give you a clear idea of what I think about the ship's appearance, facilities and services. They are based on what I consider reasonable expectations of the *average traveler*, and I'll be sure to tell you when a ship doesn't meet that standard. However, I emphasize *average traveler*, not the most demanding gourmet and connoisseur. I do not downgrade a ship's rating because a waiter (rather than a wine steward) poured the Chablis; or because there was a line for the tender. They are considerations, of course, but of more basic things are more important.

Traditional Cruise Ships

This largest category includes all motorized vessels. This section does not include those ships that can be termed "luxury yachts."

AMSTERDAM (Holland America Line)

Placed in Service: 2000
Length: 780
Passengers: 1,380
Staterooms: 378/140/172
Crew Size: 600
Officers: Dutch

Registry: Netherlands
Gross Tonnage: 61,000
Passenger Decks: 10
Stateroom Size: 182 to 1,125 square feet
Passenger/Crew Ratio: 2.3:1
Crew: Indonesian/Filipino

Meal Arrangements: Open seating in the main dining room for breakfast and lunch. Alternative dining includes the Lido Buffet for all meals (including most evenings), and an Italian restaurant for dinner.

Cruise Style: In general, there are three formal evenings on cruises of 12 nights. Other nights are evenly divided between informal and casual.

Price Range: The 12-night cruises begin at $4,109 and rise to $6,429 for staterooms. Suites start at $8,540 and run as high as $23,669. Savings of 40% or more are available for early booking. Gratuities are included.

The *Amsterdam* is the newest ship in Holland America's fleet and is the first flagship not to bear the formerly well recognized *Nieuw Amsterdam* name. In typical Holland America style, the *Amsterdam* combines modern features with traditional style. There is less glitz than on many of the newer ships and the public areas have the feel of early days of sea travel. The *Amsterdam* is good for those who appreciate fine detailing rather than eye-popping appointments. The one exception to this overall style is the main dining room, with its showy palms and heavy use of bright brass spread over two decks. However, that is nicely counterbalanced by the soothing strains of a strolling string quartet. You'll find fresh flowers throughout the ship, as well as teak decks. Many public areas are centered around a three-level atrium. There is an abundance of bars and lounges, along with quieter areas such as a library and art gallery.

Various recreational facilities are conveniently concentrated on the Lido Deck. The ship's layout is fairly conducive to good traffic flow and is made less tunnel-like by generous use of gently curving corridors. The large number of suites includes many oversized staterooms that HAL has designated as "mini-suites." But all of the rooms – even those in the lowest price category – are spacious by cruise ship standards; there are usually somewhat separated sitting and sleeping areas. The attractive décor features lots of brown and beige.

Service aboard the *Amsterdam* is excellent, in keeping with the high standards that Holland America has set over the years.

AZUR (First European)

Placed in Service: 1971 (1994)
Length: 559 feet
Passengers: 800
Staterooms: 152/208/40
Crew Size: 330
Officers: Greek

Registry: Panama
Gross Tonnage: 15,000
Passenger Decks: 7
Stateroom Size: 95 to 212 square feet
Passenger/Crew Ratio: 2.4:1
Crew: International

Meal Arrangements: A buffet breakfast and lunch is the only alternative to the main dining room.

Cruise Style: One formal night and a couple of informal evenings per cruise. The remainder of the trip is casual.

Price Range: A 10-night cruise begins at $680 and can reach $1,690; suites range from $1,450 to $1,780. The price range on a 12-night cruise is $1,360 to $2,460 for regular staterooms and $2,530 to $2,980 for suites.

Until recently, this was First European's flagship, but the *Azur* certainly won't win any awards for beauty or facilities. The exterior, although a little on the boxy side, is mostly white accented by a deep blue trim. The two large funnels look oddly out of proportion for the size of the ship. A sharply raked stern allows for a spacious main swimming pool area with plenty of deck space. The restaurant is attractive. Other facilities include a lounge, disco, multi-purpose theater, cinema, small gymnasium (with sauna and massage available) and a limited number of shops. The lower-priced staterooms are quite cramped and below the standards of most of today's ships. Upgraded rooms are somewhat larger, functional and attractive, but still nothing special. The service is friendly and efficient but, despite the relatively small size of the ship, is not as personalized as you might expect.

BLACK PRINCE (Fred. Olsen)

Placed in Service: 1966 (1999)
Length: 480 feet
Passengers: 412
Staterooms: 167/69/5
Crew Size: 200
Officers: Norwegian

Registry: Norway
Gross Tonnage: 11,209
Passenger Decks: 7
Stateroom Size: 66 to 192 square feet
Passenger/Crew Ratio: 2.1:1
Crew: British/International

Meal Arrangements: There are two separate "main" dining rooms, as well as a buffet for breakfast and lunch only.

Cruise Style: Two or three formal nights per cruise and usually double that number of informal evenings. All other times are casual.

Price Range: 14-night cruises begin at $2,465 and rise to a maximum of $4,280 for regular staterooms. Suites run $4,940.

Any time you read terms such as "timeless" and "classic" in the brochures you have to watch out! While such attributes are desirable to many travelers and evoke positive response, those words are often a disguise for the fact that the ship is old and less appealing. And that, unfortunately, is definitely the case with this vessel, the exterior of which looks like it's had a few too many run-ins with piers. The interior appointments are dreary and the facilities are limited. Even worse are the accommodations. The frighteningly small minimum stateroom size (66 square feet) are single occupancy. Unfortunately, double rooms begin at just 93 square feet. This might be alright for an overnight ferry ride, but a lot of people will be claustrophobic by the time their cruise ends. On the positive side, the service is actually better than on many newer ships and the friendly crew does a good job. All in all, this is like a budget motel without the budget prices. If the destination is your focus and you're not too fussy about the surroundings, then this ship will suffice. However, if you want the full luxury cruise experience, I suggest that you look elsewhere.

BLACK WATCH (Fred. Olsen)

Placed in Service: 1972 (1996)	Registry: Norway
Length: 674 feet	Gross Tonnage: 28,492
Passengers: 761	Passenger Decks: 8
Staterooms: 364/48/23	Stateroom Size: 150 to 200 square feet
Crew Size: 310	Passenger/Crew Ratio: 2.5:1
Officers: Norwegian	Crew: British/International

Meal Arrangements: Besides the main dining room the only other choice is a breakfast and lunch buffet.

Cruise Style: Two or three formal nights per cruise are the norm. The number of informal evenings varies from three to six, depending upon the length of the cruise. The remainder of the evenings are casual.

Price Range: Regular staterooms begin at $1,825 for a 10-night cruise and rise to $2,850, with suites ranging from $3,305 to $5,210. Two-week cruises start at $2,640 for regular staterooms and go as high as $4,115, while suites will run from $4,770 to $7,530. Prices are proportionately higher for those cruises in excess of two weeks.

Some of what I said about the *Black Prince* (above) also applies to this ship. The good news is that the *Black Watch* betters the former vessel in every way except service (where, happily, they are equally fine). The ship has a classic profile – suiting the time it was built – which a lot of travelers prefer. *Black Watch* is large enough to have all of the facilities you would want (although not with any great abundance), yet small enough to set you apart from the crowd. The staterooms are nicely decorated, comfortable and generally of a decent size, although some of the lower categories are a little small. The dining experience is adequate, but not particularly inspiring.

BRAEMAR (Fred. Olsen)

Placed in Service: 1993 (2001)	Registry: Panama
Length: 537 feet	Gross Tonnage: 19,089
Passengers: 750	Passenger Decks: 7
Staterooms: 272/124/10	Stateroom Size: 140 to 350 square feet
Crew Size: 320	Passenger/Crew Ratio: 2.3:1
Officers: European	Crew: International

Meal Arrangements: Open seating is available in the main dining room for breakfast and lunch. You also can try the buffet for those meals.

Cruise Style: The dress code is the same as on the *Black Prince* and *Black Watch*.

Price Range: For a 13-night cruise the stateroom rates run from $4,065 to $4,255, with suites ranging from $5,175 to $6,655. The 14-night cruises start at $4,510 and rise to $4,710. Suites begin at $5,730 and top out at $7,375.

Before being acquired by Fred. Olsen, this ship was known as the *Crown Dynasty*. The *Braemar* is the most attractive ship operated by this company. It has a somewhat rounded but still sleek exterior appearance and is very graceful, with its single large triangular funnel sitting almost at the very stern of the ship. The majority of the public areas are also attractive, but some tend to get a crowded feel despite the fact that this isn't an overly large ship. Likewise, the layout of some facilities could be altered for a better flow. While the *Braemar* has most of the assets associated with the larger cruise ships, they are not extravagant or plentiful.

Since the ship is new to this line. I cannot offer information about the dining areas, which were more than adequate under previous ownership. It is probable that the cuisine will be the same as on the line's other vessels. The majority of cabins are small, many far too small to be comfortable for more than a few days. Unfortunately, the number of larger cabins is low and they are in the high end of the price range.

BRILLIANCE OF THE SEAS (Royal Caribbean Cruises)

Placed in Service: 2002	Registry: Liberia
Length: 962 feet	Gross Tonnage: 90,090
Passengers: 2,100	Passenger Decks: 12
Staterooms: 744/237/69	Stateroom Size: 166 to 584 square feet
Crew Size: 859	Passenger/Crew Ratio: 2.4:1
Officers: Norwegian	Crew: International

Meal Arrangements: The Minstrel main dining room has open seating for both breakfast and lunch. *Brilliance of the Seas* has one of the largest number of options for alternative dining of any ship in the region. These range from two cafés (one buffet style , one more upscale) to a grill and even a coffee shop. There is always at least one restaurant open for dinner in addition to the main dining room.

Cruise Style: Three formal nights per cruise, with the remainder about evenly divided between informal and casual.

Price Range: The 12-night cruises start at $3,299 and rise to a maximum of $8,429. For suites you will pay from $4,349 to $22,499. This reflects the huge variation in suite types and the fact that some of the better regular staterooms are comparable to the lower category of suites.

Making its debut just in time for the 2002 sailing season, *Brilliance of the Seas*, besides fully justifying its name, is the second Royal Caribbean ship in the so-called "Radiance" class. The translation is that this ship meets the true meaning of the term mega-liner, with comprehensive facilities and excellent service. Although the ship could not be seen prior to this book going to print, it has the same configuration and features of the *Radiance of the Seas*, which hit the waters in early 2001. The following evaluation of facilities and style are made based on that. Considering its size – mammoth – *Brilliance* displays a beautiful and graceful profile, with a gently sloping superstructure in front and imaginatively designed funnel nearer to the stern. The three uppermost decks are almost entirely devoted to recreational facilities and, in addition to the usual fare, you'll find a high-tech golf simulator facility, a separate swimming pool for the teen crowd and even a climbing wall. There's a multi-level fitness center and one of the best equipped spas at sea. At the very top is the Viking Crown Club, a lounge that offers a fantastic view. There's also a forward observation point on the bow. Most ships do not allow access to this point but *Brilliance* is designed in a way that encourages passengers to go there.

The spectacular central atrium has glass-enclosed elevators and runs almost the entire height of the ship. This visually stunning area provides convenient access to most of the ship's public areas as well as to staterooms. Equally attractive is the Solarium, which sports an exotic Indian theme that includes several elephant statues. The three-level Pacifica Theater can host lavish production shows while numerous smaller and more intimate venues will keep you entertained throughout the day and night. The multi-level Minstrel Room, the main dining room, has a grand staircase. If the décor matches that on *Radiance*, with its exquisite color scheme, graceful tall columns and stunning central chandelier – it will be brilliant. At press time it was too early to comment on the dining experience and service, but Royal Caribbean has earned a reputation for being above average in both categories. Of course, with a ship of this size one cannot expect a high degree of personalized service.

All of the staterooms are of a good size, even those in the lower-priced category. Most rooms below the suite level are attractively decorated in modern furniture with cheerful colors and fabrics. Interior rooms are a little on the spartan side, but they are still comfortable and highly functional. As with most of today's large vessels, bathtubs aren't standard until suite level, but the showers in regular staterooms are larger than is commonly found.

CARONIA (Cunard Line)

Placed in Service: 1973 (1999) Registry: Great Britain
Length: 627 feet Gross Tonnage: 24,492
Passengers: 665 Passenger Decks: 9
Staterooms: 309/52/12 Stateroom Size: 67 to 872 square feet
Crew Size: 400 Passenger/Crew Ratio: 1.7:1
Officers: Norwegian/British Crew: European

Meal Arrangements: The main dining room has a single seating for all meals. The buffet is also open for all meals (on most nights), as is the Italian specialty restaurant.

Cruise Style: This is a formal ship and usually runs with three formal evenings per week. The remainder of the cruise is divided about equally between informal and casual.

Price Range: Seven-night cruises range from a low of $1,709 to a high of $4,679 for regular staterooms and from $6,119 to $9,269 for suites. For the 15-night cruise, prices begin at $3,999 and rise to a maximum of $8,899. Suites start at $12,399 and go up to $17,649. An automatic $10 per person/per day charge is added to all stateroom accounts to cover gratuities. You have the option of lowering or raising this figure. Be sure to notify the desk staff of any change no later than two days before the end of your cruise.

Until a few years ago this ship was named the *Vistafjord* and, along with its sister ship (the *Sagafjord*), was the epitome of five-star cruising. Despite recent refurbishment, time has taken its toll. Nonetheless, the *Caronia* is still a fine ship and it will satisfy many with a traditional luxury cruise experience. Because it is not large, there are limited public areas (the ballroom, for instance, doubles as the showroom), but they are both attractive and functional. Cunard has attempted to keep up with modern trends as is evidenced by the addition of an alternative restaurant. All dining is enjoyable, with beautiful table settings, excellent cuisine and fine personalized service.

All categories of accommodation are well designed with optimum use of space. While the majority of rooms are decent in size, some in the lower price categories are far too small. There are lots of nice touches in the rooms, including plush terrycloth bathrobes. The service on *Caronia*, in true Cunard fashion, is excellent in every way and compares favorably with ships in the luxury yacht class.

INTRODUCTION

CONSTELLATION/MILLENNIUM (Celebrity Cruises)

Placed in Service: 2002/2000   Registry: Liberia
Length: 965 feet   Gross Tonnage: 91,000
Passengers: 1,950   Passenger Decks: 11
Staterooms: 754/205/16   Stateroom Size: 165 to 1,637 square feet
Crew Size: 999   Passenger/Crew Ratio: 2.0:1
Officers: Greek   Crew: European

Meal Arrangements: In addition to the main dining room and lunch and breakfast buffets, there are several dining options. These are highlighted by the Cova Café Milano, a fine but small specialty eatery. You might also try the grill or pizza bar, or any of the club-like bars serving food.

Cruise Style: Per week, there are usually two formal nights and three informal nights, with the remaining two evenings being casual.

Price Range: The starting price for regular staterooms on a seven-night cruise is $1,649, which rises to a high of $2,629. Suites will go for between $5,849 and $14,099. The 11-night cruises begin at $2,549 and have a high of $3,379. For suites the range is $7,499 to $15,749. The 10-night cruises are slightly lower priced than the 11-nighters.

These wonderful twins are Celebrity's newest mega-liners. The *Millennium* is a fabulous floating resort with fantastic facilities. The exterior has a dark blue hull softened by gold stripes and a multi-colored superstructure topped by Celebrity's hallmark slanted X on the funnel. Its appearance is impressive. The spacious public decks are well laid out and beautiful, even though this ship lacks the huge atrium that is found on many of the newer large ships. There is a small atrium nuzzled between the dramatic glass elevators that provide views of the sea as you travel between decks. So many lounges are scattered throughout the ship that you may have a hard time finding time to patronize them all! Some offer entertainment, and all are great for socializing. The two-level Metropolitan Restaurant is one of the loveliest main dining rooms on the sea.

The many excellent facilities of *Millennium* include the huge and fabulously equipped *AquaSpa*, complete with its own thermal suite; *Shipmates Fun Factory* for children (has its own arcade); and the beautiful three-level theater with a large stage that features elaborate shows. The exceedingly beautiful outside pool area is much larger than on many ships and can handle the crowds. Dining options aboard *Millennium* will please even top connoisseurs of fine food. Menus feature outstanding cuisine prepared by a celebrity chef, all finely presented by a careful and attentive staff. An excellent passenger-to-crew ratio assures a high level of service on *Millennium*. Likewise, when it comes to selecting a stateroom, you can't really go wrong. Even the smallest room is a good size by cruise ship standards, and upgraded rooms are considerably bigger. The majority of outside rooms have their own veranda, some of which are two or more times the size of verandas on most other ships. All rooms are decorated in a tasteful manner with bright and cheerful draperies and bed coverings, quality furniture and plenty of storage space. You do have to get into the suite category in order to have a bathtub instead of a shower. There are plenty of amenities in all room classes, and if you opt for a suite you even have your own butler!

The *Constellation* was still in the shipyards as this book went to press and was scheduled to be placed into service in May of 2002. It will be identical in appearance and facilities to the *Millennium*. However, it is likely that some of the facility and deck names will be changed.

COSTA ATLANTICA (Costa Cruises)

Placed in Service: 2000
Length: 960 feet
Passengers: 2,114
Staterooms: 792/207/58
Crew Size: 920
Officers: Italian

Registry: Italy
Gross Tonnage: 85,000
Passenger Decks: 12
Stateroom Size: 160 to 388 square feet
Passenger/Crew Ratio: 2.3:1
Crew: Italian/International

Meal Arrangements: There is a sizable selection of alternatives to the main dining room, including the usual breakfast and lunch buffet. You may dine at Club Atlantica, a specialty restaurant, for an extra fee. More casual is the Café Florian. There's also a poolside grill and a pizzeria.

Cruise Style: For each week of cruising there is one formal night. The remainder of the cruise is casual, with at least one theme night where dressing appropriate to the theme is popular.

Price Range: Five-night cruises begin at $1,580 and rise to $2,090 for staterooms; suites start at $2,270 and rise to $2,700. For a seven-night cruise, the starting price is $2,230 and that rises to $2,950; suites range from $3,200 to $3,800.

This magnificent vessel is Costa's new flagship, but it won't be for long because additional ships are due to join the scene over the next few years. Coming soon after the well received *Costa Victoria*, the *Atlantica* marks the true entry of this line into the world of the megaship. The ship has an impressive exterior appearance and the public areas won't disappoint. The highlight is the beautiful atrium, which extends almost through the entire superstructure of the ship. Glass elevators provide good (if brief) views of the stunning décor. *Atlantica* has a full range of recreational facilities, including a well-equipped spa. The three-deck Caruso Theater is gorgeous and befitting the name (which is also used on some other Costa ships). The production shows are a bit disappointing, given the spectacular surroundings. The elegant main dining room has two stories; upper and lower sections are connected by a gracefully curving grand staircase. Quality and service is on par with competing ships. The specialty restaurant is truly excellent, but many people – including myself – strongly object to the $19 fee imposed for dining there, especially when the brochure describes it as only a "modest" surcharge. The

Café Florian is a delightful re-creation of a café by the same name in St. Mark's Square, Venice. However, a non-Italian themed lounge called Madame Butterfly might be the most beautiful spot of all in the entire ship. (Everything named on this ship has a connection to Italy, in this case the composer of the opera was Italian.) The accommodations are very good. Even the smallest rooms are more than adequate and larger than on many ships of this type. There are many levels of stateroom categories and once you get into the suite range you'll even have your own butler service. Guests staying in suites get one night at the specialty restaurant for free. The *Costa Atlantica* offers value with the elegance (mostly Las Vegas style glitz in this case) and facilities of a mega-liner in an atmosphere that is mostly casual and fun. A last reminder that won't be repeated in the rest of the Costa ship reviews: don't forget the special theme nights (especially the wild and wildly popular Bacchanal, where guests wear togas) and other elements of Italian style that make this line so attractive to many travelers.

COSTA CLASSICA (Costa Cruises)

Placed in Service: 1992 (2000) Registry: Italy
Length: 869 Gross Tonnage: 78,000
Passengers: 1,998 Passenger Decks: 10
Staterooms: 686/293/20 Stateroom Size: 185 to 431 square feet
Crew Size: 900 Passenger/Crew Ratio: 2.2:1
Officers: Italian Crew: Italian/International

Meal Arrangements: The Puccini Restaurant and outdoor Alfresco Café are the primary alternatives to the main dining room. There's also a buffet option for breakfast and lunch.

Cruise Style: For each week of cruising there is one formal night. The remainder of the cruise is casual, with at least one theme night.

Price Range: Five-night cruises begin at $1,500 and rise to $2,030 for regular staterooms. Suites will run from $2,460 to $2,710. For a seven-night cruise the fare ranges from $2,180 to a maximum of $2,750. Suites start at $3,450 and have a high of $3,700.

The recent refurbishment of this ship was much more than a new coat of paint. The entire vessel was lengthened. An old section was removed and a new and larger section that added more than 300 rooms and many public areas was inserted. The result is a ship that is on par with the other megas of this line – the *Atlantica* and *Victoria* – although the interior public facilities are not as large or eye-popping. The added capacity sometimes make things more crowded than on many ships.

The appealing Florence and Rome decks host most public areas and are well designed and well equipped. Especially nice are the two-level Colosseo Theater and the Piazza Navona Grand Bar, which is the largest of several lounges. There are two pools (one has two Jacuzzis adjacent), but the recreational facilities are not as varied as on most large ships. While the staff seems to adore children, limited facilities are common on Costa ships. You should take this into consideration if traveling with kids.

The dining experience aboard *Classica* is more fun than gourmet. There is heavy emphasis on pasta and things Italian (fine with me), but there are no dazzling culinary inventions. The alternative restaurant has good food and service.

The huge plus of this vessel is the size of the staterooms, all of which are highly functional and comfortable. There are, by ship standards, no small rooms on *Classica* and most are considerably larger than on the majority of ships. The décor is a bit too modern and sterile for my tastes, and while there's sufficient color, I found them lacking in style.

COSTA EUROPA (Costa Cruises)

Placed in Service: 1986 (2002)	Registry: See below
Length: 798 feet	Gross Tonnage: 53,000
Passengers: 1,494	Passenger Decks: 9
Staterooms: 500/252/5	Stateroom Size: 131 to 425 square feet
Crew Size: 612	Passenger/Crew Ratio: 2.4:1
Officers: See below	Crew: International

Meal Arrangements: The breakfast and lunch buffet is the only alternative to the main dining room.

Cruise Style: Week-long cruises on Costa typically have only one formal evening and the remainder of the nights are casual. Included in the latter category is at least one theme night (the Bacchanal festival), where dressing in costume is appropriate.

Price Range: Regular staterooms run $2,680-$3,550 for an 11-night cruise. Suites are priced at about $3,730. Prices for week-long cruises have yet to be determined, but will run in the same range as the line's other seven-night cruises.

Until the end of 2001 this ship was called the *Westerdam* and sailed for Holland America. It was rechristened and modestly refurbished for its transfer to Costa, where it replaced the older *Costa Riviera* as part of this line's extensive expansion and upgrading. As of press time there wasn't a lot of ship information available. With HAL, this vessel was of Netherlands registry and had Dutch officers. This will probably be changed to Italian registry and officers.

The refurbishment was aimed at making over HAL's more subdued atmosphere into the more lively Costa mold. This mid-size ship has traditional lines and styling. It was built just before the real advent of the mega-liner and, thus, has relatively fewer facilities than many of the newer ships. However, all the standards are offered, including a showroom, casino, pool and other recreational facilities, and lots of nice lounges. *Europa* features teak decks and lots of open spaces both on the deck and in public areas. Staterooms start on the small size and you have to upgrade several levels to get to a comfortable amount of room. One can assume that the cruise style and service, from food to entertainment, will change to match other Costa ships.

COSTA ROMANTICA (Costa Cruises)

Placed in Service: 1993	Registry: Italy
Length: 722 feet	Gross Tonnage: 53,000
Passengers: 1,356	Passenger Decks: 10
Staterooms: 418/226/34	Stateroom Size: 185 to 431 square feet
Crew Size: 610	Passenger/Crew Ratio: 2.2:1
Officers: Italian	Crew: Italian/International

Meal Arrangements: The only alternative to the main dining room is the buffet, which offers breakfast and lunch. For lighter snacks, there's a pizzeria and patisserie.

Cruise Style: For each week of cruising there is one formal night and the remaining evenings are casual. There is, among the casual nights, at least one theme night where dressing appropriate to the theme is the popular thing to do (you may dress in regular clothes if you prefer).

Price Range: A five-night cruise ranges from $1,550 to $2,280 for regular staterooms and $2,210 to $2,460 for suites. For a seven-night cruise, prices start at $2,460 and go to a high of $3,620. Suites range from $4,260 to $4,660.

This is a lovely ship with a sleek, modern profile. I don't care for the three straight funnels bunched together, but classic ship enthusiasts seem to enjoy it. The ship is well designed and has an easy layout to follow. The four bottom decks contain all of the accommodations, with the exception of some suites on the top decks. All public facilities are on four decks immediately above the stateroom levels. As on the *Classica*, decks are named for European cities. One of the ship's most distinct features can be seen from the outside – a large round dish-like structure sitting not too far back from the bow of the ship. This is a glass-enclosed disco called Diva and is a popular spot for the views and the party atmosphere. The recreational facilities on *Classica* are good and include two pools, a spa and fitness center, plus a fair amount of walking space. There's a good selection of retail outlets in the shopping promenade. The two-level theater is in keeping with the elaborate showrooms that the newer Costa ships all feature. As in many other cases, it is in the style of an Italian opera house. In fact, this one is called the L'Opera Theater.

The restaurants are a bit run-of-the-mill, or perhaps they seem that way because the rest of the ship is so appealing. The cuisine is standard fare for Costa, as is the service. The staterooms are all of a good size, with even the smallest being considerably larger than the industry average. Use of brighter colors in the décor would help dress things up, especially since the overwhelming majority of outside rooms have small portholes rather than big windows, as is the case on most newer ships.

COSTA TROPICALE (Costa Cruises)

Placed in Service: 1982 (2001)	Registry: Italy
Length: 672 feet	Gross Tonnage: 36,674
Passengers: 1,022	Passenger Decks: 10
Staterooms: 312/187/12	Stateroom Size: 180 to 350 square feet
Crew Size: 550	Passenger/Crew Ratio: 1.9:1
Officers: Italian	Crew: Italian/International

Meal Arrangements: Besides the main dining room, there is a buffet for breakfast and lunch. A new pizzeria and alternative restaurant have also been added as part of the ship's recent refurbishment.

Cruise Style: For each week of cruising there is one formal night and the remainder of the cruise is casual. There is, among the casual nights, at least one theme night. Costume dress is popular.

Price Range: The seven-night cruises begin at $2,150 and rise to a maximum of $2,920 for staterooms, while suites begin at $3,100 and have a maximum of $3,550.

Up until 2001 this ship sailed under the Carnival Cruise Line banner. Carnival is the parent company of Costa and with their abundance of new ships the *Tropicale* became superfluous. *Tropicale* is a better ship than some of the older ships in Costa's fleet, such as the *Costa Marina* and the *Costa Riviera*. When it changed hands between the two companies, it underwent a $25 million refurbishment of all public areas as well as staterooms. Nowadays, the ship is looking pretty good despite approaching its 20th birthday. When first launched, this ship might well have been the most modern looking ship there was and, even today, it still compares well with new ships. The biggest visible change is the replacement of Carnival's wing-shaped funnel with Costa's traditional round yellow stack. Unfortunately, despite the expensive changes, the *Tropicale* still resembles a Carnival vessel.

The *Tropicale* has a good range of attractive public facilities, although many of them are on the small side. The layout provides good flow, but the ship tends to have a crowded feel. Not so with the accommodations, however, which are unusually spacious for a ship in this price class. The very functional rooms are well designed and have a pretty, cheerful décor. This ship was designed to provide a good cruise experience at a reasonable price. It's great if you want to enjoy your time, but don't demand the absolute best. The food is less Italian than on other ships in this fleet.

COSTA VICTORIA (Costa Cruises)

Placed in Service: 1996	Registry: Italy
Length: 828 feet	Gross Tonnage: 76,000
Passengers: 1,928	Passenger Decks: 10
Staterooms: 652/292/20	Stateroom Size: 120 to 431 square feet
Crew Size: 800	Passenger/Crew Ratio: 2.4:1
Officers: Italian	Crew: Italian/International

Meal Arrangements: The main dining room is separated into two sections that have the feel and appearance of two rooms. Alternatives include the breakfast/lunch buffet, the Ristorante Magnifico by Zeffirino (additional charge); and a pizzeria.

Cruise Style: For each week of cruising there is one formal night and the remainder of the cruise is casual. There is, among the casual nights, at least one theme night.

Price Range: The starting price for a five-night cruise is $1,550, which goes up to $2,280. Suites are priced from $2,205 to $2,385. The fares for a seven-night itinerary run from $2,180 to $2,750 for regular staterooms and from $3,100 to $3,350 for suites.

This is another beautiful new ship that most travelers are proud to sail on. The exterior, except for the three bunched funnels, looks much like the slightly newer and larger *Costa Atlantica*. The decks are named after Italian operas and contain beautiful and mostly well-designed public areas. These include a dramatic multi-level atrium called the Planetarium and an excellent forward observation lounge complete with waterfall. The two-level Festival Show Lounge is a great place to take in some entertainment. The ship has numerous bars and lounges, a good-size shopping area and lots of spacious public spaces. Recreational facilities include a full spa and an outside promenade on the upper deck.

The main dining room is actually two separate rooms (the galley is in between), so it isn't as massive as on many big ships. It is quite attractive, but not spectacular. The food is largely Italian and quite tasty, if not highly imaginative. Service is typically friendly on this line and this vessel is no exception. As on the *Atlantica*, the $19 fee for the alternative restaurant is excessive, although you do get one night's complimentary dinner there if you are staying in a suite (big deal).

The only disappointment on the *Costa Victoria* is the staterooms, which are considerably smaller than on the other new ships in the line. You have to upgrade considerably to get a room that's on par with the lowest-priced rooms on the *Atlantica*. And, here again, many rooms have portholes instead of windows. On the positive side, the décor is bright and cheerful. Even the small rooms are comfortable and fairly well designed.

CROWN ODYSSEY (Orient Line)

Placed in Service: 1988 (2000)
Length: 614 feet
Passengers: 1,036
Staterooms: 388/114/16
Crew Size: 470
Officers: Norwegian/European

Registry: Bahamas
Gross Tonnage: 34,250
Passenger Decks: 10
Stateroom Size: 155 to 614 square feet
Passenger/Crew Ratio: 2.2:1
Crew: International

Meal Arrangements: In addition to the main dining room there is a buffet option for breakfast and lunch (the area is sometimes used as an alternative restaurant for dinner). There's also another small café open most evenings.

Cruise Style: This line generally has two informal nights per cruise and the rest are casual. Some longer cruises may have another formal evening, but note that "formal" on this ship means jackets and ties for men, not tuxes.

Price Range: Because of the variation in the number of days in various cruises and Orient's land-inclusive pricing policy, this is an approximate range for the cruise-only portion per week of cruise time: Regular staterooms are from $1,695 to $3,495, while suites are approximately $3,875 to $4,695.

The *Crown Odyssey* was built at a time when cruise ships were beginning to make the transition from what we would now term as "classic" to the more modern lines and styling of today's bigger vessels. The result is quite pleasant. The size is nice – big enough to include every facility you'd want and lots of space in the public areas, yet not so huge as to overwhelm. It also incorporates some traditional features that blend with today's vogue styles. All in all, if you have never taken a cruise or have only sailed on some of the older ships, you will most likely be very pleased with what you find on board *Crown Odyssey*. Don't expect a mega-liner experience – you'll be disappointed. The ship has a lovely exterior style that combines traditional elements of cruise ship design with newer trends. Public facilities are also quite attractive and are a mixture of bright brass and subdued colors. The *Crown Odyssey's* layout is easy to follow and the ship gives a spacious feel, despite not being in the mega-size category. The 500 or so staterooms offer a huge variety of accommodation levels. Even the smallest rooms are more than adequate, with a well-planned layout that makes good use of space. More expensive accommodations provide a great deal more room. The service on *Crown Odyssey* is friendly and efficient, not overbearing or fancy. Orient Line cruises devote just as much attention to intensive port activity as to the cruise experience itself.

CRYSTAL SYMPHONY (Crystal Cruises)

Placed in Service: 1995 (1999)
Length: 781 feet
Passengers: 940
Staterooms: 406/0/64
Crew Size: 545
Officers: Norwegian/Japanese

Registry: Bahamas
Gross Tonnage: 51,044
Passenger Decks: 8
Stateroom Size: 202 to 982 square feet
Passenger/Crew Ratio: 1.7:1
Crew: International

Meal Arrangements: The main dining room is supplemented by the buffet for breakfast and lunch. Dinner alternatives include two small cafés (one serving Italian and the other Chinese). Crystal Cruises suggests a cash gratuity for the waiter each time you patronize one of these cafés. An all-day bistro sells snacks and sweets.

Cruise Style: There are three formal nights on cruises of 10 days or more, while some shorter cruises may have only two. The remaining evenings are about equally divided between casual and informal. Keep in mind that within each category, Crystal Cruises tends to have a more dressed-up crowd than many other lines.

Price Range: A 12-night cruise in a regular stateroom costs from $7,925 to $10,160, while suites range from $14,515 to $27,050. The 13-night cruise starts at $8,590 and runs up to $11,010 for staterooms, and $15,730 to $29,310 for suites.

Crystal Cruises rises to the top of the large-vessel pack. The magnificent *Crystal Symphony* is a prime example of the line's superb quality.

This feels like a big ship. The passengers capacity isn't overly high and the overall cruise experience is one of luxury from start to finish. The graceful all-white exterior is beautiful, with traditional design elements such as a pointed narrow bow and a slightly rounded stern. Interior décor is even more stunning, beginning with the multi-level Crystal Plaza and its incredible statuary, columns, glass piano and an indescribable central sculpture of crystal that looks very grand. In my opinion, the public areas rank among the most beautiful at sea today.

Dining aboard the *Crystal Symphony* is a delightful experience, with elegant service and culinary delights that awaken your taste buds. It is well appreciated by gourmets and may even be a bit over the top for some. While most ships have an afternoon tea, Crystal offers its Mozart Tea, where the wait staff dresses in splendid period attire. The Sun Deck has a huge array of recreational facilities ranging from tennis to spa services. The swimming pool has a retractable glass dome should the weather turn inclement. Entertainment and lounge facilities are also extensive and varied.

The staterooms aboard *Crystal Symphony* are spacious by cruise ship standards, and all of them are thoughtfully designed and beautifully appointed. Plus, many of the rooms have a private veranda. Every room has a decent-size sitting area that includes a sofa, as well as unusually large bathrooms that all feature a tub – something rarely seen on cruise ships. Crystal has built its reputation on outstanding service and that is exactly what you will get from every member of the attentive crew.

EUROPEAN STARS/EUROPEAN VISION (First European)

Placed in Service: 2002/2001 Registry: Italy
Length: 823 feet Gross Tonnage: 58,600
Passengers: 1,500 Passenger Decks: 9
Staterooms: 379/272/132 Stateroom Size: 150 to 235 square feet
Crew Size: 711 Passenger/Crew Ratio: 2.1:1
Officers: European Crew: European/International

Meal Arrangements: There are two main dining rooms with open seating for breakfast and lunch. Additionally, there's an Italian restaurant, a buffet (breakfast and lunch) and an indoor/outdoor grill. There's also an ice cream bar and other places for light snacks.

Cruise Style: There is one formal evening and two informal nights per week of cruising. The remainder of the time is casual.

Price Range: Stateroom prices on a seven-night cruise begin at $910 and rise to $2,130, while suites range from $1,680 to $2,660. Ten-night cruises start at $1,300 and reach $2,250. Suites run from $2,400 to $2,820.

The *European Vision*, the slightly older of these two ships, debuted in the summer of 2001. Due to time constraints while researching this book, I was unable to see either of these ships. Consequently, the information given here was largely provided by the cruise line. Except for the names of the decks and some of the public rooms, these two ships are identical in every way. They represent the newest, biggest and best in First European's growing fleet. Although the twins have a somewhat boxy look (not atypical of the new generation of large ships), there is still something very attractive and impressive about their exterior appearance. The interior décor nicely juxtaposes traditional and modern styling in a colorful and comfortable way.

The ships are spacious and well laid out. In addition to a large health club and two swimming pools, the Euros have a golf simulator. You'll find two separate shopping areas, a two-level show lounge, theater and disco. The two-deck reception foyer is overlooked by the casual and pretty Caffè Quadri. Kids of all ages are well taken care of in a children's facility and in the separate teen's club. The latter group will certainly enjoy the virtual reality game room (the adults may get a kick out of it too!).

Regular staterooms are adequate in size, enhanced by cheerful color schemes, modern styling and excellent utilization of space. However, if you like to have lots of room, consider upgrading to a suite (which are not overly large themselves). First European has a reputation for friendly service and there is no reason to believe that won't hold true on these ships, which are a great deal larger than most of the rest of the fleet.

FLAMENCO (First European)

Placed in Service: 1972 (1997)   Registry: Bahamas
Length: 642 feet   Gross Tonnage: 17,000
Passengers: 850   Passenger Decks: 7
Staterooms: 262/127/12   Stateroom Size: 100 to 237 square feet
Crew Size: 350   Passenger/Crew Ratio: 2.4:1
Officers: Greek   Crew: International

Meal Arrangements: The only alternative to the main dining room is a buffet that offers breakfast and lunch.

Cruise Style: There is one formal evening and two informal nights per week of cruising. The remainder of the time is casual.

Price Range: Six-night cruises cost $700 to $1,250 for regular staterooms and from $1,290 to $1,510 for suites.

The *Flamenco* is mildly attractive to look at, featuring a yacht-shaped white hull and blue-and-gold trim. The public facilities are attractive enough, but nothing will dazzle you or inspire great comment. The layout allows for easy navigation with all facilities set on two successive decks and the outdoor facilities situated on top (the one exception is the theater, which is on the Sun Deck). To the front of the theater is an excellent observation area. The *Flamenco* offers most of the facilities that you may want, but they are often limited and cramped. Lower-priced staterooms are far too small to be comfortable, with those in the higher price bracket reaching only "adequate" status. The service is friendly and casual. Overall, this type of ship provides a good experience for the budget traveler.

GOLDEN PRINCESS (Princess Cruises)

Placed in Service: 2001   Registry: Bermuda
Length: 935 feet   Gross Tonnage: 109,000
Passengers: 2,600   Passenger Decks: 14
Staterooms: 763/332/205   Stateroom Size: 161 to 764 square feet
Crew Size: 1,100   Passenger/Crew Ratio: 2.4:1
Officers: British   Crew: Italian

Meal Arrangements: Those who like variety will enjoy the three separate formal dining rooms and the standard breakfast/lunch buffet. There are also two by-reservation restaurants; one serves Italian food (including pizza) while the other specializes in Southwestern cuisine. The latter is certainly unusual for a cruise ship. Both have a small additional charge, as do the patisserie and caviar bar. A poolside grill serves hamburgers and pizza.

Cruise Style: The main dining room has a mixture of formal, informal and casual nights, with the majority being informal. An alternative dining room is always open for dinner, so you can choose to avoid the formal nights altogether.

Price Range: Fares begin at $2,540 for 10-day cruises ($3,240 for 12 days) and rise to $4,140 for 10-day cruises ($4,440 for 12 days). Suites begin at $4,290 and run as high as $7,440 for the 10-day cruise. Twelve-night cruise suite prices range from $4,440 to $8,840.

Golden Princess is one of the newest ships in the large and growing Princess fleet. It epitomizes what the cruise line says about its "Grand Class" cruising, which is lots of everything – on a grand scale. Size allows choice, not only in dining but in activities.

This Princess is one of the biggest vessels afloat in length, width and height. Although massive in every way, it has a certain appeal too. On the upper portion of the superstructure, three distinct areas will grab your attention. At the bow, the fitness center rounds its way across the ship's beam and looks from the outside like an observation lounge. Nearer to the stern is a graceful pyramid-like structure that essentially hides the funnel. It also serves as a cover for various recreational facilities. The most controversial exterior feature, which looks like a rear spoiler on a car, sits at the stern and houses a stunning disco/nightclub that is reached from special elevators via a moving walkway 16 decks above the sea. It's worth going to just for the ride! An entire chapter could be devoted to the ship's public facilities, which include four swimming pools (one with a retractable dome), a virtual reality center and a place where passengers can star in their own videos, and bars and lounges almost too numerous to count. The theater is one of the largest at sea and lavish production shows in typical Princess style are featured.

Despite its size, the *Golden Princess* is easy to navigate. However, Princess' claim that it has a "small ship feel" is not true, in my opinion. A ship this large could not possibly have a small ship feel, regardless of the number of places in which you can lose yourself. The dining experience, other than the great variety that is offered, is commensurate with the quality level of all other ships of the fleet. That is, plenty of good food (though not gourmet) and reasonably attentive service. Accommodations are pleasant, but nothing special. The numerous classes of staterooms fall into about half a dozen general categories. The smallest are too small for my taste, but once you get up a few notches in the cost ladder they are much more roomy. More than 700 of them have a veranda. Note: Don't be led astray by the large number of suites because this includes many "mini-suites," which are, essentially, oversized staterooms. Big ships have their advantages and disadvantages. If you are among the many people who want to experience one of these new luxury megaliners, than the *Golden Princess* merits your consideration.

GRANDEUR OF THE SEAS (Royal Caribbean Cruises)

Placed in Service: 1996
Length: 916 feet
Passengers: 2,446
Staterooms: 801/402/20
Crew Size: 760
Officers: Norwegian

Registry: Norway
Gross Tonnage: 74,000
Passenger Decks: 11
Stateroom Size: 158 to 1,033 square feet
Passenger/Crew Ratio: 3.2:1
Crew: Italian

Meal Arrangements: Breakfast and lunch in the main dining room is open seating. The primary alternative dining room is the Windjammer Café (buffet breakfast and lunch), which is open most evenings for more casual dining. The Champagne Bar also serves a number of specialty items.

Cruise Style: There are two formal nights per week of sailing, with the remaining evenings split between informal and casual.

Price Range: Stateroom prices for seven-night cruises begin at $1,799 and rise to a maximum of $4,199. Suite prices range from $5,699 to a high of $11,999. Early booking discounts can be as much as $1,200 in the higher priced non-suite staterooms.

Royal Caribbean has no shortage of gorgeous ships and *Grandeur of the Seas* fits in well with their outstanding collection. Although the exterior design is in keeping with the latest trends, the massive size and general shapelessness seen in many new ships is softened in *Grandeur* by the almost triangular-shaped funnel, emblazoned with the distinctive Royal Caribbean logo, that sits at the stern. A similar structure sits in the ship's middle and contains the Viking Crown Lounge, an entertainment venue as well as a great place for viewing the passing scenery.

The interior layout is highly functional, with most facilities located off a multi-level central atrium called the Centrum. This stunning area is bathed in natural light which pours in through the large windows. The main dining room covers two levels linked by a fabulous grand staircase. All of the ship's public areas are spacious and there is a good collection of art throughout. Recreational facilities are extensive and many are housed in a glass-covered solarium. *Grandeur* also features a wealth of entertainment options ranging from elaborate shows in the two-level Palladium Theater to several lounges with live music and dancing. Although Royal Caribbean isn't in the top tier of lines when it comes to culinary delights, few will find fault with the quality or quantity of food on offer. One nice touch is that many dinners are geared toward a particular national cuisine and the wait staff dresses accordingly. It makes for a colorful sight and helps to alleviate boredom that can arise when eating in the same room night after night. The service is adequate, although hurried in the early seating.

All staterooms aboard *Grandeur* start at a decent size and work their way up to being pleasantly roomy. The room décor in the lower-priced categories is plain, but the areas are laid out in a highly functional and comfortable manner. Not surprisingly, color schemes, quality of furnishings and amenities are all much better in the suite categories.

MARCO POLO (Orient Line)

Placed in Service: 1965 (1993)   Registry: Bahamas
Length: 578 feet   Gross Tonnage: 22,080
Passengers: 848   Passenger Decks: 8
Staterooms: 287/129/8   Stateroom Size: 93 to 484 square feet
Crew Size: 356   Passenger/Crew Ratio: 2.4:1
Officers: Scandinavian   Crew: International

Meal Arrangements: The only option besides the main dining room is the breakfast and lunch buffet. This room becomes a small alternative specialty restaurant on selected evenings.

Cruise Style: Like other ships of this line, the style is generally casual with just one or two informal nights on a week-long cruise. Longer cruises may have a formal night, but the level of dress isn't generally that far above the informal.

Price Range: Orient offers cruises of various lengths and also has a land-inclusive pricing policy, which makes it hard to show a comparable price range here. These figures are for the cruise-only portion, per week of cruise time: Regular staterooms run from $1,695 to $3,495, while suites are between $3,875 and $4,695.

Despite her age, the *Marco Polo* has been nicely refitted and still looks good. Her design is classic and the overall effect is very pleasing, full of grace and charm. The *Marco Polo* has a strengthened hull and a helicopter pad as well as zodiac rafts for exploration of tight places. Because she is so well equipped, the *Marco Polo* sails to some unusual destinations, such as the Antarctic. This is in keeping with Orient Line's port-intensive cruise programs. These facilities aren't all that useful in the Mediterranean, but they do allow exploration of out-of-the-way places. Keep in mind that the tenders are small and lines can be slow moving.

Public areas aboard the *Marco Polo* are decorated in a lively and cheerful manner, but they aren't particularly special. Facilities are good for a ship of this size; of course, they cannot compare to facilities aboard a mega-liner. The food is good and is served by a friendly staff that always seems eager to please. Accommodations are functional but small. If you're taking a longer cruise, you should consider upgrading to a larger room. In summary, the *Marco Polo* offers good value and decent facilities. It features interesting itineraries but may lack some of the luxuries associated with cruising.

MELODY (Mediterranean Shipping Cruises)

Placed in Service: 1982 (1997)   Registry: Panama
Length: 672   Gross Tonnage: 36,500
Passengers: 1,076   Passenger Decks: 9
Staterooms: 381/151/6   Stateroom Size: 137 to 427 square feet
Crew Size: 535   Passenger/Crew Ratio: 2.0:1
Officers: Italian   Crew: International

Meal Arrangements: A buffet for breakfast and lunch is available as an alternative to the main dining room.

Cruise Style: Mostly casual but, depending upon length of cruise, may have up to three nights of informal dress. Mediterranean Shipping Cruises (MSC) refers to these nights as "formal," but requires only a tie and jacket for men. Dressing to the hilt is acceptable too.

Price Range: Fares for a seven-night cruise start at $1,249 and go up to $2,349 for staterooms. Suites begin at $2,149 and reach a high of $3,199.

The *Melody* is not a huge ship by any means, but she is significantly bigger than she appears at first glance. Neither a beauty nor a wallflower, the *Melody* has a fairly traditional styling and a snow-white exterior (some striping would improve the hull). Most of the public areas are located on two upper decks, one of which contains two pools, a spa and more. All are attractive and functional. Unfortunately, the main dining room (on a lower deck) has a very crowded feel, almost as though it was an afterthought. But the quality of food (mainly Italian) is very good and is served by a capable staff. One excellent facility of the *Melody* is the large children's recreation area, which even has its own pool. This ship does attract many families with children – perhaps because of those facilities – which may or may not appeal to you. Accommodations are very colorful and comfortable. The lower-priced cabins especially benefit from the thoughtful layout and good use of space. If you can afford to upgrade about four categories you'll get a sitting area and a decent amount of room. Like all other ships in the MSC fleet, this is another vessel that is good for the budget traveler who doesn't need first-class luxuries.

MERCURY (Celebrity Cruises)

Placed in Service: 1997	Registry: Panama
Length: 866 feet	Gross Tonnage: 77,713
Passengers: 1,870	Passenger Decks: 10
Staterooms: 589/296/50	Stateroom Size: 171 to 1,514 square feet
Crew Size: 909	Passenger/Crew Ratio: 2.1:1
Officers: Greek	Crew: European

Meal Arrangements: In addition to the main dining room and buffet service for breakfast and lunch, there are a couple of café-type eateries offering lighter meals.

Cruise Style: Week-long cruises usually have two formal nights. The remainder of the evenings are divided between informal (more common) and casual.

Price Range: 10-night cruises begin at $1,949 and reach $4,649 for regular staterooms. Suites start at $3,899 and have a high of $16,499.

It's hard to find fault with any of Celebrity's fabulous ships and the *Mercury* is no exception. A lot of cruisers expect a snow-white exterior and are a little disappointed when they see the large dark blue areas on the mid-hull section of the ship. Personally, I think the change of color is rather nice. The *Mercury's* profile is not particularly distinguished but, considering her size, she manages to avoid the boxy and bulky shape common in many of today's larger ships. She has well-designed deck plans with plenty of space that are easy to negotiate. Recreational facilities are highlighted by the fully equipped AquaSpa, which has become a distinctive feature of Celebrity ships and is very popular. Pampering is part of the Celebrity experience and that's illustrated by excellent service throughout the ship, especially in the dining rooms. Great care is taken to prepare a variety of imaginative cuisine and presentation is beautiful. A large art collection is scattered throughout the *Mercury*, and there are many good lounges from which to choose. My favorite is the two-deck Navigator Club, which has wrap-around windows and seating at different levels. It's a great place to gaze out upon the sea. At night it turns into a disco and remains one of the ship's most popular spots. All staterooms, regardless of category, are of a high standard and even those in the lowest category are large by cruise standards. They are attractive, functional and well designed, with lots of amenities, just as you would find in a first-class hotel. Many have verandas and floor-to-ceiling windows are also a common feature. Suites go all the way up to the super luxury level, where you get your own butler.

MISTRAL (First European)

Placed in Service: 1999	Registry: France
Length: 708 feet	Gross Tonnage: 47,900
Passengers: 1,200	Passenger Decks: 12
Staterooms: 377/221/0	Stateroom Size: 140 to 237 square feet
Crew Size: 470	Passenger/Crew Ratio: 2.6:1
Officers: Greek	Crew: International

Meal Arrangements: The main dining room is supplemented by a sizable alternative restaurant featuring casual meals. This is in addition to the breakfast/lunch buffet and a small coffee bar where sweets lovers will find much of interest.

Cruise Style: There is one formal night per week of cruising and two informal evenings. The rest of the time is casual.

Price Range: Fares for a seven-night cruise begin at $890 and go up to $2,060 for regular staterooms. Suite rates are from $1,620 to $2,580.

The *Mistral* was the inaugural ship in First European's "Premier" class (ships worthy of being called a luxury liner). She's a little smaller and less luxurious than the brand new *European Vision* or *European Star*, but still a beautiful ship providing a quality cruise experience at an affordable price. The *Mistral's* white and blue exterior (a hallmark of First European) has clean lines and a streamlined look. The unusual stern is slowly raked inward and gives the appearance of a multi-story resort hotel. Unfortunately, the design doesn't allow for much outdoor space, either bow or stern. The main outdoor area is the Cannes Deck, on the top, which has a nice pool and plenty of seating. Lounge chairs lined up on a balcony along each side of the ship provide one of the most comfortable viewing areas I've seen on any ship. Interior public areas are spacious and have an air of understated elegance, with soft colors and warm décor. The ship's layout is generally good and uncrowded. Both the quality and presentation of food is above average for this price bracket, and the service is both gracious and efficient while retaining a high degree of informality. I have many positive comments about the *Mistral*, but the staterooms are disappointingly small, especially in the lower categories. That said, their décor is lovely and their design functional. A cruise aboard the *Mistral* should be a pleasant experience. Note that the majority of passengers are European, as is the case on all ships of this line.

MONTEREY (Mediterranean Shipping Cruises)

Placed in Service: 1952 (1988)	Registry: Panama
Length: 564 feet	Gross Tonnage: 20,040
Passengers: 550	Passenger Decks: 4
Staterooms: 170/126/4	Stateroom Size: 65 to 344 square feet
Crew Size: 280	Passenger/Crew Ratio: 2.0:1
Officers: Italian	Crew: International

Meal Arrangements: As on most ships of this size, you'll find only one alternative to the main dining room – a buffet for breakfast and lunch.

Cruise Style: Mostly casual but, depending upon length of cruise, may have up to three nights informal. MSC refers to these nights as "formal," but they state that tie and jacket is acceptable. Tuxes are certainly acceptable too.

Price Range: For an 11-night cruise the regular stateroom fares are from $1,799 to $2,999. Suites start at $3,299 and rise to $3,799. Fourteen-night cruises begin at $2,499 and rise to $3,999. Suite prices are from $4,399 to $4,999.

This is a small ship by today's standards and, despite refurbishment over the years, an older and less luxurious one. The *Monterey* was originally built as a commercial vessel and even after its transformation to a recreational vessel, some common cruise amenities have been left out. There's a good-size sports deck and pleasant outdoor pool, but the fitness center is very limited. You'll also notice that the *Monterey* lacks any kind of spectacular visual centerpiece. The appealing dining room serves tasty Continental cuisine that incorporates many Italian dishes.

Of the numerous stateroom categories offered, too many are unacceptably small and you will have to upgrade considerably to get a decent-size cabin. Even the most spacious rooms lack attractiveness, but they are, at least, functional. Don't set your expectations too high and a cruise aboard the *Monterey* will be enjoyable, if not a true luxury experience.

NOORDAM (Holland America Line)

Placed in Service: 1984 (1990)	Registry: Netherlands Antilles
Length: 704 feet	Gross Tonnage: 33,930
Passengers: 1,214	Passenger Decks: 9
Staterooms: 343/194/70	Stateroom Size: 152 to 296 square feet
Crew Size: 542	Passenger/Crew Ratio: 2.2:1
Officers: Dutch	Crew: Indonesian & Filipino

Meal Arrangements: Open seating in the main dining room for breakfast and lunch. Alternative dining is offered at the Lido Buffet, open most evenings.

Cruise Style: Two formal nights on most cruises. The remainder of the time shows a slightly higher number of informal evenings than casual ones.

Price Range: For the various 10-night cruises on this ship, regular stateroom prices range from $2,799 to $4,739, while mini-suites are $5,844. Discounts for early booking run about 40%. Gratuities are included.

When the *Noordam* was placed into service she was considered a new class of ship for Holland America, and a big one at that. Although excellent maintenance has enabled this ship to retain much of its "new" feeling, many of today's cruise passengers will find some of its public areas and facilities lacking in both variety and size. But the *Noordam* retains the quiet and sophisticated elements that have made Holland America so popular. Most of the public facilities are concentrated on the Promenade and Upper Promenade decks, which makes for less walking. However, the layout of those decks isn't always intuitive. The ship's décor is subdued, in keeping with HAL's more traditional cruising style. Art and artifacts grace the public areas. The *Noordam* provides a good number of activities, including swimming and a good workout facility. The top-deck Crow's Nest Lounge, a feature of many HAL ships, makes for a nice place to imbibe and socialize with the other guests and is also an outstanding forward observation point.

Your dining experience will likely be above average, with good quality food and presentation. The service, however, is not outstanding. Staterooms are comfortable and nicely decorated. Most are of a good size, although some in the lowest categories can be small. A slight upgrade removes that potential problem. Many staterooms are categorized by HAL as "mini-suites," but they are really only slightly larger regular staterooms and because of the label you will be charged more than they are worth.

NORWEGIAN DREAM (Norwegian Cruise Line)

Placed in Service: 1992 (1998)	Registry: Bahamas
Length: 754 feet	Gross Tonnage: 50,764
Passengers: 1,748	Passenger Decks: 10
Staterooms: 564/170/140	Stateroom Size: 140 to 350 square feet
Crew Size: 700	Passenger/Crew Ratio: 2.5:1
Officers: Norwegian	Crew: International

Meal Arrangements: There is open seating for all meals, a rarity usually offered only by the most expensive liners. There are three separate dining rooms, along with a casual bistro, a pizzeria and other places where you can get light snacks.

Cruise Style: NCL's "free-style" cruising means that your voyage will be as casual or as dressy as you wish. Although there is a designated "formal" night in the main dining room, the casual alternative restaurants are open every evening too, so you can take your pick. The appropriate style for the entire cruise is "resort casual."

Price Range: Stateroom prices for a 12-night cruise start at $2,199 and rise to $3,649. For suites the range is from $3,549 to $6,899. Norwegian Cruise Line's policy regarding gratuities is to automatically charge $10 per person/ per day to your room account to cover tips. However, if you feel uncomfortable with this amount (and many people do either one way or the other), notify the staff in the lobby and they will adjust it. Cash tipping, however, is not done.

A 1998 refurbishment stretched this vessel and added some more rooms. The all-white exterior is extremely attractive, crowned by a large blue funnel near the stern. This combination of traditional features with modern trends is pleasing to the eye. The ship's layout is fairly simple. The top-most decks contain a good variety of recreational facilities, ranging from basketball courts to a gymnasium and massage facility. These facilities (other than the restaurants which I cover below) are attractive, but somewhat on the small side compared to other ships in this class. If you like dramatic open spaces the *Norwegian Dream* is not for you. Several areas have been designed specifically for children, making this a family-friendly ship. There's a nice observatory lounge at the bow end of the Sports Deck. One of the nicest features of this ship and others of NCL is the "free-style" program. Nowhere is this more evident than in the various dining rooms. They are all quite beautiful, but the showpiece is the largest room, the Four Seasons. Located amidships, the gracefully rounded room extends over the sides of the decks immediately above and below it. Walls of glass allow wonderful vistas from just about any seat in the house. Unfortunately, NCL doesn't set any records for its food and service. However, you will get tasty meals served by a competent and friendly staff.

The modern accommodations tend to be small, but they are colorful and comfortable. You have to go well up the price ladder to get what I would term "spacious" cabins. The *Norwegian Dream* provides a cruise typical of all NCL ships. It has beautiful surroundings and many of the features expected on today's modern ships but without a feeling of true luxury. It appeals to younger families and those with a mind for value.

NORWEGIAN SUN (Norwegian Cruise Line)

Placed in Service: 2001
Length: 853 feet
Passengers: 2,002
Staterooms: 650/295/56
Crew Size: 800
Officers: Norwegian

Registry: Bahamas
Gross Tonnage: 77,104
Passenger Decks: 12
Stateroom Size: 121 to 489 square feet
Passenger/Crew Ratio: 2.5:1
Crew: International

Meal Arrangements: Open seating and great selection on this ship. There are four separate dining rooms plus a bistro and other places for light snacks.

Cruise Style: Free-style dress is in force. See the details under the *Norwegian Dream*, above.

Price Range: Stateroom prices run from $1,631 to $2,437, while suites cost between $2,821 and $5,327. Gratuities are added to your account. See the details above under the *Norwegian Dream*.

When it came into service the *Norwegian Sun* was the biggest vessel in the NCL fleet. Her exterior is remarkably similar to that of the *Norwegian Dream*, but her interior layout is far different, with most of the middle decks devoted to staterooms. Public areas are found on three of the lower and middle decks and the recreational facilities are located on the two top decks. Perhaps because this ship was built for vacationing passengers (as opposed to the *Dream*, which started life as a commercial vessel), the public areas are more spacious and dramatic. There's a pretty seven-level atrium with a glass canopy and glass elevators. There's a great shopping area, a big variety of lounges, and a fairly large casino. The two-level main theater is beautiful and shows a diverse range of entertainment. Recreational facilities are extensive.

Your dining experience aboard the *Sun* – from the nature of the restaurants to service, presentation and style – is much the same as on the *Norwegian Dream*. Surprisingly, the main Four Seasons restaurant is actually nicer on the *Dream*. Accommodations are attractive but not large, with many of the low-category rooms smaller than those on the *Dream*. A large number of ocean view staterooms have private verandas.

The *Norwegian Sun* provides a good quality cruise experience and good value, but it's not in the luxury category.

ODYSSEUS (Royal Olympic)

Placed in Service: 1962 (1996)
Length: 483 feet
Passengers: 454
Staterooms: 183/43/0
Crew Size: 194
Officers: Greek

Registry: Greece
Gross Tonnage: 9,821
Passenger Decks: 7
Stateroom Size: 102 to 280 square feet
Passenger/Crew Ratio: 2.3:1
Crew: Greek

Meal Arrangements: There is open seating in the main dining room for breakfast and lunch. The only alternative is the buffet for breakfast and lunch.

Cruise Style: Each week of cruising usually has two formal evenings and one informal evening. The other nights are casual. All ships in this line include one Greek Night in the casual category. On those evenings, you are encouraged to dress Greek style, or at least wear the national colors (blue and white).

Price Range: Fares for the seven-night cruise begin at $1,830 and go to a maximum of $2,570. Three- or four-night mini cruises range in price from $655 to $1,395. Suites are priced from $1,075 to $2,195.

The *Odysseus* had been on private charter service for several years. This year marks her re-entry into the cruise world as a replacement for the *Stella Oceanis*. The ship was almost rebuilt in its entirety in 1987 and enjoyed a minor refurbishment in 1996. She doesn't look old, but does sport a traditional exterior profile. The *Odysseus* isn't very big and is relatively easy to get around. Public areas are spacious and attractive, though not dazzling. Recreation and entertainment options are somewhat limited, but this is usually overlooked as the majority of itineraries offered are short. Staterooms are attractively decorated and comfortable, but far too many of them are much smaller than is standard on most of today's ships.

OLYMPIC COUNTESS (Royal Olympic)

Placed in Service: 1976 (1998)
Length: 537 feet
Passengers: 814
Staterooms: 245/136/26
Crew Size: 350
Officers: Greek
Registry: Greece
Gross Tonnage: 18,000
Passenger Decks: 8
Stateroom Size: 87 to 265 square feet
Passenger/Crew Ratio: 2.3:1
Crew: Greek

Meal Arrangements: There is little choice other than the main dining room. Breakfast and lunch can be taken at an outdoor buffet, while a coffee bar offers light snacks.

Cruise Style: Per week of cruising there are generally two formal evenings and only one informal evening. The other nights are casual. All Royal Olympic ships have a Greek night in the casual category, when you are encouraged to dress Greek-style or at least wear blue and white, the national colors.

Price Range: Three- or four-night mini-cruises start at $655 and go up to $1,395. Suites are priced from $1,075 to $2,195.

The royal blue and white ships of Royal Olympic are a familiar sight in the Mediterranean, especially in the eastern portion. Most of their ships, including the *Olympic Countess*, are older, smaller vessels that offer casual port-intensive cruises without much in the way of luxury. Public areas are decorated in a bright manner and the all-Greek crew is similarly cheerful and friendly. There's a small fitness center, as well as a library and a few lounges. The main showroom, which doubles as a lounge and nightclub, offers enjoyable but below-average productions. All dinners must be taken in the one dining area, where the food is little better than decent. Fortunately, the itineraries are short enough that the lack of dining options is not too important. All of these shortcomings are probably bearable if your primary interest is the ports. However, the accommodations are definitely a problem. The smallest of the staterooms are oversized closets. Even the standard rooms (which represents about a third of the total) are a tiny 125 square feet – not enough room to stretch out and relax. On many ships you can forgive the small size because at least the décor is nice; on the *Olympic Countess*, plain is the order of the day. The bathrooms are also tiny. The only way to get good quality accommodations on this ship is to upgrade all the way to a deluxe suite, but that isn't a good value for your money.

OLYMPIC EXPLORER/OLYMPIC VOYAGER (Royal Olympic)

Placed in Service: 2001/2000
Length: 590 feet
Passengers: 836
Staterooms: 244/122/52
Crew Size: 360
Officers: Greek

Registry: Greece
Gross Tonnage: 25,000
Passenger Decks: 8
Stateroom Size: 140 to 258 square feet
Passenger/Crew Ratio: 2.3:1
Crew: Greek

Meal Arrangements: Eating is primarily limited to the main dining room. There is an indoor/outdoor buffet for breakfast and lunch, as well as a pizzeria and ice cream bar.

Cruise Style: Each week of cruising has two formal evenings and one informal evening. The other nights are casual (including Greek night). All ships of this line include one Greek night when passengers are encouraged to dress Greek-style (or wear the country's national colors, blue and white).

Price Range: Fares for a seven-night cruise begin at $2,250 and rise to $3,185. For suites the range is $3,850 to $5,440.

These twins mark a change in Royal Olympic's world of cruising and they represent a huge improvement over the company's other ships.

They differ sharply from most of the new cruise ships in size. Although bigger than other Royal Olympic vessels, these carry only about half of what is typically seen in contemporary vessels. Don't think that you're going to have a great deal of room just because they carry fewer passengers. Everything is relative, and the space in public areas is about par for most ships.

Both ships have a beautiful sleek design and lovely décor that is both cheerful and soft on the eyes. Flow is quite good. The ships are among the fastest on the seas today, which suits the typically port-intensive itineraries of Royal Olympic. Numerous facilities, which are in line with what you might expect on much larger ships, include a gymnasium, a spa and a well designed main lounge.

Food aboard these sister ships is more than satisfactory and is served by a friendly staff in beautiful surroundings. The accommodations also bring a new level of luxury to the line. These are the only vessels in Royal Olympic's fleet with staterooms that are comparable to those on other new ships. Although a large percentage of the rooms are still below the industry average in size, they are big enough that you won't be tripping over yourself. They are attractive and well designed.

The overall cruise experience aboard the *Explorer* and *Voyager* is a good one, with plenty of activities and the expert-in-residence program that means you're guaranteed interesting lectures about the land attractions.

PACIFIC PRINCESS (Princess Cruises)

Placed in Service: 1971 (1993)	Registry: Britain
Length: 553 feet	Gross Tonnage: 20,000
Passengers: 640	Passenger Decks: 7
Staterooms: 243/67/10	Stateroom Size: 126 to 441 square feet
Crew Size: 350	Passenger/Crew Ratio: 1.8:1
Officers: British	Crew: European

Meal Arrangements: As a much smaller ship, the *Pacific Princess* doesn't offer the "Personal Choice" options of the newer Princess vessels. Consequently, there is only a buffet for breakfast and lunch in addition to the main dining room.

Cruise Style: There are usually two formal nights per week of cruising, with the remainder of the evenings equally divided between informal and casual.

Price Range: The standard 12-day cruise stateroom prices begin at $2,805 and rise to a maximum of $3,870. Suites range from a low of $5,230 to a high of $6,210.

The original "Love Boat" just about says it all for this well known and well traveled ship which, to some extent, is responsible for the present popularity of cruising. After her current limited run in the Mediterranean, Princess Cruises will be withdrawing the *Pacific Princess* from service. For many people, including numerous couples who have romanced aboard her, that will be a sad day. Even though the ship is still attractive, there is little doubt that she has become dated and is now a poor cousin in the star-studded Princess fleet.

Rather than reviewing this ship in the usual manner (it can be considered as average in all respects), suffice to say that one last cruise on the *Pacific Princess* is primarily for those who wish to put a piece of history under their belts. For that reason alone, I'm sure that demand for this ship's final cruises will be very high.

QUEEN ELIZABETH II (Cunard Line)

Placed in Service: 1969 (1999)   Registry: Great Britain
Length: 963 feet   Gross Tonnage: 70,327
Passengers: 1,778   Passenger Decks: 13
Staterooms: 674/244/9   Stateroom Size: 107 to 1,184 square feet
Crew Size: 1,004   Passenger/Crew Ratio: 1.8:1
Officers: British   Crew: International

Meal Arrangements: Five restaurants offer full-service meals and there's also a buffet (also open for dinner, with service) and a grill that serves quick lunches. Open seating at all meals is the general rule, except for the restaurant (Mauretania), which operates on a two-seating basis.

Cruise Style: Cunard is still an old-fashioned and traditional cruise line. Expect at least three formal nights per week to 10 days of cruising, with the remainder of evenings being about equally split between informal and casual.

Price Range: Rates for the 15-night cruise begin at $3,499 and rise to $19,659. For suites the prices run from $26,519 to $42,459. A gratuity fee of $13 per person/per day is added to each stateroom account. If you wish, this amount can be either lessened or increased. If you intend to change the amount (don't be intimidated), notify desk personnel at least a full day before the end of the cruise.

When the *QE II* entered service more than 30 years ago she was, size-wise, in a class all by herself. The term mega-liner wasn't in use back then, but this ship was certainly of that genre. She's still a big ship by any standard, but only one among many. The *QE II* was getting rather tired looking and out of date, so a major refurbishment in 1999 helped spruce things up. Sadly, the dated look is still visible, especially next to newer floating resorts. Of course, traditionalists prefer that look and will state firmly that the *QE II* is still the ultimate ship afloat.

With the lines of a traditional ocean liner, the *QE II* is quite impressive. However, the décor, although classic in many ways, lacks any real pizzazz. She has only limited Mediterranean itineraries, so I'll concentrate on the features that make a *QE II* cruise unique. Although there aren't the sharp class distinctions as in the old days of cruising, there are still some vestiges of this on the *QE II*.

On a ship of this size, the facilities are extensive. Most facilities are open to all passengers but there is, for instance, one restaurant that is open only to passengers in several of the upper-grade accommodations. Likewise, certain deck spaces (with assigned lounge chairs) are restricted to upper-class passengers. Such distinctions in today's world may seem out of place and even a turn-off. But, no doubt, there will be those people who pay the premium price and expect special treatment. Additionally, those traveling in the low- or middle-price brackets may be more comfortable dining and talking with other passengers who share a similar lifestyle. Food and service is of a high standard no matter where you dine, and is considered one of the ship's stronger points. The same cannot be said for the staterooms, which are usually adequate but quite unimaginative in décor and style. Many rooms are far too small, despite the fact that this ship was designed for trans-Atlantic cruising and passage aboard comes with a high price tag.

RHAPSODY (Mediterranean Shipping Cruises)

Placed in Service: 1977 (1997)	Registry: Panama
Length: 541	Gross Tonnage: 17,495
Passengers: 750	Passenger Decks: 8
Staterooms: 276/127/22	Stateroom Size: 87 to 265 square feet
Crew Size: 350	Passenger/Crew Ratio: 2.1:1
Officers: Italian	Crew: Italian

Meal Arrangements: The main dining room is the only full-service restaurant on board. There is a buffet for breakfast and lunch.

Cruise Style: Mostly casual but, depending upon length of cruise, may have up to three nights informal. MSC refers to these nights as "formal," but a tie and jacket are acceptable for the men.

Price Range: The five-night cruises cost from $849 to $1,199 for regular staterooms and from $1,249 to $1,399 for suites. For seven nights the range is $1,249 to $2,199 for staterooms and from $2,299 to $2,499 for suites. The 11-night cruises begin at $1,599 and go up to $2,699. Suites are from $2,899 to $3,199.

This ship is quite similar in appearance to the other ships in the line (the *Melody* and the *Monterey)*. It is not very large and lacks the luxury appointments that are common on today's vessels. However, it is attractive and provides a pleasant cruise experience without busting your budget.

Public areas are surprisingly pleasing to the eye, with lots of open space and cheerful décor. A multi-functional room that doubles as the ship's show lounge is one of the most popular areas, a gathering spot for all. A separate club has dancing. Recreational facilities are somewhat limited, but you will find a small gym and sauna, along with a relatively large, pleasing pool area that features a jogging track above. The dining room is also pretty, but the food, which emphasizes Italian cuisine, is standard. The wait staff is jolly and eager to please, though the service is not white glove. Although the staterooms are colorful, functional and pleasantly furnished, many of them are too small and you will almost certainly be feeling cramped by the end of a week-long cruise. Accommodations at the high end of the price scale are bigger, but most people would choose this line for value and you'll lose that element if you upgrade on your room.

ROTTERDAM (Holland America Line)

Placed in Service: 1997
Length: 778 feet
Passengers: 1,316
Staterooms: 378/120/160
Crew Size: 593
Officers: Dutch

Registry: Netherlands
Gross Tonnage: 62,000
Passenger Decks: 12
Stateroom Size: 182 to 1,125 square feet
Passenger/Crew Ratio: 2.2:1
Crew: Indonesian/Filipino

Meal Arrangements: Open seating in the main dining room for breakfast and lunch. Alternative dining includes the Lido Buffet for all meals (including most dinners), and a specialty restaurant serving Italian food in the evenings.

Cruise Style: Two formal nights and three informal nights per cruise. The rest of the time is casual.

Price Range: Standard staterooms for a 12-night cruise run from $4,529 through $6,429; suites begin at $8,540 and rise to $23,669. HAL offers discounts in excess of industry norms for those who book very early. Gratuities are included.

Old name, new ship. Holland America likes to do things in a traditional way and that includes keeping the names of its former ships – some of which have reached almost legendary proportions in the annals of pleasure cruising.This is the sixth ship to carry this name. If you look at the *Rotterdam*, you will immediately notice its similarities with the *Amsterdam*. They are virtually identical. See page 22 for a complete description of the *Amsterdam*. There are only small statistical differences between the two and the layout is the same. The only easily noticeable difference is that the *Rotterdam's* main pool is on an extended version of the recreation-oriented Lido deck instead of being to the rear of an accommodation deck. Public facilities are the same on both ships, and even the deck names and facilities are usually identical.

ROYAL PRINCESS (Princess Cruises)

Placed in Service: 1984 (1995)
Length: 757 feet
Passengers: 1,200
Staterooms: 560/0/40
Crew Size: 520
Officers: British

Registry: Great Britain
Gross Tonnage: 45,000
Passenger Decks: 9
Stateroom Size: 168 to 805 square feet
Passenger/Crew Ratio: 2.3:1
Crew: Italian

Meal Arrangements: This ship does not feature the "Personal Choice" dining option offered on larger Princess ships. However, besides the main dining room (open seating for breakfast and lunch), there is a buffet/café and pizzeria.

Cruise Style: There are two formal evenings per cruise, with the remainder of the nights equally divided between informal and casual.

Price Range: Regular stateroom rates for 10-night cruises begin at $2,490 and rise to $3,990. Suites run from a low of $5,040 up to $8,470. For 12-night cruises stateroom fares have a base of $3,040 and reach a high of $4,590. The range for suites is from $5,590 to $9,070.

The *Royal Princess* looks good, considering her age. She's smaller than any of the "Grand Class" ships that Princess now operates, but still large enough to incorporate all the facilities and amenities that today's cruise passengers expect. Her outline is graceful, with a superstructure that curves gently upwards at the bow and outward and then upward at the rear. The large funnel, often the most unattractive feature on ships, actually enhances her overall appearance. A good amount of open teak deck space allows people space to jog or walk under covered promenades. The ship's beautiful atrium spans three decks and was one of the first to be incorporated into a liner. All of the public areas are well designed and attractive. They have served as prototypes for Princess' larger vessels and are essentially smaller versions of what has now proved to be popular with cruise travelers. The entertainment program is good and the *Royal Princess* offers an activity-filled schedule, as is common on all Princess vessels. The dining experience is only average. Perhaps the strongest feature of the *Royal Princess* is the accommodations, which are all located on the outside, a rarity on a ship of this size. Plus, a large percentage of them have private verandas. The rooms are larger than is common (especially in the lower price categories) and there are enough options if you want more room and luxury.

SEVEN SEAS MARINER (Radisson Seven Seas Cruises)

Placed in Service: 2001	Registry: France
Length: 713	Gross Tonnage: 50,000
Passengers: 708	Passenger Decks: 9
Staterooms: 354 (outside suites)	Stateroom Size: 301 to 1,076 square feet
Crew Size: 440	Passenger/Crew Ratio: 1.6:1
Officers: French	Crew: International

Meal Arrangements: Open seating for all meals in a choice of four different restaurants.

Cruise Style: Two formal nights per week of cruising. The remainder of the evenings are equally divided between informal and casual. Radisson is considered to be one of the dressier lines.

Price Range: Seven-night cruises run from a low of $3,395 to a high of $15,195. The 10-night price range is from $4,795 to $21,295; while 11-night cruises begin at $5,295 and rise to a maximum of $22,095.

The *Mariner* is Radisson Seven Seas' newest and largest ship. It has all the attributes of the luxury yacht class, but is just too large to be included in that category. This vessel was the first of its size to offer all outside suites with balcony. Her bright snow-white exterior has the appearance of a much larger ship in style and also maintains some traditional features – it's neither boxy nor too rounded. The *Mariner* has all of the facilities associated with the biggest of ships. A central atrium spans all of the passenger decks. There's a beautiful two-level theater, a casino and numerous recreational facilities, including a full-service spa and fitness center, and a jogging track. You're not likely to feel crowded aboard as there is plenty of space. The *Mariner's* dining options deserve special attention. The elegant Compass Room is the largest dining area. An alternative, called Signatures, serves fine gourmet cuisine that competes with that of the best European cities. Latitudes is a smaller specialty restaurant, and La Veranda is a Mediterranean-style bistro featuring buffet meals from several well-stocked and nicely displayed food islands. All of the food is excellent and service is top notch. Wine is complimentary, as are the drinks in the wet bar in your stateroom. The *Mariner* also has several elegant lounges styled after private European clubs.

The spacious staterooms are ooh la la! The décor is exquisite and the amenities and comfort levels are unmatched in the cruising world. In a delightful departure from the standard, gratuities, drinks and whatever else are extra on most ships are all included in the price of your cruise aboard the *Mariner*. If you like to have more than a couple of drinks, you should get your money's worth! Cruisers disembark knowing they have enjoyed first-class luxury all the way.

STELLA SOLARIS (Royal Olympic)

Placed in Service: 1953 (1999)	Registry: Greece
Length: 544 feet	Gross Tonnage: 18,000
Passengers: 628	Passenger Decks: 8
Staterooms: 166/82/66	Stateroom Size: 96 to 226 square feet
Crew Size: 320	Passenger/Crew Ratio: 2.0:1
Officers: Greek	Crew: Greek

Meal Arrangements: Open seating in the main dining room for breakfast and lunch. There is the option of regular service or buffet for breakfast. The ship has recently added a grill room as an alternate to the main dining room.

Cruise Style: There are usually two formal evenings and only one informal evening per week of cruising. The other nights are casual. All ships of this line feature one Greek Night in the casual category where you are encouraged to dress to match the theme.

Price Range: Seven-night cruise fares for regular staterooms start at $1,830 and reach a high of $2,570. For suites the range is $3,220 to $4,095.

Unfortunately, I think some passengers will feel embarrassed when this vessel anchors next to one of the newer beauties of the sea. The *Stella Solaris* is the oldest ship in the Royal Olympic fleet and the oldest of any major cruise line in this market. Although it has been refurbished several times, it is past its best. It has a traditional profile and thus looks better from a distance than upon close examination. But the *Stella Solaris* has positive attributes, including some attractive public areas. The main lounge, which doubles as a showroom, doesn't allow for extravagant productions, but does feature entertaining cabaret-style shows. There's also a sizable spa, disco and several lounges in addition to a fairly spacious and comfortable theater. The outdoor swimming pool, also large, has plenty of deck space around it. Surprisingly, the dining room aboard the *Stella Solaris* is probably the best of the Olympic fleet, excluding its two newest ships.

Despite my complaints, the *Solaris* has a good repeat rate due to a combination of factors – the friendly and attentive crew and the relative value for money are two. The homemade potato chips served at the ship's bars have contributed too. Staterooms are generally small and the décor somewhat stale. Still, if you upgrade one or two notches you can get about 180 square feet – more than decent by any ship standards.

TRITON (Royal Olympic)

Placed in Service: 1971 (1999)	Registry: Greece
Length: 486 feet	Gross Tonnage: 14,000
Passengers: 676	Passenger Decks: 7
Staterooms: 202/110/26	Stateroom Size: 110 to 270 square feet
Crew Size: 300	Passenger/Crew Ratio: 2.3:1
Officers: Greek	Crew: Greek

Meal Arrangements: Open seating for breakfast and lunch in the main dining room. There is a buffet for breakfast and lunch with both indoor and outdoor seating.

Cruise Style: Two formal evenings and one informal evening per week. The other nights are casual. All Royal Olympic vessels have a Greek Night and you are encouraged to dress Greek style or at least wear blue and white.

Price Range: Fares on a seven-night cruise start at $1,605 and rise to $2,270 for regular staterooms. Suites begin at $2,855 and top out at $3,255. For a 10-night cruise prices range from $2,295 to $3,245 for staterooms and from $4,080 to $4,650 for suites.

The majority of Royal Olympic's older vessels have a presentable exterior with traditional, graceful lines and decent color schemes. In general, the décor of this ship is pleasant, but some areas need refurbishment. This ship is popular with the budget set and is usually crowded. It doesn't have a great deal of open space, but is very well laid out, with nearly all staterooms on the lower decks and all public areas on the upper four decks, three of which are quite small. The ship has a good selection of the usual facilities, including fitness center, disco and theater. The Nine Muses Nightclub at the fore end of the top deck is especially nice. A fairly small pool, which lacks significant deck space, is surrounded by an attractive walking promenade/jogging track. Meals aboard the *Triton* are nothing to write home about. However, you certainly won't go hungry. Since this is one of Royal Olympic's older ships, the accommodations are lacking, particularly in size. Most rooms are plain and lack functionality. In order to get sufficient room, you have to upgrade to one of the top three price categories. However, many rooms in the higher categories have a tub instead of a shower.

WORLD RENAISSANCE (Royal Olympic)

Placed in Service: 1966 (1996)
Length: 492 feet
Passengers: 474
Staterooms: 163/59/15
Crew Size: 230
Officers: Greek

Registry: Greece
Gross Tonnage: 12,000
Passenger Decks: 8
Stateroom Size: 110 to 275 square feet
Passenger/Crew Ratio: 2.1:1
Crew: Greek

Meal Arrangements: There is no alternative to the main dining room.

Cruise Style: Two formal evenings and one informal evening per week of cruising. The other nights are casual. All ships in this fleet feature a Greek Night when guests are encouraged to wear Greek dress.

Price Range: Three- and four-night mini-cruises are priced from $635 to $1,395 for regular staterooms and from $1,075 to $2,195 for suites.

The *World Renaissance*, one of the smaller vessels plying the Mediterranean, suffers from many of the same problems as the other older ships of the Royal Olympic line. See the above description for specifics. Let's take a look at the good things. Sun worshippers are likely to enjoy this ship as there is an abundance of outside deck space for walking, jogging or sunbathing by the pool. There are two reasonably sized pools. Décor in the public areas is mildly attractive, but public facilities are lacking. Although there is a tiny disco, the only other significant public area besides the restaurant is the multi-purpose lounge, which doubles as a showroom. It isn't particularly well designed for either function. The staff is quite friendly, especially in the dining room, where you will be surprised to see more Indonesian cuisine on the menu than Greek. That's because this ship served several years in Asia and the menu seems to be a holdover. The range of accommodations runs the gamut from too small to better than average. The number of rooms that offer at least 165 square feet is numerous.

Luxury Yachts

There is no industry-wide standard or official classification for the luxury yacht class. So, I get to determine the requirements. I have included here only those ships that meet all of the following criteria:

- ⚓ Maximum length under 625 feet
- ⚓ Maximum passengers under 400
- ⚓ *Average* stateroom size in excess of 200 square feet
- ⚓ Passenger/crew ratio of 1.8:1 or better
- ⚓ Fine reputation for service and style

Admittedly, the last requirement is subjective, but you'll soon learn that these operators receive very few complaints.

RADISSON DIAMOND (Radisson Seven Seas Cruises)

Placed in Service: 1992
Length: 420
Passengers: 350
Staterooms: 175
Crew Size: 200
Officers: Finnish

Registry: Bahamas
Gross Tonnage: 20,295
Passenger Decks: 6
Stateroom Size: 220 square feet
Passenger/Crew Ratio: 1.8:1
Crew: European

Meal Arrangements: There is open seating for all meals in the main dining room. The Grill offers informal buffet breakfasts and lunches and converts into an Italian-style trattoria at night.

Cruise Style: Two formal nights per week of cruising. The remainder of the evenings are divided between informal and casual. Radisson is, by reputation, one of the dressier lines in operation.

Price Range: Seven-night cruises are priced from $3,495 to $7,395. The nine-night cruise costs between $4,595 and $9,495.

The *Radisson Diamond* is definitely the most unusual looking cruise ship in service. Its twin-hulled design helps to give it the stability of a much larger ship but, unlike small catamarans, it is not fast. In fact, it is one of the slowest cruise ships around. Most guests don't seem to mind because they are surrounded by luxury. No other cruise ships have followed suit in design, partly due to the sometimes awkward interior layout that is caused by facilities being located on opposite sides of the hulls. The *Diamond* is a very pretty ship with facilities that sparkle, including a moderately sized five-deck atrium. The big spa offers massage, aromatherapy and other indulgent services. Cabaret shows are held in the Windows Lounge, a magnificent crystal and glass area. There's also a piano bar and piano entertainment on some nights in the main dining room. The Grand Dining Room, two decks high and surrounded by rich draperies, is as elegant as I have seen. The *Diamond* even has its own "wine cellar," offering fine vintages to complement the classy Continental cuisine and fine service. Accommodations are uniform and wonderful. Beautifully decorated staterooms are very big by ship standards and feature a fully stocked refrigerator. Each room has a separate sitting area and most have a private veranda. The fairly small bathrooms have lots of marble and manage to include a cozy tub.

SEABOURN GODDESS I/II (Seabourn Cruise Line)

Placed in Service: 1984/5 ('97/8)
Length: 344 feet
Passengers: 116
Staterooms: 58 (outside suites)
Crew Size: 90
Officers: European

Registry: Norway
Gross Tonnage: 4,250
Passenger Decks: 5
Stateroom Size: 179 to 410 square feet
Passenger/Crew Ratio: 1.3:1
Crew: European/American

Meal Arrangements: Open seating for all meals in the main dining room. You may dine in an outdoor café for breakfast and lunch; it's a buffet, but waiters carry your tray.

Cruise Style: Seabourn uses the term "elegant casual" to describe its dress code aboard the *Goddesses*. That seems like a contradiction in terms, but it does mean you don't have to worry about tuxedos, gowns or ties on board these ships.

Price Range: Seven-day cruises run from $4,999 to $13,709. Longer cruises are proportionately higher. Early booking savings run 25-30%. All gratuities are included.

The twins have been around awhile, but are back among the top luxury yachts now that they've received major make-overs. Even for this class of ship, these intimate luxury yachts are small in size and number of passengers. Discriminating travelers will likely find everything they could wish for, from spacious and beautiful accommodations to the first-rate service found only on ships with impressive passenger-to-crew ratios like this. These vessels have a considerably larger array of facilities than the Renaissance ships described above. Besides the pool with its adjoining whirlpool and several lounges, there's a good fitness center complete with sauna. There's also a bar on the spacious sun deck. One of the more unusual features of the *Goddesses* is the watersports platform, where you can use equipment such as JetSkis at no extra charge. All of the public areas are elegantly furnished. The dining salon serves quality food with sophisticated white glove service. Flambé desserts are a specialty and caviar is available all day long. Wine is included in the price, although the highest quality vintages warrant an additional fee. The accommodations are all beautiful and come with a separate living area and well-stocked refrigerator. The bathrooms are very nice, although on the small side, and you'll find bathrobes hanging there. I noted that several categories of accommodations are no larger than on a regular cruise ship. However, this is a luxury experience all the way. Children under the age of 16 are not allowed on these ships.

SEABOURN LEGEND/SEABOURN PRIDE/ SEABOURN SPIRIT (Seabourn Cruise Line)

Placed in Service: 1992 (1999)/1988 (1997)/1989 (1999)
Registry: Norway
Length: 440 feet
Passengers: 208
Staterooms: 104 (outside suites)
Crew Size: 150
Officers: Norwegian

Gross Tonnage: 10,000
Passenger Decks: 6
Stateroom Size: 205-590 square feet
Passenger/Crew Ratio: 1.4:1
Crew: European/International

Meal Arrangements: There is open seating for all meals in the main dining room. An alternative café is available daily for breakfast and lunch and on all non-formal evenings.

Cruise Style: There are only two dress categories on these Seabourn ships: Formal (two nights for each week of cruising); and the "elegant casual" (see description above) on all other nights.

Price Range: Seven-day cruises are priced from $4,749 to $13,999. Longer or shorter cruises are proportionally higher or lower. Early booking savings run in the neighborhood of 25-30%. Gratuities are included.

These ships are sleeker and more modern than the *Goddesses.* They offer a slightly lower level of luxury, although the personal service and pampering still far exceeds what you will find on regular cruise ships. Onboard facilities include a complete spa with fitness center, massage, sauna and steam room and many personal wellness programs. There's also an outdoor whirlpool, swimming pool, a small casino and a watersports marina (it has fewer facilities than its counterpart on the *Goddesses*). Dinner is a gourmet delight, with outstanding food, wonderful service and quality linens and tableware. Accommodations are equally superb, with plush bedding and soothing natural colors. All categories are well designed and filled with lots of amenities (including the best soaps and body lotions) but, considering the price, some are not nearly as roomy as you would expect.

What's in a Name?

Ships change from one cruise line to another quite regularly. As lines upgrade their fleets, they often sell ships to another line or assign them to a subsidiary company lower on the luxury scale. Many of best-known luxury ships wind up as budget carriers in Asia, but some still cater to the American and European markets. The *Crown Odyssey, Braemar* and *Costa Tropicale* are some examples. It's the cruise lines' version of musical chairs. With the help of a name change and a new itinerary, some ships keep going forever!

Some readers, especially true cruise lovers, might be wondering why they can't find the *Seabourn Sun*, the largest and most luxurious ship in the Seabourn fleet, in this book. This ship regularly cruised in the Mediterranean and did so as recently as the summer of 2001. Having completed a world cruise, the vessel is being sent to join the Holland America Line fleet in the summer of 2002 and will be renamed the *Prinsendam*. HAL's intention was to have the ship sail in Europe but, according to their website, the vessel will offer only Northern and Western European itineraries. Keep checking www.hollandamerica.com for updates.

SILVER SHADOW & SILVER WHISPER (Silversea Cruises)

Placed in Service: 2000/2001   Registry: Bahamas
Length: 610 feet   Gross Tonnage: 28,258
Passengers: 382   Passenger Decks: 7
Staterooms: 194 (outside suites) Stateroom Size: 287 to 1,435 square feet
Crew Size: 295   Passenger/Crew Ratio: 1.3:1
Officers: Italian   Crew: International

Meal Arrangements: There is open seating for all meals in the main dining room. Alternative dining options are open only for breakfast and lunch and include the Terrace Café, which has both indoor and outdoor seating areas, and a small poolside grill.

Cruise Style: There are usually two formal nights per week of sailing, while the remainder of the evenings are evenly split between informal and casual.

Price Range: For a seven-night cruise, prices range from a low of $6,095 to a high of $13,995. Twelve-night cruises run from $9,495 to $22,395. All rooms are suites. Gratuities are included, as are all beverages, even wine and champagne. On many sailings, one standard shore excursion is offered at no charge.

These marvelous ships are identical (except for the one year difference in their year of construction) and each offers a top-notch luxury cruising experience. They accommodate more than twice as many passengers as the preceding Seabourn entries and measure just over 600 feet, which puts them at the limit of the luxury yacht class. But their style and feel alone would distinguish them from "ordinary" cruise ships. No other ships have a better space ratio, and personalized service (the hallmark of Silversea) is expected with the absolutely superb passenger-to-crew ratio, a number that you rarely see. Public areas are remarkably beautiful. There's a library, several lounges of varying size (including a cigar bar), and a casino. The shows at the two-level theater are good, although not as elaborate as those on bigger ships. The limited selection of shops includes Bulgari. The top deck has a wonderful observation lounge and a full-service bar. Dinner aboard is a gourmet experience that will be appreciated by those with sophisticated tastes and fine service.

I have yet to find ship accommodations that beat these all-suite rooms. Spaciousness is only the beginning. The décor is beautiful and features generous use of light woods, lots of glass and luxury furnishings. All bathrooms have tubs and most have double vanities. The larger suites are on a par with those you'd expect in an expensive land-based resort. The amenities are too numerous to mention. Of course, all this privacy, room, attention and luxury does come at a price, and budget cruisers need not apply to Silversea. Discriminating travelers who can afford the tariff will adore it.

SILVER WIND (Silversea Cruises)

Placed in Service: 1995   Registry: Bahamas
Length: 514 feet   Gross Tonnage: 16,800
Passengers: 296   Passenger Decks: 6
Staterooms: 148 (outside suites) Stateroom Size: 240 to 1,314 square feet
Crew Size: 210   Passenger/Crew Ratio: 1.4:1
Officers: Italian   Crew: International

Meal Arrangements: Open seating for all meals in the main dining room. Limited alternative dining options for breakfast and lunch.

Cruise Style: There are usually two formal evenings per week of sailing. The remaining nights are evenly split between informal and casual.

Price Range: All units are suites. They run from $6,195 to $12,995 for a seven-night cruise, all the way up to $$9,695-$21,295 for a 12-night cruise. Gratuities are included in the fare, as are all beverages (even wine and champagne) and, often, one shore excursion is often complimentary.

The *Silver Wind* is not quite as big as the above Silversea entries, but it's every bit a luxury yachting vessel. Its passenger-to-crew ratio is an undetectable notch below that of the other ships and, therefore, still beats the remainder of the competition. Ship facilities are almost the same as those on the other ships, but they are proportionately smaller to match the number of passengers. Rooms match those found aboard the *Shadow* and *Whisper* and, although they average 10% smaller, they have plenty of room and plenty of luxury. The dining experience is almost identical, too. The *Silver Wind's* beautiful twin ship, the *Silver Cloud*, is one year older and has a Bahamian registry. It is not scheduled to sail in the Mediterranean during 2002, but has been there frequently in the past.

SONG OF FLOWER (Radisson Seven Seas Cruises)

Placed in Service: 1986 (1990)   Registry: Bahamas
Length: 408   Gross Tonnage: 8,282
Passengers: 180   Passenger Decks: 6
Staterooms: 80/0/20   Stateroom Size: 183 to 398 square feet
Crew Size: 144   Passenger/Crew Ratio: 1.3:1
Officers: Norwegian   Crew: European

Meal Arrangements: There is open seating in the main dining room for all meals. An alternative restaurant is available for dinner.

Cruise Style: There are generally two formal nights per week of cruising. The remainder of the evenings are about equally divided between informal and casual. Radisson has a reputation of being one of the "dressier" lines frequented by well-dressed and well-heeled passengers.

Price Range: The lowest rate for a seven-night cruise is $3,095, the highest, $5,795. The range for an eight-night cruise runs from $3,595 to $6,795.

The size tells you it's a luxury yacht, but the profile looks just like a graceful miniature mega-liner. The *Song of Flower* has a good selection of recreational and other facilities for its size, but they are more limited than you will find on other ships. However, entertainment is well tended to, with two dance floors, a nightclub and show lounge. The Galaxy Dining Room is a delightful room decorated with masses of flowers, presumably to suit the ship's name. All of the public areas are attractive and cheerful, although a refurbishment might be due shortly. The dining experience maintains the high standards of the line and you'll find that Angelo's Italian trattoria is especially good. The accommodations are more varied than on most ships of this size and type, but they are all well designed and pleasing to the eye. There are lots of amenities, such as terrycloth robes, slippers, a stocked refrigerator and more. Many bathrooms have tubs.

Sailing Ships

The sailing ships listed here are by no means the only ones serving the Mediterranean. Numerous (often much smaller) sailing vessels and yachts ply the waters of several countries, most notably Greece and Turkey. They tend to concentrate on limited geographic areas. I have therefore chosen to include in this category only those vessels that offer a more broad-based Mediterranean experience and whose facilities are more in line with those found on the traditional cruise ships.

ROYAL CLIPPER (Star Clippers)

Placed in Service: 2000	Registry: Luxembourg
Length: 439 feet	Gross Tonnage: 5,000
Passengers: 228	Passenger Decks: 5
Staterooms: 92/6/16	Stateroom Size: 100 to 320 square feet
Crew Size: 105	Passenger/Crew Ratio: 2.2:1
Officers: International	Crew: International

Meal Arrangements: Open seating for all meals in the Dining Room (there is no alternative). At some ports an outdoor barbecue is held on shore at lunchtime.

Cruise Style: Happily, you can leave your formal attire at home when sailing on this ship. Dress is casual at all times. The only restriction is that no shorts or tees are allowed at dinner time.

Price Range: For seven-night cruises the tariff for staterooms is from $1,950 to $2,975, while suites are $3,970 to $4,970.

It goes to show how little the country of registry really means – Luxembourg is landlocked! The *Royal Clipper* is an elegant five-masted vessel with 42 billowing sails that soar to a height of 197 feet. It is the largest true sailing ship in the world today. "True" means that it has no engine back-up as most of today's sailing ships do (they usually rely on sail for about 75% of their cruise time). The *Royal Clipper* has very up-to-date facilities, but everything about its look and style is a throwback to centuries past. The elegance of the public facilities will surprise most guests. There's a beautiful three-deck atrium that allows natural light into the elegant multi-level dining room. The huge open sun deck has three pools and there is also a fitness center with spa. The marina, at the ship's stern, is the launching point for numerous water-based recreational adventures. Quiet times can be spent in the library or in the observation lounge. For the best views, climb up the mast to the real old-fashioned crow's nest. Safety harnesses are provided. The main dining room is filled with pictures of famous sailing ships and the cuisine is expertly prepared and presented. Service is excellent without being overbearing. Cabins are tastefully appointed but are only small to average in size. The top accommodations are more spacious and have a bathtub. The experience of travel aboard a sailing ship is unique and cannot be compared to a regular cruise. The beauty of the *Royal Clipper* is nothing short of magnificent and few people will go home unsatisfied.

STAR FLYER/STAR CLIPPER (Star Clippers)

Placed in Service: 1991/1992	Registry: Luxembourg
Length: 360 feet	Gross Tonnage: 2,298
Passengers: 170	Passenger Decks: 4
Staterooms: 78/6/1	Stateroom Size: 95 to 150 square feet
Crew Size: 72	Passenger/Crew Ratio: 2.4:1
Officers: International	Crew: International

Meal Arrangements: See the details under the *Royal Clipper*.

Cruise Style: Casual all day and night, as on the *Royal Clipper*.

Price Range: Regular staterooms run from $1,850 to $2,970 for the seven-night cruise. Suites are priced at $3,970.

Each of these identical and beautiful four-masted sailing ships is smaller than the *Royal Clipper* and has fewer public facilities. There's still lots of room and you shouldn't feel cramped. Public areas are few, limited to the restaurant, deck space, two swimming pools on the sun deck and a library. The lovely dining room serves as a multi-function room during non-meal times. My one complaint is that the rooms are tiny at worst and adequate at best. Nautical décor in the rooms and public areas is a delight and gives the feel of a 19th-century vessel.

WIND SPIRIT/WIND STAR (Windstar Cruises)

Placed in Service: 1988/'86 ('95/'96)
Registry: Bahamas

Length: 440 feet	Gross Tonnage: 5,350
Passengers: 148	Passenger Decks: 5
Staterooms: 74/0/0	Stateroom Size: 188 to 220 square feet
Crew Size: 90	Passenger/Crew Ratio: 1.6:1
Officers: Norwegian/British	Crew: Indonesian/Filipino

Meal Arrangements: The one restaurant has open seating for all meals.

Cruise Style: Take your pick of terms – resort casual, casual elegant, or whatever. The big news is no ties and jackets for men and no gowns for women.

Price Range: Staterooms are priced at between $5,020 and $5,220 for a seven-night voyage, while a suite is $6,719. The gratuity policy on this line is not clear. They don't say that tips are included, but tipping is not encouraged. Most people do leave gratuities and it would, therefore, be better if the line made a clear decision on how it wants gratuities to be handled.

These identical ships (there's a third sister called *Wind Song* which cruises elsewhere) provide an unhurried and luxurious way to cruise. The four tall masts gracefully rise almost 170 feet above the deck. Each vessel has a fairly good number of facilities, although they are not on a par (quantity-wise) with the big ships or even most of the luxury yachts. You will find a library, casino, swimming pool with hot tub and a fitness center with sauna. Unlike most ships, the *Wind Spirit* and *Wind Star* have no scheduled activities. You can do whatever you like, whenever you like.

The highly functional staterooms are of a good size and are nicely decorated, although the bathrooms are a little on the small side. Service is excellent and attentive throughout the cruise. Be aware that there are no elevators, which make these ships unsuitable for the physically challenged.

WIND SURF (Windstar Cruises)

Placed in Service: 1990 (1998)	Registry: Bahamas
Length: 617 feet	Gross Tonnage: 14,745
Passengers: 312	Passenger Decks: 7
Staterooms: 125/0/31	Stateroom Size: 188 to 376 square feet
Crew Size: 185	Passenger/Crew Ratio: 1.7:1
Officers: British/Dutch	Crew: International

Meal Arrangements: There is open seating for all meals in the main dining room. The alternative bistro has buffet meals, including dinner.

Cruise Style: Informal, as described for the ships above.

Price Range: Staterooms are priced between $5,020 and $5,220 for a seven-night cruise, while suites are priced at $7,718. See the above listing for gratuity policy.

The newest and largest of the four ships in the Windstar fleet, the *Wind Surf* has five 164-foot masts that carry seven sails. Don't expect to see the crew hoisting the sails like in a pirate movie – all of the action is electronically controlled from the bridge. This is high-tech sailing! This ship has a good array of recreational activities. A watersports platform offers easy access for scuba divers and zodiac rafts also depart from here. The surprisingly large and well-equipped WindSpa has a staff of 10 ready and willing to pamper you. After you've relaxed at the spa, head for the ship's lounge, which has a piano bar. The main dining room is nice and serves high quality continental and California cuisine – a good option for health-conscious cruisers. The bistro is best when the weather is good and you can dine outside on the patio. All of the accommodations are first class and range from large to very spacious. Amenities such as bathrobes and stocked mini-bar are standard.

A Peek Inside The Shipyards...

The shipbuilding boom is still very much in progress, and may even be accelerating if current construction activity is any indication. Almost all major cruise lines have ships on order and shipyards are humming with activity all over the world. While not everyone agrees that bigger is better, the mega-liner trend is much in evidence on the construction roster. Passenger capacity of more than 3,000 and gross tonnages in excess of 100,000 (a rarity now) will soon become commonplace. In case you're thinking ahead on your cruise planning, here's a brief rundown on ships scheduled to be delivered beginning after the 2002 Mediterranean season ends. Many of these are sure to see service in the Mediterranean. Most lines are adding to their fleet, but I've only included in this list those lines that are currently serving the Mediterranean.

⚓ Costa: A sister ship to the *Atlantica,* called the *Costa Mediterranea*, due for delivery in the summer of 2003; plus two ships of 105,000 tons each in 2003 and 2004.

⚓ Crystal: An unnamed 68,00-ton, 1,080-passenger ship scheduled for June, 2003.

⚓ Cunard: *Queen Mary II* will carry 2,620 passengers. Due December, 2003.

⚓ First European: Two *Mistral*-class ships, names and details to be determined.

⚓ Holland America: The *Zuiderdam* is due in September, 2002, and the *Oosterdam* in July, 2003. Both will carry 1,848 passengers. Three other ships are scheduled between January, 2004 and May, 2005.

⚓ Mediterranean Shipping Cruises: A 1,600-passenger ship is scheduled for completion in 2003 and another one will arrive in 2004.

⚓ Norwegian: *Norwegian Star,* a 2,300-passenger ship will be due in December, 2002.

⚓ Princess: Two 2,600-passenger ships – the *Diamond Princess,* July, 2003; and *Sapphire Princess,* May, 2004. Princess also has two 1,950-passenger ships, the *Coral Princess,* due in October, 2002, and the *Island Princess,* June, 2003.

⚓ Royal Caribbean: Two ships in the *Brilliance of the Seas* class are due for June, 2003, and June, 2004. Also, three 3,100-passenger ships are in the works for later.

Ocean Voyager

As this book was set to go to press, Orient Lines announced that it had acquired the 1981-built luxury liner *Europa* from Hapag-Lloyd and that the vessel would start service as the *Ocean Voyager* in the spring of 2002. The 37,301-ton vessel is moderately sized, holding a total of 626 passengers. It has an outstanding passenger-to-crew ratio of 1.5:1. Staterooms are large (beginning at 180 square feet for singles and a minimum of 230 square feet for doubles). There will be single open seating for all meals in four different restaurants. The 655-foot-long ship has nine decks and is designed for long cruises. And that, unfortunately, is the problem for many travelers. *Ocean Voyager's* two Mediterranean departures are parts of 68-day cruises and the minimum segment length is 17 days. Because of the nature of these voyagers and their limited departures, I suggest that you contact your travel agent or Orient Lines for further information. Prices, which include gratuities, begin at $3,995 for a 17-day cruise. The *Ocean Voyager,* with its space and style, is well suited for lengthy stays at sea that are reminiscent of a time long past.

Choosing a Stateroom

*N*ow that you have chosen a ship that fits your needs, it's time to decide on the type of stateroom you want. This is the primary cost determinant and the price range is considerable on every ship. The best accommodations are generally more than twice as expensive as the lowest-priced, and that doesn't even count the larger and more luxurious suite facilities.

Two important factors to consider when selecting a room are size and location. The bigger the room the higher the price, with the top category being, of course, a suite. You'll need to determine whether additional space is worth the money, keeping in mind that you'll probably spend much time elsewhere. On the other hand, cruise ships don't usually offer hotel-sized rooms either, so you probably won't want the smallest room. Be sure you know what size room you are booking to avoid disappointment. Remember that an *average* hotel room is at least 300 square feet, and most luxury hotel rooms these days are 500 square feet or larger. That means they are substantially larger than the standard room on even the most spacious ships.

More modern ships (as well as some of the smaller ones) usually have the majority of their rooms located on the outside, which means you wake up to beautiful scenery passing by your porthole or window each morning. If you're not squeamish about sleeping in a windowless room, an inside stateroom (where available) can save money and might do just as well from a comfort standpoint. Inside rooms aren't always smaller, either, and you might opt for a larger inside room rather than a smaller outside one. The middle section of any ship gives the smoothest ride, although rough passage is rarely a problem unless you're unfortunate enough to encounter a major Mediterranean storm – which is relatively uncommon even during the winter months. Rooms on the higher decks cost more than those on the lower decks.

After evaluating all of these factors, consult the ship diagram to help you pick out the room class you want.

Ship Itineraries

N̲ow that you're ready to step aboard just about any ship, it's time for me to burst the bubble and tell you why some cruises just aren't as good as others. For each itinerary, this section will show the number of nights you will spend on board, embarkation city, ports of call during the cruise (including the all-important amount of time allotted at each) and disembarkation city. Sometimes, the number of hours spent in port can be misleading. For example, you will see many port calls lasting between 12 and 19 hours, and not all of this time is daylight. It usually means that the ship leaves port late at night, which is well past the useful shore time unless you plan to party (and that's a waste of money since you can do so on the ship). In many cases you will see "overnight," instead of a number of hours. This means that the ship arrives on one day and leaves on the next.

The duration of port calls given below is based on the scheduled arrival and departure times and does not allow for any port formalities, lines getting onto tenders or other possible delays. Nor does it take into account that most cruise lines require you to be back on board one hour prior to sailing. When figuring out how much time you actually have in port, *subtract two hours* from the shore time listed.

My evaluation is based on how well shore time is used and whether the ports are worthwhile stops. As for the way in which the cruise is conducted, including availability and pricing of shore excursions, there isn't much difference from one line to another. All shore excursions are well run, usually by the same local tour operators regardless of which line you travel on.

Repositioning Cruises & Other Options

Not every ship that comes here in summer stays in the Mediterranean for the entire cruise season. Many vessels do stay within other areas of Europe for several months, incorporating just one or two Mediterranean voyages during the season. If you choose a ship that is operating this type of schedule, you'll need to determine the available sailing dates to see if they fit your needs. You may find that your vessel of choice is in the Mediterranean only at the beginning or end of the season. This may affect your decision if sunny weather is important to you.

Few ships spend the entire year in the Mediterranean, and most have two or more "repositioning" cruises. Ships that cruise in the Caribbean during the winter, for example, will have a repositioning cruise to get to the Mediterranean, or the other way around. To reduce down time, cruise lines usually open their trans-Atlantic cruise to guests, often at bargain rates. Although such cruises may have several Mediterranean ports, I have excluded them from the itinerary descriptions because the majority of time is spent at sea, crossing the Atlantic. However, if this type of cruise appeals to you, contact the cruise line or your travel agent and they should be able to tell you which ships are relocating at the time you want to travel. Every line has at least one ship doing a trans-Atlantic run in each direction every season.

Traditional Cruise Ships/Luxury Yachts

AMSTERDAM

> *Itinerary 1: Embarks at Venice after overnight on board. 12 nights. Ports of call: Katakolon (11 hours); Piraeus/Athens (11 hours); Kusadasi (11 hours); Malta (8 hours); Naples (10 hours); Civitavecchia/Rome (14 hours); Monte Carlo (10 hours); and Marseille (12 hours). Disembarks at Barcelona. The reverse itinerary is also available.*

Evaluation: This is a good selection of ports as it includes many major stops, such as Athens, Rome and Kusadasi (Ku-SHAH-DAH-si), while also stopping at some more unusual places – Katakolon (Mount Olympus) and Malta. The overnight in Venice allows plenty of time to explore, and you may opt to take extra days in Venice at the beginning of your cruise. The major negative is the single day in Rome, the Eternal City, which warrants two days. Athens also gets just one day and could use more.

> *Itinerary 2: Embarks at Venice after overnight on board. 12 nights. Ports of call: Dubrovnik (10 hours); Nauplion (17 hours); Piraeus/Athens (11 hours); Santorini (11 hours); Kusadasi (11 hours); Yalta (11 hours); Odessa (10 hours); and Nessebur (7½ hours). Disembarks at Istanbul.*

Evaluation: This is a good eastern Mediterranean itinerary with three ports of call in the Black Sea. It also allows for a good exploration of the mainland of Greece, since the long day in Nauplion (NO-plee-on) can be put to good use in visiting many ancient historic sites. If you're interested in seeing the Greek Islands, pick another cruise – Santorini is the only island stop. Dubrovnik is a worthwhile port. Consider spending some time in Istanbul at the end of the trip. One could easily spend a week in this interesting city.

> *Itinerary 3: Embarks at Istanbul. 12 nights. Ports of call: Sanis (9 hours); Rhodes (6 hours); Alexandria (10 hours); Haifa (15 hours); Kusadasi (11 hours); Piraeus/Athens (16 hours); and Dubrovnik (9½ hours). Disembarks at Venice after overnight on board.*

Evaluation: Other than the fact that you might have trouble finding what to do on Sanis for a full day (if you don't like lying on the beach or shopping), this has some good ports. The time in Alexandria is more than sufficient for that city, but don't let them talk you into an excursion to Cairo – the time is much to short for that. The Haifa area is quite interesting and, given the single day, you might be better off staying there rather than heading for Jerusalem. If you want to see just the highlights of Jerusalem, you should head out of Haifa as soon as you arrive in port. The time allotments for Rhodes and Kusadasi are acceptable, but would have been better if they were reversed because Rhodes requires more time to explore. You should also be able to accomplish the main highlights of Athens, but not much beyond that. As I mentioned above, Istanbul require more than a day, so consider arriving a day or two before your embarkation.

This ship also has several different itineraries that combine some Mediterranean ports with those on the Atlantic coast as far north as Rotterdam and even Scandinavia.

AZUR

> *Itinerary 1: Embarks at Genoa. 10 nights. Ports of call: Katakolon (5½ hours); Alexandria/Port Said (see below for details); Haifa (overnight); Rhodes (4½ hours); and Piraeus/Athens (5 hours). Disembarks at Venice.*

Evaluation: You can only get off the ship at Alexandria if you are going to take a guided all-day excursion to Cairo and the Pyramids. You then rejoin the ship at Port Said. These excursions make for a long and tiring day without spending enough time at the places you came to see. The overnight in Haifa is good, but the time in Athens is totally inadequate. Even Rhodes could use more time if you wanted to get out of the walled city area. This cruise does transit the pretty Corinth Canal. A variation of this itinerary spends 14 hours at Port Said (Port SAY-eed). It doesn't stop at Alexandria, but at least everyone can get off the ship! This version also embarks at Venice as well as returning there at the end of the cruise.

> *Itinerary 2: Embarks at Venice. 12 nights. Ports of call: Dubrovnik (5 hours); Corfu (5 hours); Kusadasi (6 hours); Port Said (11 hours); Haifa (overnight); Rhodes (5 hours); Piraeus/Athens (6 hours); and Naples (5 hours). Disembarks at Genoa.*

Evaluation: While this cruise hits a lot of good ports, the time allotments are low. There's barely enough time allocated to Dubrovnik and Rhodes, and far too little in Athens, where you get just 3½ hours to see the sights. That means you can see the Acropolis, but nothing else of importance. In Naples, the time constraint means you won't see the city and Pompeii or the island of Capri. The only strong point of this itinerary is the overnight in Haifa. Sailing time is saved by making two transits of the Corinth Canal.

> *Itinerary 3: Embarks at Genoa. 11 nights. Ports of call: Katakolon (5½ hours); Alexandria/Port Said (see below for details); Haifa (overnight); Rhodes (4½ hours); Piraeus/Athens (5 hours); and Civitavecchia/Rome (11 hours). Disembarks at Genoa.*

Evaluation: Another itinerary with excellent stops but poor time allocation. The only places where you get adequate time are Katakolon and Haifa. In Rhodes, you'll be able to rush through the walled city, but that's all. The times for Athens and Rome, once you take transportation to and from the port into account, are insufficient. (The tour to Cairo via Alexandria to Port Said is described above, in the first itinerary.) This cruise also transits the Corinth Canal.

> *Itinerary 4: Embarks at Genoa. 12 nights. Ports of call: Barcelona (5½ hours); Catania (5 hours); Katakolon (6 hours); Alexandria/ Port Said (see below for details); Ashdod/Jerusalem (11 hours); Piraeus/Athens (5 hours); and Civitavecchia/Rome (12 hours). Disembarks at Genoa.*

Evaluation: At first glance, this list of ports is very impressive, but closer examination reveals what is actually a very poor itinerary. Catania and Katakolon are not allocated sufficient time to explore the sights. Like many cruises on this line, you will be transiting the pretty Corinth Canal.

> *Itinerary 5: Embarks at Venice. 10 nights. Ports of call are Catania (10 hours); Malta (10 hours); Sousse/Gabes, Tunisia (10 hours); and Dubrovnik (6 hours). Disembarks at Venice after two nights on board.*

Evaluation: This itinerary finally allows you adequate exploring time in most places, and more than enough time for a thorough visit to Venice. The best ports along the way are Dubrovnik and Malta, where you're allotted more time than on most cruise lines. Plus, there's enough time in Catania to take excursions to other places along the eastern Sicilian coast. Sousse and nearby Gabes are fairly interesting, but not nearly so much as a visit to Tunisia would have been.

Itinerary 6: Embarks at Venice after overnight on board. 10 nights. Ports of call are Katakolon (5 hours); Port Said (14 hours); Ashdod/Jerusalem (12 hours); and Piraeus/Athens (5 hours). Disembarks at Venice.

Evaluation: This trip doesn't have many ports, considering its length. It allows sufficient time in Venice and Katakolon, but the other allocations aren't long enough. Again, the time in port at Athens is not nearly enough. And, although the Ashdod stop offers a trip to Jerusalem, once you subtract the time in transit, there's precious little time for any serious sightseeing. The 14 hours in Port Said is more then you need. Of course, you could do an excursion to Cairo, but it makes for a long day with limited time to visit the major sites. This cruise transits the Corinth Canal.

BLACK PRINCE

Itinerary: Embarks at Dover. 14 nights. Ports of call are Malaga (12 hours); Cagliari (10 hours); Tunisia (12 hours); Cartagena (11 hours); Gibraltar (6 hours); and Lisbon (12 hours). Disembarks at Dover.

Evaluation: This is a reasonable western Mediterranean itinerary, but for the six days spent at sea getting to and from Dover. That is why there are so few port calls in such a long cruise. Some of the ports are only average – Malaga, Cartagena, Cagliari – but they do offer enough to keep you busy for the time allocated. Gibraltar is very tiny and most ships that stop there allow a similar amount of time, but there's much to do and see, so a couple of hours more would have been better. Lisbon cannot be properly visited in a single day. This is only a good trip for those who like the cruise experience and don't want a port-intensive vacation.

BLACK WATCH

Itinerary 1: Embarks at Dover. 18 nights. Ports of call: Lisbon (12 hours); Cartagena (15 hours); Salerno (12 hours); Civitavecchia/Rome (15 hours); Livorno [Pisa/Florence] (15 hours); Villefranche (11 hours); Mahon, Menorca (11 hours); Gibraltar (8 hours); and La Coruña (8 hours). Disembarks at Dover.

Evaluation: All the ships of this line sail to and from England, which consumes valuable cruise time. Times in each port are generally adequate, except that both Lisbon and Rome need more than a single day to explore. The time in Cartagena could be lowered, but there are a number of excursions to interesting destinations nearby.

Itinerary 2: Embarks at Dover. 14 nights. Ports of call: Almeria (10 hours); Ibiza (9 hours); Barcelona (15 hours); Sète (7 hours); Palma de Mallorca (13 hours); Gibraltar (10 hours); and Guernsey, Channel Islands (9 hours). Disembarks at Dover.

Evaluation: This is one of just a few itineraries that allow almost a full day in Gibraltar (and that's not bad by any means). It is largely a resort port trip, including Ibiza, Palma, Sète (pronounced Set) and even Guernsey (a non-Mediterranean port). The long call at Barcelona should allow most visitors to see most of what is important in that city. Almeria itself is very interesting and you probably will find yourself with extra time on your hands if you don't take an excursion. The *Black Watch* also has a 10-night itinerary (Southampton to Southampton) that visits La Coruña, Cadiz, Casablanca and Gibraltar, as well as Brest in France.

BRAEMAR

Itinerary 1: Embarks at Dover. 13 nights. Ports of call: Lisbon (8 hours); Malaga (9 hours); Barcelona (15 hours); Mahon, Menorca (10 hours); Ceuta (4 hours); Gibraltar (4 hours); and La Coruña (9 hours). Disembarks at Dover.

Evaluation: For both itineraries the biggest drawback is the length of time spent getting to and from England. You are spending twice as long (and, therefore, spending roughly twice as much money) to see the same number of ports that are usually seen on a week's Mediterranean cruise. Unless your main purpose is to enjoy the cruising experience, these vessels aren't the best choice. But the *Braemar* is a nicer ship to be on than either the *Black Prince* or the *Black Watch*. The ports on this itinerary are interesting and there is enough time allotted, except for Lisbon. Gibraltar could use a couple of extra hours as well, but you can see most of the highlights in four hours if you're quick.

Itinerary 2: Embarks at Dover. 14 nights. Ports of call: Alicante (7 hours); Barcelona (10 hours); Sète (10 hours); Ajaccio (8 hours); Palma de Mallorca (10 hours); Ceuta (9 hours); and Guernsey, Channel Islands (9 hours). Disembarks at Dover.

Evaluation: One port on this itinerary (Guernsey) isn't even in the Mediterranean. However, the selection of ports is varied and the times allotted are suitable.

BRILLIANCE OF THE SEAS

Itinerary 1: Embarks at Barcelona. 12 nights. Ports of call: Villefranche (10½ hours); Livorno [Pisa/Florence] (11 hours); Naples (12 hours); Venice (overnight); Dubrovnik (7 hours); Corfu (10 hours); and Civitavecchia/Rome (12 hours). Disembarks at Barcelona.

Evaluation: All two week cruises in the Mediterranean cover enough ports to make it a worthwhile adventure and this is no exception. The best features are the overnight stay in Venice and two interesting ports (Dubrovnik and Corfu) that aren't often visited. The brief stop in Rome is disappointing, and in Livorno there's enough time to adequately see Florence or Pisa, but probably not both. Villefranche (Veel-fronsh) is nicely situated between Monte Carlo and Nice (pronounced Nees) so you could visit either of those destinations and possibly even both if you're quick. The time allowed in Naples affords the choice of a number of day-trip excursions, including Pompeii, Capri or the Amalfi coast.

Itinerary 2: Embarks at Barcelona. 12 nights. Ports of call: Villefranche (10½ hours); Livorno [Pisa/Florence] (11 hours); Civitavecchia/Rome (12 hours); Santorini (8 hours); Kusadasi (13 hours); Piraeus/Athens (11 hours); Mykonos (8 hours) and Naples (12 hours). Disembarks at Barcelona.

Evaluation: The pluses and minuses of the preceding itinerary apply here too. Time in the Greek island ports is adequate and in Kusadasi you may have extra time on your hands. Although you can see the highlights of Athens in a single day, the time allotted doesn't allow for a thorough exploration.

CARONIA

Itinerary 1: Embarks at Barcelona. 7 nights. Ports of call: Mahon, Menorca (6 hours); St. Tropez (10 hours); Villefranche (overnight); and Livorno/Portofino [Pisa/Florence] (see below for details). Disembarks at Civitavecchia/Rome.

Evaluation: With additional time on land at both ends of the cruise, this is a nice trip that visits worthwhile ports. The overnight in Villefranche will allow you to take an excursion to just about any part of the Côte d'Azur, including Monte Carlo. Passengers taking excursions to Florence disembark in Livorno and rejoin the ship in Portofino. From there, it's possible to arrange a visit to Pisa. So, with some planning of your shore time, this itinerary allows you to see a fair number of sights.

> *Itinerary 2: Embarks at Civitavecchia/Rome. 7 nights. Ports of call: Dubrovnik (9 hours); Venice (overnight); and Katakolon (7 hours). Disembarks at Piraeus/Athens. The reverse itinerary is also available.*

Evaluation: There aren't many ports on this cruise, but those that are included are all highly worthwhile. The time in Dubrovnik is generous and can be put to good use, and there's plenty of time in Katakolon to visit Mt. Olympus. Similarly, the overnight in Venice allows you to see most of the significant sights in that city. Do add some time on at each end of the trip to see Rome and Athens.

> *Itinerary 3: Embarks at Civitavecchia/Rome. 7 nights. Ports of call: Sorrento (9 hours); Malta (4 hours); Palermo (7½ hours); Porto Vecchio, Corsica (5 hours); Marseille (9 hours); and Palma de Mallorca (5 hours). Disembarks at Barcelona. The reverse itinerary is also available.*

Evaluation: This is another interesting collection of ports and the time allotments are reasonable, although a couple of extra hours in Malta would be preferable. In Marseille, you can opt to see the city quite thoroughly or take an excursion to Avignon. Only beach lovers would need more time in Palma.

> *Itinerary 4: Embarks at Civitavecchia/Rome. 7 nights. Ports of call: Zakinthos, Greece (8 hours); Mykonos (9 hours); and Istanbul (overnight). Disembarks at Piraeus/Athens.*

Evaluation: Zakinthos is an Ionian island off the Peloponnese and it's visited only by this ship. It's a quiet, pretty, out-of-the-way place where you can explore for a few hours. Unless you head for the beach, though, you might find yourself looking for things to do. The time set aside for Mykonos allows you to get over to Delos, if you wish. Also, the overnight in Istanbul enables you to see a large part of the city's most important sights. Again, pre- and post-cruise time is recommended to properly see Rome and Athens.

Itinerary 5: Embarks at Civitavecchia/Rome. 14 nights. Ports of call: Sorrento (5 hours); Malta (4 hours); Palermo (7½ hours); Porto Vecchio, Corsica (5 hours); Marseille (9 hours); Barcelona (14 hours); Mahon, Menorca (6 hours); St. Tropez (10 hours); Villefranche (overnight); Livorno [Pisa/Florence] (12 hours); and Portofino (6 hours). Disembarks at Civitavecchia/Rome.

Evaluation: The first week of the cruise is identical to that in Itinerary 3, so look above for details. The second week begins on a pretty good note in Barcelona, where you get enough time to see many of the city's sights. Other time allocations are generally good, although the time in Livorno is minimal and may not be enough for a thorough excursion to Florence. The overnight in Villefranche means plenty of opportunity to visit other Riviera ports.

Itinerary 6: Embarks at Piraeus/Athens. 6 nights. Ports of call: Kusadasi (15 hours); Rhodes (5½ hours); Catania (9 hours); and Naples (9 hours). Disembarks at Civitavecchia/Rome. The reverse itinerary is also available.

Evaluation: This relatively short cruise visits some interesting ports, but in trying to do too much – i.e., the Aegean and Italy – you miss some important ports in both places. The amount of time in Kusadasi is too much; everything of interest there can be seen in under 10 hours. The time would have been better spent in Rhodes, where the allotment is sufficient to see only the walled city. In Naples, time allows for a trip either to Pompeii or Capri, but not both.

CONSTELLATION

Itinerary 1: Embarks at Civitavecchia/Rome after overnight on board. 10 nights. Ports of call are Livorno [Florence/Pisa] (10 hours); Naples (11½ hours); Malta (6 hours); Palma de Mallorca (8 hours); Marseille (12 hours); and Villefranche (11 hours). Disembarks at Rome.

Evaluation: This is a good itinerary. The one complaint I have is the time in Livorno, which is among the shortest of any ship and barely allows time for a trip to Florence. (Pisa is a better choice for the day and would also allow time for seeing the sights in Livorno itself.) Time in Naples is sufficient for an excursion to either Capri or Pompeii (in addition to some highlights in Naples), but not both. Marseille is a little far from the heart of the Riviera to make a shore excursion worthwhile, but you can always visit from Villefranche, which gets a generous time allotment. Malta is a great little place and although a few hours more here would be nice, you can see all of the highlights in the six hours provided. Consider an overnight in Barcelona.

Itinerary 2: Embarks at Barcelona. 7 nights. Ports of call: Villefranche (13 hours); Ajaccio (11 hours); Civitavecchia/Rome (12 hours); Naples (12 hours); and Malta (6 hours). Disembarks at Barcelona.

Evaluation: As above, the time in Naples is sufficient for an excursion to either Capri or Pompeii (in addition to some highlights in Naples), but not both. Again, I'd prefer to have additional time in Malta. The time in Rome is totally insufficient – I call it a tease, rather than a port call. Villefranche is not a great Riviera port, but it serves as a great base for shore excursions to several others (the nearest is Nice). Ajaccio provides a pleasant change of pace from the mainline ports.

Itinerary 3: Embarks at Civitavecchia/Rome. 11 nights. Ports of call are Santorini (9 hours); Mykonos (13 hours); Rhodes (8 hours); Istanbul (overnight); Kusadasi (9 hours); Piraeus/Athens (10 hours); and Naples (12 hours). Disembarks at Civitavecchia/Rome.

Evaluation: This essentially Aegean cruise itinerary also takes in Italy. I recommend that you spend more time in Rome either prior to or after the cruise. The overnight in Istanbul is a big plus because single-day visits are almost as inadequate in this city as they are in Rome, even though the port is close to everything you'll want to see. Even picky sightseers will be able to fill two days in Istanbul. The Santorini-Mykonos-Rhodes trio is probably the most common island combination on Aegean trips and the times in port are adequate. The long stay in Mykonos will allow you to catch a local boat to Delos, if you wish. The one negative is the time allowance for Athens, which may not be sufficient.

COSTA ATLANTICA

Itinerary 1: Embarks at Venice. 7 nights. Ports of call: Bari (3 hours); Katakolon (5 hours); Kusadasi (6 hours); Istanbul (10 hours); and Piraeus/Athens (5½ hours). Disembarks at Venice.

Evaluation: These ports are all worthwhile, with the exception of Bari, which has little of interest. Fortunately, the time allotment there is short. Time given at Katakolon and Kusadasi is more than sufficient to see the nearby ancient ruins of, respectively, Olympus and Ephesus (EF-feh-siss). While a 10-hour visit is enough to see most ports, Istanbul requires more. I suggest that you concentrate your sightseeing on the city's Sultanahmet section, which is near the cruise ship dock. The time given in Athens is totally insufficient for independent tours and you will probably see more by taking a city tour offered by the cruise line.

> *Itinerary 2: Embarks at Genoa. 5 nights. Ports of call: Naples (7 hours); Malta (6 hours); Corfu (6 hours); and Dubrovnik (6 hours). Disembarks at Venice.*

Evaluation: This mini-repositioning cruise calls on excellent ports, with the exception of Corfu, where the hours ashore are kept to a minimum. The times in both Malta and Dubrovnik are typical and, while you could easily spend more time in each, are both adequate to see the major sights. The Naples stop may not be long enough for you to explore the Bay of Naples area, but you'll have time for either the city and Pompeii, or a trip to the Isle of Capri. Consider taking additional days before and after the cruise in Genoa and Venice.

> *Itinerary 3: Embarks at Venice. 5 nights. Ports of call: Bari (6 hours); Corfu (5 hours); Malta (6 hours); and Naples (6 hours). Disembarks at Genoa.*

Evaluation: This itinerary is considerably weaker than the preceding one of the same length. Bari is a poor substitute for Dubrovnik and you have even less time in Naples, which means that even a visit to Pompeii would be rushed.

COSTA CLASSICA

> *Itinerary 1: Embarks at Venice. 7 nights. Ports of call: Bari (4½ hours); Katakolon (5½ hours); Santorini (5 hours); Mykonos (4½ hours); Rhodes (10 hours); and Dubrovnik (5 hours). Disembarks at Venice.*

Evaluation: Costa is the only line with several itineraries stopping at Bari. Maybe they know something I don't. The time spent here is enough to explore whatever the town has to offer. Because this itinerary does Santorini and Mykonos on the same day, you will be a little short of time on the first island. Port time in Mykonos is probably adequate for the island itself, but because you are there during the evening, you can't get over to see Delos. Dubrovnik's port time could be lengthened by a couple of hours, although you should be able to see the old city fairly well in the time allowed. There is ample time on Rhodes to explore both the city and the island. You may consider spending additional nights in Venice at the end of the cruise.

Itinerary 2: Embarks at Genoa. 11 nights. Ports of call are Naples (6 hours); Alexandria (13 hours); Limassol (6 hours); Antalya (10 hours); Rhodes (12 hours); Santorini (10 hours); and Katakolon (5 hours). Disembarks at Genoa.

Evaluation: This is an interesting collection of ports, some good, and some weaker ones. The shore allotments in almost all places are sufficient, with only Naples getting inadequate time for the area's major sights. Alexandria has been given too much time for just the city itself, yet not enough time to make a worthwhile excursion to Cairo. In Antalya (an-TAL-ya) you have time to take excursions to neighboring towns. Oddly, this Aegean itinerary skips both Kusadasi and Athens.

Itinerary 3: Embarks at Venice. 5 nights. Ports of call are Bari (5 hours); Corfu (5 hours); Malta (5 hours); and Naples (6 hours). Disembarks at Genoa.

Evaluation: This is virtually identical to *Costa Atlantica's* Itinerary 3, but you have an hour less in Bari and Malta. That's good in the case of Bari, but not good in the case of Malta which, although small, has much to see.

Itinerary 4: Embarks at Genoa. 5 nights. Ports of call are Naples (7 hours); Malta (6 hours); Corfu (6 hours); and Dubrovnik (6 hours). Disembarks at Venice.

Evaluation: See *Costa Atlantica's* Itinerary 2 for an evaluation of this routing.

COSTA EUROPA

Itinerary 1: Embarks at Savona (near Genoa). 11 nights. Ports of call are Naples (6 hours); Alexandria (13 hours); Limassol (5 hours); Antalya (10 hours); Rhodes (11 hours); Heraklion (8 hours); and Civitavecchia/Rome (11 hours). Disembarks at Savona.

Evaluation: This is the only large ship using Savona, a short distance from Genoa, as an embarkation and debarkation point. This cruise has an interesting assortment of ports and the time allocations are quite good for most. However, you don't get enough time in Naples and, as you'll constantly be reading, a single day in Rome just isn't sufficient for properly seeing even the highlights. The long calls on Rhodes and Heraklion allow for thorough exploration of those islands. As above, the duration in Alexandria is more than enough to see the city, but not long enough to see Cairo (don't take the expensive excursion where you spend most of the day on the bus).

> *Itinerary 2: Embarks at Savona (near Genoa). 11 nights. Ports of call are Naples (6 hours); Istanbul (10 hours); Yalta (6 hours); Odessa (10 hours); Piraeus/Athens (6 hours); and Katakolon (6 hours). Disembarks at Savona.*

Evaluation: Costa's Black Sea cruise is pretty good, except for the short times in Naples and especially Athens, where you will barely have time to see the Acropolis. Likewise, a single day in Istanbul is never enough, but you should be able to see many of the highlights. There is sufficient time in both of the Black Sea ports. The time allotments would be better if reversed, since there is more to see for most people in Yalta than in Odessa.

> *Itinerary 3: Embarks at Savona (near Genoa). 11 nights. Ports of call are Barcelona (5 hours); Casablanca (14 hours); Lanzarote, Canary Islands (10 hours); Tenerife, Canary Islands (9 hours); Madeira (9½ hours); and Malaga (6 hours). Disembarks at Savona.*

Evaluation: I've included this itinerary for those who are interested in the Atlantic islands. There is more than enough time allowed at the three ports of call. Likewise, the time allotment in Malaga is sufficient to see the city (but not to take excursions inland) and you will probably find yourself with some extra time in Casablanca. The short call in Barcelona is definitely not enough time to see the city, but many sights are near the port and, with proper planning, you can see quite a bit.

COSTA ROMANTICA

> *Itinerary: Embarks at Genoa. 11 nights. Ports of call: Naples (6 hours); Alexandria (13 hours); Limassol (6 hours); Antalya (10 hours); Rhodes (12 hours); Santorini (10 hours); and Katakolon (5 hours). Disembarks at Genoa.*

Evaluation: This trip has some similarities to the 11-night cruise of the *Europa*, but it doesn't go to Istanbul and Rome. The cruise offers sufficient time in all of the ports except for Naples. Limassol and Antalya are rarely incorporated in eastern Mediterranean cruises. Rhodes and Santorini are probably the best Greek islands to visit, with lots of things to see and do.

This ship also has two repositioning cruises from Genoa to Amsterdam and the reverse. The nine-night cruises make several port calls in Spain and Portugal, but also spend a day at sea after Atlantic Spain and stop at Dover, England before arrival in Amsterdam. As such, these aren't true Mediterranean cruises and I haven't offered a full evaluation.

COSTA TROPICALE

Itinerary 1: Embarks at Venice. 7 nights. Ports of call: Bari (4½ hours); (5½ hours); Santorini (5 hours); Mykonos (4½ hours); Kusadasi (10 hours); and Dubrovnik (5 hours). Disembarks at Venice.

Evaluation: Fortunately, little time is spent in Bari, one of the least glamorous of the Mediterranean's ports. Because Santorini and Mykonos are seen on the same day, you will find your visit to Santorini too short and will also miss the opportunity to see Delos. There is certainly more than enough time spent in Kusadasi to see the ruins of Ephesus and much of the area's other sights. Although Dubrovnik could easily warrant a full day, you'll have enough shore time to adequately explore the old city. Venice, too, can be explored fully if you plan your time before or after the cruise.

The *Tropicale* also has two five-night repositioning cruises that are exactly the same as Itineraries 2 and 3 for the *Costa Atlantica.*

COSTA VICTORIA

Itinerary 1: Embarks at Genoa. 7 nights. Ports of call: Naples (7 hours); Palermo (10 hours); Tunis (6½ hours); Palma de Mallorca (13 hours); Barcelona (10½ hours); and Marseille (11 hours). Disembarks at Genoa.

Evaluation: This is an interesting itinerary that hits some popular ports, along with a few that aren't as heavily visited. As with most Costa itineraries, the seven-hour port time in Naples should be longer, although it is long enough to visit either Capri or Pompeii as well as the city itself. Palermo is too far away from the eastern side of Sicily, where some of the island's better sights are located, but there's enough time for you to fully explore this city. A few hours more in Tunis would allow you to see both the modern city as well as the ruins of Roman Carthage. The ship arrives in Palma at one in the afternoon and departs in the wee hours of the morning, but that's sufficient for most cruisers to see the major sights. From Marseille you can either see the city or take an excursion to Avignon and Nimes, but not both.

Itinerary 2: Embarks at Genoa. 5 nights. Ports of call: Naples (5e hours); Tunis (7 hours); Palma de (11 hours); and Barcelona (6 hours). Disembarks at Genoa.

Evaluation: This mini-cruise is different than the other short cruises offered by Costa and is a variation of the above itinerary. The selection of ports is highly satisfactory but none has adequate port time, except for Palma. Your visit to Tunis will be satisfactory, given the time restriction, but time in Barcelona and Naples is definitely too little.

CROWN ODYSSEY

Almost every cruise line offers pre- and post-stays in the embarkation and disembarkation cities, but Orient Lines goes a step farther and has built these features into all of the following cruises. You *can*, in all cases, opt for the cruise-only portion, and that is what I have evaluated below. Contact the cruise line directly or ask your travel agent for more details if you are interested in their land arrangement.

Itinerary 1: Embarks at Istanbul. 9 nights. Ports of call: Delos (8 hours); Bodrum (17 hours); Rhodes (12 hours); Antalya (17 hours); Port Said (14½ hours); Alexandria (6½ hours); and Heraklion (6 hours). Disembarks at Piraeus/Athens.

Evaluation: This interesting itinerary combines a couple of Greek islands with numerous places in Turkey and a visit to Egypt. There's plenty to see in just about every place visited, although the times in Bodrum and Antalya could easily be cut down. I recommend that you take the overnight excursion to Cairo, leaving the ship in Port Said and reboarding at Alexandria. Otherwise, there is too much time in Port Said and not enough in Alexandria.

Itinerary 2: Embarks at Piraeus/Athens. 5 nights. Ports of call: (4 hours); Mykonos (8 hours); Santorini (11 hours); Rhodes (12 hours); and Kusadasi (6 hours). Disembarks at Istanbul.

Evaluation: This is a short cruise if you don't take the various land options that are available. But if time or money is limited, it is a good port-intensive trip. Delos and Mykonos are visited on the same day (they are only an hour apart) and the time allotment for each island and for Kusadasi is excellent, neither too long Nor too short. The routing is typical of many Aegean cruises, but this one is done with unusual efficiency.

> *Itinerary 3: Embarks at Barcelona. 7 nights. Ports of call: Monte Carlo (6 hours); Civitavecchia/Rome (12 hours); Sorrento (11 hours); Malta (5 hours); and Santorini (11 hours). Disembarks at Piraeus/Athens.*

Evaluation: A generally good selection of ports. Unfortunately, it offers less than eight actual sightseeing hours in Rome. From Sorrento there is time to visit part of the Amalfi Coast and either Capri or Pompeii, but not both. Calls in Malta and Monte Carlo could be improved with a little more time.

> *Itinerary 4: Embarks at Civitavecchia/Rome. 5 nights. Ports of call: Livorno [Pisa/Florence] (13 hours); Portofino (6 hours); Cannes (overnight); and Palma de Mallorca (9 hours). Disembarks at Barcelona.*

Evaluation: Thirteen hours in Livorno is just about enough time for an adequate visit to Florence, while the times in Portofino and Palma are adequate. A late arrival in Cannes (pronounced Kahn) makes the overnight there not really as long as it seems, but there's definitely time to take in the local sights and perhaps make a side excursion.

> *Itinerary 5: Embarks at Istanbul. 7 nights. Ports of call: Kusadasi (9 hours); Delos (4 hours); Mykonos (9 hours); Piraeus/Athens (17 hours); Malta (5½ hours); and Sorrento (11 hours). Disembarks at Civitavecchia/Rome. A variation of this itinerary substitutes Santorini (10 hours) for Piraeus/Athens.*

Evaluation: Another good itinerary with plenty of time in ports. Few day stops at Athens will give you this much time (although some of it is in the evening after the major sights close) and you should be able to see most of the important places. If you like island-hopping, try the Santorini variation.

> *Itinerary 6: Embarks at Barcelona. 12 nights. Ports of call: Monte Carlo (6 hours); Civitavecchia/Rome (12 hours); Sorrento (11 hours); Malta (5 hours); Santorini (two calls, each 11 hours); Piraeus/Athens (12 hours); Delos (4 hours); Mykonos (8 hours); Rhodes (12 hours); and Kusadasi (5 hours). Disembarks at Istanbul.*

Evaluation: This itinerary visits a lot of interesting places and combines the Greek islands and Turkey with parts of the French Riviera. The shortcomings are the day call in Rome and the double stop at

Santorini (once in each direction), which is one of the nicer Greek islands but still requires only one 11-hour stop.

CRYSTAL SYMPHONY

> *Itinerary 1: Embarks at Piraeus/Athens.12 nights. Ports of call: Taormina (9 hours); Sorrento (10 hours); Cagliari (9½ hours); Tunis (9 hours); Corfu (9 hours); and Dubrovnik (15 hours). Disembarks at Venice after overnight on board.*

◆ NOTE: Each of the *Crystal Symphony's* Mediterranean itineraries are done only once. If you like one, find out if it fits your available dates and book it fast!

Evaluation: This first itinerary has a nice selection of ports even without cruising the Aegean (Corfu, although in Greece, is not an Aegean Isle). There is ample time in all ports and even a little extra in Cagliari and Dubrovnik. Enough time is spent in Taormina so that you can head to other parts of Sicily on a day-trip. The itinerary includes an overnight in Venice, so there's no need to book additional hotel time there, but we recommend an early arrival in Athens to allow some sightseeing time.

> *Itinerary 2: Embarks at Venice after overnight on board. 12 nights. Ports of call: Dubrovnik (14 hours); Bari (9 hours); Taormina (9 hours); Sorrento (10 hours); Livorno [Florence/Pisa] (13 hours); Portofino (9 hours) and Portoferraio, Elba Island (7 hours). Disembarks at Civitavecchia/Rome.*

Evaluation: This interesting cruise stays mostly in the Adriatic. Bari and Elba are the least desirable of the ports. Bari has little of interest, and you'll find it hard to fill the long amount of time you have there. Elba, although quaint and pretty, could also be visited in less time than is allotted. In Livorno, you're given just enough time to take a side trip to Florence. You could also do Pisa along with Livorno, but you won't have time to see all three locations. The overnight in Venice allows sufficient time to see the city. Taking extra land nights in Rome would be a great way to finish up this generally fine cruise.

> *Itinerary 3: Embarks at /Rome. 13 nights. Ports of call: Venice (overnight); Dubrovnik (13½ hours); Rhodes (10 hours); Kusadasi (9 hours); and Istanbul (overnight). Disembarks at Piraeus/Athens.*

Evaluation: This route takes in fewer ports than some of the other *Symphony* itineraries, but all of them are first rate. Also, the time allotments are good, beginning with an overnight stay in Venice. Most cruise lines don't allow so much time at Kusadasi (often a half-day port call to see Ephesus). With the extra time you could well explore some of the area's other points of interest beyond the Roman ruins. The overnight in Istanbul means you're able to take in the city's many remarkable sights, but there still isn't enough time to do everything that's worthwhile. Try finishing up the trip with an extra night or two on land in Athens.

> *Itinerary 4: Embarks at Piraeus/Athens. 12 nights. Ports of call: Istanbul (overnight); Kusadasi (10 hours); Thessaloniki (12½ hours); Sorrento (8 hours) and Livorno [Florence/Pisa] (13 hours). Disembarks at Civitavecchia/Rome.*

Evaluation: This option has a good amount of port time plus overnights, which give you even more freedom to explore. However, I'd prefer to see one or two Greek islands substituted for Thessaloniki (Tess-ah-loh-nee-kee), where the allotted time may be excessive for many visitors. Again, sufficient time has been allowed in Livorno so you get to see the highlights of Florence, but you should consider adding on time when in Rome. The time in Sorrento is sufficient to explore the Amalfi Coast.

> *Itinerary 5: Embarks at Civitavecchia/Rome. 12 nights. Ports of call: Sorrento (10 hours); Malta (10 hours); Portofino (10 hours) and Palma de Mallorca (10 hours). Disembarks at Barcelona after overnight on board.*

Evaluation: This is another good itinerary, enhanced considerably if you add extra days to properly see Rome. With a full day at Sorrento you have the option of seeing the Amalfi Coast, Naples or Pompeii, but certainly not all. Numerous excursions can also be made from Portofino to places on the Italian Riviera (or you could travel as far as Pisa) and the amount of time in Palma is just about right. You can even get around the island quite a bit. The overnight in Barcelona should allow sufficient time for you to see the most important sights without having to add on additional days.

This ship also has one last itinerary that departs from Barcelona and ends in Lisbon. However, it includes the Canary Islands and several ports on the northwest coast of Africa, so it isn't a true Mediterranean cruise according to the definition used for this book. The *Crystal Symphony* also has two transitional Mediterranean cruises with the first beginning in Southampton, England. In the Mediterranean it stops at Lisbon, Gibraltar, Alicante, Palma and Taormina before ending in Athens. At the end of the season a cruise departs from Barcelona and goes to Malaga, Cadiz, Casablanca, and two stops in the Canary Islands before ending in Lisbon.

EUROPEAN STARS

Itinerary 1: Embarks at Barcelona. 7 nights. Ports of call: Marseille (10 hours); Genoa (9 hours); Naples (6½ hours); Palermo (10 hours); Bizerte, Tunisia (9 hours); and Palma de Mallorca (11 hours). Disembarks at Barcelona.

Evaluation: This is a good itinerary, except for the relatively short time allotted for Naples, where you can opt to see the city's sights or take an excursion to Pompeii, but not both. A tour to Capri is also out of the question because by the time you sail there and back there's no time to see the island. In Marseille you can either tour the city or take a tour to Avignon and Nimes. Bizerte is a rarely visited port that doesn't offer too much, but the stop here allows enough time for a decent excursion to Tunisia. The cruise starts and finishes at Barcelona, so you may not feel the need for additional time there.

Itinerary 2: Embarks at Genoa. 11 nights. Ports of call: Katakolon (8 hours); Heraklion (5 hours); Alexandria (13 hours); Piraeus/Athens (9 hours); Naples (7 hours); Ajaccio (7 hours); and Marseille (8 hours). Disembarks at Genoa.

Evaluation: The first two ports of call are interesting, although I'd prefer less time in Katakolon and longer in Heraklion, where the surrounding area has more to offer. Still, there's enough time ashore to see the ruins of Knossos without rushing. Time allotments in other ports are long enough to see the most important things, although more time in Naples and Athens would be an improvement. The time in Marseille can be well spent in the city and surrounding areas, but a trip to Avignon may leave you rushing your visit.

EUROPEAN VISION

Itinerary 1: Embarks at Venice. 7 nights. Ports of call: Dubrovnik (6 hours); Corfu (5 hours); Santorini (5 hours); Mykonos (5 hours); Rhodes (8 hours); and Piraeus/Athens (8 hours). Disembarks at Venice.

Evaluation: This cruise makes a number of interesting stops. The time in Dubrovnik is standard, although an extra hour or two would be helpful. Times in Corfu and Rhodes are both very good, the latter allowing for exploration of other parts of the island in addition to Rhodes city. The stop in Santorini could be longer and would allow you to see all parts of the island. Unfortunately, the call in Mykonos is short and in the evening, which rules out sightseeing. Eight hours for Athens is barely enough to see the main highlights.

> *Itinerary 2: Embarks at Venice. Ports of call: Dubrovnik (6 hours); Katakolon (5 hours); Piraeus/Athens (10 hours); Kusadasi (5 hours); Istanbul (9 hours); Alexandria (12 hours); Catania (5½ hours); and Naples (6 hours). Disembarks at Genoa.*

Evaluation: The major flaws in this itinerary are the short days in Naples and, especially, Istanbul. In the latter, head for the Sultanahmet section of the city, where you can see a lot of attractions in a very small geographic area. You certainly won't be able to explore the city as a whole. And, although you still will have to miss much that is worthwhile, you'll be able to take in the major highlights in Athens. Other port times are adequate.

FLAMENCO

> *Itinerary : Embarks at Genoa. 4 nights. Ports of call: Mahon, Menorca (6 hours); Palma de Majorca (5½ hours); Ibiza (5 hours); and Barcelona (5 hours). Disembarks at Genoa.*

Evaluation: This is an interesting short cruise through the Balearic Islands. The times in port are generally sufficient, although you may find yourself wishing for a few more hours in Palma, the largest city of the island group. The only mainland port of call is Barcelona and the time there is too short. You will have to rush through the sights in the port area, while places farther away are not even an option.

The *Flamenco* also has several "holiday" itineraries that stop at several ports along the coast of Spain. They run to the Atlantic isles and farther down the coast of North Africa on the Atlantic coast. Call the cruise line if you'd like to learn more.

GOLDEN PRINCESS

> *Itinerary 1: Embarks at Barcelona after overnight on board. 10 nights. Ports of call: Livorno [Florence/Pisa] (11 hours); Naples (10½ hours); Venice (overnight); and Piraeus/Athens (10 hours). Disembarks at Istanbul after overnight on board. The reverse itinerary is also available.*

Evaluation: The overnight on board at both ends of the trip provides much needed time for exploring (especially Istanbul). The time in Livorno and Athens is tight if you want to see even the major area sights. Overnight stays in Naples and Venice are more than adequate. In Naples, you'll have time to explore the city and either Capri or Pompeii (but not both). This itinerary hits some good ports and wisely doesn't waste time with a day-stop at Rome. It reaches both Athens and Istanbul, but may disappoint some cruisers because it doesn't offer a chance to see Ephesus or visit any Greek islands. Perhaps the addition of Venice will make up for that!

> *Itinerary 2: Embarks at Barcelona after overnight on board. 12 nights. Ports of call: Monte Carlo (12 hours); Livorno [Pisa/Florence] (11½ hours); Naples (10½ hours); Venice (overnight); Piraeus/Athens (10½ hours); and Kusadasi (10 hours). Disembarks at Istanbul after overnight on board. The reverse itinerary is also available.*

Evaluation: This is a stretched version of the previous itinerary, with two bonus ports – Monte Carlo and Kusadasi, where time ashore is adequate to do the major sights. If you have the time and money to take this one, I'd recommend it. You get to see Ephesus, but there's still not a Greek isle on the list. The addition of Monte Carlo with time to see not only that city but some of the surrounding Riviera is a big plus.

GRANDEUR OF THE SEAS

> *Itinerary 1: Embarks at Barcelona. 7 nights. Ports of call: Villefranche (13 hours); Livorno [Florence/Pisa] (11 hours); Civitavecchia/Rome (12 hours); Naples (12 hours); and Malta (5 hours). Disembarks at Barcelona.*

Evaluation: The strong point of this itinerary is the adequate time allotted for most ports of call. The port of Villefranche is convenient for excursions to Monte Carlo and/or Nice, and from Livorno you have enough time to see Florence or Livorno and Pisa (you won't be able to hit all three). The full day in Naples allows you to see the many sights in and around the city. The five hours in Malta is adequate, but you may wish you had a couple more. The only significant negative – and one I always complain about – is the single day in Rome. Many cruise lines have increasingly been stopping overnight in Venice and Istanbul. Why not Rome?

Itinerary 2: Embarks at Barcelona. 7 nights. Ports of call: Villefranche (13 hours); Ajaccio (10 hours); Livorno [Pisa/Florence] (10 hours); Naples (10 hours); and Malta (6 hours). Disembarks at Civitavecchia/Rome.

Evaluation: This cruise isn't much different from the previous itinerary, but it has the big advantage of ending at Rome, where you can add a day or two to explore the Eternal City. The addition of a stop in Corsica offers a nice change of pace from the more famous locations and is made possible by the fact that you don't have to spend a lot of time at sea returning to Barcelona. Given the general similarities, I prefer this routing to the previous one.

Itinerary 3: Embarks at Civitavecchia/Rome. 7 nights. Ports of call: Naples (12 hours); Malta (6 hours); Barcelona (11 hours); Villefranche (13 hours); and Livorno [Pisa/Florence] (11 hours). Disembarks at Civitavecchia/Rome.

Evaluation: Try to take a day or two in Rome before this cruise begins. The itinerary has a suitable amount of time in each port. Barcelona can easily fill more than a day, but you could certainly see all of the most important sights in the allotted time. I give this itinerary high marks, but would rate it even higher if it followed a more logical and compact sequence, ending in another port rather than returning to Rome.

Itinerary 4: Embarks at Civitavecchia/Rome. 7 nights. Ports of call: Santorini (9 hours); Mykonos (11 hours); Kusadasi (10 hours); and Piraeus/Athens (10 hours). Disembarks at Civitavecchia/Rome.

Evaluation: This is a somewhat standard Aegean cruise, with stops at Santorini and Mykonos, as well as a land trip to Ephesus. There's also enough time in Mykonos to take a side-trip to the island of Delos. Since the cruise starts and finishes in Rome, a lot of time is spent getting to and from that port, which means some of the more interesting ports are skipped, notably Istanbul. On the other hand, it does allow you ample opportunity to add on as much time as you need in Rome. In my view, a long single day is barely adequate for seeing Athens' highlights, and the 10 hours offered here means even less touring time (take off almost two hours for getting into the city and back). A couple of extra hours would avoid having to rush to see the main points of interest.

MARCO POLO

See the preliminary information preceding the itineraries for *Crown Odyssey*, as this ship's land/sea packages are handled in the same manner.

> *Itinerary 1: Embarks at Civitavecchia/Rome. 5 nights. Ports of call: Livorno [Pisa/Florence] (13 hours); Portofino (6 hours); Cannes (overnight); and Palma de Mallorca (9 hours). Disembarks at Barcelona.*

Evaluation: This is the same cruise as *Itinerary 4* for the *Crown Odyssey*, detailed on page 83.

> *Itinerary 2: Embarks at Civitavecchia/Rome. 7 nights. Ports of call: Cannes (7 hours); Palma de Mallorca (11 hours); Gibraltar (5 hours); Tangier (5 hours); Casablanca (10 hours); and Cadiz (10 hours). Disembarks at Lisbon.*

Evaluation: The time allotments in each port are adequate, although an extra hour or two would be good in Cannes and Gibraltar. Cadiz can be seen in less than 10 hours but there's not enough time to make an excursion to Seville. Tangier (also spelled Tangiers) is a little redundant since the ship also visits Casablanca.

> *Itinerary 3: Embarks at Barcelona. 6 nights. Ports of call: Monte Carlo (6 hours); Civitavecchia/Rome (12 hours); Sorrento (7 hours); Corfu (8 hours); and Korcula (6 hours). Disembarks at Venice after overnight on board.*

Evaluation: Six hours is enough for most people to see the sights of Monte Carlo, but it doesn't allow additional time for shopping, gambling or people watching – all things that are so popular in this port – or excursions to nearby Riviera towns. Time allotments are good for Corfu and Korcula, but the stop in Sorrento is a little too short if you wanted to more fully explore the area. It's enough time for a trip to Pompeii or Capri, but not both, especially if you want to also see the Amalfi Coast. The time in Rome is a tease.

> *Itinerary 4: Embarks at Venice after overnight on board. 7 nights. Ports of call: Dubrovnik (5 hours); Santorini (12 hours); Delos (4 hours); Mykonos (9 hours); and Kusadasi (6 hours). Disembarks at Istanbul.*

Evaluation: Santorini and Mykonos are two good islands to visit. Delos is thrown in for good measure, which makes this a pretty good Greek itinerary. However, Athens is notably missing. The time in Kusadasi is just right to see Ephesus and maybe one or two other area attractions, but Dubrovnik could use an extra couple of hours.

> *Itinerary 5: Embarks at Barcelona. 14 nights. Ports of call: Monte Carlo (6 hours); Civitavecchia/Rome (12 hours); Sorrento (6 hours); Corfu (8 hours); Korcula (6 hours); Venice (overnight); Dubrovnik (7 hours); Santorini (12 hours); Delos (4 hours); Mykonos (9 hours); and Kusadasi (6 hours). Disembarks at Istanbul.*

Evaluation: This trip combines the previous two itineraries into a single trip and thus visits a lot of ports. While it is good overall, it does suffer from a few of the disappointments noted above in the individual itineraries.

MELODY

> *Itinerary: Embarks at Genoa. 7 nights. Ports of call: Naples (5 hours); Palermo (10 hours); Tunis (5 hours); Palma de Mallorca (overnight); Barcelona (10 hours); and Marseille (12 hours). Disembarks at Genoa.*

Evaluation: The *Melody* spends virtually the entire season running this one route, which covers the central Mediterranean area nicely. However, the times in both Naples and Tunis are not adequate. In Naples you'll have time only to see the city sights or go to Pompeii – you certainly can't do both – and Capri is out of the question unless you do little more than ride there and back on the hydrofoil. In Tunisia there's time to see Carthage, but not enough to fully explore the modern city. The time spent in Barcelona is standard, although I'd prefer a few hours more. The 12-hour stop in Marseille is enough for you to take an excursion to Avignon or Nimes.

> *Itinerary 2: Embarks at Genoa. 9 nights. Ports of call: Malaga (9 hours); Funchal, Madeira (9 hours); Tenerife, Canary Islands (9 hours); Casablanca (13 hours); Cadiz (11 hours); and Barcelona (4 hours). Disembarks at Genoa.*

Evaluation: If you're interested in the Atlantic islands off the coast of Spain and Portugal, this is a pretty good itinerary. (I do not offer evaluations of these non-Mediterranean destinations, but you can refer to the general information on page 289.) Port times are generally adequate, although the time in Cadiz isn't enough to get to Seville and back. More seriously, four hours in Barcelona is extremely limiting, even though the port is close to some major attractions.

MERCURY

> *Itinerary 1: Embarks at Barcelona. 10 nights. Ports of call: Villefranche (12½ hours); Livorno [Pisa/Florence] (11 hours); Rome (12 hours); Santorini (8 hours); Kusadasi (9 hours); and Piraeus/Athens (12 hours). Disembarks at Barcelona. An 11-night version of this itinerary adds a stop in Naples (12 hours).*

Evaluation: At first glance, this looks like a good itinerary with a decent selection of ports. However, because it starts and finishes in Barcelona and makes the trip all the way to Athens, a lot of time is spent at sea. Of course, for some travelers this will not be a disadvantage at all. The port times are generally adequate (you can see neighboring Nice from Villefranche) except for the one-day stop in Rome. Likewise, some additional time in Livorno is warranted if you want to take your time exploring Florence. Additionally, you may feel cheated because your ship makes it all the way to Kusadasi in Turkey but misses Istanbul. I recommend taking the 11-day version of this trip, which includes Naples.

> *Itinerary 2: Embarks at Barcelona. 11 nights. Ports of call: Villefranche (12½ hours); Livorno [Pisa/Florence] (11 hours); Rome (12 hours); Naples (12 hours); Ajaccio (7 hours); Palma de Mallorca (8½ hours); Malaga (10 hours); and Tangier (6 hours). Disembarks at Lisbon. The reverse routing is also available; it stops at Ceuta instead of Tangier.*

Evaluation: While this itinerary starts with the same ports as the previous route (see review above), it then reverses direction after Rome and concentrates on the western Mediterranean, taking in more ports. Every stop from Ajaccio through Tangier is at least mildly interesting and the time allocations are sufficient. I would add a day in Lisbon at the end of your cruise (or the beginning if you're heading in the opposite direction). You might also consider that in Barcelona. Ceuta (SOO-tah) is just as interesting as Tangier, but it may disappoint those who have seen too many "exotic" or "romantic" movies based here.

MILLENNIUM

Itinerary: Embarks at Istanbul. 12 nights. Ports of call: Kusadasi (9 hours); Piraeus/Athens (12 hours); Katakolon (10½ hours); Venice (overnight); Naples (11 hours); Civitavecchia/Rome (14 hours); and Villefranche (7 hours). Disembarks at Barcelona. The reverse itinerary is also available.

Evaluation: This is an ambitious itinerary combining a number of major ports with some smaller ones. The time in Katakolon is sufficient for an excursion to Mt. Olympus and there is more than enough time to do more than just the ruins of Ephesus while in Kusadasi. The overnight in Venice is a plus. The 14-hour allotment in Rome dwindles to just 10 hours after travel to the city, which is enough to offer just a taste of what the city has. From Naples, you'll have time to visit either Capri or Pompeii, but not both. The seven hours in Villefranche allows time for a trip to Nice, but not any other Riviera localities.

MISTRAL

Itinerary 1: Embarks at Marseille. 7 nights. Ports of call: Genoa (7 hours); Katakolon (5 hours); Kusadasi (5 hours); Mykonos (4 hours); and Naples (5 hours). Disembarks at Marseille. A variation of this itinerary disembarks in Genoa.

Evaluation: This cruise is advertised as an "Aegean experience." However, you spend two full days at sea before you reach the Aegean and, as a result, the port experiences are severely limited. Seven hours in Genoa is adequate to explore this historically interesting town. Times at Katakolon (Mount Olympus) and Kusadasi are also sufficient. The call on Mykonos is in the evening, which means you don't get to sightsee too much, and the short call in Naples is even a bigger problem because you won't have time to do Capri (in fact, you'll have to rush to see only Pompeii). I recommend that you use the time to see the highlights of Naples itself. The variation that disembarks at Genoa is not a significant difference. However, it has a slight advantage in that it does allow you to see Genoa in greater detail.

Itinerary 2: Embarks at Marseille. 6 nights. Ports of call: Genoa (7 hours); Mahon, Menorca (5 hours); Tunis (8½ hours); Malta (6 hours); and Naples (5 hours). Disembarks at Marseille.

Evaluation: With a port call on every day this is a fairly intensive itinerary that visits a variety of interesting places. While the times allotted in Mahon and Malta are both good, and that in Genoa and Tunis adequate, once again the time spent in Naples is far too short. Overall, this is a good trip for those with limited time.

MONTEREY

Itinerary 1: Embarks at Genoa. 11 nights. Ports of call: Naples (5 hours); Alexandria/Port Said (see below for explanation); Beirut (8 hours); Tartous (13 hours); Piraeus/Athens (10 hours); and Capri (5 hours). Disembarks at Genoa.

Evaluation: This itinerary goes to a lot of beautiful and interesting places. Although time is short in some of them, advance planning will allow you to make the most of your visits. On most trips to Naples, I encourage you to make a trip to Capri, but this cruise makes a separate stop at Capri so you can use the time in Naples to see either the city itself or to go to Pompeii. You won't be able to do both. The times in Beirut and Tartous are sufficient, but 10 hours in Athens is only enough for a quick tour of the highlights. The itinerary allows you to disembark in Alexandria and re-board the ship in Port Said *only* if you are going on the full-day excursion to Cairo and the Pyramids. Unfortunately, a day trip doesn't allow enough time for seeing the magnificent sights. *Note: Those passengers who do not wish to take this excursion cannot leave the ship during the two hours spent at each of the Egyptian ports.*

Itinerary 2: Embarks at Genoa. 11 nights. Ports of call: Mahon, Menorca (5 hours); Cadiz (11 hours); Lisbon (9 hours); Casablanca (overnight); Gibraltar (5 hours); Valencia (7 hours); Barcelona (6 hours); and St. Tropez (14 hours). Disembarks at Genoa.

Evaluation: If you haven't already noticed, the ships of MSC (including the *Melody*, above, and the *Rhapsody*, below) all visit too many ports and offer too little time in each. Put on your running shoes! Time allotments for Mahon, Gibraltar and Valencia are all adequate, but there's not enough time in Barcelona or Lisbon. You can use the long day in St. Tropez to explore other areas of the French Riviera.

Itinerary 3: Embarks at Genoa. 10 nights. Ports of call: Almeria/Malaga (see below for explanation); Funchal, Madeira (9 hours); Tenerife, Canary Islands (9 hours); Casablanca (14 hours); Cadiz (11 hours); and Barcelona (5 hours). Disembarks at Genoa.

Evaluation: This is similar to an itinerary on *Melody* (see above) and it comes with all of the same shortcomings. What's different are the stops for Almeria and Malaga. You can leave the ship at Almeria if you take a shore excursion and rejoin it a little farther down the coast at Malaga. Otherwise, you have to stay on the ship (you can get off at Malaga during the four-hour stop there). Also, this route offers an extra hour in Barcelona.

> *Itinerary 4: Embarks at Genoa. 14 nights. Ports of call: Naples (5 hours); Santorini (5 hours); Yalta (10 hours); Odessa (8 hours); Istanbul (overnight); Piraeus/Athens (10 hours); Heraklion (9 hours); Malta (5 hours); and Capri (5 hours). Disembarks at Genoa.*

Evaluation: This long cruise visits a lot of exceedingly interesting places. If you're interested in the Ukrainian ports this is a good trip, with suitable time allotments for each port. Again, this cruise makes a call at Capri so you can use the time in Naples to visit Pompeii or just stay in the city. Athens will be rushed in 10 hours, and the overnight in Istanbul is timed in such a way that you don't get all the time to sightsee. The stop in Santorini is shorter than on most other cruise lines and doesn't allow for a full exploration of the island.

NOORDAM

> *Itinerary 1: Embarks at Istanbul after overnight on board. 10 nights. Ports of call: Kusadasi (9 hours); Samos (16 hours); Mykonos (10 hours); Santorini (11 hours); Katakolon (6 hours); Loutraki/Itea (11 hours); and Naples (11 hours). Disembarks at Civitavecchia/Rome. This itinerary can also be done in the reverse order.*

Evaluation: An Aegean cruise with a little Italian thrown in for good measure, this generally good trip has one important omission – Athens. Going to the Aegean without seeing Athens is like visiting England without seeing London. For first-time Aegean cruisers, it's a concern. I would prefer to stop in Rhodes rather than Samos. But those who prefer a change of pace in an out-of-the-way location will like the mix, even if they have time to kill in Samos. While in Mykonos you'll have time to see Delos on a pleasant side-trip. The Loutraki/Itea stop allows for some further exploration of the mainland (you'll also see some of the mainland on your stop at Katakolon), but it's probably not enough time to make a run for Athens. You start this trip with an overnight in Istanbul. I recommend you add a day or two in Rome at the end to round out this very pleasant trip.

Itinerary 2: Embarks at Civitavecchia/Rome. 10 nights. Ports of call: Rhodes (10½ hours); Limassol (8½ hours); Haifa (overnight); and Alexandria (12 hours). Disembarks at Istanbul.

Evaluation: The overnight at Haifa gives you time to explore that area and also spend some time in Jerusalem. Rhodes is always a great stop and the full day will allow you to get around the island and explore the old walled city. The time allotment for Limassol is adequate, as it is for Alexandria (assuming you don't attempt to visit Cairo). You will need to add time at the end in Istanbul if you're to see any significant amount of what that city has to offer. Also available is a reverse itinerary, which has a 12-hour call in Haifa (rather than an overnight) and an additional call at Ashdod/Jerusalem (13 hours). This option provides a little more total land time in Israel.

Itinerary 3: Embarks at Lisbon. 10 nights. Ports of call: Casablanca (13½ hours); Gibraltar (7½ hours); Palma de Mallorca (10½ hours); Barcelona (10½ hours); Marseille (12 hours); Monte Carlo (17 hours); and Livorno [Florence/Pisa] (13 hours). Disembarks at Civitavecchia/Rome. The itinerary in the reverse direction omits Gibraltar and stops at Cadiz instead (9½ hours).

Evaluation: A very good itinerary, enhanced if you add time in Lisbon at the beginning and in Rome at the end. There's plenty of time in Palma and Marseille, and adequate stopover time in both Gibraltar and Livorno (where you can head off to Florence or Pisa). A few more hours in Barcelona would be better, although it isn't critical. The extra-long day in Monte Carlo will allow you to see everything in the Principality and even take an excursion to Cannes or Nice. The evening will probably be spent clearing out your wallet in the casino! The reverse itinerary (which substitutes Cadiz for Gibraltar) is equally good. However, there's more of interest in Gibraltar than in Cadiz (and there's not enough port time here to allow for a trip to Seville).

NORWEGIAN DREAM

Itinerary 1: Embarks at Civitavecchia/Rome. 12 nights. Ports of call: Livorno [Florence/Pisa] (11 hours); Genoa (14 hours); Cannes (14 hours); Marseille (9 hours); Barcelona (9 hours); Cadiz (10 hours); Lisbon (8 hours); and LeHavre (12 hours). Disembarks at Southampton (London).

Evaluation: Most of the *Norwegian Dream's* time in Europe is spent outside the Mediterranean and its one "Mediterranean" cruise spends several days in other parts of Europe. The full-day stop in

LeHavre could be spent on a trip to Paris, but seeing the City of Light on a day trip is just a tease. The Mediterranean ports on this trip have sufficient time allotments with the exception of Lisbon, where there's so much to see. Many cruisers opt to use the Cannes stop to visit Monte Carlo. This routing is different from the majority of Mediterranean itineraries, spending a lot of time sailing to northern France and England. A pleasant trip.

NORWEGIAN SUN

Itinerary 1: Embarks at Istanbul. 12 nights. Ports of call: Kusadasi (10 hours); Piraeus/Athens (10 hours); Venice (overnight); Naples (10 hours); Civitavecchia/Rome (10 hours); Cannes (11 hours); and Marseille (10 hours). Disembarks at Barcelona. The reverse itinerary from Barcelona to Istanbul stops at Livorno [Florence/ Pisa] (11 hours) instead of Marseille.

Evaluation: The ports you'll visit on this itinerary are excellent, but the amount of time you'll spend in each is barely adequate. Only the stops in Venice (overnight), Marseille and Kusadasi are sufficient, with perhaps a little too much time in the latter. And although the allotment for Cannes is sufficient, you won't want to attempt a trip to Monte Carlo. The times for Naples is enough only if you stay in the city, but your sightseeing will be a rush to see anything else if you take in Pompeii or Capri. The big letdown is in Rome, where you barely get five hours for sightseeing. The reverse route stops at Livorno, where you could make a very tightly scheduled trip to Florence. In either direction I recommend you add days on land before and after the cruise, especially in Istanbul, which has a lot to offer.

Itinerary 2: Embarks at Istanbul. 7 nights. Ports of call: Mykonos (6½ hours); Heraklion (6 hours); Alexandria (overnight); and Santorini (7 hours). Disembarks at Istanbul.

Evaluation: This trip starts and ends in Istanbul, so be sure to add some extra time for exploration. The overnight in Alexandria is great if you want to visit Cairo, but it's too long if you're not. The call at Mykonos is sufficient for island sightseeing, but there isn't time to take a relaxed trip to Delos. Santorini and Heraklion round out the generally short port calls on this trip.

Itinerary 3: Embarks at Civitavecchia/Rome. 7 nights. Ports of call: Genoa (14 hours); Cannes (10 hours); Barcelona (10 hours); Malta (5 hours); and Sorrento (9 hours). Disembarks at Civitavecchia/Rome.

Evaluation: You'll probably want to book a hotel night or two in Rome despite the fact that this cruise begins and ends there. Genoa is an interesting stop in itself, but the long call allows you many alternative excursion opportunities. The time in Cannes is more than adequate if you're staying in Cannes itself, but barely allows enough time for a good excursion to Monte Carlo. Likewise, Barcelona and Malta could each use a few more hours. Sorrento and the Amalfi Coast can be seen in the time given, but a trip to Pompeii, for example, would be out of the question if you do any sightseeing in and around Sorrento itself.

Itinerary 4: Embarks at Istanbul after overnight on board. 7 nights. Ports of call: Kusadasi (9 hours); Piraeus/Athens (10 hours); Katakalon (9 hours); Messina (6 hours); and Naples (10 hours). Disembarks at Civitavecchia/Rome. The reverse routing is also available.

Evaluation: This is an Aegean and Italy cruise for those who don't mind skipping the Greek islands. It has several strong points. The overnight in Istanbul is a good start and the time in Kusadasi allows you to see more than the ruins at Ephesus. The Athens stop is short, but the time in Katakalon is generous. Messina isn't the most interesting of the Sicilian ports, but six hours will allow for sufficient exploration in town or even a rush trip over to Taormina. The stop at Naples would be better with a few extra hours so you could see the surrounding area. I recommend that you add some time in Rome at the end of your cruise.

Itinerary 5: Embarks at Istanbul. 12 nights. Ports of call: Sochi (9 hours); Yalta (10 hours); Odessa (10 hours); Dikili (10 hours); Kusadasi (9 hours); Rhodes (10 hours); Heraklion (10 hours); Santorini (10 hours); and Mykonos (10 hours). Disembarks at Piraeus/Athens.

Evaluation: This Black Sea and Aegean cruise has many interesting ports. Despite its length, you'll still need to add on days at both ends to see Istanbul and Athens. All ports of call have sufficient time allotments. Sochi, an uncommon stop, makes a nice addition to the usual Yalta and less-usual Odessa. Dikili, in Turkey, is not frequently visited either, but it has enough for a day of sightseeing in the area. The 10-hour Rhodes stop allows time to get around the island as well as time to explore some of Crete in addition to Heraklion. And, while on Mykonos, you'll have more than enough time to take an excursion to Delos. This interesting itinerary is quite different than most.

> *Itinerary 6: Embarks at Piraeus/Athens. 12 nights. Ports of call: Santorini (10 hours); Rhodes (10 hours); Haifa (12 hours); Ashdod/ Jerusalem (overnight); Port Said (14 hours); Alexandria (12 hours); and Kusadasi (9 hours). Disembarks at Istanbul.*

Evaluation: This trip is primarily a Holy Land cruise with a dose of Aegean ports thrown in. It has a good itinerary that will be enhanced if you add days at both ends for seeing Athens and Istanbul. The time spent at the two Greek islands is more than sufficient for major sights, and the same is true for the Kusadasi stop. Israel can be explored quite well in the three days you have at the Haifa/Ashdod ports of call. In the Egyptian ports, I recommend you use the time in Alexandria to see the city and take an excursion to Cairo from Port Said. If you don't plan to go to Cairo from Port Said, you'll probably find you have time on your hands in this port.

ODYSSEUS

> *Itinerary 1: Embarks at Piraeus/Athens. 7 nights. Ports of call: Istanbul (overnight); Kusadasi (10 hours); Patmos (5 hours); Mykonos (6 hours); Rhodes (9 hours); Heraklion (4½ hours); and Santorini (4½ hours). Disembarks at Piraeus/Athens.*

Evaluation: The overnight in Istanbul is a good start, although this wonderfully interesting city still needs more time to be fully explored. You'll have plenty of time in Kusadasi, Patmos and Rhodes, but the port calls in Heraklion and Santorini are short. Unfortunately, the cruise stops in Mykonos in the evening, which means you can't see Delos. A similar itinerary starts with an overnight in Istanbul and returns there at the end of the cruise. The ports of call are the same (with 13 hours allowed at Piraeus/Athens). Some sailings switch the order of port calls.

> *Itinerary 2: Embarks at Piraeus/Athens. 7 nights. Ports of call: Mykonos (4 hours); Kusadasi (5 hours); Patmos (4½ hours); Rhodes (11 hours); Heraklion (4½ hours); and Santorini (4 hours). Disembarks at Piraeus/Athens.*

Evaluation: This Greek islands cruise adds a bonus stop in Kusadasi. Time is somewhat short in Heraklion, Mykonos and Santorini, and the latter two port calls are both in the evening. While these towns are simply charming at that time, the only attraction is the Crafts Museum, which opens in the evening.

> *Itinerary 3: Embarks at Piraeus/Athens. 4 nights. Ports of call: Mykonos (4 hours); Kusadasi (5 hours); Patmos (4½ hours); Rhodes (11 hours); Heraklion (4½ hours); and Santorini (4 hours). Disembarks at Piraeus/Athens.*

Evaluation: Like the previous two itineraries, this one has many evening port calls so you miss out on sightseeing time. And, as above, the total time allotted in Mykonos, Heraklion, and Santorini is just enough for a cursory visit, rather than a trip to points of interest.

> *Itinerary 4: Embarks at Piraeus/Athens. 3 nights. Ports of call: Mykonos (4 hours); Rhodes (6½ hours); Bodrum (5 hours); Amorgos (5 hours); and Santorini (5 hours). Disembarks at Piraeus/Athens.*

Evaluation: Ditto everything from the previous itinerary. This is a good example of the mini-cruise concept that has too many ports crammed into a short time period. Bodrum and Amorgos are not usually visited on short cruises like this. However, they require minimal time to see, which may be an advantage with this tight schedule.

OLYMPIC COUNTESS

The *Olympic Countess* does the same routes as described in Itineraries 1 through 3 of the *Odysseus*.

OLYMPIC EXPLORER

> *Itinerary: Embarks at Lisbon. 12 nights. Ports of call: Malaga (7 hours); Ibiza (7 hours); Cagliari (8 hours); Civitavecchia/Rome (17 hours); Livorno [Pisa/Florence] (13 hours); Villefranche (3 hours); Barcelona (7½ hours); Gibraltar (5 hours); Casablanca (13 hours); Cadiz (16 hours); and Portimão (12 hours). Disembarks at Lisbon.*

Evaluation: This western Mediterranean voyage has many excellent features and interesting ports of call. There's a good combination of exotic North Africa, resort islands and ports, and historic cities. Generally, the time allotments in each aren't too bad. There's enough time in Cadiz to pay Seville a quick visit, and in Livorno you can easily take an excursion to Florence. Although this is one of the longest single-day visits to Rome on offer, you still have only about nine hours of sightseeing available. It may sound like a lot, but there's so much to see in Rome that you barely scratch the surface of the treasures to be seen. The short call in Villefranche allows time to explore town, but is too short for a trip to neighboring Nice. Portimão is a good place to see Portugal's Algarve resort coast.

OLYMPIC VOYAGER

Itinerary 1: Embarks at Piraeus/Athens. 7 nights. Ports of call: Santorini (6 hours); Alexandria (4½ hours); Rhodes (5 hours); Istanbul (6 hours); Yalta (5 hours); and Mykonos (6 hours). Disembarks at Piraeus/Athens.

Evaluation: One of the reasons that this itinerary has such short port times is because so much time is spent at sea getting to and from Egypt and the Ukraine. And the trip hardly seems worth it, considering the short visits in those places. The six hours in Istanbul is a tease, as there's so much to see and so many interesting places to discover. The time on Rhodes is short too, probably enough to see the walled city but not to explore towns around the island, such as Lindos. The evening call in Mykonos means you can't visit Delos, which is a shame.

Itinerary 2: Embarks at Istanbul. 7 nights. Ports of call: Yalta (5 hours); Mykonos (6 hours); Piraeus/Athens (15 hours); Santorini (6 hours); Alexandria (4½ hours); and Rhodes (5 hours). Disembarks at Istanbul.

Evaluation: The ports of call and their time allotments are very similar to the previous itinerary, but this one starts and ends in Istanbul, rather than Athens. If you're not going to add time in those cities (but you really should), this is the better of the two itineraries because you have more time in Istanbul and a reasonable number of hours to explore Athens.

PACIFIC PRINCESS

Itinerary: Embarks at Athens after overnight on board. 12 nights. Ports of call: Volos (11 hours); Alexandria (13½ hours); Port Said (12 hours); Rhodes (11 hours); and Kusadasi (11 hours). Disembarks at Istanbul after overnight on board.

Evaluation: The port calls are mostly Aegean, but the addition of two Egyptian ports gives this cruise a twist. That said, there's too much time in both Alexandria and Port Said, yet still not enough to manage an unrushed trip to Cairo. The times in the other ports are all sufficient. You have time to take excursions from Volos and to see more than just Ephesus while in Kusadasi. In addition, note that the *Pacific Princess* will also be doing some Mediterranean cruising as part of several lengthy (21- or 30-day) transatlantic and European cruises. This is the ship's last year in service with Princess and I'm sure there are people who will want to sail on it one last time.

QUEEN ELIZABETH II

Itinerary : Embarks at Southampton. 15 nights. *Ports of call:* Vigo, Spain (10 hours); Lisbon (10 hours); Palma de Mallorca (10 hours); Ajaccio (10 hours); Livorno [Pisa/Florence] (12 hours); Marseille (10 hours); Barcelona (12 hours); Malaga (10 hours); and Gibraltar (4 hours). Disembarks at Southampton.

Evaluation: If you don't mind spending a full week at sea getting to and from Southampton (usually cost is a deciding factor), this is a pretty good itinerary. The ports are all interesting, with Malaga being the one exception. The time allotments are generally good, although a little more time could be used in Livorno in order to fully explore Florence. Of course, a single day is too little for Lisbon and the amount of time in Gibraltar is overly generous. But it is, after all, a British colony!

RADISSON DIAMOND

Itinerary 1: Embarks at Civitavecchia/Rome. 7 nights. *Ports of call:* Livorno [Florence/Pisa] (12 hours); Portofino (10 hours); Monte Carlo (16 hours); St. Tropez (9 hours); Marseille (10 hours); and Sète (10 hours). Disembarks at Barcelona. The reverse itinerary is also available with minor variations in the time spent in some ports.

Evaluation: Add time at both ends for exploring the major cities and this is a good itinerary that covers several Riviera-type ports. Times ashore are sufficient and you may even find yourself with time to kill in Monte Carlo. A few extra hours in Livorno would have allowed you to properly see Florence.

Itinerary 2: Embarks at Piraeus/Athens. 7 nights. *Ports of call:* Santorini (10 hours); Rhodes (10 hours); Mykonos (13 hours); Kusadasi (13 hours); and Çanakkale (5 hours). Disembarks at Istanbul after overnight on board.

Evaluation: This is a fairly typical Aegean cruise with the exception of an unusual stop in Çanakkale (Cha-nak-kah-lay). It stops at all of the most heavily visited Greek isles. Port times are very good and there is certainly enough time to visit Delos while on Mykonos. The overnight in Istanbul is also a plus, and you might want to consider staying a day in Athens before you join the ship.

Itinerary 3: Embarks at Istanbul. 8 nights. Ports of call: Dikili (5 hours); Kusadasi (9 hours); Santorini (9 hours); Corfu (6 hours); and Dubrovnik (7 hours). Disembarks at Venice after overnight on board. The reverse itinerary is also available; It substitutes Çanakkale for Dikili.

Evaluation: An interesting itinerary with a mix of major and less visited ports. Time slots in each day port are just right and sometimes a little generous. You should be able to fill up your port excursions quite nicely. Although Dikili and Corfu aren't the most exciting of places, they are good for those who like less-visited sites. I'd prefer to have the overnight in Istanbul, rather than Venice.

Itinerary 4: Embarks at Venice. 9 nights. Ports of call: Dubrovnik (6 hours); Corfu (5 hours); Taormina (9 hours); Capri (8 hours); Civitavecchia/Rome (11 hours); and Livorno [Florence/Pisa] (12 hours). Disembarks at Nice.

Evaluation: I like all of the ports on this route, but there's just too little time in Rome. Livorno and Dubrovnik could also benefit from longer stops. Capri can be well explored in eight hours, but you won't have time to see Pompeii *and* Naples. A short trip to one of these places is all you'll have time for.

Itinerary 5: Embarks at Nice. 7 nights. Ports of call: Monte Carlo (overnight); Cannes (11 hours); Portofino (11 hours); Livorno [Florence/Pisa] (11 hours); Porto Cervo, Sardinia (6 hours); and Sorrento (9 hours). Disembarks at Civitavecchia/Rome.

Evaluation: You have to really like resort towns and cities to appreciate this itinerary, which has a heavy emphasis on the ports of the Côte d'Azur and the Italian Riviera. There is plenty of time in all of those ports and perhaps too much in some, notably Monte Carlo. All Radisson cruises make a long stop here, which is great if you want to hit the casino but will leave non-gamblers twiddling their thumbs to kill time when the sights are all done. The Livorno call could benefit from a few extra hours. However, with the allotted 11 hours, I suggest you make a trip to Pisa in addition to exploring Livorno itself. The time in Sorrento allows for a good exploration of the Amalfi Coast. As always, consider taking more time in Rome at the end of your cruise.

> *Itinerary 6: Embarks at Civitavecchia/Rome. 7 nights. Ports of call: Sorrento (8 hours); Taormina (9 hours); Dubrovnik (10 hours); and Split (6 hours). Disembarks at Venice after overnight on board.*

Evaluation: Begin your vacation with a couple of days in Rome before boarding the ship. This itinerary is a good one, allowing a reasonable amount of time for exploring the Amalfi Coast, Taormina and Dubrovnik. Split is an uncommon stop in the cruising world and, although it's attractive and interesting, some people may find it too similar to Dubrovnik to be worthwhile.

> *Itinerary 7: Embarks at Istanbul. 7 nights. Ports of call: Dikili (5 hours); Kusadasi (14 hours); Patmos (4 hours); Samos (6 hours); Rhodes (10 hours); Mykonos (15 hours); and Santorini (10 hours). Disembarks at Piraeus/Athens.*

Evaluation: For a seven-night Aegean cruise this itinerary gets you to a lot of ports. All of the time allotments are appropriate too, with the smaller ports given just a few hours. The generous amount of time at the major islands can be put to good use, but you may find yourself with a spare hour or two in Kusadasi. There's plenty of time on Mykonos to get over to Delos. I suggest you add a night or two in Athens at the end.

> *Itinerary 8: Embarks at Istanbul. 7 nights. Ports of call: Dikili (5 hours); Kusadasi (11 hours); Santorini (10 hours); Taormina (8 hours); and Sorrento (9 hours). Disembarks at Civitavecchia/Rome.*

Evaluation: The universal problem with week-long cruises that combine the Aegean with Italy is that they just can't cover all of the most important islands in that time. Santorini is interesting, but you will miss out on several other popular Greek isles. Times in port are all appropriate. In Sorrento, however, you won't have the luxury of seeing Naples and the Amalfi Coast– it's one or the other. Again, consider adding hotel time at the beginning and end of the cruise.

> *Itinerary 9: Embarks at Venice after overnight on board. 7 nights. Ports of call: Dubrovnik (5 hours); Corfu (5 hours); Taormina (9 hours); and Capri (8 hours). Disembarks at Civitavecchia/Rome.*

Evaluation: While none of the ports of call is among the most visited, this is a great collection of destinations. The only exception is Corfu, which is not terribly interesting. Still, your time there is kept to a minimum so you won't get bored. A couple more hours in Dubrovnik would be helpful, but not essential. Add on some time in Rome and you have a nice trip here.

> *Itinerary 10: Embarks at Civitavecchia/Rome. 10 nights. Ports of call: Portofino (9 hours); Cannes (10 hours); Barcelona (overnight); Malaga (10 hours); Cadiz (9 hours); and Casablanca (9 hours). Disembarks at Funchal, Madeira Islands.*

Evaluation: A good combination of Riviera resort ports (Portofino and Cannes) and historic cities of Spain and North Africa. The 10 days includes the rather long voyage to the pretty island of Madeira. The time in Cadiz isn't long enough to visit Seville and is too much for the sights in the city. Try an excursion to the nearby sherry producing countryside. The overnight in Barcelona means you don't have to rush through the many things to see and do there. Overall, port time allotments are very good.

ROYAL PRINCESS

> *Itinerary 1: Embarks at Barcelona. 10 nights. Ports of call: Civitavecchia/Rome (12 hours); Naples (11 hours); Malta (6 hours); Piraeus/Athens (11 hours); Santorini (11 hours); and Kusadasi (6 hours). Disembarks at Istanbul after overnight on board. Reverse itinerary is also available.*

Evaluation: A nice itinerary with a varied selection of ports that provides a good Mediterranean introduction. The distance from Barcelona to the next port call is fairly long, so I recommend this itinerary only to those who enjoy the cruising days. There's too little time in Rome and Athens, of course, but adequate time in Naples and Malta. The overnight in Istanbul is a necessity.

Itinerary 2: Embarks at Piraeus/Athens after overnight on board. 12 nights. Ports of call: Volos (11 hours); Santorini (10 hours); Alexandria (13½ hours); Port Said (10 hours); Rhodes (11 hours); and Kusadasi (7 hours). Disembarks at Istanbul after overnight on board. Reverse itinerary is also available in a shorter 10 night version. It omits Volos and Santorini and does not have an overnight in Athens.

Evaluation: Since you already have the overnight in Istanbul, you only have to add one in Athens to make this a good trip. Volos is an interesting stop. Although you can't possibly fill 11 hours in town, you will have time to visit some of the fascinating cliff monasteries in the vicinity. The time in Santorini, Rhodes and Kusadasi is excellent. Your 10 hours in Port Said is more than enough to visit the Suez Canal and related sites. The 13-hour stop in Alexandria may tempt you to take a Cairo excursion. Don't do it. Even with this amount of time your trip will not allow for proper exploration and you'll return to the ship frustrated. On the other hand, there's not enough to see in Alexandria to fill the time. The shorter version of this cruise misses some interesting ports and doesn't provide enough time in Athens (but you can always add it on yourself).

Itinerary 3: Embarks at Istanbul after overnight on board. 12 nights. Ports of call: Kusadasi (6 hours); Rhodes (11 hours); Santorini (11 hours); Piraeus/Athens (12 hours); Malta (11 hours); Taormina (11 hours), Naples (12 hours), and Livorno [Pisa/Florence] (12 hours). Disembarks at Civitavecchia/Rome.

Evaluation: This is a generally good itinerary that visits many interesting ports. You will need to add a day or two in Rome and may opt to do the same in Istanbul. The times in the various day ports are excellent, with the exception of Athens, where you have barely enough time to see the major sights. From Livorno, you can get to Florence and back, although it's a bit of a rush. If you're limiting this call to Pisa and Livorno, then it's more than enough. Your time in Naples can include a visit to Pompeii and possibly even Capri (you'll need to keep your in-town sightseeing to a bare minimum).

Itinerary 4: Embarks at Barcelona after overnight on board. 12 nights. Ports of call: Monte Carlo (12 hours); Livorno [Pisa/Florence] (11 hours); Naples (nine½ hours); Piraeus/Athens (11 hours); Kusadasi (6 hours); and Istanbul (10½ hours). Disembarks at Venice after overnight on board. The reverse itinerary is also available.

Evaluation: This itinerary is plagued by too many weak points. These include the short time allotments in Livorno, Athens and especially Istanbul. The ports are among the best in the Mediterranean, but that doesn't do much good if you don't get enough time to see them.

> *Itinerary 5: Embarks at Civitavecchia/Rome. Ports of call: Livorno [Pisa/Florence] (12 hours); Monte Carlo (10½ hours); Barcelona (14 hours); Gibraltar (9 hours); Casablanca (13 hours); Cadiz (10 hours); Lisbon (8½ hours); Vigo (7½ hours); and Le Havre (12 hours). Disembarks at London (Southampton).*

Evaluation: Although this itinerary goes out of the region, it is still essentially a Mediterranean cruise. The non-Mediterranean portion begins at Vigo in northern Spain. Port times for Le Havre and Civitavecchia are totally inadequate if you were planning to visit either Paris or Rome, respectively. Time allocations in most of the other ports along the way are reasonable, except for Lisbon, where you will be hard pressed to see even the major sights.

SEABOURN GODDESS I

> *Itinerary 1: Embarks at Tenerife, Canary Islands. 9 nights. Ports of call: Lanzarote, Canary Islands (6 hours); Casablanca (13 hours); Malaga (overnight); Cartagena (10 hours); and Palma de Mallorca (6 hours). Disembarks at Nice.*

Evaluation: This trip spends a fair amount of time in the Canary Islands – not exactly in the Mediterranean region. However, the Canaries are pleasing islands, with fine beaches, resorts and scenery. The time in Casablanca is more than sufficient, and the allotments for Cartagena and Palma are both adequate. Malaga itself, while being a well-known resort, doesn't have nearly enough to justify being an overnight stay. However, you can use the extra time for a worthwhile excursion to Granada or even Gibraltar. Disembarking in Nice gives you the opportunity to add time as you like it along the French Riviera.

> *Itinerary 2: Embarks at Nice. 7 nights. Ports of call: Le Lavandou (10 hours); Portofino (10 hours); Livorno [Florence/Pisa] (15 hours); Portoferraio, Elba Island (8 hours); Sorrento (10 hours); and Ponza (10 hours). Disembarks at Civitavecchia/Rome.*

Evaluation: This cruise is one of many on smaller ships that concentrates on less-visited ports. It is well suited to the repeat Mediterranean traveler or those who prefer out-of-the-way places. Le Lavandou, Portofino and Sorrento are all pleasant ports and the reasonable time allowances are generally long enough that you can make interesting excursions to the better-known places nearby. The long day in Livorno is a plus if you're planning on seeing Florence. Elba Island is interesting, although eight hours may be hard to fill. Similarly, Ponza has little to fill your 10 hours there. Consider going to a nearby beach to relax. Finally, you'll need additional time in Rome, so add a day or two at the end.

Itinerary 3: Embarks at Civitavecchia/Rome. 7 nights. Ports of call: Capri (9 hours); Taormina (10 hours); Cephalonia (9 hours); Nauplion (16 hours); and Hydra (9 hours). Disembarks at Piraeus/ Athens.

Evaluation: To reach the mainland from the isle of Capri you have to take a boat or hydrofoil, which is time consuming. Unfortunately, the nine hours you get doesn't allow sufficient time for an exploration of the Naples area other than Capri itself, where you can certainly fill a day. There's adequate time in Taormina, but perhaps too much time in quiet Hydra and Cephalonia (Seh-feh-low-nyeh). The long day in Nauplion allows for a choice of optional excursions to the nearby ancient sites. Additional time is needed at both embarkation and debarkation points in order to make this a good sightseeing itinerary. Otherwise, it's more of a relaxing cruise with little activity.

Itinerary 4: Embarks at Piraeus/Athens. 7 nights. Ports of call: Nauplion (16 hours); Monemvasia (10 hours); Santorini (12 hours); Mykonos (11 hours); and Kusadasi (17 hours). Disembarks at Istanbul.

Evaluation: As in the above itinerary, the Nauplion call allows you a chance to explore the nearby ancient sites. Too much time is given in Kusadasi and Monemvasia. I love Kusadasi, but it doesn't warrant a 17-hour stop. Of course, you'll certainly be able to explore the surrounding area by guided excursion. More than enough time is also allowed in Santorini. In Mykonos you'll have a chance to take the ferry to pretty Delos. Consider adding time before and after the cruise, especially in Istanbul.

Itinerary 5: Embarks at Istanbul. 7 nights. Ports of call: Volos (11 hours); Skiathos (9 hours); Samos (10 hours); Rhodes (15 hours); and Bodrum (8 hours). Disembarks at Piraeus/Athens.

Evaluation: This trip visits several unusual ports (Volos, Skiathos, Samos and Bodrum). The time in each is either enough or, possibly, too much (unless you're going to the beach). This itinerary has one of the longest port calls in Rhodes. You can easily fill up a long day with interesting sights here. Once again, more time is needed in the cities at the start and end of your trip.

> *Itinerary 6: Embarks at Piraeus/Athens. 7 nights. Ports of call: Hydra (17 hours); Cephalonia (16 hours); Corfu (10 hours); Dubrovnik (15 hours); and Korcula (4 hours). Disembarks at Venice.*

Evaluation: This cruise has a limited appeal, stopping at quiet ports (Hydra and Cephalonia) and less-visited places (Korcula). There's more than enough time in Corfu and Dubrovnik and even the short time in Korcula is adequate for what there is to be seen. The time in Hydra and Cephalonia is excessive even for avid sightseers. Again, take more time at the start and finish.

> *Itinerary 7: Embarks at Venice. 7 nights. Ports of call: Hvar (5 hours); Dubrovnik (12 hours); Corfu (overnight); and Korcula (4 hours). Disembarks at Venice.*

Evaluation: This variation of the previous itinerary is somewhat better because you don't have the long days in some of the less interesting ports. Korcula and Hvar are similar, and the time allotment for each is reasonable. The full day in Dubrovnik is great. The weakest point on this cruise is the overnight in Corfu, which isn't justifiable on a seven-day cruise. Since you will be in Venice twice, there might well be enough time to see the famous sights of that city (depending upon your airline connections) without having to add on a hotel night.

> *Itinerary 8: Embarks at Venice. 7 nights. Ports of call: Korcula (4 hours); Corfu (13 hours); Cephalonia (10 hours); Itea/Delphi (5 hours); and Hydra (17 hours). Disembarks at Piraeus/Athens.*

Evaluation: Most of what was said about Itinerary 6 also applies here. However, the exclusion of Dubrovnik – which you pass by – is inexcusable. The relatively short stop at Itea allows enough time to see the amazing ancient site of Delphi. In Hydra, plan to spend some time on the beach because there aren't enough sights to fill the 17 hours you have there.

Itinerary 9: Embarks at Istanbul. 7 nights. Ports of call: Volos (11 hours); Hydra (13 hours); Mykonos (11 hours); and Kusadasi (17 hours). Disembarks at Istanbul.

Evaluation: Even with some time in Istanbul at both ends of the trip, try to schedule an additional night or two to see Turkey's largest metropolis. This trip spends too much time in places like Hydra and Kusadasi. The 11-hour Mykonos stop, however, is just about the right length. Be sure to get to Delos.

Itinerary 10: Embarks at Nice. 7 nights. Ports of call: Monte Carlo (16 hours); Cannes (overnight); St. Tropez (overnight); Le Lavandou (10 hours); Cassis (9 hours); and Port Vendres (10 hours). Disembarks at Barcelona.

Evaluation: Except for the fact that this trip ends in Barcelona (where more time is probably needed), this is a Riviera-only itinerary. If you want to spend a week cruising the Riviera and making an in-depth exploration of its ports, then this trip is almost perfect.

Itinerary 11: Embarks at Barcelona. 7 nights. Ports of call: Port Vendres (10 hours); Mahon, Menorca (9 hours); Palma de Mallorca (10 hours); Alicante (10 hours); Cartagena (10 hours); and Motril (4 hours). Disembarks at Malaga.

Evaluation: Compare this to Itinerary 1. Except for the fact that it doesn't stop in the Canaries or Casablanca, it is essentially a Costa del Sol cruise. In addition to time in the mainland ports themselves, you should try a few excursions into the interior. Granada is a bit far from any of the day ports but since you're ending in Malaga, it's a logical inland destination. (You're probably not going to be flying home directly from Malaga anyway.) The relatively long calls in both Menorca and Palma are good for the resort lover.

Itinerary 12: Embarks at Malaga. 7 nights. Ports of call: Puerto Banus (overnight); Ceuta (10 hours); Seville (overnight, but number of hours varies greatly due to tidal conditions at this inland port); Cadiz (10 hours) and Portimão, Portugal (10 hours). Disembarks at Lisbon.

Evaluation: Seaborn runs several trips along the Iberian Peninsula, but this one has some poor qualities. A long stay in Cadiz is generally warranted for those heading off to Seville, but this trip does a separate port call in Seville, so you have time on your hands in Cadiz.

Puerto Banus is a little known port (because there isn't much to see and it's not one of the better Costa del Sol resorts), but a great place from which to visit Gibraltar and other places. Too much time is allowed for the North African Spanish enclave of Ceuta. Portimão is another uncommon port of call, but from there you can explore portions of Portugal's famous Algarve resort coast. If you can, add a couple of nights in Lisbon.

> *Itinerary 13: Embarks at Lisbon. 11 nights. Ports of call: Seville (overnight, but number of hours varies greatly due to tidal conditions at this inland port); Cadiz (10 hours); Malaga (10 hours); Ceuta (7 hours); Casablanca (8 hours); Agadir, Morocco (8 hours); and Lanzarote, Canary Islands (5 hours). Disembarks at Tenerife, Canary Islands.*

Evaluation: This itinerary combines the previous itinerary with some of the more popular ports in the Canary islands. The only additional port is Agadir, which doesn't have a great deal to see. The best aspects of this trip are the number and variety of ports. Note that many of these ports are quiet and not suited to those looking for nightlife.

SEABOURN GODDESS II

> *Itinerary 1: Embarks at Monte Carlo. 9 nights. Ports of call: St. Tropez (10 hours); Marseille (12 hours); Porquerolles (8 hours); Portoferraio, Elba Island (10 hours); Bonifacio (Corsica) (9 hours); Mahon, Menorca (6 hours); and Palma de Mallorca (9 hours). Disembarks at Barcelona after overnight on board.*

Evaluation: If you enjoy exploring a limited area in detail, especially places away from hordes of visitors, then this cruise will be to your liking. There are plenty of Riviera ports, all with adequate time allotments. Both Corsica and Elba are interesting stops, although there's a little too much time in the latter. Those who appreciate nice islands will appreciate the stops in Menorca and Palma. The overnight in Barcelona allows two days to take in the sights.

> *Itinerary 2: Embarks at Monte Carlo. 7 nights. Ports of call: Porquerolles (9 hours), Portovenere (10 hours); Livorno [Florence/ Pisa] (12 hours); Cannes (16 hours); Cassis (10 hours); and St. Tropez (16 hours). Disembarks at Monte Carlo.*

Evaluation: This cruise is definitely for the Riviera enthusiast and not the general traveler. The only non-resort port is Livorno, which could use a few more hours in order to allow time for a trip to Florence. The times in most of the small Riviera ports are great for shoppers and beach-lovers, but may be too long for sightseers.

> *Itinerary 3: Embarks at Monte Carlo. 7 nights. Ports of call: Le Lavandou (10 hours); Portofino (16 hours); Livorno [Florence/Pisa] (15 hours); Portoferraio, Elba Island (8 hours); Sorrento (10 hours); and Ponza (10 hours). Disembarks at Civitavecchia/Rome. The reverse routing is also available; however, this itinerary substitutes Capri (11 hours) for Sorrento.*

Evaluation: I like this better than the previous itinerary because it's more diverse and allows time for excursions from Livorno. Both the Sorrento or Capri versions are good, although keep in mind that any excursion from Capri will involve a trip back and forth to the mainland. Ponza is a weak link and you'll have a hard time filling 10 hours there. Book a hotel for additional time in Rome.

> *Itinerary 4: Embarks at Monte Carlo. 7 nights. Ports of call: Calvi, Corsica (10 hours); Porto Cero, Sardinia (10 hours); Civitavecchia/ Rome (12 hours); Sorrento (10 hours); Giannutri (8 hours); and Portofino (16 hours). Disembarks at Monte Carlo.*

Evaluation: This cruise is for those who want to get off the beaten track. Calvi and Porto Cero don't offer much in the towns themselves, but there's enough time to explore some of the lovely interior regions of Corsica and Sardinia. These two islands offer great scenery. Giannutri is little more than a beach and doesn't have enough to warrant an eight-hour stop. You may also have time to kill in Portofino. You should have enough time before and after the cruise to properly see Monte Carlo, but in Rome you won't have enough. The port call in Sorrento could possibly include a trip as far away as Pompeii.

> *Itinerary 5: Embarks at Monte Carlo. 7 nights. Ports of call: Cannes (16 hours); St. Tropez (16 hours); Porquerolles (8 hours); Cassis (9 hours); Marseille (10 hours); and Sète (10 hours). Disembarks at Barcelona.*

Evaluation: Another mostly Riviera option. The generous length of the calls allows for exploring neighboring areas as well as the ports themselves. You'll spend quite a bit of time traveling to Monte Carlo, but may not have enough time for sights and activities once you get there. You can choose to spend a night before the cruise in Monte

Carlo, or use some of the excess time in nearby ports to go back and visit. Of course, that isn't the most efficient way of doing things. Finally, consider taking additional time on land in Barcelona at the end of your cruise.

> *Itinerary 6: Embarks at Barcelona. 7 nights. Ports of call: Port Vendres (10 hours); Mahon, Menorca (8 hours); Palma de Mallorca (9 hours); Alicante (10 hours); and Cartagena (10 hours). Disembarks at Malaga after overnight on board.*

Evaluation: The selection of ports on this cruise is less than distinguished. Plus the time allotments in Alicante and Cartagena don't allow for decent excursions inland.

The *Seabourn Goddess II* has a few other itineraries that I haven't included because they are primarily trips to the Atlantic islands (such as the Canaries) and Atlantic ports of North Africa.

SEABOURN LEGEND

> *Itinerary 1: Embarks at Tenerife, Canary Islands. 9 nights. Ports of call: Lanzarrote, Canary Islands (6 hours); Agadir, Morocco (5 hours); Casablanca (10 hours); Ceuta (10 hours); Malaga (10 hours); Cartagena (10 hours); and Palma de Mallorca (10 hours). Disembarks at Barcelona.*

Evaluation: This is essentially the same routing as the *Seabourn Goddess I's* Itinerary 1 (page 108), but it disembarks at Barcelona rather than Nice.

> *Itinerary 2: Embarks at Barcelona. 7 nights. Ports of call: Port Vendres (11 hours); Cassis (10 hours); Le Lavandou (11 hours); Porquerolles (10 hours); Cannes (10 hours); and St. Tropez (18 hours). Disembarks at Nice. This itinerary can be done back-to-back with Itinerary 1 for a 16-night cruise.*

Evaluation: Once you sail from Barcelona this is another Riviera port-hopping extravaganza. If you enjoy these resort ports, you can't go wrong. For many, however, the land excursions are not interesting enough. The ports are very similar.

> *Itinerary 3: Embarks at Nice. 7 nights. Ports of call: Sorrento (overnight); Capri (9 hours); Porto Cervo, Sardinia (8 hours); Livorno [Florence/Pisa] (12 hours); and Portofino (16 hours). Disembarks at Cannes.*

Evaluation: This itinerary would be better with more time in Livorno and less in Portofino. Cervo is rarely visited by cruise sips and makes a nice change of pace between standard ports of call. The overnight at Sorrento should give you sufficient time to explore the Amalfi Coast and even Pompeii or Naples, which means you can spend all of the time while in Capri on the island.

> *Itinerary 4: Embarks at Cannes. 7 nights. Ports of call: Barcelona (14 hours); Port Vendres (11 hours); Cassis (10 hours); Porquerolles (9 hours); and St. Tropez (19 hours). Disembarks at Nice. This itinerary can be done back-to-back with Itinerary 3 for a 14-night cruise.*

Evaluation: As with most of the Riviera cruises, the ports of call on this one are somewhat similar and you have to enjoy resorts to appreciate a cruise like this. This itinerary gives a fair amount of time in each place. The long day in Barcelona allows you to see all of the city highlights. A slightly different version of this itinerary stops at the same port calls (with the same time allocations). The only difference is that it embarks and disembarks in Nice.

> *Itinerary 5: Embarks at Cannes. 7 nights. Ports of call: Barcelona (10 hours); Palma de Mallorca (10 hours); Alicante (10 hours); Cartagena (10 hours); and Gibraltar (5 hours). Disembarks at Malaga.*

Evaluation: The ports on this cruise are all interesting, although Alicante and Cartagena are similar. Inland excursions are possible from most stops, but reaching anyplace worthwhile with enough time to see it is a challenge with such short port calls. An extra hour or two in Gibraltar would be an improvement.

> *Itinerary 6: Embarks at Malaga. 8 nights. Ports of call: Ceuta (10 hours); Seville (overnight, but hours vary greatly according to tidal conditions); Cadiz (8 hours), Casablanca (12 hours); Agadir, Morocco (5 hours); and Lanzarote, Canary Islands (5 hours). Disembarks at Tenerife, Canary Islands.*

Evaluation: This is very similar to Itinerary 1 with the major difference that it embarks at Malaga rather than Barcelona. Unless you spent some time at nearby Granada, the Barcelona difference makes the other itinerary preferable to this one.

SEABOURN PRIDE

Itinerary 1: Embarks at Malaga. 7 nights. Ports of call: Cartagena (10 hours); Alicante (10 hours); Valencia (11 hours); and Palma de Mallorca (8 hours). Disembarks at Nice.

Evaluation: This route would be better if a different port were substituted for either Cartagena or Alicante, which are very similar. The times in all ports are adequate.

Itinerary 2: Embarks at Nice. 7 nights. Ports of call: Porquerolles (10 hours); Cannes (10 hours); Monte Carlo (overnight); and Livorno [Florence/Pisa] (12 hours). Disembarks at Civitavecchia/ Rome. This itinerary can be done back-to-back with Itinerary 1 for a 14-night cruise.

Evaluation: This selection of ports is much better than the majority of other Seabourn itineraries because it doesn't visit too many similar ports. Time allotted in each place is generally good, although a few more hours in Livorno would help and you will have to add on time in Rome.

Itinerary 3: Embarks at Civitavecchia/Rome. 7 nights. Ports of call: Sorrento (10 hours); Taormina (9 hours); Dubrovnik (14 hours); and Korcula (5 hours). Disembarks at Venice.

Evaluation: If you can stay for a day or two at the outset in Rome and in Venice at the end (depending upon your flight connections), this is a good itinerary. The ports are quite varied and interesting and the time allotments are just about right for each. Unfortunately, the Sorrento stop isn't long enough for you to explore the Bay of Naples region.

Itinerary 4: Embarks at Venice. 7 nights. Ports of call: Corfu (10 hours); Galaxidhi/Delphi (5 hours); Kusadasi (15 hours); Mykonos (10 hours); and Monemvasia (10 hours). Disembarks at Piraeus/ Athens. This itinerary can be done back-to-back with Itinerary 3 for a 14-night cruise.

Evaluation: The short call at Galaxidhi is more than enough time to take a tour of ancient Delphi. The stay in Corfu is a little longer than needed. The 10-hour stop in Monemvasia is necessary if you're going to take excursions to the wonderful rock monasteries in the vicinity. However, the very long call in Kusadasi could have you scavenging for things to see after Ephesus and the other local attractions. Be sure to get over to Delos from Mykonos – you have plenty of time to do so. I recommend checking into a hotel in Athens upon disembarkation and taking a day or two to see more of the city.

Itinerary 5: Embarks at Piraeus/Athens. 7 nights. Ports of call: Nauplion (10 hours); Santorini (8 hours); and Dubrovnik (7 hours). Disembarks at Venice.

Evaluation: This route reverses the beginning and ending points of the previous itinerary, but it doesn't duplicate any port. Santorini is actually quite a bit more interesting than Mykonos (although you won't get to Delos). During your stop in Nauplion, many worthwhile ancient sites are within easy reach (Delphi is a bit too far). Dubrovnik is a great place to visit.

Itinerary 6: Embarks at Venice. 7 nights. Ports of call: Corfu (14 hours); Cephalonia (4 hours); Taormina (10 hours); and Sorrento (overnight). Disembarks at Civitavecchia/Rome. This itinerary can be done back-to-back with Itinerary 5 for a 14-night cruise.

Evaluation: The strong points on this itinerary are the overnight in Sorrento and a generous day call on Taormina (arguably the best place to go ashore in Sicily). However, Cephalonia is a waste of your time and far too many hours are dedicated to Corfu unless you plan to plop yourself down on a beach.

SEABOURN SPIRIT

Itinerary 1: Embarks at Alexandria. 6 nights. Ports of call: Antalya (10 hours); Marmaris (16 hours); Bodrum (10 hours); and Aghios Nikolaos (7 hours). Disembarks at Piraeus/Athens.

Evaluation: For a short cruise this one has a disproportionate amount of sailing time because it starts in Alexandria. Keep in mind that Alexandria isn't an easy connection to make, and I'd only suggest this cruise if you're spending some time in Egypt prior to embarkation. The three Turkish ports of Antalya, Bodrum and Marmaris are all interesting, but you'll be looking for things to do in the latter, which doesn't justify a 16-hour stop. Aghios Nikolaos (AH-gee-ohs Neeko-layohs), on the east side of Crete, has some interesting sights. Unfortunately, the port call isn't long enough for a trip to Knossos.

Itinerary 2: Embarks at Piraeus/Athens. 7 nights. Ports of call: Santorini (10 hours); Mykonos (10 hours); Rhodes (10 hours); and Kusadasi (14 hours). Disembarks at Istanbul. This itinerary can be done back-to-back with Itinerary 1 for a 13-night cruise.

Evaluation: This is a generally good Aegean itinerary that hits three of the most popular Greek islands. The time in each is just about right, and you'll even have enough time to visit Delos from Mykonos. The full day in Kusadasi is probably more than you need to see the important sights. You will definitely need to add on nights in Istanbul.

Itinerary 3: Embarks at Istanbul. 7 nights. Ports of call: Mykonos (16 hours); Patmos (9 hours); Aghios Nikolaos (10 hours); and Nauplion (overnight). Disembarks at Piraeus/Athens.

Evaluation: Compared to the previous itinerary, this one is quite poor. Few people will need 16 hours on Mykonos, even with a side-trip to Delos. Patmos has even fewer points of interest and doesn't require that much time either. It's quaint and attractive and less commercialized than Mykonos, which is a big plus. There's an overnight in Nauplion, but most of the nearby ancient sites can be seen on a typical day port call. Even with the overnight on board, you won't be able to reach the more distant places, such as Delphi. Adding a hotel stay in Athens will be necessary for most visitors as airline connections are typically for early afternoon, which would only allow a few hours for sightseeing after disembarkation.

Itinerary 4: Embarks at Piraeus/Athens. 7 nights. Ports of call: Santorini (11 hours); Kusadasi (14 hours); Rhodes (9 hours); and Volos (10 hours). Disembarks at Istanbul. This itinerary can be done back-to-back with Itinerary 1 for a 14-night cruise.

Evaluation: This route has only slight and non-critical time allotment changes from Itinerary 2, but the only major difference is that this trip substitutes Volos for Mykonos. Deciding which is a better choice is difficult. Mykonos is one of the "typical" Greek islands and is justly popular. A stay here allows you to see one of Greece's outstanding ancient sites on Delos. However, Volos has its own delights, including some nearby ancient ruins, as well as the famous Greek monastery sites. You'll have plenty of white-washed houses on Santorini, so my vote goes to this itinerary.

Itinerary 5: Embarks at Istanbul. 7 nights. Ports of call: Skiathos (10 hours); Galaxidhi/Delphi (7 hours); Corfu (10 hours); and Dubrovnik (10 hours). Disembarks at Venice.

Evaluation: In order to make this a worthwhile trip you'll need to add a few days in Istanbul and at least a day in Venice at the end. Even so, this cruise is lacking in many respects. There's a lot of sailing. Also, Skiathos and Corfu are not the most interesting places in Greece and each could be done with fewer hours in port. The pluses are the daytime stop in Galaxidhi, which allows you to visit the Delphi ruins, and an adequate amount of time in delightful Dubrovnik.

Itinerary 6: Embarks at Venice. 7 nights. Ports of call: Korčula (7 hours); Taormina (9 hours); Naples (overnight); and Sorrento (10 hours). Disembarks at Civitavecchia/Rome. This itinerary can be done back-to-back with Itinerary 5 for a 14-night cruise.

Evaluation: Although there are only two distinct areas covered in this itinerary (the Adriatic and southern Italy), the collection of ports and time allocations make this a most pleasant cruise. The island of Korcula can be explored in fewer than seven hours, but you'll still enjoy this port call. As mentioned above, I feel that Taormina is "the place" in Sicily, offering the ancient Greek theater and an excursion to Mt. Etna. With the overnight in Naples plus the time in Sorrento, you should be able to do a thorough exploration of the Bay of Naples region. Use the time in Naples to include visits to Pompeii and/or Capri. Then devote the time in Sorrento for exploring the Amalfi Coast. Now, you all you have to do is add on time in Rome and Venice).

Itinerary 7: Embarks at Civitavecchia/Rome. 7 nights. Ports of call: Syracuse (10 hours); Dubrovnik (10 hours); and Hvar (8 hours). Disembarks at Venice.

Evaluation: Syracuse is a good port call, and there's enough time to visit Taormina while you're there. And Dubrovnik is sure to be a favorite. Hvar, like Korcula, is an interesting island, although eight hours may be more than you need there.

Itinerary 8: Embarks at Venice. 7 nights. Ports of call: Korcula (7 hours); Itea/Delphi (4 hours); and Samos (9 hours). Disembarks at Istanbul. This itinerary can be done back-to-back with Itinerary 7 for a 14-night cruise.

Evaluation: The long distance between Venice and Istanbul means this seven-night cruise has only a few port calls. Samos is not one of the more interesting Greek isles and the time there is excessive, but it does enable you to see Delphi. Korcula is generally considered one of the less important ports, but on this trip it becomes one of the highlights, which doesn't say too much for the itinerary. Of course, you will have to add some time in Istanbul and Venice.

Itinerary 9: Embarks at Istanbul. 7 nights. Ports of call: Volos (10 hours); Mykonos (10 hours); Aghios Nikolaos (8 hours) and Nauplion (overnight). Disembarks at Piraeus/Athens.

Evaluation: Except for the inadequate time in the embarkation and disembarkation points (which you can do something about), this is an interesting itinerary. It does only one of the main Greek island ports, but Aghios Nikolaos on the island of Crete is becoming increasingly mainstream too. From Nauplion you can take any number of excursions to nearby ancient sites, while Volos has both ancient and medieval wonders.

Itinerary 10: Embarks at Piraeus/Athens. 5 nights. Ports of call: Kusadasi (14 hours); Bodrum (8 hours); and Antalya (9 hours). Disembarks at Alexandria. This itinerary can be done back-to-back with Itinerary 9 for a 12-night cruise.

Evaluation: This short cruise doesn't visit any part of Greece once departing from Athens. If you don't mind missing the islands, it still has something to offer. The Turkish ports are all of great interest, and although times in each are a little long, you can find enough to fill your day. The key to this trip is planning a few days at your disembarkation port. If you take a couple of days to explore Egypt, then the combination land/sea tour can be a real delight.

SEVEN SEAS MARINER

Itinerary 1: Embarks at Barcelona. 7 nights. Ports of call: Sète (10 hours); Marseille (11 hours); St. Tropez (12 hours); Monte Carlo (16 hours); Portofino (11 hours); and Livorno [Florence/Pisa] (10 hours). Disembarks at Civitavecchia/Rome.

Evaluation: The ports of call are almost exclusively set along the French and Italian Rivieras. Time allotments in all of them are adequate and sometimes slightly too long. Unfortunately, there is far too little time in Livorno to allow for a worthwhile trip to Florence. Try heading for Pisa instead. Additional nights in Rome are, as usual, a necessity here and, depending upon your flight schedule, you may or may not have to do the same in Barcelona .

Itinerary 2: Embarks at Civitavecchia/Rome. 7 nights. Ports of call: Monte Carlo (10 hours); St. Tropez (9 hours); Barcelona (14 hours); Malaga (11 hours); and Casablanca (6 hours). Disembarks at Lisbon.

Evaluation: I like the port selection on this trip. You get a smattering of the Riviera (two ports, both with sufficient time), and a couple of Spanish cities. The long day in Barcelona should be adequate for most visitors to see a good number of attractions. Likewise, the time in Casablanca is just about right. If you add some days to sightsee in Rome and Lisbon, this is a great trip.

Itinerary 3: Embarks at Istanbul. 7 nights. Ports of call: Mykonos (5 hours); Kusadasi (10 hours); Santorini (10 hours); Taormina (10 hours); and Sorrento (10 hours). Disembarks at Civitavecchia/ Rome.

Evaluation: This trip packs quite a bit into its week of cruising, including Kusadasi and two of the better Greek islands. Unfortunately, the time in Mykonos is not enough to see both it and Delos. You'll have to decide which one is more important to you. The time in both Taormina and Sorrento is reasonable. Land time will be needed both before and after the cruise to see Istanbul and Rome.

Itinerary 4: Embarks at Monte Carlo. 7 nights. Ports of call: Civitavecchia/Rome (11 hours); Sorrento (10 hours); Santorini (10 hours); Kusadasi (15 hours); and Mykonos (7 hours). Disembarks at Istanbul.

Evaluation: Since you're embarking at Monte Carlo, you will have to decide how much time you'll need before the trip to see the French Riviera. Keep in mind that there should be enough time on the day of departure to see Monte Carlo itself. The Rome call is too short by far, and with barely adequate time in Mykonos you'll have to rush to see both it and Delos. There's too much time in Kusadasi. The only appropriate time allotments are in Sorrento and Santorini. Much more time is needed in Istanbul.

INTRODUCTION

Itinerary 5: Embarks at Piraeus/Athens. 10 nights. Ports of call: Rhodes (9 hours); Kusadasi (10 hours); Yalta (10 hours); Sevastopol (10 hours); Odessa (9 hours); Varna (9 hours); and Constanta (10 hours). Disembarks at Istanbul after overnight on board.

Evaluation: While this trip is essentially a Black Sea cruise, it does stop at Kusadasi and Rhodes, two great ports with good time allocation. Both Yalta and Odessa are quite interesting. Sevastopol is a very unusual port call and a stop here adds little to what you'll see in the previous two ports. Varna and Constanta are standard Black Sea day ports. There is sufficient time in all of these ports, and perhaps too long in Sevastopol. Overall, this is a good, if unusual, trip. Be sure to add a night in Athens prior to embarkation. You might also find it necessary to add a day in Istanbul.

Itinerary 6: Embarks at Civitavecchia/Rome. Ports of call: Livorno [Florence/Pisa] (11 hours); Portofino (9 hours); Sète (9 hours); Barcelona (12 hours); Marseille (9 hours); and Cannes (10 hours). Disembarks at Monte Carlo.

Evaluation: This is another Riviera-oriented cruise from Radisson. Time allotments in the Riviera ports are adequate or better, and there's little need for out-of-town excursions to other nearby towns. The time in Barcelona allows you to see most of the important sights. However, the Livorno port call is too short if you want to see Florence. You won't have to add on a night in Monte Carlo unless you have an early flight home, but you will want to take an extra day or two in Rome.

Itinerary 7: Embarks at Civitavecchia/Rome. 11 nights. Ports of call: Sorrento (9 hours); Taormina (9 hours); Venice (overnight); Dubrovnik (6 hours); Corfu (5 hours); Piraeus/Athens (9 hours); and Kusadasi (15 hours). Disembarks at Alexandria.

Evaluation: This cruise is a long one, but it lacks focus. For example, it goes to Greece, but doesn't visit any of the main islands (the time in Corfu is alright); it goes to Turkey but doesn't visit Istanbul (too much time is allowed for Kusadasi). Also, it spends a longer than usual amount of time at sea for a Mediterranean cruise. Most of the port times are sufficient, and the overnight in Venice is a bonus. The nine hours in Athens is definitely not long enough. A few more hours in Dubrovnik would also be better.

Itinerary 8: Embarks at Alexandria. 10 nights. Ports of call: Rhodes (10 hours); Heraklion (9 hours); Malta (9 hours); Tunis (10 hours); Cagliari (5 hours); Palma de Mallorca (9 hours); and Sète (9 hours). Disembarks at Barcelona.

Evaluation: This itinerary suffers from similar shortcomings as the previous one – it spends a lot of time at sea and passes close to many important ports without stopping at them. But the first four ports are all among the more interesting in the region and the time in each is quite good. The times in the last three ports are sufficient.

Itinerary 9: Embarks at Barcelona. 7 nights. Ports of call: Malaga (12 hours); Cadiz (11 hours); Casablanca (8 hours); Agadir (11 hours); and Lanzarote, Canary Islands (9 hours). Disembarks at Las Palmas, Canary Islands.

Evaluation: Some of this route lies outside my Mediterranean definition for this book. It's not a bad trip, although the time allotments for Cadiz and, especially, Agadir are too long. The port call in Malaga is long enough that you could take a trip to Granada and see the famous Alhambra (see page 170 in the port chapter).

SILVER SHADOW

Itinerary 1: Embarks at Haifa. 10 nights. Ports of call: Alexandria (17 hours); Alanya (3 hours); Antalya (4 hours); Marmaris (10 hours); Rhodes (overnight); Nauplion (10 hours); and Mykonos (15 hours). Disembarks at Athens/Piraeus.

Evaluation: This interesting itinerary has quite a bit to offer. It combines the eastern Mediterranean and Holy Land with some Aegean cruise standards and allows plenty of time for what may very well be the most interesting of the Greek islands (Rhodes). The stop at popular Mykonos is long enough for a side trip to Delos and then some -- you may have extra hours to kill in this small port. How much can you shop and sit at the seaside cafés? Alanya and Antalya are two lovely, less visited Turkish ports – a few more hours in each would be better. Nauplion makes a good base for exploring ancient sites. The amount of time in Alexandria is so long that even I would concede that a trip to Cairo may be a good idea (few itineraries allow enough time for a decent trip there). Spend some time in Israel before embarking in order to see Jerusalem (it's very close to Haifa) and do the same at the end in Athens.

> *Itinerary 2: Embarks at Istanbul. 10 nights. Ports of call: Dikili (9 hours); Volos (10 hours); Piraeus/Athens (8 hours); Katakolon (9 hours); Taormina (10 hours); and Livorno [Florence/Pisa] (15 hours). Disembarks at Genoa.*

Evaluation: Neither Dikili or Volos are among the most frequently visited ports, but they each have enough of interest to fill your time ashore. The same is true for Katakolon (see Mount Olympus) and Taormina. The time in Livorno is about cruise industry standard and does allow for a whirlwind visit to Florence. However, there is definitely too little time spent in Athens – enough for a quick run to the Acropolis and back.

> *Itinerary 3: Embarks at Civitavecchia/Rome. 12 nights. Ports of call: Livorno [Florence/Pisa] (11 hours); Marseille (15 hours); Palma de Mallorca (14½ hours); Tarragona (15 hours); Malaga (16 hours); Gibraltar (8 hours); and Casablanca (16 hours). Disembarks at Lisbon.*

Evaluation: The Rome-to-Lisbon run isn't common in the Mediterranean cruise inventory, so that makes this route a little unusual. The selection of ports is fine, but the time allotments in almost every case are not appropriate. Too much time is allotted in Palma, Tarragona and Casablanca (and Malaga, unless you're going to take an excursion to Granada); and too little is given in Livorno. Gibraltar's port time is just right. Even though this is a fairly long trip, don't miss out on the sights in Rome and Lisbon – book a night or two in each.

SILVER WHISPER/SILVER WIND

These two ships have, respectively, 19 and 17 different itineraries in the Mediterranean. No two trips are alike and each itinerary is done only once, which makes useful evaluations impossible. Cruises range from seven to 14 days and follow basic patterns that are similar to one of the four itineraries described for the *Silver Shadow*. They generally combine some of the more heavily visited ports with several places that few cruise lines visit. If the itineraries for the *Silver Shadow* are of interest to you, contact the cruise line (see *Addendum*) or your travel agent for more detailed itinerary information.

SONG OF FLOWER

> *Itinerary 1: Embarks at Istanbul. Seven nights. Ports of call: Dikili (5 hours); Kusadasi (10 hours); Santorini (9 hours); Taormina (9 hours); and Sorrento (10 hours). Disembarks at Civitavecchia/ Rome.*

Evaluation: Some Turkey, some Greece, some Italy. Add some land-based days at both ends to properly see Istanbul and Rome. The biggest drawback with this itinerary is that it doesn't visit Athens. Time allotments are quite good for each port. In Sorrento, you'll be able to see the Amalfi Coast area, but probably not Pompeii as well. Dikili is probably the weakest link, but you have only five hours there and you'll have no problem keeping busy.

> *Itinerary 2: Embarks at Civitavecchia/Rome. Seven nights. Ports of call: Livorno (11 hours); St. Tropez (9 hours); Sète (9 hours); Barcelona (11 hours); Marseille (10 hours); and Nice (10 hours). Disembarks at Monte Carlo. A reverse itinerary is also available. It adds Portofino (11 hours), but generally has an hour less in many other ports.*

Evaluation: Of all the cruise lines, Radisson Seven Seas seems to neglect Livorno, allowing only minimal time there. You'll find yourself rushing to see just a little of Florence. This is another mostly Riviera cruise with Barcelona thrown in for good measure. The route is a bit indirect, so there is more time at sea than would normally be necessary to visit these ports. The reverse routing isn't very different, but it does add the pretty town of Portofino.

> *Itinerary 3: Embarks at Monte Carlo. Seven nights. Ports of call: Marseille (10 hours); Sète (10 hours); Barcelona (12 hours); and Malaga (10 hours). Disembarks at Lisbon after overnight on board.*

Evaluation: Depending upon when you arrive in Monte Carlo you may need to schedule an evening there on land. Even if your flight times don't necessitate that, you should consider it anyway as it allows you time to see other parts of the Côte d'Azur. Sète sits at the opposite end of France's Mediterranean coast and is not often visited by cruise ships, especially large ones. There's too much time allowed here, but allotments for the other ports are sound. The best feature of this itinerary is the overnight in Lisbon.

> *Itinerary 4: Embarks at Lisbon. 8 nights. Ports of call: Cadiz (7 hours); Malaga (11 hours); Barcelona (12 hours); Marseille (10 hours); and St. Tropez (14 hours). Disembarks at Monte Carlo.*

Evaluation: This itinerary is similar to the previous one, done in reverse. It adds Cadiz (sufficient port time) and St. Tropez (too much port time). Remember, this trip ends in Monte Carlo and from there you can explore the Riviera. In order for this to be as good as the preceding itinerary you would have to add on time on your own in Lisbon.

> *Itinerary 5: Embarks at Monte Carlo. Seven nights. Ports of call: Civitavecchia/Rome (10 hours); Sorrento (10 hours); Taormina (9 hours); Santorini (9 hours); and Kusadasi (9 hours). Disembarks at Piraeus/Athens.*

Evaluation: Many cruises give you 10 hours at Civitavecchia and have the nerve to say that you can see Rome. You'll have a maximum of six hours to see it. Rather than make a rushed trip there, I recommend that you use the time in Civitavecchia to see some of the ancient sites around that city. The other ports on this trip are varied and interesting, with suitable time allotments in each. Be sure you add a day in Athens at the end.

> *Itinerary 6: Embarks at Piraeus/Athens. Seven nights. Ports of call: Itea/Delphi (6 hours); Santorini (10 hours); Rhodes (10 hours); Mykonos (16 hours); Kusadasi (12 hours); and Dikili (5 hours). Disembarks at Istanbul. The reverse itinerary is also available.*

Evaluation: This fairly standard Aegean cruise doesn't have any major drawbacks. Just be sure to add a few days on land to see Athens and Istanbul. This route stops at a good selection of islands and the time allotments are generally adequate. However, your stop in Mykonos is too long, even if you include time for a trip to nearby Delos. Your stop in Itea – an unusual port of call – gives you the chance to see Delphi. Dikili isn't particularly interesting but makes for a pleasant brief stop. Another nice feature of this cruise are the several hours you will spend going through the picturesque Corinth Canal.

STELLA SOLARIS

In addition to the itineraries listed here, the *Stella Solaris* also does the routings as described in Itineraries 1 through 3 of the *Odysseus* (pages 100-101).

> *Itinerary 1: Embarks at Piraeus/Athens. Seven nights. Ports of call: Lesvos (8 hours); Istanbul (16 hours); Nessebur (5 hours); Odessa (9 hours); and Yalta (5 hours). Disembarks at Piraeus/Athens.*

Evaluation: The day stop in Istanbul is long, but still is not enough to see much more than the sights of the Sultanahmet section of the city. The island of Lesvos (or Lesbos) is rarely visited by cruise ships and doesn't have much to offer aside from pretty beaches and seclusion.

The three Black Sea ports are all interesting but the time allotments would be better if Odessa and Yalta were reversed.

Itinerary 2: Embarks at Piraeus/Athens. Seven nights. Ports of call: Kos (6½ hours); Alexandria (5½ hours); Port Said (16 hours); Limassol (6 hours); Antalya (6 hours); and Izmir (5 hours). Disembarks at Piraeus/Athens.

Evaluation: This interesting itinerary has a good combination of ports, many of which aren't the usual Mediterranean stops. That's the good part. The problem, as is the case all too often with this cruise line, is the short times allotted at each. Kos (a Greek island) and the Turkish port of Izmir are infrequently visited by cruise ships and times at both are sufficient. You can also see a good deal of what is worthwhile in Alexandria and Antalya in the scheduled stop. However, the call in Limassol is short (given the time it takes to get back and forth to Nicosia, a popular side trip). The time in Port Said is too long for the city itself, yet too short for a meaningful excursion to Cairo and the Pyramids.

TRITON

In addition to the itineraries listed here, the *Triton* also does the routings as described in Itineraries 1 through 3 of the *Odysseus* (pages 100-101).

Itinerary 1: Embarks at Piraeus/Athens. Seven nights. Ports of call: Messina (4½ hours); Civitavecchia/Rome (8 hours); Naples (6½ hours); Katakolon (4½ hours); Santorini (7 hours); Kusadasi (5 hours); and Mykonos (4½ hours). Disembarks at Piraeus/Athens.

Evaluation: Messina is an appropriately short call, with enough time to see the limited sights of the city. Alternatively, make a quick trip over to Taormina. In Naples you'll be able to see either Pompeii, Capri or Naples itself, but only one. The time allotments in the Greek ports are alright, with the exception of the early evening call at Mykonos, which means you can't take a trip to nearby Delos. Eight hours for Rome is not worthwhile. Once you spend four hours getting back and forth and having a bite to eat, you will have only four hours to see the Eternal City. Try visiting some of the sights in and around Civitavecchia instead.

> *Itinerary 2: Embarks at Civitavecchia/Rome. Seven nights. Ports of call: Naples (6½ hours); Katakolon (4½ hours); Santorini (7 hours); Kusadasi (12 hours); Mykonos (4½ hours); Piraeus/Athens (7 hours); and Messina (4½ hours). Disembarks at Civitavecchia/Rome.*

Evaluation: This is essentially the same itinerary as the one above except for the embarkation and disembarkation points. You have two shots to visit Rome (including before and after the cruise), but only seven hours in Athens. Since most people will find more to see in Rome, this version has an edge over the previous one.

WORLD RENAISSANCE

In addition to the itineraries listed here, the *World Renaissance* also does the routings as described in Itineraries 1 through 3 of the *Odysseus* (pages 100-101).

> *Itinerary: Embarks at Piraeus/Athens. Seven nights. Ports of call: Heraklion (4½ hours); Santorini (4 hours); Rhodes (12 hours); Patmos (3½ hours); Kusadasi (6 hours); Istanbul (overnight); and Mykonos (8 hours).*

Evaluation: This cruise deviates from the standard Aegean itinerary by adding stops at Patmos and Heraklion. However, in so doing it also shortens the times spent in other ports. You can see Patmos in the time allotted, but Santorini requires more, as does Heraklion. The overnight in Istanbul allows just one day of sightseeing because you arrive in the evening.

Sailing Ships

Sailing ships do not travel as fast as regular cruise ships. This is not necessarily a disadvantage. It all depends upon what type of experience you are looking for.

ROYAL CLIPPER

> *Itinerary 1: Embarks at Cannes. Seven nights. Ports of call: Costa Smeralda, Sardinia (4 hours, plus additional three-hour beach stop at Ile de Mortorio); Calvi, Corsica (8 hours); Livorno [Florence/Pisa] (16 hours); Portovenere (13 hours); and Monte Carlo (14 hours). Disembarks at Cannes.*

Evaluation: This itinerary combines several Riviera ports with stops at the islands of Corsica and Sardinia. I don't care for "beach" stops, but you might. The time in Livorno and Monte Carlo is sufficient, while you may get a little bored in Portovenere. This trip can be combined with the following itinerary to create a two-week cruise.

Itinerary 2: Embarks at Cannes. Seven nights. Ports of call: Hyères Islands (5 hours); Mahon, Menorca (5½ hours); Palma de Mallorca (6½ hours); Barcelona (9 hours); Cap Creus, Spain (8 hours); and St. Tropez (6 hours). Disembarks at Cannes.

Evaluation: I don't particularly like the combination of ports on this trip, especially since some of the port times are kind of short. Although this is okay in Mahon, St. Tropez, and the infrequently visited Hyères Islands, Palma and Cap Creus could use some more time. (There isn't much to see in Cap Creus, but there are some good excursions; unfortunately, you don't have enough shore time to do any of them justice.) You can see the highlights of Barcelona in a day port of call, but not a detailed exploration.

STAR CLIPPER

Itinerary 1: Embarks at Civitavecchia/Rome. Seven nights. Ports of call: Paestum, Italy (9 hours); Taormina (11 hours); Lipari/Aeolian Islands (9 hours); Sorrento (11 hours); and Palmarola, Italy (5 hours). Disembarks at Civitavecchia/Rome.

Evaluation: Most of the ports on this itinerary are not visited by large cruise ships, so this can be an interesting experience if you're looking for something out of the ordinary. Paestum is a little known but fascinating ancient site, and the Aeolian Islands provide plenty of great scenery. Taormina is one of the better, if not the best, ports of call in Sicily and Sorrento can be a good base for exploring the Bay of Naples area or the Amalfi Coast. Palmarola hasn't much to offer, but with only five hours there it doesn't really detract from the overall itinerary. Do try to add time in Rome before or after the cruise. This trip can be combined with the following itinerary to make a two-week cruise.

Itinerary 2: Embarks at Rome. Seven nights. Ports of call: Bonifacio (7 hours); Monte Carlo (11 hours); Portofino (8 hours); Livorno [Florence/Pisa] (14 hours); and Portoferraio, Elba Island (7½ hours). Disembarks at Civitavecchia/Rome.

Evaluation: Even the round-trip to Rome doesn't allow time for properly seeing the city unless you add on a couple of nights on your own. There's a nice balance of ports between the most "in" spots (such as Monte Carlo) and the out-of-the-way places, like Elba Island. The time allotments are all reasonable and help to make this an enjoyable trip.

STAR FLYER

Itinerary 1: Embarks at Piraeus/Athens. Seven nights. Ports of call: (9 hours; preceded by a 4½-hour beach stop at Camlimani); Güllük (8 hours); Patmos (9 hours); Mykonos (12 hours); and Serifos (6 hours). Disembarks at Piraeus/Athens.

Evaluation: Covering a limited Aegean area, this cruise combines some popular stops, such as Mykonos, with plenty of lesser known places. Güllük is a great call because you have the opportunity to relax or swim if you are a leisure lover, or to see some more ancient sites in the area. Both Patmos and Serifos are of only minor interest. This trip can be combined with the following itinerary to make a two-week cruise.

Itinerary 2: Embarks at Piraeus/Athens. Seven nights. Ports of call: Rhodes (13 hours); Bodrum (8 hours); Dalyan River/Fethiye (10 hours); Santorini (12 hours); and Hydra (6 hours). Disembarks at Piraeus/Athens.

Evaluation: Like the preceding itinerary, this Athens round-tripper combines popular ports of call with some destinations that are off the beaten track. Rhodes and Santorini are among the best of the Aegean islands, superior even to Hydra. Bodrum is mildly interesting, and the Fethiye (FEH-tee-ye) area has a wide assortment of recreational activities and unusual scenery. The time allotments in each port are suitable.

WIND SPIRIT/WIND STAR

Itinerary 1: Embarks at Lisbon. Seven nights. Ports of call: Portimão (5 hours); Tangier (8 hours); Marbella (12 hours); Ibiza (13 hours); and Palma de Mallorca (8 hours). Disembarks at Barcelona. The reverse itinerary is also available.

Evaluation: Portimão, a rarely visited port on Portugal's southern Algarve resort coast, is a very pleasant destination. There's enough time in Marbella for you to make a trip to either Malaga or the more interesting Gibraltar (the port city of Marbella has little of interest).

Ibiza, another uncommon port of call in the Balearic Islands, is a pleasant stop, although the time spent there could be shorter. The times in the other ports are good, but you should definitely add on time before the cruise in Lisbon and possibly in Barcelona as well.

Itinerary 2: Embarks at Barcelona. Seven nights. Ports of call: Port (10 hours); Marseille (15 hours); Nice (7 hours); Monte Carlo (9 hours); Portofino (10 hours); and Portoferrario, Elba Island (10 hours). Disembarks at Civitavecchia/Rome. The reverse itinerary is also available.

Evaluation: This is a thorough exploration of the French and Italian Rivieras. If you're not overly thrilled with resort towns ranging from quaint to sophisticated, it could get a little boring. On the other hand, if you love resort towns, then this is an excellent itinerary. Since there is a lot of time spent in Marseille you could explore the city as well as take an excursion to Avignon or Nimes. The itinerary as listed arrives in Monte Carlo in the evening and so is more suited to those who want to enjoy the gaming and nightlife of the town. The reverse trip spends all day there, which allows for more sightseeing. Do be sure to add some time in Rome.

Itinerary 3: Embarks at Civitavecchia/Rome. Seven nights. Ports of call: Capri (7 hours); Messina (7 hours); Gythion (8 hours); Nauplion (10 hours); and Ermoupolis (7 hours). Disembarks at Piraeus/Athens. The reverse itinerary is also available.

Evaluation: This cruise offers adequate time in all ports. Gythion and Ermoupolis are remote Greek ports that are only of mild interest. This trip is best for those who prefer to escape the crowds. You'll need to add pre- and post-cruise time in the major cities.

Itinerary 4: Embarks at Piraeus/Athens. Seven nights. Ports of call: Mykonos (15 hours); Santorini (8 hours); Rhodes (15 hours); Bodrum (11 hours); and Kusadasi (8 hours). Disembarks at Istanbul. The reverse itinerary is also available.

Evaluation: This is a very good Aegean cruise, assuming that you allow additional time in Athens and Istanbul. The times spent in all the ports are adequate or better. There's more than enough time in Mykonos to get over to Delos. The reverse itinerary – which I prefer – spends more time at Santorini, where you won't have trouble filling the extra hour or two.

WIND SURF

The *Wind Surf*, in addition to the itineraries below, also does *Wind Spirit's* and *Wind Star's* Itineraries 1 and 4 (see pages 130 and 131 respectively).

> *Itinerary 1: Embarks at Barcelona. Seven nights. Ports of call: Mahon (8 hours); Port Vendres (7 hours); Marseille (15 hours); Sanary-sur-Mer (9 hours); Porquerolles (9 hours); and Cannes (16 hours). Disembarks at Nice. The reverse itinerary is also available.*

Evaluation: Almost all of the calls on this trip are mainland or island resorts. However, this is not your standard selection, with many less common stops included. Times in each port are adequate and several allow for exploration of the surrounding area.

> *Itinerary 2: Embarks at Nice. Seven nights. Ports of call: Monte Carlo (overnight); St. Tropez (9 hours); Portofino (10 hours); Portovenere (16 hours); Portoferraio, Elba Island (9 hours); and Porto Vecchio, Corsica (9 hours). Disembarks at Civitavecchia/ Rome. The reverse itinerary is also available.*

Evaluation: Again, because sailing ships are slower, they tend to stop at more small ports along the way in order to avoid excessive time at sea. Although some of the ports on this itinerary are definitely mainstream, others are not. The long time spent in Portovenere can be used to get to Florence. Port times are all at least adequate.

> *Itinerary 3: Embarks at Civitavecchia/Rome. Seven nights. Ports of call: Capri (10 hours); Sorrento (9 hours); Lipari/Aeolian Islands (6 hours); Tunis (6 hours); Porto Empedocle, Sicily (10 hours); and Gozo, Malta (4 hours). Disembarks at Malta (Valletta). The reverse itinerary spends an overnight in Sorrento after an evening arrival.*

Evaluation: This is a very interesting itinerary. The only major problem with this one (and the one that follows) is that it either starts or ends in Malta, where it can be difficult to make air connections. Between the time spent in Capri and Sorrento you should also be able to see a good portion of the Bay of Naples area, including Pompeii and the Amalfi Coast. Lipari is a relatively unvisited but pleasant port of call. A few more hours in Tunis would be helpful, but in the six hours provided you can hit the highlights (i.e., ancient Carthage). Out-of-the-way Porto Empedocle is a quaint village on the southern Sicilian coast and is not visited by any other cruise line. No other line stops at Gozo, either, one of the smaller islands of Malta. Four hours is enough to see it. Add time at the end for Rome.

> *Itinerary 4: Embarks at Malta. Seven nights. Ports of call: Taormina (7 hours); Cephalonia (9 hours); Corfu (7 hours); Dubrovnik (12 hours); and Hvar (7 hours). Disembarks at Venice after overnight on board. The reverse itinerary is also available.*

Evaluation: This is another good itinerary that visits quite a few interesting places. The time in each port is generous (few itineraries allow so long in Dubrovnik, for example). The only unusual place is Cephalonia, which doesn't have a whole lot to offer but provides a pleasant break from the more popular ports.

Ship Activities

*P*eople often describe cruise ships as "floating hotels" – a pretty appropriate description. But perhaps "floating resorts" might be a more accurate term because of the extensive facilities and activities that are found on every ship. Generally, the larger the ship, the more diverse the available activities. However, even the smaller vessels will usually have more than enough on the agenda to keep you busy during time spent at sea. So, if you've never cruised and are worried that you'll be bored after a few days, put it out of your mind. You may find that you don't even have enough time to do everything you want to do. For some people, of course, the option to just relax and do nothing is an attractive aspect of a cruise. But you can always swim, exercise, walk or jog around the deck, dance the night away, watch a movie, wine and dine until you explode, or be entertained by singers, dancers, comedians, magicians and who knows what else. (Most ships have an early and late entertainment show each evening.) You'll have the opportunity to learn more about the upcoming ports of call from onboard experts. Perhaps you're feeling lucky. Casinos are a mainstay of every cruise ship and you'll find slot machines as well as table games. The casino is almost always closed when the ship is in port because of local regulations, but it comes alive at night when the ship is out on the open sea. And many people cruise to meet new friends. After a few nights, you'll almost certainly get to know your dinner table companions quite well. Something about cruising encourages comradery and friendships (and romances) develop as you travel from port to port together. It's up to you. No one is going to force you to take part in the many get-togethers.

It's safe to say that there is always something happening on board. Every ship publishes a daily calendar that will be brought to your room. It will inform you of scheduled activities from dancing lessons and card games to a dozen other activities, one or more of which is sure to whet your appetite. The calendar also has useful information on procedures for port calls and other events, so read it carefully each day. Entertainment and recreational activities are largely self-explanatory. But let's look at those that are unusual or unique to Mediterranean cruising.

Over the years cruise directors have become more focused on the educational aspects of visiting foreign ports. More time and attention is devoted to making sure that you have the opportunity to learn about your destinations. These travel education programs take two forms. The first is the **port briefing**. Prior to arrival at each port you can attend a session where explanations of local culture and sights are given. (On some ships the talk will be given for all ports at the outset of the cruise.) Although these are generally quite useful and informative, keep in mind that these sessions also have a business purpose – namely, to encourage cruisers to sign up for shore excursions. As you will learn in the *Ports of Call* chapter of this book, that isn't always necessary. Ask questions about excursions and use that information to plan your own trip, if you wish. Every ship also has a tour office, where you can make enquiries about available shore excursions. Don't expect for them to have a great deal of advice about setting out on your own. That's where this book comes in.

A second educational program that will frequently be encountered is a **lecture** by one or more natives of the region. Often accompanied by slides or videos, they can be an interesting way to learn more about the local culture. Many cruise lines also offer talks on topics unrelated to the cruise. These can cover anything ranging from personal finance to personal health and fitness and everything in between. There are even some cruises with a "theme," where many programs are based on a particular type of activity.

There are several activities that I classify under the category of "touring" the ship. Take some time during the early part of the cruise to walk around and explore. This will acquaint you with the ship so you can negotiate it with ease after a short time on board. Moreover, many ships are spectacular in design and often filled with works of art. A careful exploration of your vessel can be an entertaining and eye-opening experience.

A lot of ships offer passengers the opportunity to look behind the scenes and see some aspects of how the ship is operated. Probably the most popular of these is a visit to see the bridge. Open house on the bridge is always a well-attended event where both children and adults can make believe they are the Captain for at least a few moments. This tour is almost always announced in advance and is sometimes so popular that they have to give out tickets to keep the number of visitors at any one time more manageable. Some of the smaller ships – especially luxury yachts and sailing vessels – may even have an open bridge policy (exceptions are when the ship is leaving or entering a port). Touring the kitchens is another event, although it's rarely advertised and you may have to ask your dining room steward. They may be given for those passengers who are interested, often at the very end of the cruise.

Increased security after September 11, 2001 is likely to decrease the number of vessels offering bridge tours.

Options in Port

Unless you have come to Europe to simply cruise, the ports you visit will be the most important aspect of your trip. Selecting the itinerary was only the first step in planning your land activities. Now it is time to decide how you are going to see what you have traveled thousands of miles to reach. There are two basic choices: either you use the cruise line's shore excursion program of guided tours, or you head out on your own. (Complete cruise tour packages are another option which will be explored later.) As with everything else, there are advantages and disadvantages to each approach, depending upon your interests, planning capabilities and spirit of adventure to go it alone. Of course, you may have every reason to take an organized shore excursion in one port and to go on your own in the next port. Some places are well suited to individual exploration, while others are not.

Organized Shore Excursions

Every cruise line will present you with a lengthy list of optional shore excursions that they have arranged with local tour operators. Some lines will let you book these in advance, while others make you wait until you board ship to make the arrangements. While certain lines have more choices than others, there will always be more options in every port than you could ever have time for.

The primary advantage of organized excursion is that they are easy. All of the planning has been done. You will be picked up at the dock and transported to the sights included on the excursion itinerary and then be taken back to the ship. Also, some time is saved because you don't have to wait in line to buy tickets at museums and other attractions. However, efficient travelers who can get around on their own can usually see far more during the time allotted in port than those who take the organized tours. But if you're the type who can't read a map or tends to get easily lost, you will probably be better off with a tour.

When it comes to cost, organized tours are no bargain, and some are outright rip-offs. Because the tour operator has to make a profit and the cruise line has to get its cut, it is *almost always* considerably less expensive to go it on your own. Follow this simple example as an indication of the possible cost differential. On Rhodes there is a half-day excursion (between four and five hours) that goes to the Acropolis of Lindos on another part of the island. The cost for this trip when booked through a cruise ship is about $40 per person. You could do it on your own for less than $10 a person, which includes round-trip local bus transportation and admission to the Acropolis.

In each port described in this book I will clearly indicate whether or not I believe an organized shore excursion is worthwhile. If you can't book shore excursions prior to departure (or haven't done so), make sure you are aware of the sign-up deadline. Some cruise lines want all the arrangements done right at the beginning of the cruise, while others have the deadline nearer to the time of each excursion. Always try to get as many details about the trip as you can before booking. Find out what the tour *visits*, as opposed to *passes by*. A busy guided itinerary sometimes makes only one or two lengthy stops and simply whizzes by a number of attractions that really warrant further attention.

On Your Own

Self-travel in port is best done in larger ports where most of the sights are close by or where public transportation is good. In those cases where you have many hours in port and it includes lunch time, you may be able to have the option of returning to the ship to eat or trying some of the local cuisine on shore. Either of those options has to be better than being herded in as a group to a restaurant chosen by the tour operator.

One possible disadvantage of going it on your own is that if you get lost, or lose track of time, the ship isn't going to wait for you. It will, however, always wait for the rare late excursion. Whenever you venture out on your own (except in those tiny ports where you'll always be within a few minutes walk of the ship), take the telephone number of the ship's port agent. If you are going to be a little late, you can phone ahead and see if the ship can wait. *Don't* use this as a means of getting more time in port. It should be used only when genuinely needed. The telephone numbers should be provided in your daily program or by some other means. If not, ask for them.

Complete Cruise Tours

Each cruise line offers complete tour packages that include guided sightseeing in cities before and/or after the cruise itself. While these tours don't include port excursions during the course of the cruise, the principle is the same. You have to weigh the advantages and disadvantages of individual vs. group travel as they relate to your specific situation. Again, the tour packages are usually more expensive than individual travel, whether it be for one or two days, or a full week pre- or post-cruise. One of the reasons for this is that the cruise lines usually select luxury class hotels; you may well be satisfied with something simpler. If you are the type of traveler who usually takes package tours, then it probably makes sense to take the complete cruise tour. But if you're confident traveling independently, don't let the travel agent talk you into a cruise tour package.

Practical Information

*E*ven if you have cruised in Alaska or the Caribbean, a European cruise is different. And travelers who have been to Europe but haven't cruised will find a trip aboard a floating resort quite different. So, whether you are a first-timer or an experienced voyager, the various topics in this A to Z section should help to answer many of your questions.

Accommodations on Land

*O*ne of the nicest things about a cruise is that you may not have to even think about choosing a hotel. On the other hand, a large number of Mediterranean cruise passengers will have either a pre-cruise or post-cruise land extension, perhaps both. If you sign up for the extensions that are run by the cruise lines, the hotel accommodations will be selected for you. It will usually be a first class option, with prices to match. You may be willing to stay at a place that isn't as fancy. If you choose to make arrangements on your own, you can opt for an inexpensive hotel, and you can sometimes get a better rate at the top hotels than what the cruise line is offering. It's beyond the scope of this book to provide information on accommodations in the gateway ports, but I can offer several suggestions to make the search process easier.

⚓ If you want accommodations that are similar to those you are familiar with in the United States, then Mediterranean nation properties affiliated with the major American chains are the first place to look. Even here, though, expect some differences. Make your reservations through the American toll-free reservation numbers.

⚓ Another possibility is to use some of the better and larger European chain hotels. The quality is usually on a par with their American counterparts and reservations can easily be made from the United States by telephone (with English-speaking reservation agents).

⚓ The Internet has opened up a whole new world for hotel reservations. With a little research, you'll be able to find a hotel or inn with local flavor and often at a cost well below that of the big chains. The number of sites is almost endless. I suggest that you use your favorite search engine and enter the name of the city or country and "hotels." Take some time to evaluate the rating system used to be sure you get the quality you're looking for. Reservations are sometimes made directly on-line, although it is just as common for them to be handled via e-mail. E-mail is an excellent way to "chat" with the proprietors. There's a good chance you'll save even more money this way since there is no middleman getting a cut of the action. There is seldom any language difficulty, and in cases where language is a problem you can use a free web translation service (such as http://babelfish.altavista.com) to put your words into a foreign language.

In the *Addendum* you will find a list of chain hotels with a strong Mediterranean presence.

Clothing On & Off Ship/Weather

*T*he largely agreeable weather of this region has its own name wherever it occurs throughout the world – a Mediterranean climate. What that means is you can count on comfortable to warm weather during the spring and fall, as well as hot summers. During the warmest months, the comfort level is improved by cooling sea breezes. The amount of rainfall varies quite a bit from one Mediterranean location to another. The summer sees frequent showers in many areas, but lengthy storms usually take place in the winter months.

Take a look at the average high and low daily temperatures as well as the normal monthly rainfall in several popular Mediterranean destinations in the table below.

TEMPERATURE CHART				
All temperatures are listed in degrees Fahrenheit, but be aware that local weather conditions will be quoted in Celsius. To convert the temperature from Celsius to Fahrenheit simply multiply the Celsius temperature by 1.8 and then add 32.				
	APRIL High/Low/Rain	JUNE High/Low/Rain	AUGUST High/Low/Rain	OCTOBER High/Low/Rain
Alexandria	75/59/0.1	83/69/0.0	87/75/0.0	83/68/0.3
Athens	68/52/0.9	86/68/0.3	92/73/0.3	75/60/2.1
Barcelona	64/52/1.9	77/64/1.5	82/70/1.7	70/59/3.8
Haifa	78/55/0.2	82/64/0.0	86/70/0.0	81/60/0.1
Istanbul	60/45/1.7	77/60/1.1	82/66/1.2	68/55/2.6
Lisbon	67/53/2.3	77/60/0.7	82/63/0.2	72/58/2.9
Malta	68/55/1.1	84/67/0.5	90/74/0.1	65/52/3.0
Monte Carlo	63/50/2.5	75/61/1.5	80/66/1.2	70/57/4.4
Naples	64/47/3.0	79/60/1.5	84/64/1.2	71/53/5.2
Odessa	56/44/1.3	76/62/1.9	80/65/1.4	60/48/1.2
Rome	66/50/2.6	82/63/1.3	82/67/1.0	71/55/4.5
Venice	61/46/2.9	77/60/3.1	80/63/3.1	64/48/3.0

PRACTICAL INFORMATION

Also keep in mind that the majority of Mediterranean locations are quite humid, although if you're in port or near the shore this will be mitigated to some extent by sea breezes.

During the day on-board dress is highly casual and comfortable. How you dress after dinner depends upon what you are going to be doing. If you're going to take in a show or dance the night away, the general rule is to remain dressed as you were for dinner. Otherwise, you can return to your cabin and change into more casual attire. The dress codes for dinner attire are almost universally referred to as formal, informal and casual. Let's take a closer look at what each one means.

⚓ **Formal attire** means a tuxedo for men and gowns for women. However, that's only a recommendation. Men will be admitted on formal evenings (even the most formal Captain's dinner) if they wear a dark suit. The majority of men do wear tuxedos, however, so you might feel underdressed in a suit. For ladies, a nice dress (but not slacks) will be acceptable in lieu of a gown. A lot more of the cruising public prefers to be casual these days, so the number of formal nights is far lower than it used to be. Alternative restaurants are another means of avoiding formal and even informal dress. If you don't have a tuxedo but decide that you want to wear one on formal evenings, just about every cruise line will have one for rent. Call the cruise line ahead of time and your tux will be waiting in your stateroom upon your arrival. The daily rates are usually better than those you'll find at a local tuxedo rental store, but you are forced to rent for the entire cruise.

⚓ **Informal attire** varies from one line to another. It used to mean jackets for men (usually with a tie) and a dress or pant suit for women. This is still common in many cases, but a number of cruise lines have now downgraded informal dress so that men are not required to wear a jacket. A shirt with a collar will be fine; no shorts are permitted. For women, any smart attire will certainly be appropriate.

⚓ **Casual dress** has two meanings, depending upon the time of day. In the afternoon, it refers to resort wear. However, at dinner time it translates to what most people call business casual, and not everything goes. Specifically, jeans (even "dress" jeans), shorts, halter tops and beach wear are definite no-nos at dinner time.

How you dress when in port depends not only on the weather, but also on your activities. Casual and comfortable is generally the best way to dress. Ship officials will always have a local weather forecast available before you disembark, so check it out. Casual and even sloppy attire is usually alright when touring, but more conservative dress is appropriate when visiting churches, mosques or temples. Be respectful. Men will not be allowed to enter a mosque if they are wearing shorts and women must always be modestly dressed. Halter tops, sleeveless blouses and short skirts are frowned upon. Entry is frequently denied to those who are underdressed even at churches, especially those in smaller towns and conservative areas.

I recommend packing light. However, if there is an exception it is on a cruise, for two reasons. You will be in one place for a length of time so you don't have to worry about packing and unpacking. Also, although the trend has been towards more casual dress, there is still a great deal of dressing up and many people, especially women, will want to make sure that they have a different outfit for each night of the cruise. Heaven forbid the possibility that your table mate might see you in the same outfit more than once!

In addition to your clothing, don't forget to pack the following items.

⚓ Sunscreen

⚓ Insect repellent (brands containing DEET may be some-what more effective, but DEET-less brands are safer, especially for children)

⚓ Sunglasses

⚓ Hat

⚓ Binoculars

⚓ Camera and/or camcorder with plenty of extra film, tapes and battery packs. Although you will be able to purchase film and other needs in port (and often on board ship), the prices are much higher than they are at home.

⚓ Medications. Bring a copy of your prescription along as well, not only because you might lose your medication, but to assist in the customs process. Although it is rare to be challenged by customs officials about this, a prescription will help clear things up rapidly.

⚓ Credit cards are a good choice for port purchases as well as settling your account on board ship. Bring a small amount of cash. Traveler's checks are widely accepted.

Cruising Season

Because the Mediterranean has a generally warm climate, the cruise season extends from the beginning of April through November, and some itineraries run throughout the year. Some lines don't operate for the full eight-month span, but they are all available during the key months of May through October. If you are considering a winter cruise, you should be aware that some Mediterranean ports are chilly at that time of year and the worst storms occur during the winter.

Costs are often lower during the beginning and end of each cruising season. The middle of the summer usually commands the highest prices, but some lines charge their premium fares during June and September knowing that some people want to avoid the hottest months of the year.

PRACTICAL INFORMATION

Dining

*D*ining on board is one of the biggest pleasures of cruising. You'll savor wonderfully prepared cuisine (often from renowned chefs), including delicacies from the area of the world in which you are cruising. In the case of the Mediterranean that's a wonderful treat in itself. Be prepared to put on some extra pounds during the course of your cruise!

In the old days of cruising ship-board dining was straight forward. You took most of your meals in the main dining room and perhaps had a buffet for breakfast and/or lunch. How things have changed. In addition to the main dining room, almost all of today's ships have at least one alternative restaurant. This can take the form of a bistro, café, or just about anything else. It is usually open only for dinner, although you'll find some ships with, for example, a pizzeria open during lunch. Alternative restaurants almost always have a casual or informal dress code. The larger the ship, the more alternative restaurants there are – some of the largest vessels offer three or more. Unfortunately, it is becoming more common for the cruise lines to charge a fee for one or more alternative restaurants. Sometimes it is only a few dollars, but it can range as high as $20 per person. I think that is a rip-off and hope it doesn't become a trend. Select cruise lines do not operate their alternative restaurants on the night of the Captain's dinner, when they want everyone to be in the main dining room. There may be other restricted evenings for specialty restaurants.

The main dining room is usually the most formal of the ship's restaurants in terms of atmosphere and service. It is extremely rare to have "single seat" dining – that is, everyone is served at the same time. More common is to have two seatings, called early and late. The early seating commonly begins around 6 pm, although it could be adjusted to fit with port calls. Late seatings generally start about 2½ hours after the early seating. Some people avoid the early seating for fear that it will be rushed, but I haven't found that to be a problem. You will be given a choice of which seating you want at the time you book your cruise and every effort will be made to accommodate your wishes. "Better" tables (that is, those closer to the captain or with a better view) are usually given to guests in the higher priced staterooms, but you can request to be reseated if you don't like what you are given. Depending upon capacity and other factors, these requests may sometimes be granted.

Dinner in the main room is always a multi-course affair and, although the portions in each course aren't big, nobody walks away hungry. In fact, most ship dining room staff will gladly accommodate requests for additional servings. Don't be afraid to ask. Try not to overeat at these meals because, as you'll soon see, there are plenty of other eating opportunities on board. Some lines offer complimentary wine or other alcoholic beverage one or two times during a cruise, but drinks (including soft drinks) usually have additional cost. All cruise ships have a good selection of wines and champagnes and your wine steward will be happy to assist you in making the right choice to accompany your dinner. The more upscale lines, obviously, have a better selection of wines. Spirits of all types are available throughout the day at numerous bars and lounges and, of course, during evening entertainment performances.

You may choose to eat breakfast and lunch in the main dining room, but many ships have a separate buffet for these two meals. Buffets are casual and allow you to make a quick getaway from the ship at port. You will *not* receive any credit for meals missed while on shore excursions, although guided full-day excursions will routinely include a nice sit-down lunch in a carefully chosen local restaurant. Independent travelers can return to the ship for lunch, find a lunch spot on their own or just skip lunch. Buffets vary in size and quality, and they can be spectacular affairs. Cruise lines close the buffet before dinner, except on special nights when they offer a dinner buffet.

Three meals a day doesn't seem to be enough for hungry cruise passengers. Two other standard features these days are the afternoon tea (usually about 4 pm) and the midnight buffet. The former is generally comprised of small sandwiches, pastries and fruits, in addition to coffee or tea. As is the case with meals, however, there is usually a charge for drinks. The midnight affair is heavy on sweets, often sinfully so. Even if a late night cheesecake isn't your cup of tea, do at least look at one of these often beautiful and bountiful displays. See if you can resist taking something! There are plenty of other opportunities to eat, too. Sweets, such as ice cream, are often served out on deck in the afternoon. Again, some cruise lines have begun to charge for this treat. So far, at least, those lines are in the minority.

Disabled Travelers

*T*here has been some controversy in recent years about just how far the cruise lines have to go in order to meet requirements for handicapped persons. Public relations staff working for the cruise lines will be quick to point out amenities for the handicapped are provided "voluntarily," but the fact of the matter is that cruising can present some difficulties for the disabled traveler.

Almost all major cruise lines can offer rooms suitable for handicapped guests. This is especially true on the larger, more modern vessels. Also, crew members will go out of their way to assist those with physical limitations. That's the good news. The bad news is that, by their very nature, ships impose limitations for the disabled traveler. Even though you can get from one deck to another by elevator, corridors are often narrow and negotiating some areas is difficult. But the biggest problem is in port, when it's time to go ashore, as very few ports have airport-style ramps to get on and off the ship. Of course, there are numerous ports where you can simply take a small ramp to get off the ship, but at the majority of calls you'll need to use the ship's gangplank, which is often narrow, has open spaces between steps and sways while you're on it. It gets worse. The gangplank may end on the dock, but more often it leads the way to the ship's tender, which is waiting to run guests ashore. Negotiating this route may be impossible for those with physical challenges. As a safety precaution, ship lines or captains reserve the option to prohibit physically handicapped passengers from disembarking at certain port calls.

If you have any questions, call the cruise line and ask specific questions about facilities, including access at ports of call.

Discounts

Seeing is not believing when looking at prices listed in cruise brochures. Every line offers a price reduction for booking early. Some offer a straight cash discount, which may begin at around $400 for lower-priced staterooms and rise to well in excess of $1,000 for the more expensive accommodations. Other lines give a percentage off the regular fare, as much as 40% in some cases, although 10% is more common. Additionally, your discount will vary within the same cruise line depending upon how far in advance you book. The earlier you do it, the greater the discount. Refer to the individual cruise line brochures or your travel agent for specific cruise-sponsored discounts. You can also sometimes get a bargain by waiting until the last minute. If there's room available, you can sometimes get aboard at a greatly reduced rate. I don't recommend this method if your heart is set on a particular cruise – if sales are brisk a last-minute discount may never happen.

Another way to cut costs is to book through a discount cruise travel agent, who buys large blocks of staterooms. Newspaper travel sections are filled with advertisements for such agents. To ensure that you are dealing with a reputable company, make sure they are a member of CLIA (Cruise Lines International Association), NACOA (National Association of Cruise Only Agencies), ASTA (American Society of Travel Agents), or some other major reputable travel organization. Consult your local phone book to find the cruise-only travel agents in your area. Among the larger national cruise agencies are **Cruises of Distinction**, ☎ (800) 434-5544 and the Internet-based **Cruise.com**, www.cruise.com.

Package deals that include air sometimes work out to be less expensive than booking the air and cruise sections separately (see the next section for more details on flight information). But no pricing system is ever static in the travel world. Do some research. Price things separately and as part of a package deal and see which is the best price at the time.

Since all of the cruise lines are anxious to have your repeat business, it's standard practice for them to offer discounts to travelers who have sailed with them before. These discounts can be substantial, and some lines even increase discounts according to how many cruises you have taken. An example of this is the Crystal Society of Crystal Cruises, which offers completely free cruising. You have increasingly better discounts all the way up to 100 cruises, at which point you travel for nothing! Of course, if you have the time and money to take 100 Crystal cruises, you probably don't need a free cruise! Another way that you can get credit towards reduced fares is by traveling with their cruise partners. The "Vacation Interchange Privileges" is offered by Costa, Holland-America, Cunard, Seabourn, Carnival and Windstar, all of which are owned by the same company.

The variety of discounts available is so great that you should rarely have to pay the full fare.

Driving & Car Rentals

A lot of American travelers won't consider driving a rental car in Europe. But if you can drive in the States, then you can scoot all over Europe as well. Roads are generally excellent, although highway systems may be lacking in the less-developed countries away from Western Europe. And although the language may be different, all roads in Europe use easily learned and recognizable symbols. Make sure that you have good maps and a route plan (it's easier to spot signs for specific towns, attractions, etc.) and you'll do fine. As far as the way Europeans drive, don't believe everything you read in most guidebooks, which make it seem like life on the roads in Europe is akin to a gladiatorial contest. It's really not that different than in the United States. However, some driving customs are different. In Italy, drivers will tailgate you if you're going what they consider to be too slow. Also, most European countries do follow the rule of passing only on the outside lane, so don't stay in that lane unless you are passing other vehicles. It's unlikely you'll want to drive in any of the European cities, which are filled with heavy traffic and narrow streets, and have limited parking. Even small towns can be troublesome, but renting a car for the day is a great way to get out in the country.

Most major American rental companies have offices in the popular ports, but it can be cheaper to use foreign firms such as Auto Europe or Kemwel. Make reservations prior to your trip and as far in advance as possible. This is especially important in smaller communities (where the supply of cars is limited) and is always the case if you want an automatic transmission (Europeans love their manual transmissions). Note that you'll be charged more for a car with automatic transmission. Gas prices are much higher in Europe too, but you can minimize costs by driving as small a car as you feel comfortable with. Some of the roads in rural areas are narrow and winding, so a smaller car is advantageous. It should be obvious but is worth mentioning that mileage and speed are given in kilometers. One mile is equivalent to approximately 6/10 of a mile; 100 kph is about 60 mph. Finally, while the majority of countries in the Mediterranean region honor a valid US driver's license, I recommend that you secure an international driving permit before your trip if you plan to rent a car. They are available at AAA offices and cost $10 (plus a processing fee if you're not a AAA member). Good for one year from the issue date, an IDP does *not* replace your state-issued license – rather, it must accompany it.

Electrical Appliances & Other Technical Tidbits

*T*aking a cruise in Europe means that you avoid dealing with all the different electrical issues that land travelers encounter. Cruise ships usually have the same 110-volt system found in the US and their outlets accept the two-pin plug found on all of your appliances. However, some of the European cruise lines have 220-volt electrical systems and use the two-round-pin plug that is used throughout Europe. Even these ships may have dual voltage systems. If the ship you're traveling on has only a 220-volt system, you'll need a transformer.You might also encounter a few ships with 110-volt systems that have the European-style outlets, in which case you'll need a plug adapter. These are sometimes provided on board, but it's best to bring your own.

To ensure that you're properly equipped, ask in advance what kind of system is in use on the ship you have selected. The cruise line brochures usually have this information. If not, contact the cruise line directly.

Financial Matters & Foreign Currency

The cashless society of on-board ship life is simple. Just about the only expenses on board are tips and any meals you might wish to take at the alternate dining rooms. A large percentage of lines use US dollars as their on-board currency, while some of the foreign ones use their own national currency. Only a few cruise lines allow you to charge tips to your shipboard account.

It is always best to carry as little cash as possible – you won't use it, especially if you return to the ship for lunch or plan to take guided shore excursions, which often include meals. If you plan to explore independently, your major expenses will be local transportation, admissions to museums and other sights, perhaps a snack or drink, and these will be minimal. Try to assess what you might spend in advance so that you don't exchange too much money into local currency. You can often use American money for store purchases overseas, but you won't receive a good exchange rate. It is always better to deal in the local currency. Cruise ships have exchange offices where you can get a small amount of foreign currency. If yours doesn't, use an ATM (which are ubiquitous in port call towns), which will allow you to withdraw a small amount of money and get an excellent rate of exchange. ATM machines provide the best rates of exchange . Credit cards are almost universally accepted throughout this region in stores that sell expensive wares. It is less common for them to be accepted in local shops in a small town, where bargaining with cash is the usual means of doing business. The farther east you travel in the Mediterranean, the more difficulty you will have using credit cards. The same is true for traveler's checks. Also, for things like transportation and admissions, credit cards and travelers checks are almost never accepted.

PRACTICAL INFORMATION

Currencies

Let's look at the various foreign currencies that you might encounter during your Mediterranean cruise. Keep in mind that the equivalent US dollar values given here were correct as of press time. Exchange rates fluctuate a great deal, so use this only as a rough guide and always inquire as to the current exchange rate just prior to your departure. The 2002 introduction of the Euro as a uniform currency in 12 European Union nations makes things a whole lot easier.

Currency Exchange Chart		
Country	Currency	Equivalent to US $1
European Union	Euro *	1.12
Bulgaria	Lev	2.16
Croatia	Kuna	8.26
Cyprus	Pound	0.65
Egypt	Pound	4.56
Gibraltar	Pound	0.69
Israel	New Shekel	4.34
Malta	Lira	0.46
Morocco	Dirham	11.45
Romania	Leu	32,429
Tunisia	Dinar	1.45
Turkey	Lira	1,509,000
Ukraine	Hryvnia	5.36

* The Euro (€) is scheduled to phase out the national currencies of five countries – France (franc), Greece (drachma), Italy (lira), Portugal (escudo) and Spain (peseta). The transition to actual cash use of the Euro took place on January 1, 2002.

In countries such as Turkey, where the value of the currency is so low, it is common practice to omit the last three digits. Thus, something that costs 5,000,000 Turkish lira will be marked on store signs as 5,000. You should always be careful when counting your foreign currency, but especially so in situations like this where large numbers are involved for even a tiny purchase and it's easy to get confused.

Determining money needs for longer stays on land is also a good idea. Make the exchange only when you arrive in the country where you will be needing the cash. ATMs and banks are always the best places to do the transaction, but keep in mind that you pay a fee at your home bank for using a foreign ATM.

Flight Arrangements

*A*ll cruise lines offer the option to include air transportation with your cruise fare. In fact, many price lists show the air-inclusive rate and you then have to subtract an "air credit" if you intend to book your own transportation.

Using the cruise line's air program will certainly be your easiest option. Everything will be taken care of for you and transfers from the airport to your cruise ship will be included. If you make your own air arrangements, you will almost certainly have to make your way to the ship on your own. Also, if several guests are arriving via a cruise-sponsored air program and the plane is late, the ship's departure may be delayed in order to accommodate those passengers. Don't expect that courtesy if you're traveling on your own.

So far it sounds like a really good deal to go with the cruise air program. But there are some potential disadvantages to consider. The air fares offered are good, but most often not the cheapest. Comparison is the key; you'll probably be able to find a cheaper air fare. What makes your task more difficult is that cruise lines don't usually give you detailed departure times until final documents are issued (usually about two to four weeks before your departure). You'll probably book your flight long before that, and you could wind up on a flight that is inconvenient. Weigh the advantages and disadvantages, and don't let the travel agent or the cruise line bully you into something that you would prefer not to do.

Getting to Your Ship

I've already touched on the subject of transfers from the airport to your ship. It's easy if the cruise line will be providing the transfers (that is, you book through their air program). Otherwise, the best bet in most places is to take a taxi, which can cost a considerable amount. Although public transportation (trains, buses) is usually available, it isn't a practical solution because you'll probably have considerable luggage. If you choose to take part in a pre-cruise tour of the gateway city, all transportation to the ship will be included. Independent travelers will once again have to make their own way but can minimize inconvenience by choosing a hotel that is relatively close to the cruise ship terminal. Occasionally, cruise lines offer an option that allows you to make your own flight arrangements and add on, for a fee, ground transfers to and from the ship. Inquire at the time you book.

In each of the destination ports described in Part III, I have indicated the location of the port and given some information on getting there. If you are traveling on your own, the best way to insure that you don't miss your cruise is to be in the embarkation city the day before the cruise departs. If you do plan to fly in on the day of the cruise itself, allow at least six hours as a bare minimum between the scheduled flight arrival time and the ship's departure time.

Health

*E*very cruise ship has a doctor on board and a well equipped medical facility that can handle routine medical care and even minor emergencies. In the event of an emergency that cannot be handled on ship, you'll be transferred to a land hospital. If you take prescription medicine, make sure that you have a supply sufficient for the entire trip (and even a few extra). The ship's medical center is not a pharmacy.

In Western Europe you shouldn't encounter any unusual health problems. The most common complaint is traveler's diarrhea caused by strange foods and your system's unfamiliarity with the local water. Of course, if you eat your meals on board the ship, this won't affect you. While on land, avoid food from street vendors and drink bottled water (bring water from the ship). In eastern Europe, North Africa and the Middle East you should never drink the water (Israel is the only exception, and even there you should stick to bottled water) and be especially careful of where you eat.

As of press time travelers to the Mediterranean weren't required to be inoculated, but ask the cruise line or consult your physician before leaving. Be aware that some types of inoculations (hepatitis, for example) must be taken many months prior to the time you travel. If you plan to spend an extended period of time on land in less developed areas, secure additional information on what health precautions may be in order.

Passports, Customs & Other Considerations

*C*ruise lines will not issue tickets until you have provided proof of necessary paperwork to get into the country of embarkation and to get back home. The information below assumes that you are an American citizen. All other nationals should consult the proper authorities in their country to determine what documentation and other requirements must be met.

United States citizens must have a valid passport to enter any Mediterranean country. In most cases, the foreign nation will require that the expiration date of your passport be at least six months beyond the time your visit ends. Don't wait for the last minute to get your passport; applications are available at most post offices. For detailed information, visit www.travel.state.gov/passport_services.html. Applications can take eight to 10 weeks to process. Most of the countries you'll visit do not require that you have a visa for short visits. The exceptions (at press time) include Egypt, Syria, Turkey and the Ukraine. Always confirm visa restrictions at the time of booking. Cruise line personnel usually have up-to-date information on this, but you can also consult the embassy or consular office of the foreign country for more detailed information. You can get visas on your own through the embassy or consulate, or you can let the cruise line make all the arrangements for you. This is much more convenient, although every cruise line charges what I consider to be an exorbitant fee (as much as US $60) for doing so.

Customs procedures in most European countries have been streamlined and you can usually get through the airport formalities quickly. This is especially so in the western European nations. In the Middle East and some areas of eastern Europe, expect thorough inspections and more paperwork. If you do get stopped, be polite and courteous; any rude behavior on your part is only likely to slow down the process.

It is standard operating procedure for your passport to be collected upon boarding of your cruise ship and you likely won't get it back until the morning of your disembarkation at the end of the cruise. Ship personnel will handle all customs formalities as you enter each new country, and customs officials come on board the ship and will check passports and do whatever else they have to do without your even knowing that it happened. You do not need your passport with you for day-long stops, but you should always carry proper identification, including the ship ID that was issued to you. That is the most important item to carry at all times. It is also wise to make a photocopy of the ID pages of your passport to carry with you at all times.

Upon disembarkation you will receive your passport back and your luggage will have already been brought into the cruise ship terminal, where you will reclaim it and present it – along with your passport – to the local customs officials.

Staying in Touch

*B*eing on a cruise ship doesn't mean that you have to lose touch with friends and family (or, perish the thought, business contacts) back home. In the old days it was a complicated and expensive procedure to place a call. Today it's just expensive, not because of technology limitations, but because the cruise lines make some extra money on the deal. It's hard to find a stateroom without a direct-dial telephone that can be used to call anywhere in the world. Dialing procedures vary from ship to ship, so consult the information guide in your room or ask for assistance from the ship's operator. Prior to departure, you will be given a telephone number (usually toll free) that people in the United States can dial to reach your cruise line's overseas telephone operator. All they then have to do is inform the operator which port you are in and the call can be completed. Note that the recipient (that is you) is charged for incoming calls.

A less expensive alternative for calling home is to wait until you are in port, where you can invariably purchase a calling card. Just make sure which countries are valid origination points for a call on the card you intend to use. Also, in some countries the public phones have a fee for you to access your calling card system. In such cases the cost is minimal and the easiest way to have the proper amount is to purchase a small denomination local calling card. Remember, that you have to dial the international access code for the United States (001) before the area code and local number.

Computer lovers will be glad to hear that more and more ships now have cyber cafés. Fees for PC use vary, but you can do everything you can at home, including e-mail.

Time Zones

*M*ost of the western Mediterranean is six hours ahead of the Eastern time zone in the United States. So, when it's noon in

New York it will be 6 pm throughout most of this region. The eastern Mediterranean is seven hours later. It's usually easy to keep track of the time when you're on land. If you cross into another time zone, adjust your watch at the next port of entry (you won't know when you cross into another time zone while on the water). Your ship's daily program gives notice of any time zone changes each day, and announcements are sometimes made too. For your general information and convenience when in ports, here is the rundown on time zones by country.

Time Zone Chart	
Difference from Eastern Time Zone (New York)	
5 hours later	Portugal, England
6 hours later	Croatia, France (including Corsica), Gibraltar, Italy (including Sardinia and Sicily), Malta, Morocco, Spain and Tunisia
7 hours later	Bulgaria, Cyprus, Egypt, Greece, Israel, Romania, Turkey and the Ukraine

As a rule, Daylight Savings Time is observed. However, the exact beginning and ending days for this time of the year may vary slightly from one country to the next.

Tipping

Except for a few lines (mostly the top-dollar luxury cruise lines), tipping of ship personnel is *not* included in your fare. And, as is the case throughout the travel and leisure industry, tipping is a way of life. Most ship personnel that will be directly serving you (dining room waiters, cabin attendants, etc.) do not earn a great salary and tips provide a substantial portion of their income. The question of how much to tip involves your evaluation of the service provided and your own personal preferences and beliefs regarding gratuities.

Cruise line management often provides written suggestions as to what is an acceptable tip amount. Tip envelopes are usually given to you near the end of your cruise, sometimes with the suggested amount written on the envelope. Remember, these are guidelines only. Don't be intimidated into giving more than you think is warranted or is above what you can afford. Here are some commonly accepted guidelines:

⚓ *Dining Room Staff:* $3-3.50 per day for your waiter and about half that for his assistant. Most cruise lines also suggest tipping the restaurant manager (i.e., the maitre'd), but I don't see the need for that unless he performs some special service for you. If you frequently ask advice from the wine steward then he should also receive a tip of a dollar per day.

⚓ *Cabin Attendant:* $3-3.50 per day is acceptable. Some sources recommend a small amount for the chief housekeeper but, as above, I don't see the need for that unless he or she has handled a particular problem well for you.

⚓ *Other Staff:* The only other people you will likely tip are bartenders, cocktail waiters or waitresses and deckhands who help out with the lounge chairs. These people should be tipped a dollar for each time you use their services. Be aware that some lines now include a 15% gratuity for these people. If so, do not feel obligated to give anything additional.

No tipping of waiters and stewards takes place during the course of the cruise. You leave your tip for all services toward the very end, perhaps the last time you dine for your waiter or the evening before disembarkation for your cabin steward.

A few cruise lines pool their tips. You leave the entire gratuity in one envelope and it will be shared among those who provided services for you.

There are still relatively few cruise lines that include gratuities in the cost of the cruise. (Advertisements of "free tips" are simply not true – the price has been raised to reflect this cost – it just relieves you of the burden of doing it on your own.) If you're traveling with a line that does this, there's no need to tip any more. On the other hand, if you feel that a particular crew member's service has been outstanding, show your appreciation by providing an additional gratuity.

As this book went to press the lines that *did include* gratuities in the fare were Holland America, Radisson Seven Seas, Seabourn and Silversea. Several other lines automatically charge your account with a set amount each day for tips. However, you always have the option to change this amount. Always confirm the policy at the time of booking and even just prior to departure.

Traveling with Children

Although children are much more commonly seen on cruises these days than in the past, this is still an activity that appeals more to adults than to the little ones. This is not meant to discourage you from bringing your children, but to give you advance warning that it might not be their favorite vacation. Some cruise lines are more child-friendly than others. In general, the more sophisticated the cruise (look at the dress codes and prices), the less child-friendly the ship. But there are many aspects of Mediterranean cruising that will delight children old enough to appreciate some of the sights, and just about every ship now has at least a few programs for children. Most have supervised activities all day long and into the evening. These are usually grouped by age so that teens don't have to be bored by activities that appeal to younger children. Teens can join in special social programs and dances for their age group and usually find these a good way to meet new friends. Any specific questions you may have about children's facilities and activities should be directed to your cruise line *before* you book.

So, It's Your First Time Cruising...

No, it's not a spelling error. Remember, I did say this section was going to cover things from A to Z, now didn't I? Seriously, being a rookie cruiser is no need for concern, although newcomers will have additional questions. Vacationing on a cruise ship is really like staying at a full-service resort that's on the move. Most things are done for you, including the handling of your baggage to and from your room upon embarkation and disembarkation. You'll find that cruises are unusually well organized and managed. If you have any questions or concerns, just ask a crew member – they're always more than happy to help. Here are a few things that first-time cruisers should be aware of:

⚓ **Seasickness** is uncommon, especially in the Mediterranean, which has far fewer storms (almost always in the winter) than the Caribbean. Even in unsettled weather, cruise ships are big enough and stable enough to provide a comfortable ride. If you're prone to motion sickness, an ounce of prevention can be useful. Remedies such as Dramamine and Meclazine are available over the counter or by prescription, but they're effective only if you take them several hours prior to getting on board.

Symptoms can be minimized by focusing on the horizon, which helps you regain your balance. Some people say that placing an ice cube behind the ear may relieve symptoms.

⚓ Cruise lines are known for their punctuality, but delays can occur. At each port you will be provided with a **time schedule** that tells you when to be back on board. Comply with this schedule as the ship will not wait long, if at all.

⚓ Every cruise line today operates with a sophisticated system for keeping track of who is on board and who is not. You will be issued a **form of identification** that permits you back on board at each port. Be sure that you have it with you before disembarking.

⚓ **Safety** is of utmost importance to the ship's crew. Pertinent safety instructions are posted in each stateroom, and every cruise will have a lifeboat drill soon after embarking (some might even have it before the ship leaves from its gateway port). *You are required to attend*. You should be fully aware of emergency procedures, as should your children. The drill (you don't actually get into the lifeboats) is kind of fun and colorful.

The Cruise Line Corporate Office

*O*ver the past several years there has been a major consolidation within the cruise industry. While the number of cruise lines out there makes it seem like there are plenty of choices, the reality is that most ships are owned by just a few big players. Here's the rundown:

By far the largest company is **Carnival Cruises**. Although they don't cruise the Mediterranean under that name, they are well represented by all of their subsidiary companies, which include Costa Cruises, Cunard, Holland America, Seabourn and Windstar. They have almost 50 ships in service. **Royal Caribbean** has ships under that name and also owns Celebrity Cruises. Norwegian Cruise Line and Orient Lines are both owned by a company called **Star Cruises**. The parent company operates under that name primarily in Asia. Princess Cruises is the largest company operating only under one name. Even so, nine of the 19 lines cruising the Mediterranean are owned by just three firms. Given recent trends it wouldn't be at all surprising to see further acquisitions by the largest corporations.

It was announced in late 2001 that Princess and Royal Caribbean lines had agreed to merge. In response, Carnival Cruises made a hostile counter bid for Princess. Nothing has been finalized as this book goes to press, but a new company created by such a merger would be the largest cruise line in the world.

PRACTICAL INFORMATION

Ports Of Call
& Cruise Sightseeing

*T*his part of the book focuses on the real meat and potatoes of your cruise. More than 120 different ports (and cities that can be reached from those ports) are profiled here, including destinations that are always – or almost always – visited and some unusual stops. Cruise lines are always trying to go one better than their competitors, so it is possible that, if you scan all of the cruise brochures, you may come up with a port or two that isn't included here. But that should be the rare exception.

The port profiles are grouped by country or area, starting with the western end of the Mediterranean and working east along the northern coast before heading back west on the south side. Within each region or country section, ports are profiled in alphabetical order.

To give a detailed description of *every* port visited by a cruise ship, this book would reach encyclopedic proportions. Therefore, if a port of call is on the destination list of only a few ships, it will be described in a section at the end of each country or regional section under the heading *Less Visited Ports*. Note that some of these "less visited ports" aren't such unusual places to stop anymore, although they are almost always among the smaller ports visited.

You will notice that not all countries bordering the Mediterranean Sea are included here. That's because either they are not on any current cruise ship itineraries or because they are not considered safe destinations. The primary countries in this category are Libya, Algeria and the western Balkan states of Montenegro and Albania. Although all of them do have worthwhile sights, you probably won't be comfortable visiting any of them. However, you will find some ships that visit Lebanon and Syria, primarily cruise lines whose passengers are not predominantly American. If you are particularly interested in seeing these destinations, you can certainly find a ship that goes there. Also excluded from these port listings are destinations near the Mediterranean which lie outside of it (with the exception of Lisbon, Portugal and Morocco). Among this group are places such as La Coruña and Vigo in Spain, Funchal (island of Madeira), the Canary Islands, and the Azores. However, do see the aside on these islands at the conclusion of this chapter.

On-Board Sightseeing

Not all sights are located in the ports. Scenic cruising is another aspect of a Mediterranean trip and there are many sights that you'll be able to take in from the deck of your ship. Some of the best scenic attractions are visible as you arrive in a port, and I have noted especially good port views at the outset of each port description. Even nighttime arrivals can offer spectacular views, particularly as you arrive in a large city. Because of the large open sea spaces of the Mediterranean, general scenic cruising between ports is more limited than you'll find in, say, Alaska or the Norwegian coastal fjords. But there are some spots worth being on deck for, including:

- ⚓ Strait of Gibraltar
- ⚓ Strait of Bonifacio (separating Corsica and Sardinia)
- ⚓ volcanic Stromboli Island and the other small islands nearby
- ⚓ Strait of Messina between Sicily and the Italian mainland
- ⚓ the islands along the Dalmatian Coast between Split and Dubrovnik
- ⚓ almost all cruising between mainland Greek ports, including the Corinth Canal
- ⚓ the Dardanelles and the Bosporus
- ⚓ along the Turquoise Coast of southern Turkey

Considerations

While many businesses and attractions in tiny ports may adjust their opening times to suit cruise passengers, it's not the same in the cities. Just because *your* ship is in port on a certain day and time doesn't mean that the most important attractions will be open. And I have yet to see a cruise line work its itinerary around the schedules of museums or other points of interest. It is up to you to make sure that the places you want to see will be open during your available port call time. In the following pages I provide information on days and hours of operation during the summer season (May through September). If you cruise at other times of the year, expect reduced hours at some attractions. Also, note that many museums and historic sites close one day per week (frequently Monday) and are closed on holidays. If your visit coincides with a holiday, inquire about opening times before traveling any great distance. I'll provide you with the addresses (or descriptive location) for each attraction. If no opening and closing time is mentioned then the attraction is either always open or will always be open when your ship is in port.

Finally, admission prices change quite quickly. I have used the following codes to give you the approximate price for one adult as follows:

$$	US $5 or less
$$$	US $6-10
$$$	more than US $10

You will, of course, have to pay the admission in local currency. If there is no symbol, then admission is free. With the exception of a few places, you'll see that admission prices are much lower than at comparable attractions in the United States.

Gateway Ports vs. Day Ports of Call

There are two types of ports that you will encounter as you take your cruise through the Mediterranean. The first are those ports in which your cruise either embarks or disembarks. I will refer to these as "gateway" ports. The other type are the "day" ports that you stop at during your journey. Almost all day port calls are a day or less, usually between five and 10 hours of actual time for sightseeing, shopping or other activities. While that time allotment is sufficient for many ports, it is less than adequate to see many of the city's interesting destinations. In the case of embarkation and disembarkation ports, you have the opportunity to spend additional days to see and do more, and almost every cruise line can handle those bookings for you (see page 137 for more details). For clarification, each port description that follows is listed as follows:

- ⚓ *Gateway*: Embarkation/disembarkation port for the majority of cruises.
- ⚓ *Gateway/Day*: Wide variation in status. It can be a gateway, but will be a day port just as often.
- ⚓ *Day:* Almost always a stop en route during a cruise.

All of the suggested activities are based on your visit being a day call. Highlight what you should try to see, taking into account the amount of time it will take to get to and from the ship (while this is sometimes a short ride or walk, it can involve longer distances). If the port is a gateway (either most or some of the time), the "One Day Highlights Tour" will be followed by a section headed "More Sights & Excursions." This covers worthwhile excursions that require spending more than a day in port.

Ports of Call Tourism Information

I give a lot of information about attractions in this book. However, what should you do if you want some general assistance about one or more sights? Calling the place is a chore in a foreign country, and the chances of you reaching an English-speaking staff member to answer your questions are slim. Plus, you'll need a phone card or local currency, and you'll have to figure out the local phone system. It's not easy. In lieu of telephone numbers I give the address and telephone number for the nearest tourist information office. If you have to travel some distance to get into the "port of call," I have listed the office that is most convenient to the most popular sights. (Small ports, especially in less developed countries, do not always have tourist offices.) When this phone number is preceded by two to four digits in parentheses, that portion of the number is the city code, the equivalent of US area codes. You need not dial it if you are calling locally, but should include it if you are calling from outside the local calling area within the same country.

The usefulness of tourist offices varies a great deal from one locality to another. The offices in western Europe are the best, with plenty of information and a trained staff with at least one English-speaking person. Offices in North Africa and eastern Europe generally have less printed information available and may or may not have an English-speaking staff member. In some places, notably the Ukraine, you won't find any English and the attitude of the staff can be less than pleasant.

Portugal

Lisbon

Port type: Gateway

Tourist information office: In the Palacio Foz at Ave. Duque d'Avila 185, Restauradores, ☎ (01) 1050-082. There is also an official tourist information kiosk in Belém opposite the Jeronimos Abbey.

The beautiful and interesting city of Lisbon (and the rest of Portugal, for that matter) lies on the shores of the Atlantic Ocean. However, because of its proximity to the Mediterranean, its historic ties to the region, and the fact that many Mediterranean cruises begin or end in Lisbon, a detailed description is necessary. Lisbon, which sits alongside the broad, picturesque Tagus River, has long been a departure point for sea travelers. Today's large and modern cruise ship terminal is part of the vast Alcantara Docks, which are situated about half-way between downtown Lisbon and Belém. You can reach either area from the port via the #15 tram which runs along the waterfront. The tram stop is only a short walk from the passenger terminal. Within Lisbon it is easy to get around on foot or by Metro.

Lisbon's attractions are divided into two major areas – those within the city center and those in Belém, a riverside district several miles to the west of downtown. In a day visit you'll be able to see some highlights in each area. The tram that runs from the city center along the river to Belém is convenient and offers a pleasant ride in and of itself. Save time and money by purchasing the "Lisbon Card," which provides unlimited use of the public transportation system as well as admission to most museums. The Lisbon Card is valid for periods of from one to three days and is available from the Tourist Information Office.

Highlights Tour

The major city sights begin with the cathedral and the castle, both located in an area known as **Alfama**. This charming neighborhood (along with the Bairro Alto or Madragoa) is one of the older sections of the city, with winding streets, hills and interesting architecture. It's a great place to walk around. The cross-shaped **Se Catedral de Lisboa** (on the Largo da Se) dates from the 12th century. It has three naves, along with the Treasury and the Monstrance of Dom Jose which is used in the Eucharist and contains more than 4,100 precious stones. The Gothic-style chapel is considered one of the masterpieces of the interior. *Open daily except Sunday from 10 am until 5 pm. The*

Cloister and Sacistry are open daily except Monday from 10 am until 1 pm and from 2 until 6 pm.

Nearby, towards the River Tagus, is the **Castelo de Sao Jorge** (Castle of St. George), one of Lisbon's most famous sights. Also dating from the 12th century, the fortress reflects the country's history and was rebuilt in the 1940s to its original appearance. The crenelated walls and battlements are a stirring sight – and so, too, is the view of the city and river from atop those walls. The castle contains many historical exhibits. *Open daily from 9 am until 9 pm. There is no charge except for special exhibits.* Not far from the castle at the river's edge is the commercial heart of the city known as the **Praça do Comercio**. In this area you should see the **triumphal arch** and the attractive **steps** to the river.

Other Lisbon sights (to the northwest of the Comercio) that you might have time for on a day trip are the **Basilica da Estrela**, on Largo da Estrela. *Open daily from 8 am until 12:30 pm and 3 to 7:30 pm.* This 18th-century church is notable for its two bell towers. The **Aguas Livres** is an 11-mile long aqueduct constructed in the 18th century. It is supported by 109 masonry arches in the neo-classical style. The **Elevador de Santa Justa** is a strange looking elevator that ascends one of Lisbon's many hills, from the top of which you'll have an excellent view of the remains of the **Convento do Carmo**, a late medieval convent. The *elevador*, which operates most of the time, is located on the Rua de Santa Justa. *$.*

Belém has a wonderful assortment of museums and historical sites, all located in close proximity to one another. Your first stop along the waterfront should be the impressive white **Monument to the Discoveries** (Padrao dos Descobrimentos), built in 1960 to commemorate the 500th anniversary of the death of Henry the Navigator. Henry was the greatest driving force behind the age of the Portuguese Discoveries. The monument is shaped like the prow of a ship and is adorned with huge statues of Henry and other important discoverers. *Avenida de Brasilia. Open daily except Monday from 9:30 am until 6:30 pm; $.* The **Tower of Belém** (Torre de Belém) was constructed to defend the Tagus by King Dom Manuel I at the turn of the 16th century. The beautiful structure has definite Moorish architectural influences and has been declared a UNESCO World Heritage Site. *Avenida de Brasilia. Open daily except Monday, from 10 am until 5 pm; $.* **Jeronimos Abbey** (Mosteiro dos Jeronimos) is across the *Praça* (or square) from the Monument to the Discoveries. This vast structure (another UNESCO site) was built in1502 – around the same time as the Tower of Belém – to commemorate the discovery of the sea route to India. The wide façade fronts a beautiful garden with a magnificent central fountain. The sculptures and other detail on the exterior make the Abbey the foremost example of the so-called Manueline style of architecture. The equally ornate interior houses the tombs of explorer Vasco de Gama and other notable figures. *Praca do Imperio. Open daily except Monday, 10 am until 5 pm; $.* Just east of here is the **National Coach Museum** (Museu dos Coches). This fine structure houses one of the largest and most impressive collections of royal coaches and paraphernalia to be found anywhere. *Calçada da Ajuda,* ☎ *(01) 361-0850. Open daily except Monday, 10 am until 5:30 pm; $.*

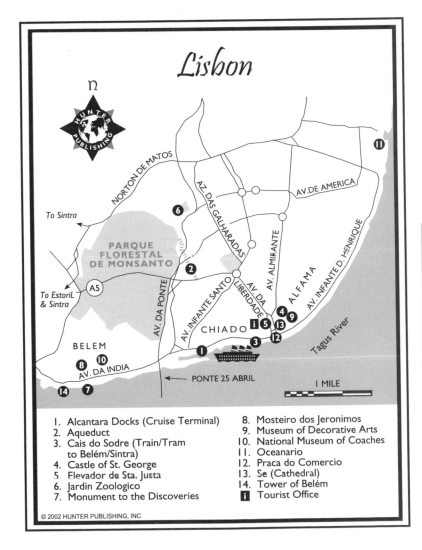

Lisbon

1. Alcantara Docks (Cruise Terminal)
2. Aqueduct
3. Cais do Sodre (Train/Tram to Belém/Sintra)
4. Castle of St. George
5. Elevador de Sta. Justa
6. Jardin Zoologico
7. Monument to the Discoveries
8. Mosteiro dos Jeronimos
9. Museum of Decorative Arts
10. National Museum of Coaches
11. Oceanario
12. Praca do Comercio
13. Se (Cathedral)
14. Tower of Belém
i Tourist Office

© 2002 HUNTER PUBLISHING, INC

PORTS OF CALL

More Sights & Excursions

There are a host of other places to visit within the city of Lisbon. The **Casa do Fado** is an interesting little museum that highlights the history of Portugal's haunting "Fado" music. There is also much about the famous Portuguese guitar. *Largo do Chafariz de Dentro 1. Daily except Tuesday, 10 am until 5 pm; $.* Another good stop is the **Decorative Arts Museum** (Museu-Escola de Artes Decorativa), located in the former Palace of Azurara in the Alfama quarter. It has an excellent collection of art work and household items from the 15th through 19th centuries. *Largo das Portas do Sol 2. Daily except Monday, 10 am until 5 pm; $$.* The **Zoo** (Jardim Zoologico) has been delighting visitors for more than 100 years with one of the finest animal collections in Europe. Many activities in the zoo are especially suitable for children. *Estrada de Benfica 158. Daily, 10 am until 8 pm; $$.* If you enjoy animal life, consider a stop at the modern **Oceanarium** (Oceanario), the most popular holdover attraction from the 1998 World Expo held in Lisbon. Depending upon how you figure such things, this is the second largest aquarium in the world. It has an outstanding collection of marine species, and the building itself is a striking example of post-modern architecture. *Parque das Nacoes. Daily, 10 am until 7 pm; $$.* Finally, a brief visit to Portugal's **National Pantheon**, the Panteao Nacional, will make a nice way to close out your city visit. It is housed in a gleaming white-domed church called the Igreja de Santa Engracia. *Campo do Sonia Clara. Daily except Monday, 10 am until 5 pm.*

Outside the City

If you have an extra day here, use it to explore a few of the splendid palaces near the suburban community of **Sintra**. You can't possibly do them all in one day, even if you have your own car. The very best one is the outlandish and colorful **Palacio Nacional da Pena**, built in medieval style. It's a fanciful masterpiece, with fairytale-like turrets and a sumptuous interior. The huge gardens and park are also worth exploring if you have the time. Also worthwhile is the **Palacio Nacional de Sintra**. If you don't want to rent a car or take a guided tour, try the train service from Lisbon's Rossio station, which runs frequently. Once in Sintra station, a moderately priced shuttle bus connects all of the major sights, including the aforementioned palaces and the Castle of the Moors (discussed below). Ask at the tourist office for schedules and other information. The Palacio Nacional de Sintra was the palatial home of many Portuguese kings, although it was constructed by the Moors. In addition to Moorish architecture there are elements of Gothic, Manueline and Renaissance. Check out the highlight of this splendid treasure – the famous blue tile panels (*azulejo*). *North end of Sintra-Vila at the Praca de Republica. Open daily except Wednesday, 10 am until 1 pm and 2 to 5 pm; $.*

Not too far from Sintra is the **Palacio Nacional de Queluz**, in the town of Queluz (also reached by train from Rossio station). *South of Sintra. Open daily except Monday, 10 am until 1 pm and 2-6:30pm; $.* This structure has often been compared to Versailles because of its outstanding gardens with many fountains and statues. The palace itself is not as elaborate as Versailles or even the other major palaces within Sintra. However, it is closer than the others and makes for a nice little trip of a few hours. *Between Lisbon and Sintra in the town of Queluz. Open daily except Tuesday, 10 am until 1 pm and 2 to 5 pm; $.*

Within Sintra, buses and taxis are available, but not as convenient as renting a car. If you have any additional time to explore, there are several other sights well worth seeing. The exotic gardens of the **Parque de Monserrate** are three miles west of Sintra via Estrada de Monserrate. *Open daily from 1 am until 6 pm, $.* At **Castelo dos Mouros**, an eighth-century Moorish fortification, you'll see the remains of this hilltop fortress and castle. Equally rewarding is the panoramic view from atop. Some people think this is the best place to photograph the nearby Pena Palace in all its glory. *Estrada da Pena. Open daily, 10 am until 6 pm.* If driving, consider making a short detour past Sintra to stop at **Cabo da Roca**, a rugged, wild and sometimes eerie spot that overlooks the pounding surf of the Atlantic Ocean. This is the most westerly point of land in mainland Europe and – if you wish – you can purchase an inexpensive certificate attesting to that fact. On the way back you may want to take a brief look at the seaside resorts on the coast around **Estoril**, which has one of Europe's biggest casinos with Las Vegas-style entertainment nightly.

Less Visited Portuguese Port

PORTIMÃO: Situated on Portugal's famous Algarve coast, this is an attractive little seaside resort which can also be used as a base for exploring some of the more famous southern coastal towns, such as **Faro**.

Spain/Gibraltar

Almeria

Port type: Day.
Tourist information office: Parque Nicolás Salmerón, ☎ *950-274-355.*

The beaches in Almeria – another coastal resort town – are attractive and usually less crowded than other Costa del Sol ports. If you want to spend some time on the beach, this might be the best place to do it. The coastal scenery around Almeria is quite pleasant. Granada is about 100 miles away, and shore excursions to the Alhambra are also a possibility. The large port is not far from the heart of the city, although it's not an easy walk so consider taking a taxi. The main point of interest in town is the impressive 10th-century **Alcazaba** that rises on a hill just opposite the port area. *Open daily, 10 am until 2 pm and from 5:30 to 8 pm; $.* The requisite **cathedral** is also worth seeing. It's located just a few blocks northwest of the port – look for the spire. *Open daily from 10:30 am until noon.*

The Balearic Islands (Ibiza, Mallorca & Menorca)

Port type: Day.
Tourist information office (Palma):
Carrer de Santo Domingo 11, ☎ *971-724-090*

These island playgrounds are about 80 to 140 miles off the coast of the Spanish mainland (depending upon which island). Favorable climate and nice scenery make them popular resorts, and a lot of cruise passengers choose to partake in the resort-related recreational activities (swimming, watersports, etc.). The largest and most popular of the Balearic Islands is **Mallorca** (Ma-york-ah). Its capital city, Palma (frequently referred to as Palma de Mallorca) receives more than five million visitors each year.

All three of these ports have good port facilities and tendering is rarely necessary. The docks are within a very short walk of the center of town in all cases, although taxis are always available for distant destinations, which includes some of the better beaches. To explore the interior of the larger islands, consider taking a guided excursion. Car rentals are expensive and often unavailable, and the islands are filled with winding roads. Each of the main islands has something unique to offer.

The big island of Mallorca also is home to the largest city in the islands – Palma de Mallorca, which boasts many beautiful beaches both in and out of the city, as well as a number of sights. These are all within close proximity of one another and near the port. The four places detailed below are practically lined up one after the other along the north side of the Parc de la Mar, which parallels the waterfront. All this means that you can explore the points of interest and avoid the confusing maze of streets only a few blocks away. Begin at the west end of the park with the beautiful **Palace of Almudaina**. It was built in the 13th century as a Moorish castle but was later used by Spanish monarchs. Even today it is sometimes closed if being used by the royal family. Entry is only via guided tour (on the half-hour). *Open 9:30 am to 1:30 pm and 4-6:30 pm; closed Sunday; Saturday tours 9:30-1:30 only).* Your next stop is **La Seo Cathedral**, located across the Plaza Almundaina from the palace. It is easily the most recognizable structure on the island and you will no doubt have noticed it sitting majestically on a hill near the waterfront as your ship pulled into Palma. It is the second largest Gothic cathedral in Spain and was constructed over a period of nearly 500 years beginning in 1230. Upon entry you will first visit the cathedral's small but interesting **museum**. *Open daily except Sunday, 10 am to 12:30 pm and 4-6:30 pm (10-1:30 on Saturday).* Also in this vicinity is **La Llotja**, a beautiful Gothic structure which now serves as an exhibition center. Take a few minutes to look around here. The **Museum of Mallorca** (Museu de Mallorca) presents an interesting review of the city's history and culture. *Carrer Portella 5; open daily except Monday, 10 am to 2 pm and 4-7 pm (only 10-2 on Sunday); $.* The **Arab Baths** are just north of the park (walk up a gated street called the Portella and then turn right on Can Serra). The baths are in excellent condition and, despite their small size (two small chambers remain), are one of the more interesting sights in town. Considering that the Moors ruled Mallorca for several centuries, it is odd that the Arab baths are the only remaining evidence of that era. Portions of the columns which support the baths are from Roman times. *Open daily, 9 am to 6 pm; $.* Palma also has a **Spanish Village** displaying architectural representations of building styles throughout the country (it isn't as good as the one in Barcelona, detailed on page 176). West of downtown is a 14th-century fortified palace called the **Bellver Castle**. Situated in a large park, it's an attractive place to stroll and take pictures.

Outside of Palma the island of Mallorca offers a treasure trove of activities. The mountains known as the Serra e Tramuntana dominate the island, which is covered with extensive olive groves and pine forests. The coast is rugged and beautiful. As mentioned before, you can rent a car (with some difficulty) and explore places that the guided tours pass by. The drive to **Sa Calobra** and the wild **Cape Formentor** is one of the most scenic in all the Mediterranean. The winding road rises and falls precipitously but shouldn't present a problem as long as you take it slow. There is also a train that connects Palma with Soller but this limits your flexibility so that even a guided bus excursion would be better.

Ibiza (ee-bee-thah) receives only about a quarter of the visitor volume that Mallorca gets, but it can still be quite crowded. The natural scenery is just as pleasant here, although most people come for the wilder nightlife and the great shopping, found mostly in the port area of **Sa Penya** and also in the old town. The old town has a well preserved section of walls as well as the **Archaeological Museum** (Museu Arqueologic). *Placa Catedral 3; open daily except Sunday, 10 am to 1 pm; $.* You can also take a boat ride from the town's harbor to **Formentera**, the smallest of the Balearics. It has really great beaches.

The major settlement on the island of **Menorca** is **Mahon** (or Maó in the local tongue). There isn't anything of great importance to see in the town, although the **Xoriquer Gin Distillery** attracts its share of visitors who like to sample the wide variety of products made here. *Moll de Ponent 93; open Monday through Friday, 8 am to 7 pm, Saturday, 9 am to 1 pm.* The most enjoyable thing to do on Menorca is rent a car and drive around through small towns, by beautiful beaches and stop at some of the small but interesting archaeological sites. These sites aren't well developed for visitors and it's advisable to hire an archaeological guide from the tourist office in Mahon. If you don't want to plan that, join one of the excursions arranged by your cruise line.

Barcelona

Port type: Gateway/Day.
Tourist information office: Plaça de Catalunya 17-S, ☎ 933-043-135

Spain's second largest city has about three million inhabitants and is one of the most beautiful, interesting and vibrant cities in the world. Its history encompasses rule by Phoenicians, Carthaginians, the Romans, Visgoths and Moors before the independence of Spain as a nation. It is the capital of Catalonia, an autonomous region of Spain that even has its own language (so don't be surprised to see a lot of words you don't recognize as Spanish). Barcelona has an intense but mostly friendly rivalry with Madrid as Spain's cultural, business and tourist capital.

The international cruise ship port here is called Moll de Adossat and is located just southeast of downtown in an area known as Las Ramblas, near the junction of the Ronda Litoral. This is great for those who have just one day to explore. You can reach many of the major sights on foot, or by taxi or public transportation, including the fast and efficient metro. Some cruise lines even provide free courtesy bus service into the city center. All of these factors make shore excursions an unnecessary expense unless you have an urge to explore the outlying areas. Pick up a good street and public transportation map from the cruise ship terminal or tourist office before you start exploring.

Highlights Tour

Our one-day tour is divided into two sections, one along **La Rambla** and the other concentrating on the **waterfront**. **La Rambla** runs from the waterfront north into the city center. It's a broad tree-lined pedestrian mall that's always humming and filled with activity. It's packed with interesting shops, markets and people, and is a great place to stroll and people watch.

The sights begin with the **Columbus Monument**, which stands on top of a rather tall pedestal. It can be reached via an elevator for a small fee. Note: Claustrophobics may find the elevator too small and enclosed. Nearby is the **Maritime Museum** (Museu Maritim), an excellent facility that explores the relationship of Barcelona with the sea. The museum occupies an area that was once the extravagant royal shipyards constructed in the 14th century. *Placa Portal de la Pau 1. Open daily except Monday, 10 am to 2 pm and 4 pm to 6 pm (10-2 on Sunday); $$.* Continuing north on La Rambla, note the extravagant façade on the **Liceu Grand Theater** (Gran Teatro del Liceu) at the Placa Boqueria.

Head east on Ferran for a few blocks through the narrow maze-like streets of the **Gothic Quarter** to the splendid **cathedral** and its beautiful cloister. Head up in the elevator, as the views from the cathedral's roof-top are splendid. *Pla de la Seu. Open daily, 8:30 am to 1:30 pm and 4-7:30 pm (closes at 5 pm on Sunday); $ only for elevator to roof.* In the adjacent **Placa del Rei** you'll find the not-to-be-missed **City History Museum**, which occupies several buildings of the medieval Aragonian kings. The best parts of the museum complex are the royal chapel and the tunnel that gives a glimpse into the former Roman- and Visgothic-era ruins. It is on these ruins that modern Barcelona is built. *Carrer del Veguer 2. Open daily except Monday, 10 am to 2 pm and 4 to 8 pm (10-2 on Sunday); $.*

Go back toward the waterfront in the vicinity of Port Vell, the yacht harbor formed by the hook-shaped Moll D'Espanya which juts into the ocean. Walk to the west along the waterfront and you will soon enter a series of gardens – **Jardin de Miramar, Jardin de Mossen Gosta i Llobera** and **Jardin del Mirador**. But these pretty spots are just a prelude of what is to come. Take the **cable railway up to Montjuic**, Barcelona's most famous hilltop. The ride itself is spectacular and at the top is **Castell de Montjuic** and its **Military Museum**. Both offer a fascinating look – architecturally and through exhibits – at the history of the city. *Open daily except Monday, 10 am to 2 pm and 4 to 7 pm (10-2 on Sunday); $. The railway operates daily from 11 am to 10 pm and the fare is nominal.* Other funiculars and chair lifts lead to different parts of Montjuic, including several other gardens and museums, but you will not have time to visit them.

Back down at the shore level, head back up Ronda del Litoral and you'll soon come to the **Aquarium** (L'Aquarium), one of the largest, most modern and entertaining aquariums in Europe. *Port Vell, Moll d'Espanya. Open daily, 9:30 am to 9 pm; $$.*

Go back to the main street along the waterfront and continue on Ronda del Litoral until you come to **Parc de la Ciutadella** (Little City Park). The park contains a museum of modern art and a zoo (which require more than a day trip to see) and the fabulous **cascada** – a series of waterfalls, statues and wonderful urban park landscaping.

No trip to Barcelona (even a day trip) would be complete without seeing the famous **Holy Family (Sagrada Familia)**. Construction on this awesome cathedral was begun in 1882 and it still isn't finished. It has eight towers, each exceeding 325 feet in height, which are the first installment of a planned 18 towers (one for each of the apostles). You can ascend them via spiral staircases or elevators. La Sagrada Familia is known for its majestic vast spaces and extravagant sculptured style. They are the hallmarks of its architect, Antoni Gaudi y Cornet, known to the world as Gaudi (1852-1926). Gaudi was educated in Barcelona and lived here most of his life. He is Spain's most famous architect and his works combine elements of neo-Gothic and Art Nouveau with cubism and surrealism. This is, without a doubt, one of the most unusual church structures in the world. *Open daily, 9 am to 6 pm; $$.* Many of Gaudi's other buildings and landscape projects grace Barcelona. If you'd like to learn more about them, visit the tourist office and ask the helpful staff.

More Sights & Excursions

You could easily spend five days in Barcelona sightseeing, but most cruise passengers allow just three nights at most. There are plenty of excursions and worthwhile sights to fill your days here. The **Parc**

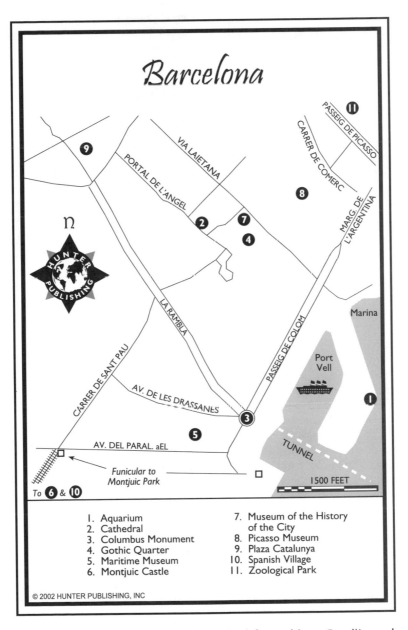

Barcelona

1. Aquarium
2. Cathedral
3. Columbus Monument
4. Gothic Quarter
5. Maritime Museum
6. Montjuic Castle
7. Museum of the History of the City
8. Picasso Museum
9. Plaza Catalunya
10. Spanish Village
11. Zoological Park

© 2002 HUNTER PUBLISHING, INC

Guell north of downtown is where to look for architect Gaudi's work at its best. Here, man has improved on nature as the beautiful park setting is enhanced with arches, ironwork, stone trees, fountains and more. In the **La Ribera** section of town you will find two museums of great interest. The first of these is the **Picasso Museum** (Museu Picasso), housed in a medieval mansion. *Carrer Montcada 15-19; open daily except Monday, 10 am to 8 pm (till 3 pm on Sunday); $.* The other worthwhile stop is the **Textile & Costume Museum**. Although it may not sound particularly inviting, it is well known for its fine collection of tapestries. *Carrer de Montcada 12; open daily except Monday, 10 am to 5 pm (until 2 pm on Sunday); $.*

Atop Montjuic (see page 174) you'll find two more museums. There's the excellent **National Museum of Art of Catalunya**. *Mirador del Palau 6; open daily except Monday, 10 am to 7 pm (till 9 pm on Thursday and till 2 pm on Sunday); $$.* The second attraction is the **Archaeological Museum**. *Passeig Santa Madrona 39-41; open daily except Monday, 9:30 am to 1 pm and 4:30-7 pm (9:30-1 on Sunday); $.*

The **Spanish Village** (Pueblo Español) is a good place to see craftspeople at work and the area is very much alive with activity during the evening. Note the unusual façades on the village's buildings, which represent various architectural styles of Spain's historic regions. *Open daily, 9 am until at least 8 pm, but much later on most evenings; $$.* A second trip to La Rambla during the evening will allow you to see and partake in the goings on.

A half-day excursion to **Tibidubo** is a very enjoyable trip. This hill stands at 1,765 feet (the highest surrounding Barcelona) and is reached by a funicular railway. Among the sights on Tibidubo is a church with a giant statue of Christ and a communications tower that is over 900 feet high. You can reach the observation deck via an outside elevator. Take this trip only on a day when the weather forecast is clear. Another great excursion is to **Montserrate** and its monastery, some 35 miles from the port. You can do this either on your own (rental car, commuter train or bus can get you there) or via your cruise line's excursion office. Located within a gorge-like section of the beautiful Sierra de Montserrat mountains, the **monastery** (Monestir de Montserrat) draws the faithful and the nature lover alike. The former come to see the Black Madonna (La Moreneta), the patron saint of Catalunya and the icons in the museum. Those who appreciate scenery will just love riding the system of funiculars that lead up to the monastery and beyond, where there are great views and plenty of hiking trails at an elevation of 3,500 feet. *Open daily, 6 am to 10:30 am and noon to 6:30 pm. The museum has shorter hours and is closed on Monday. There is a small fee for each funicular.*

Cadiz

Port type: Day
Tourist information office: Plaza de San Juan de Dios 11,
☎ 956-241-001

Cadiz is one of a seemingly endless number of historic Spanish cities. Although there are some interesting things to see here, the town certainly doesn't rank among the greatest attractions of Spain. Depending upon your ship's other ports of call you might, therefore, want to inquire about guided shore excursions to either **Seville** (80 miles to the north) or **Gibraltar**, which is about the same distance in the opposite direction (see separate port description, page 179). Seville is one of Spain's biggest, most beautiful and interesting cities. Although it is located inland, some of the smaller yacht-style cruise ships can navigate up the river to reach Seville. If you visit, be sure to see the main **cathedral** and it's accompanying **Giralda Tower**, the **Royal Alcazar** with its fabulous gardens, and the colorfully ornate **Plaza de España**. Excursions to the nearby sherry-producing areas are also popular.

Cadiz is the oldest continually inhabited city in Western Europe, dating back more than 3,000 years to the Phoenicians. The Cadiz Bay Port (also called the City Dock) is within a short distance of the city center. Most ships use the town dock, so tenders are not in use. The city is actually crowded onto a small island just off the mainland. It has a popular beach, **Playa de la Caleta**, located on the west end of town.

Start by exploring the ring road, which circles the island. This will give you a good overview and also offers many scenic viewpoints. The biggest attraction is the huge 18th-century **cathedral** that sits opposite the waterfront on the south side of town. *Cathedral museum open daily except Monday, 10 am until 1 pm; $.* Adjacent to it are the ruins of a **Roman theater**. Another sight of interest is the **Castillo de Santa Catalina** (Santa Catalina Castle), a fortress that dates from the end of the 16th century. It's adjacent to the Playa de la Caleta, off Avenida Duque de Najera. *Open Monday to Friday, 10 am to 6 pm and on weekends from 10 am to 2 pm.* The **Cadiz Museum** (Musee de Cadiz) has galleries covering both archaeology and fine arts. *Plaza de Mina. Tuesday from 2:30 pm to 8 pm; Wednesday through Saturday from 9 am to 8 pm and Sunday from 9:30 am until 2:30 pm; $.* Perhaps the most unusual attraction within Cadiz is the **Torre Tavira**, an old watchtower that now has, in addition to some fine views, a *camera obscura*. This periscope-like device projects panoramic images of the city on a large screen. *Intersection of Calles Sacra-*

mento & Marqués del Real Tesorio. Daily from 10 am to 8 pm. $ for camera obscura only.

Cartagena/Alicante

Port type: Day.
Tourist information offices:
Cartagena, Plaza Almirante Bastarreche, ☎ 968-506-483;
Alicante, Explanada de España 2, ☎ 965-200-000

These two ports are separated by a distance of only 75 miles. A stop in one could be used to see either or parts of both. Stopping in both doesn't offer you the best variety of ports, but some ships do just that. Alicante (ALEE-can-tee) is the larger port. Cartagena has the advantage that it is closer to **Murcia**, approximately 35 miles to the north of town, which has some interesting sights. The port of Cartagena has two quays that accommodate some cruise ships, but larger ships have to anchor and there is a good chance you will have to go by tender to shore. The port is just an eighth of a mile from the city center, so you may choose to ignore the taxis that will be lined up at the port. In Alicante even the biggest ships can be accommodated at the modern passenger terminal, a short walking distance from the main part of town.

Alicante has almost 300,000 residents and is another popular resort area. The **Playa de Postiguet** is the main beach in town, while farther out is the **Playa de San Juan**. A major thoroughfare called the **Explanada de España** runs parallel to the harbor and makes for a great place to stroll. Several interesting attractions are in the city center just to the north of the Explanada. These include the **Museum of Fine Arts** (Museo de Bellas Artes), an old museum in a new location (an 18th-century mansion). *Calle Gravina, $*; and the **Museo de la Asegurada**, which has an excellent collection of modern art, including works by Dali and Picasso. *Plaza Santa María.Open daily except Monday, 10 am to 5 pm.* Another sight that might interest you is the **Concatedral de San Nicolas**, a cathedral. Unfortunately, it's open only during mass, so you'll probably see just the exterior. The **Archaeological Museum** (Museo Arqueologico) has just moved into a brand new facility on Avenida de la Estación. But truly the best way to see Alicante is to cross the footbridge by the Playa de Postiquet and ride the funicular (*ascensor*) up to the 16th-century **Castillo de Santa Barbara**. This is a stunning fortress and palace complex and also offers outstanding views overlooking both the city and the sea. *Open daily except Saturday, 10 am to 7 pm; $.*

Cartagena's sights are conveniently located within a relatively small area between the waterfront on the south and the Paseo de Alfonso

XIII on the north. (Don't be fooled by the Paseo de Alfonso XII – this is by the harbor and is *not* the same street.) Some good sights are the small but interesting Archaeological Zone, **Zona Arqueologica**, which has some fairly well-preserved Roman ruins. *East of Puertas de Murcia; open daily except Monday*; and a **Roman amphitheater** and a good viewpoint overlooking the city walls. The **Plaza de Toros** is also in this area. If you're in town when there's a bullfight taking place, drop by to see this Spanish tradition. Cartagena's main attraction, **Castillo de la Concepción**, is just east of the harbor. This long structure was once a Moorish fortress. *Located in the park near the harbor, north of Paseo de Alfonso XII.*

Spain is filled with the architectural and historical heritage from the era of Moorish control. You just can't see too many of these wonderful treasures!

Ceuta

See the listing for Ceuta under Morocco

Gibraltar

Port type: Day
Tourist information office: Duke of Kent House,
Cathedral Square, ☎ 45000

The famous British enclave lies at the southernmost tip of Spain and constitutes one of the two ancient Pillars of Hercules that marked the entrance to the Mediterranean Sea. Tiny Gibraltar (2.3 square miles) is an interesting land and it played a major role in European history. The Rock's English name is a corruption of the original Arabic name *Jabal Tariq*, which means Mount of Tariq. (Tariq was the name of the Muslim general who successfully invaded Spain in 711.) Gibraltar has been under British rule since 1704. The Rock's silhouette is famous throughout the world. Hopefully, your ship's arrival will be in daylight and you'll be able to take in this wonderful sight as you approach. It is a limestone monolith that rises abruptly from the sea on the east side to a height of 1,396 feet. The slope on the west is much more gradual, creating the almost triangular shape seen so often in photographs.

Gibraltar's Cruise Liner Terminal was completed in 1995 in what used to be an unused warehouse. It can accommodate several large ships so the use of tenders to get to shore is quite rare. Conveniently, it's only a 15-minute walk from the center of town. About five million visitors come to tiny Gibraltar each year, mostly via the land crossing from Spain. Because of the location of the port and the compact nature of Gibraltar, guided tours aren't necessary; getting around Gibraltar on your own is a breeze either on foot or by local bus or taxi. The amount of time needed to see the major attractions is almost perfectly tailored for a single day visit.

The town of Gibraltar is centered around pretty **Cathedral Square** and its **Anglican Cathedral of the Holy Trinity**. Also in the vicinity are the **Governor's Residence**, where changing of the guard ceremonies are sometimes held (but it's unlikely to be while you are in port); and the **Casemates Square**, where public executions used to take place. Cannons line the waterfront promenade and park. Just off Main Street on Bomb House Lane is the **Gibraltar Museum** and its collection of everything from cannon balls to things salvaged from shipwrecks. Housed in what was once a Moorish bath, the museum also has an excellent model of the Rock showing fortifications as they existed in the 18th century. *Open daily except Sunday, 10 am until 6 pm (till 2 pm on Saturday); $.* Nearby are the **Alameda Gardens** – they are pretty but can be skipped if your time is limited. At the southern end of Main Street on either side of the **Southport Gate** you'll get a good view of the remains of the 16th-century walls that were built to defend against attacks by pirates.

The highlight of Gibraltar, however, is not the town but the area known as the **Upper Rock**. The easiest way to get there is via **cable car**, one of Gibraltar's most famous and popular attractions. The scenic trip to the top is a great little ride. There is an intermediate station between the bottom and top where you can get off to do a little further exploration. I recommend taking the cable car to the top station and wandering down to the middle station, where you can jump back on for the trip to the bottom. The views from the top are awesome and include all of Gibraltar, nearby Spain, and (on clear days) the coast of North Africa. On the way down to the middle station you'll see the **Ape's Den**, where more than 150 Barbary apes reside on the cliff. They're Europe's only native monkeys. Legend has it that as long as they remain on the Rock, Gibraltar will remain English. If you're here at either eight in the morning or four in the afternoon, be sure to stay and watch the monkeys being fed. Also along the route is **St. Michael's Cave**, the largest of Gibraltar's natural caverns. It is filled with beautiful formations, including stalactites and stalagmites. Evening concerts are held in one portion of the caverns. Experienced cave explorers can get permission (inquire at the ticket office) to climb around in the Lower Caves. In the opposite direction from the middle station (and a lengthy walk) are the **Galleries & Great Siege Tunnel**. This is where the British army engineers blasted fortifications out of the limestone rock The interior is now a sort of wax museum that will give you an idea of what life was like for the soldiers who manned the huge gun emplacements that once occupied this site. Nearby are the remains of a **Moorish Castle** that can be entered. It is sometimes referred to as the **Tower of Homage** because practically all that is left is one large tower. All attractions in this paragraph are located in the Upper Nature Reserve. *Hours for all attractions in the Upper Nature Reserve are daily from 9:30 am until sunset; $$.*

No tour of Gibraltar would be complete without a drive around the Rock. Although you can rent a car to do this, it's cheaper to hire a taxi. A guided excursion is the most expensive option. On the lower road by the sea is **Nelson's Anchorage** and its 100-ton gun installation, which could fire a one-ton shell for almost nine miles. Head south from the town to the bottom of Gibraltar at **Europa Point** (a lighthouse marks the spot). Nearby is the beautiful **Ibriham Mosque.**

If you decide to take a guided excursion then the best choice is a two-hour sea trip around Gibraltar. You'll likely see various species of dolphins. You can sign up for these excursions on your own in town but because of schedule limitations it is easier to book directly through your ship.

Malaga

Port type: Day.
Tourist information office: Pasaje de Chinitas 4, ☎ 952-213-445.

Malaga, home to over a half-million people, is part of Spain's famous resort area called the Costa del Sol (the Sun Coast). Unless you want to spend your time in the sun and sand, excursions out of the town itself are the best way to go. Look into the availability of guided day trips to fascinating **Ronda** (70 miles), with its beautiful gorge, or to **Antequera** (40 miles), which has a nearby national park and bird refuge. A little bit farther (and more rewarding) would be a trip to Granada (80 miles) to see the incomparable **Alhambra**. You can rent a car to reach these places, although it is difficult to get into the Alhambra without advance reservations; a guided tour might be the best choice. From the port, Malaga itself is only a five-minute ride to the city center via taxi or shuttle service. You could even walk it. Use of tenders for ships anchored outside the port is rare.

In-town sightseeing can fill a few interesting hours and everything is quite close to the port area. The Paseo de España and the Paseo del Parque are separated by a broad park-like mall that runs parallel to the port. Just north of Parque are the 16th-century **Cathedral** (*Molina Larias; open daily except Sunday, 9 am to 6:45 pm; $*) and the **Alcazaba**, the impressive palace and fortress of the Moors (*off Calle Alcazabilla; open daily except Tuesday, 9:30 am until 7 pm*). A series of walls connect the Alcazaba with the **Gibralfaro**, a hilltop castle that now serves as a historical museum and also offers a beautiful vista of Malaga and the Mediterranean Sea. *Open daily except Tuesday, 9:30 am until 6 pm.* If you have time, make your final stop in Malaga the **Picasso Museum**, designed to honor the famous artist who was born here. This facility is so new that hours had not yet been set at press time. *Calle San Augustín. $$.*

Valencia

Port type: Day.
Tourist information office: Plaza del Ayuntamiento, ☎ 963-510-417

Although Valencia has around three-quarters of a million residents, it gets lost in the shadow of Barcelona. However, this big port can handle the largest of ships and it is unlikely that your cruise ship won't find a spot on the dock. From the port, it's about 2½ miles into the center of the city. Take a taxi or bus to get into the downtown area if you plan to explore independently. The heart of the city is bordered on the northern edge by the former course of the Turia River. Although still crossed by a large number of bridges, the river bed is now the attractive **Turia Gardens** (Jardines del Turia). Nearby is the **Museum of Fine Arts** (Museo de Bellas Artes), with a fine collection that includes works by many well known Spanish and other European artists, among them El Greco, Goya and Velazquez. *San Pio V. Open Tuesday through Saturday, 10 am to 2 pm and 4 to 6 pm; $.* The **cathedral** in town is a stunning example of architecture but not one particular style. Each of its three portals is a different style – baroque, gothic and Romanesque. Within the cathedral museum is, supposedly, the "real" Holy Grail, but other places also lay claim to this piece of Biblical history. *Plaza de la Virgen. Open daily, 10 am until 1 pm and 4:30 to 7 pm.* If you're in town on a Thursday, aim to be in the cathedral area at noon to witness a tradition that goes back more than a thousand years. The **Water Court** (Tribunal de las Aquas) takes place on the plaza adjacent to the cathedral. Farmers in the region meet to resolve issues over use of water in this dry area. Although the decisions are not legally binding, it is traditional to abide by the court's decision. Next stop should be the **Plaza del Arzobispo**, where a 25-minute multi-media presentation on the history of Valencia and San Vicente (its patron saint) is of mild interest. A final downtown stop is the **Palace of the Marquis of Two Waters**

(Palacio del Marqués de Dos Aquas), a former palace that now houses the **National Museum of Ceramics** (Museo Nacional de Ceramica). Ceramic arts from all over the world are on display here, but the museum concentrates on ceramics produced in the surrounding region, one that is well known for quality work. *Calle del Poeta Querol. Hours vary; $.*

About half-way between downtown and the waterfront is a new museum complex called the **City of Arts and Sciences** (Ciudad de las Artes y de las Ciencias). Not all of the facilities are open as yet, but you can visit some of these modern high-tech museums, including a planetarium, IMAX theater and laser-light show. All of the exhibits are first rate and this, despite a lack of signs in English, can be very educational for children. *L'Hemistéric, Calle del Arzobispo Mayoral 14. Open daily except Monday, 10 am to 5 pm; $$.*

Less Visited Spanish Ports

Although the town centers of these communities are close to the port area, you will almost always have to reach the dock via tender.

CAP CREUS (CABO DE CREUS): This occupies a small peninsula on Spain's northeastern coast not far from the French border. It's a relaxing place but there's little to see or do

MARBELLA: One of many alternative stopping places on the Costa del Sol for a few ships. There's a good beach but the town itself has little to offer the visitor. Take an excursion up the coast to Malaga or, better yet, inland through the scenic mountains to Ronda.

MOTRIL: A small Costa del Sol town between Malaga and Almeria. Other than soaking up that famous sunshine there's little to do in Motril but Malaga and Almeria are good destinations. It's also within striking distance of Granada... if your ship allows enough time to get there.

PUERTO BANUS: Situated between Malaga and Algeciras, Puerto Banus is a small resort town that hasn't gained much notoriety because it is a bit away from the heart of the Costa del Sol. It can be used as a base for excursions to Gibraltar in addition to the two cities that flank it.

PALAMOS: North of Barcelona on the Costa Brava (Wild Coast), the rugged and rocky promontories that jut out into the sea hide tranquil and beautiful bayside beaches. A walk around the 13th-century town is a pleasant way to spend a few hours. The town rises high above the harbor. If you're here in the afternoon, take in the colorful and boisterous fish market.

PORTS OF CALL

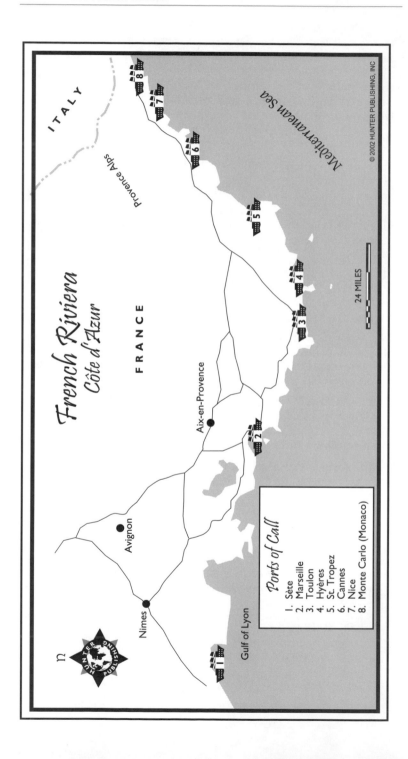

French Riviera
Côte d'Azur

ITALY

FRANCE

Provence Alps

Mediterranean Sea

© 2002 HUNTER PUBLISHING, INC

Aix-en-Provence

Avignon

Nîmes

Gulf of Lyon

24 MILES

Ports of Call
1. Sète
2. Marseille
3. Toulon
4. Hyères
5. St. Tropez
6. Cannes
7. Nice
8. Monte Carlo (Monaco)

France & Monaco
(The French Riviera)

*T*he list of ports on the French Riviera is a long one and most ships will stop at only one or two. However, some cruises (mostly luxury yachts and sailing vessels) that concentrate on this portion of the Mediterranean might make even more port calls from among this group. Among the most frequented of the Riviera ports are Cannes, Villefranche, Nice and Monte Carlo. The majority of these ports can be fully explored in less than a day, so you may have time to see more than the one or two ports you stop at. Although there is public transportation in the form of buses and trains between virtually all of these places, schedules are rarely convenient and the route is often slow due to traffic and winding roads. The best way to see other towns (in addition to the one at which you dock) is by guided shore excursion. No matter where you stop, there will always be a selection of other towns to visit. The information that follows will help you choose those that are of the most interest to you. First, a brief geography lesson. Port Vendres is near the Spanish border, while Sète (pronounced Set) is about 100 miles up the coast. Both of these are fairly removed from other ports in this section. St. Tropez, Villefranche, Cannes, Nice and Monte Carlo are relatively close to each other – the total distance between the two farthest towns is only 90 miles. Marseilles is roughly halfway between Sète and St. Tropez.

Now, let's take a look at these romantic ports in more detail.

Cannes

Port type: Day
Tourist information office: Palais des Festivals, ☎ (04) 9339-2453

Famous for its international film festival in May, as well as its resorts and beaches, Cannes is a town of about 70,000 residents and sits in a picturesque natural setting. The port of Cannes (Kahn) is quite modern, but it's not large enough to accommodate most of today's larger ships; tender service is necessary. Once you arrive at the dock, you'll be within a short walk of the city center. Taxis are available for getting around and the railroad station is only a third of a mile away from the port. The rectangular shaped **Vieux Port** (where you'll be dropped off) is usually filled with a large number of mega-yachts belonging to the rich and famous. Dominating the scene on the east side of the port is the **convention center**, Palais des Festivals et des Congres. This facility is generally not of interest unless one of Cannes' many festivals is taking place. But many visitors will be here anyway because it is the location for the local tourist office. Speaking of festivals, the entire area around the Vieux Port has a festive atmosphere and makes for an interesting place to stroll. Beyond the convention center via Boulevard de la Croisette are Cannes' many beautiful and often famous resort hotels. A walk along this promenade and into some of the properties is worthwhile. Beach lovers may be disappointed to find out that the waterfront beaches by the hotels are open only to hotel guests. There is one public beach near the Palais and a number of others in the opposite direction can be reached by taxis.

Just west of the Vieux Port is **Le Suquet**, a hill that affords wonderful views of Cannes. It can be reached by a number of stairs or winding streets off rue Georges Clemençeau. Atop the hill in a beautiful chateau is the **Cultural Museum** (Musée de la Castre). It is a good ethnographic museum with a good display of antiquities from all over the Mediterranean and Middle East regions. *Place de la Castre; open daily except Tuesday, 10 am until noon and 3 to 7 pm; $.* The island of **Ile Ste. Marguerite** is less than a mile offshore and worth a trip. It was made famous by the hero of Alexander Dumas' novel, *The Man in the Iron Mask*, who was held captive here. Many eucalyptus and pine trees grow on this pretty island and an extensive network of paths meanders around. Ferries leave from the northeast corner of the Vieux Port and the ride takes only about 15 minutes each way.

Marseille

Port type: Day
Tourist information office: 4 La Canebière, ☎ (04) 9113-8900

Well, I was off the mark a little earlier when I said that all of the ports of the French Riviera are romantic. Marseille (sometimes spelled Marseilles) is a large, heavily industrialized and mostly unattractive city with more than 1¼ million residents. Excursion possibilities from Marseille (pronounced Mar-say) are numerous. The surrounding region of **Provence** includes the elaborate 14th-century papal home of **Avignon** (65 miles); the celebrated Roman ruins at **Nimes** (75 miles), including the fabulous **Maison Carrée**, a marvelously preserved temple from the first century AD and the nearby **Pont du Gard** aqueduct that is almost 900 feet long and more than 150 feet high; and quaint **Aix-en-Provence** (25 miles). Consider renting a car for a day trip to these sites rather than signing on for a guided tour. If you have a full day in Marseille and decide to use it for an excursion (either guided or on your own), you can probably reach all of the aforementioned places. But let's not dismiss Marseille out of hand, for it has many interesting places to visit. The port of Marseille, known as the Porte Joliette, is large enough that you'll never have to tender ashore. It isn't very far from the city center either, and the easiest way to get there and around town is by metro. There's a station right at the port on Line 2, which is only two stops from the heart of the city and the transfer point to the other line. You should use the metro to avoid paying for overpriced city tours or taxis. Our city tour will start closest to the harbor and work its way out.

Just a few blocks southeast from the port via rue de l'Evêche is the **Old Charity Center** (Centre de la Vieille Charité), which contains two excellent museums, one featuring Mediterranean archaeology and the other the art of Africa, Oceana and the Americas. *2 rue de la Charité; open daily except Monday, 11 am until 6 pm; $ for each museum.* From Port Joliette it is only one subway stop to metro station Vieux Port/Hotel de Ville. A couple of blocks east in the Centre Bourse shopping complex is the **Marseille Historical Museum** (Musée d'Histoire de Marseille). It covers the entire gamut of local history, but the exhibits on the Roman era (including a second century AD merchant ship) are the best part of this excellent facility. *Enter on rue de Bir-Hakeim. Open daily except Sunday, noon until 7 pm; $.* Back nearer the metro station is the old port, or **Vieux Port** (not to be confused with Port Joliette). The entire area is a lively place and you might want to return here when things really get going in the evening, depending upon what hours your ship is in port. The activity is centered around the pedestrian-only Place Thiars. A few blocks south of Place du Général de Gaulle (on the east edge of the Vieux Port) is the **Cantini Museum** (Musée Cantini), which features both modern and contemporary works of art. *19 rue Grignan; Monday to Friday, 10 am to noon and 2-6 pm; $.* Working your way back to the Vieux Port, follow along its southern edge via the Quai de Rive Neuve all the way to the attractive **Pharaoh Gardens** (Jardin du Pharo). Just before you reach the garden, and its lovely grounds and port views, are two fortresses, **Bas Fort St. Nicolas** and **Fort d'Entrecasteaux**. From here you can see a third fort, Fort St. John, across the narrow western end of the old port. The whole thing gives you an excellent perspective of Marseille in centuries gone by.

Before returning from this part of the city you might consider a little side-trip to the **Church of Our Guardian Lady** (Basilique Notre Dame de la Garde), located on top of a hill about a half mile south of the Vieux Port (take a bus if you don't want to walk). The impressive structure dates from the 19th century and offers an excellent panorama of Marseille and the harbor. The hill is the highest point in town. *Open daily, 7 am until 8 pm.* On your way back to (or from) your ship, take a small boat ride. Along the Quai des Belges (near the Vieux Port/Hotel de Ville metro station) you can board one of the frequently departing boats that make the 20-minute ride to **Château d'If**. This splendid 16th-century fortress became a prison and was forever etched into history by the Alexandre Dumas novel, *The Count of Monte Cristo. Open daily, 9 am until 7 pm; $$ for the château and $$$ for the round-trip boat fare.*

A bit northeast of the city center (best reached by the metro to the Longchamp-Cinq station) is the splendid **Palais de Longchamp**, which was built in the middle of the 19th century. Two graceful colonnaded wings of the "palace" house a museum of art and a natural history museum. *Blvd. Longchamp & Blvd. Philippon. Open daily except Monday, 10 am to 5 pm; $.*

Monte Carlo (Monaco)

Port type: Day
Tourism information office: 2a Blvd. des Moulins, ☎ (377) 9216-6166

When you think of the French Riviera, Monte Carlo comes to mind. Monaco, of which Monte Carlo is the capital, is a tiny principality (population of 30,000) that is independent of France even though it is thoroughly French in just about every way. Romantic couples will find this luxury enclave of exquisite shopping, casinos and exciting events to be heaven, and travelers who appreciate fine scenery and interesting sights will get equal pleasure from a stop at this fascinating port. The passenger ship terminal is better than you'll find in many ports of call but, unfortunately, it isn't long enough to accommodate most of today's larger ships; there's a strong possibility that you'll be tendered ashore. The good news is that the heart of the city and almost all of the sights are only a quarter of a mile away from your landing point. If you decide to stay within Monte Carlo, there is no need for a guided tour and you can even do without the services of the local taxi drivers who'll congregate at the dock.

Monte Carlo has many sights that can easily fill up an entire day even though it covers less than two square miles. The old city, called **Rocher de Monaco**, sits on top of a nearly 200-foot-high hill and has fine views of Port de Monaco, the area where most of the action takes place. You can avoid climbing the steep hill by taking the incline that begins at the Place Saint Devote, off the northwest corner of the port area. Another way to get to the top is to take the Number 2 bus from the tourist office (near the casino) to the end of the line. Atop the hill you can also visit the fabulous **Exotic Gardens** (Jardin Exotique), which boasts more than 7,000 species of flora from all over the world in addition to its fine views. From the gardens

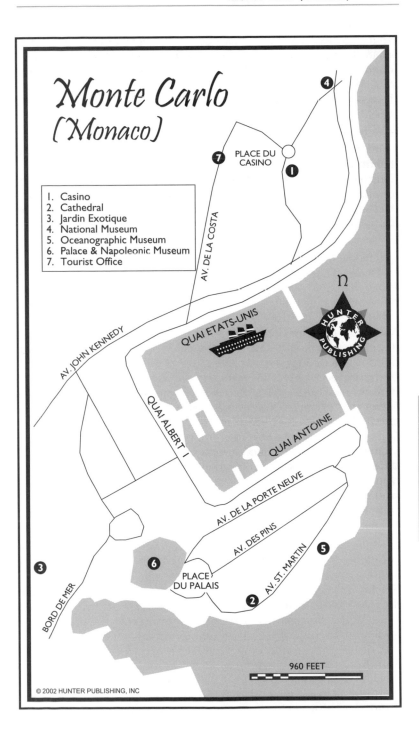

Monte Carlo (Monaco)

1. Casino
2. Cathedral
3. Jardin Exotique
4. National Museum
5. Oceanographic Museum
6. Palace & Napoleonic Museum
7. Tourist Office

PLACE DU CASINO

AV. DE LA COSTA

QUAI ETATS-UNIS

AV. JOHN KENNEDY

QUAI ALBERT I

QUAI ANTOINE

AV. DE LA PORTE NEUVE

AV. DES PINS

AV. ST. MARTIN

PLACE DU PALAIS

BORD DE MER

960 FEET

© 2002 HUNTER PUBLISHING, INC

you can access the **Observatory Caves** (Grottes de l'Observatoire), a small system of lovely caves. Be advised, however, that the caves are reached by a series of almost 300 steps so those with difficulty in walking should skip this part. The two attractions are inter-connected and have a combined admission. *62 Blvd. de Jardin Exotique; open daily, 9 am to 7 pm; $$.*

Back down in the lower town be sure to visit Monte Carlo's beautiful and famous **Casino de Monte Carlo** (proper dress is required – this isn't casual Las Vegas!) adjoining the impressive **Place du Casino**. *Casino open noon through 4 am.* You should concentrate the rest of your shore visit in the area called **Monaco Ville**, located on the southeast side of the harbor. Here are the Palais du Prince, the Monaco Cathedral and the Oceanographic Museum (Musée Océanographique), all within a quarter-mile of each another.

The **Palais du Prince**'s state apartments offer tours in English that last about a half-hour and are given at frequent intervals. *Daily from 9:30 am to 6:30 pm; $$.* The **Napoléan Museum** (Musée des Souvenirs Napoléoniens) is located in one of the palace wings. This interesting museum houses a display of items that once belonged to Napoleon. *Daily, 9:30 am to 6:30 pm; $.* If you're outside the palace just before noon you'll witness the colorful changing of the guard ceremony which takes place five minutes before the hour. **Monaco Cathedral** is not particularly impressive by European standards, but is heavily visited because it contains the grave of beloved Princess Grace – better known to Americans as Grace Kelly. The crypt also contains other members of Monaco's royal family. *Avenue St. Martin.* On a less somber note the **Oceanographic Museum** is a world-class facility with a wonderful collection of marine species in almost 100 different sea-water tanks of varying sizes. *Ave. St. Martin; open daily, 9 am to 7 pm; $$$.* End your visit with a walk along the waterfront streets surrounding Monaco Ville. A lovely park at the tip features **Fort Antoine** at the end of the small peninsula that juts out into the Mediterranean.

If you're in Monte Carlo during the latter part of May you may get caught up in the crowds and excitement of the famous **Grand Prix** auto race. While this could be a thrill for some, it might be an interference for others. Check out the exact dates at www.monaco-tourism.com if your cruise is in Monaco around this time. Your walks through town will almost certainly take you along the route of the race.

Nice

Port type: Day
Tourist information office:
5 Promenade des Anglais, ☎ (04) 9214-4800

Fashionable Nice is considered the capital of the French Riviera. (The Riviera name isn't used in France itself – rather the region is known as the Côte d'Azur or the Blue Coast.) Nice Harbor is fairly large and the docks can handle ships up to about 600 feet in length. Unfortunately, that means that the overwhelming majority of today's cruise liners have to anchor in the harbor and passengers must tender to shore. Once on land you'll be in the heart of the city and are free to explore on foot. For longer distances there are taxis available and the train station is under two miles from the harbor.

Considering that Nice is one of the Riviera's bigger cities, its beach certainly isn't one of the more attractive playgrounds. Lying just east of the nearby Vieux Nice along the Promenade des Anglais, the beach has pebbles underfoot rather than sand. But don't be disappointed – there are far better things to see and do when in port. The area known as **Vieux Nice**, near the port, is a good place for strolling. You can explore the pretty **Parc du Château**, which has good views from **Bellanda Tower**. If you don't want to walk up the hill, take the elevator which connects just beneath the tower. On the northwest side of Vieux Nice is the park-like Promenade du Paillon which, heading west, winds up at the pretty **Albert I Garden**. For those who insist on going to the beach despite my advice, the southern edge of the promenade touches on the Promenade des Anglais, which runs along the main beach. Just northwest of Vieux Nice by Place Garibaldi is the fine **Museum of Modern and Contemporary Art** that houses an astounding collection of works from the 1960s on. Even if you don't usually admire this genre of art, you're sure to find at least part of the collection interesting. *Promenade des Arts; open daily except Tuesday, 11 am until 6 pm (until 10 pm on Friday); $$.*

Nice's other sights are located a little farther from the sea, most of them about two miles from Vieux Nice. To begin exploring them, start at the main train station (Gare Nice Ville). Adjacent to the train station is the **Cathedral of St. Nicholas**. This Russian Orthodox church and its six onion-shaped domes look entirely out of place in these surroundings. Nonetheless, it is a beautiful sight. *Ave. Nicolas II; open daily, 9:30 am to noon and 2:30-5:30 pm (no afternoon opening on Sunday); $.* Farther northwest of the station is the excellent **Chagall Museum** (Musée Chagall). Marc Chagall is best known for his paintings of scenes from the Old Testament whose vivid lifelike style is hard to beat. *4 Ave. Dr. Ménard; open daily except Tues-*

day, 10 am to 6 pm; $$. Slightly further away from downtown via Boulevard de Cimiez is the **Matisse Museum** (Musée Matisse), which houses the works of Henri Matisse. *164 Ave. des Arènes de Cimiez; open daily except Tuesday, 10 am to 6 pm; $$.* Right next door is the **Archaeology Museum** *(same hours and prices as the Matisse Museum)*, a decent facility with some interesting Roman ruins. Among them are the remains of public baths and a reasonably well-preserved amphitheater.

Port Vendres

Port type: Day.
There is no tourist information office here,
but some information is usually available at the port.

Port Vendres (VON-drah) is not far north of the Spanish border, in an area that is known as French Catalan. In fact, many people are more Catalan than French and you might think you're not even in France in some places. Tender service will be required from your ship's anchorage to the port, which is right in the center of town. Port Vendres is part of a region known as the **Vermilion Coast**, or Côte Vermeille. Port Vendres itself is located in what most people would say is the nicest stretch of the Côte Vermeille. It is an attractive place with several small ports and resorts, and far less crowded than the more famous Riviera ports to the north. A port call in Vendres can make for a pleasant afternoon of strolling along the waterfront and in winding alleyways. Excursions can take you to surrounding towns and to see some of the better scenery close up. Guided trips can also take you to **Perpignan**, the region's largest community, with local museums, a palace and a large cathedral.

St. Tropez/Toulon

Port type: Day
Tourist information offices:
St. Tropez, Quai Jean Jaurès, ☎ (04) 9497-4521;
Toulon, Place Raimu, ☎ (04) 9418-5300

These two communities are about 35 miles apart so you can visit both in a shore excursion to one. Most ships will anchor at smaller St. Tropez. Upon tendering into port you'll be right in the heart of town. It was French sex-kitten Brigitte Bardot who first put St. Tropez on the map back in the mid-1950s. While the town hasn't grown much since then (it has fewer than 6,000 residents), it has become a famous resort. St. Tropez is a place of contrasts. Some of the narrow winding streets haven't changed much in a hundred years, but the harbor is filled with luxury yachts. Many visitors crowd the beaches in St. Tropez, but the best ones are actually located a few miles outside of town (you can reach them by taxi). Other than taking some sun and strolling through the quaint streets, St. Tropez doesn't have a lot to see. Two decent museums are the **Naval Museum** (Musée Navale) and the **Museum of Modern Art** (Musée de l'Annonciade). The former chronicles the maritime history of the region and is only of mild interest, but its setting – in the dungeon of the old citadel – is unique! *Rue de la Citadelle; open daily except Tuesday, 10 am until noon and 2 to 4:30 pm; $$.* The second museum was once a church and is now a museum of modern art that has works by several known artists. *Quai de l'Epi; open daily except Tuesday, 10 am until noon and 3 to 7 pm; $$.* Spend some time wandering around the town and along the beaches; it's a relaxing way to pass the day. St. Tropez has an excellent market selling fresh foods and flowers. It's located in the main square, Place des Lices, and is open Tuesday and Saturday mornings.

Toulon is unlike St. Tropez, and not only because it's 30 times as large! The entire city is a bit rundown, and seems very much out of place on the Côte d'Azur. That's why the passengers on most ships that do stop here wind up taking excursions elsewhere. However, if you decide to stay in town there are several museums to visit, including the **Toulon Museum** (Musée de Toulon). *113 Ave. du Maréchal Leclerc; open daily from 9:30 am to noon and 2-6 pm (1-6 pm on Sunday; $.* There's also the **Marine Museum** (Musée de la Marine), a decent naval museum housed in a building that once served as an arsenal. *Place Monsenergue; open daily except Tuesday, 9:30 am to noon and 3-7 pm; $$.* The best way to spend some time, though, is to take the cable car up to **Mont Faron**, which offers a fantastic view. From this vantage point even Toulon looks pretty good. Near the summit is the **Tour Beaumont**, a memorial to those who were killed in the Allied invasion that occurred near to here in August of 1944.

Sète

Port type: Day
Tourist information office: 60 Grand rue Mario Roustan,
☎ *(04) 6774-7171*

As in many of Mediterranean France's small resort towns, you will probably have to travel by ship's tender to reach land. The dock here can accommodate ships of up to around 750 feet in length, a size that is exceeded by an increasing number of the newer vessels. However, the center of town is only a few blocks from the dock and everything of interest is close by. You can even walk to the nearby railroad station. Excursion possibilities from Sète include Avignon and Nimes (see page 186, under Marseille) and **Montpellier**, only 35 miles away. Montpellier has about a quarter of a million residents. It has several museums, including one with the works of famous artists and one devoted to regional archaeology. Sète (pronounced Set) itself has a population of a little more than 40,000 and is an extremely pretty town (the best views are from nearby **Mont Ste. Clair**).

Villefranche

Port type: Day
There is no tourist information office, but numerous sources of information are available in shops and kiosks around the port area.

Your ship's tender will drop you off in Villefranche (Veel-fronsh) within steps of the city center. Taxis are available, although everything is close enough to reach on foot. A train station is about a half-mile from the port. Villefranche-sur-Mer (the full name of the town) sits between Nice and Monaco. As such, it's a starting point for excursions to those places more than a destination in and of itself. Trips to these towns are via a series of mountain roads that offer spectacular views of the coast and its picturesque villages. They are collectively known as the **Grand Corniche** and are subdivided into the Upper, Middle and Lower Corniche roads. But don't immediately head out of this town if your ship stops here – it's a delightful little place with one of the loveliest settings in the area. The old city dates from the 14th century and is a wonderful place for walking, especially around rue Obscure. Many of the streets here are actually steps, which attest to Villefranche's dramatic location.

Less Visited French Ports

CASSIS, LE LAVANDOU, PORQUEROLLES & SANARY-SUR-MER: These four towns are lined up one after the other on the Côte d'Azur between Marseille on the west and St. Tropez on the east. They are delightful little places where you can spend a short time strolling through the village and more time shopping or sunning yourself on the beach. Cassis is the best of the group because the precipitous cliffs above the sea are some of the most beautiful in the Riviera. Excursions to the more heavily visited Riviera destinations are available from these ports.

HYERES ISLANDS: The group consists of three small islands – Porquerolles, Port Cros and Levant. Half of Ile du Levant is reserved for naturists and those who wear clothes on the beach aren't particularly welcome. **Port Cros National Park**, a marine life reserve with lots of butterflies and hiking opportunities, occupies the entire island of the same name. Only a couple of cruise ships call on the Hyères Islands, but if you're eager to visit them, boats run from the mainland at Toulon as well as the smaller Riviera towns of Le Lavandrou and Hyères.

Corsica (France) & Sardinia (Italy)

The second- (Sardinia) and fourth-largest (Corsica) islands in the Mediterranean offer a pleasant way to experience the more rural aspects of Mediterranean Europe. The people and customs on each of these islands is quite different than from what you will experience in France and Italy proper. This is especially so on Corsica, where most people are not of French extraction. Many long for their own independent state and there is occasional agitation for it.

Corsica

Port type: Day

Tourism information office: 1 Place Foch (Ajaccio), ☎ *(04) 9551-5303*

A mountainous island, Corsica measures about 100 miles from north to south (not counting a narrow point in the northeast that extends another 20 miles) and averages 40 miles in width. It is possible to get to just about anywhere in Corsica regardless of where your ship docks. Most vessels stop at Ajaccio on the west coast and the largest town on the island (55,000 people). Other ports include Calvi (north of Ajaccio); Bonifacio at the southernmost point; Porto-Vecchio, a little northeast of Bonifacio; and Bastia in the northeast. The port of Ajaccio can accommodate ships up to about 650 feet in length. Once you hit the shore you'll find yourself within a few hundred feet of the town's center. Taxis are readily available to take you to places farther afield. At the other ports you'll tender to shore and be right in the heart of any of the port towns once you get on land.

Exploring the countryside of Corsica is a great way to spend the day. Although there are higher mountain peaks in the Mediterranean, of all the islands of the region, Corsica is the most mountainous. The highest point is around 8,800 feet. Much of the interior consists of the **Corsica Regional Natural Park** and, besides mountain scenery (winter skiing) and views of the sea, the park offers some stunning gorges. The most famous of these natural chasms is the **Prunelli**

Gorge. On the way to Prunelli be sure to stop for a view of beautiful **Tolla Lake.** The **Spelunca Gorge** is also quite scenic. But some of Corsica's best scenery is near the tiny coastal town of **Porto**, where you'll see a series of red granite outcroppings known as the **Calanches of Piana.** The rocks resemble some of the weird formations common to the American Southwest.

Corsica is a wine-making region and most day tours will stop at one of the local wineries. Trips to the island's interior are best done as a guided shore excursion, since car rentals aren't always available and the roads need improvement. If you decide to opt for a guided tour, make sure it visits a good number of the places mentioned above.

Ajaccio is most widely known as the birthplace of Napoleon and you won't lose sight of that when you're in town. In addition to many statues of Nappy, you'll find the **Maison Bonaparte,** *rue St. Charles; open Monday from 2 to 5 pm, Tuesday through Saturday from 10 am until noon and 2 to 5 pm, and on Sunday from 10 am until noon; $$.* The modest structure is the house where he was born and raised. The **Salon Napoléonien** is a good museum about the emperor and is located in the town hall (Hôtel de Ville). *Place Foch; open Monday through Friday, 9 am to 11:45 am and 2-4:45pm; $.* The **Musée Fesch** has a lot more stuff on Napoleon and some more diverse topics, including a decent art collection. *50 rue Fesch; open daily except Tuesday, 9:30 am until noon and 3-6 pm; $$.* Finally, the **Musée a Bandera** is a museum dedicated to Corsican military history. *1 rue Général Lévie; open daily except Sunday, 9 am to noon and 2-6 pm; $.* The most famous Napoleon statue in town is on the **Place d'Austerlitz**, which is a a replica of the one outside the Palace des Invalides in Paris. In the Place des Palmiers, Napoleon's statue is flanked by four heroic lions. Nearby is another monument to the emperor, this one on horseback accompanied by his four brothers. Keep in mind that Napoleon is still very much revered throughout France and in no place more so than on Corsica. Don't show any anti-Napoleonic tendencies if you want to befriend the locals.

Take some time to wander around Ajaccio and experience its laid-back lifestyle. In many ways, things haven't changed much here in the past several hundred years.

If you're docked at **Bonifacio**, you should definitely visit the striking **Citadelle.** Perched about 225 feet above the sea on a small promontory, it was selected as the location of a fortress because of its naturally defensible position. Sheer limestone cliffs here plunge to the sea. **Calvi** is a nice place to dock because of its location on Corsica's rugged northwest coast – one of the most scenic areas of the entire island. The other possible port towns have little to offer by themselves but, as was mentioned, make fine jumping-off places for visits around the island.

Sardinia

Port type: Day
Tourism information office: Via Goffredo Mameli 97 (Cagliari)
☎ *(800) 013-153*

Mountainous Sardinia (or Sardegna, in Italian) is almost rectangular in shape and extends 166 miles from north to south and 75 miles east to west, making it the second biggest of the Mediterranean's many islands. The highest point on the island is over 6,000 feet. Seemingly always on the invasion route of Mediterranean empires, Sardinia has been under many different flags. Even today, however, the people of Sardinia don't regard themselves as Italian.

The primary port is **Cagliari**, on the southern coast, and most cruise ships visiting Sardinia will drop anchor here. Alghero in the northwest is another port of call you may stop at. Seeing the natural scenery of Sardinia's interior calls for taking a guided shore excursion since the roads are not particularly good, places aren't that well signed and car rentals are not always easy to get. Cagliari has over 200,000 residents, which makes it far bigger than any other community on the island. Alghero, for instance, has only 40,000. In either port you'll most likely arrive in port, via tender, and find most things quite nearby. Cagliari's port is a short walk from the city center, although all of the sights on my suggested tour are north of downtown and as far as 1½ miles from the harbor. So, while you could walk, a taxi might be in order for some.

Let's first explore **Cagliari**. In the northeast corner of downtown is the **Piazza Constituzione**, behind which are the extensive walls of the old city. Good views from various points along the fortifications are available. Near the Piazza is the single best portion of the fortifications, the **Bastione di San Remy**. Continuing north from that point you'll soon reach the 13th-century **cathedral** (*duomo*) and then the **Piazzas Indipendenza** and **Arsenale**, the latter with the **Torre di San Pancrazio**, a Pisa-style tower. Sardinia's ancient past comes alive at the **National Museum of Archaeology** (Museo Archeologico Nazionale). *Piazza Arsenale; open daily except Monday, 9 am to 7 pm, $.* This is also true in the **Roman amphitheater**, which is so well preserved that it is still used for theater productions. Nearby, west of the walls is the pretty **Orto Botanico** gardens.

Alghero is a quaint old city and it's worth walking around the oldest part of town. The highlight of this part of the island is the scenic coastline with its stark cliffs, precipitous drops to the sea and isolated beaches. The single most popular attraction is **Neptune's Caves**. These can be reached either by boat or bus from Alghero (both offer several departures daily). The caves are certain to be a part of the organized guided tour too. *Guided tours of the cave hourly from 9 am to 7 pm; $$-$$$ for transportation to cave and $$ for cave itself.* The northwest section of Sardinia around the town of **Olbia** is among the most picturesque areas in the Mediterranean. It isn't highly developed and that makes it even more attractive for many visitors. Few cruise ships stop here, but it can be reached from Alghero by bus. Other Sardinian ports that are sometimes called on by cruise ships include Porto Cervo, in the extreme northern portion of the island (convenient for trips to Olbia), and Costa Smeralda, a resort town on the lovely Emerald Coast.

Italy's West Coast

Genoa

Port type: Gateway/Day
Tourism information office: Palazzina Santa Maria, ☎ (010) 248-711

Genoa has a long and glorious history. Many people don't think of it as a tourist attraction because it is one of Italy's most heavily industrialized cities. While there's no denying that, the fact also remains that Genoa has quite a bit to offer the visitor in addition to being a gateway to other areas of Italy. Genoa's passenger ship terminal was reconstructed in 1991 from the original "maritime station" and is one of the most modern and efficient terminals in the world. It is large enough to accommodate up to five cruise ships at one time, which means you'll be able to walk off the ship directly into town. The port is located along the Via della Mercanzia. It's not within walking distance of the city center, but you can hop a bus, taxi or metro to whisk you there in just a few minutes. If you are limiting your time on shore to the city itself, there is no need for an organized tour.

Depending upon the other port calls your cruise is scheduled to make while in the northern part of Italy, you might want to travel out of Genoa rather than concentrating on the city sights, some of which are similar to those in other Italian ports. Within day-excursion distance are **Milan** (90 miles), **Pisa** (110 miles) and several communities of the **Italian Riviera** (such as **San Remo**) to the west or the **Ligurian coast** to the south. The Ligurian coast is a particularly beautiful area with many wonderful villages, including the oft-sketched Portofino. But Portofino is a cruise destination in itself, as is Pisa (via Livorno), so those places are discussed separately a little later. The Italian Riviera isn't nearly as famous as its French counterpart. It just doesn't seem to have the same kind of charm. Milan is the type of place that people either love or hate, but it definitely has some worthwhile sights, most famous of which is its cathedral. But, for now, let's look at Genoa.

Highlights Tour

All of the attractions in this day tour are contained within the city's central core, which covers under a square mile. A good place to begin is the beautiful **Via Garibaldi**, lined on both sides with impressive structures, many of which were former palaces. Along this street are the **Palazzo Bianco** (White Palace) and **Palazzo Rosso** (Red Palace). Dating from, respectively, the 16th and 17th centuries, both palaces are now fine art galleries with works by European masters. *Via Garibaldi 11 & 18; both are open Tuesday through Saturday, 9 am to 1 pm (to 7 pm on Wednesday and Saturday) and on Sunday from 10 am to 6 pm; $ each.* Also along this street is the **Palazzo Doria Tursi**, the former palace of a wealthy Genoan family that now houses the city hall. It was originally built in 1564. *Via Garibaldi 9; open weekdays, hours vary.* A few blocks south of the Via Garibaldi is the **Galleria Nazionale di Palazzo Spinola**, another palace turned art museum. This one specializes in Renaissance artists. *Piazza Pellicceria 1; Monday through Saturday, 9 am to 7 pm (to 1 pm on Monday), Sunday, 2 to 10 pm; $$.* The area of the Spinola is also the beginning of the old town or old port, so wander over to the waterfront to visit the **Aquarium** (Acquario). This fine facility is one of the biggest in Europe (the largest according to Genoans but, then again, everyone measures these things differently). Most visitors spend their time in the dolphin area. *Ponte Spinola; open daily from 9:30 am to 6:30 pm (till 8 pm on Saturday and Sunday); $$.*

Head back away from the water to the large and attractive **Piazza Matteotti** and the adjacent **Piazza de Ferrari**. Dominating the squares is the **Palazzo Ducale**, which was originally the seat of Genoan government. Although it is now used for exhibits and conventions, you can still get a feel for the elaborate interior by walking inside. There are many restaurants located there now. On the opposite side of the Piazza Matteotti is the 12th-century **Cattedrale di San Lorenzo**. This magnificent structure was built of local marble (both black and white) and the elaborate exterior façade is worth a detailed look to appreciate all of the details. The interior isn't quite as marvelous, although the museum in the sacristy has some interesting items. *Piazza San Lorenzo; open daily except Sunday, 9 am to noon and 3-6 pm; $.*

More Sights & Excursions

Unlike most other gateway cities, Genoa can be adequately seen in a single day by the majority of visitors. If this is your gateway, I would suggest you use any extra days here to make some of the side-trips, as outlined above. If you want to stay in Genoa a little longer, I suggest visiting some of the **wall remains** that surround the city. The walls are set up in the hills and the best way to explore the "high" town is via some of the many funiculars that dot the city. Get a map from the tourist office and plan a route. Also of interest back in the old port and city center are several more museums and churches. Try the **National Museum of the Antarctic** (Museo Nazionale dell'Antardide), an interesting facility about Antarctic exploration set on the waterfront. *Ponte Embriaco; open daily except Sunday, $.* You can also visit the **Royal Palace & Gallery** (Palazzo Reale & Galleria), a former royal residence now in use as a museum. *Via Balbi 10; open daily except Monday, 9 am to 1:45 pm (some days until 7 pm); $$.* Finally, the **Churches of San Matteo** (at Piazza San Mateo) and **San Siro** (off via St. Lucia) are both worth a brief look.

Livorno/Pisa

Port type: Day

Tourism information offices: Livorno, Piazza Cavour 6, ☎ (0586) 898-111; Pisa, Piazza Manin, ☎ (050) 560-464

The port of Livorno can accommodate even the largest ships and you'll be tendered ashore only when there are several ships at dock. The passenger terminal is just over a quarter-mile from the center of Livorno. Taxis are available and the railroad station is about two miles from the port. Livorno has some interesting sights, but its proximity to Pisa is what draws people. Even more important is the fact that it is the closest major port to Florence. Before tackling those locations, let's explore the things to see and do in Livorno itself.

Livorno (sometimes called Leghorn, in English) has about 60,000 residents and, compared to most other localities in this region, is mildly unattractive. Yet, there are a few things to see. The main part of town, located behind the port, is island-like because it is blocked from the mainland by a canal known as the **Fosso Reale**. The local tourist office likes to call it *piccola Venezia* or "little Venice," but the comparison ends with the fact that both cities have canals! The canal area is home to the **New Fortress** (Fortezza Nuova), the larger and more interesting of Livorno's two fortresses. It was built by the powerful Medici family in the 16th century. The other fortress, called the "Old Fortress" (Fortezza Vecchia), is on the waterfront near the port.

Livorno's cathedral is in the Piazza Grande, almost exactly in the middle of the main loop of the Fosso Reale, the canal.

Pisa

It is only about 20 miles from Livorno to **Pisa** and, despite the great popularity of Pisa as a guided shore excursion, you can just as well get there on your own by rental car, bus or train. Pisa, with a population of less than 60,000, would be a provincial backwater were it not for the famous **Leaning Tower**. That's what people come to see. The *Torre Pendente* (its Italian name) is only one part of a magnificent complex known as the **Field of Miracles** (Campo dei Miracoli). This is one of Europe's most fabulous municipal squares, located just northwest of the city center and about a half-mile north of the Arno River which sweeps gracefully through Pisa. Spread out on the beautifully manicured lawns and open spaces of the Campo are the Leaning Tower, the baptistery (*battistero)* and the cathedral (*duomo*). The Leaning Tower was the bell tower (*campanilei*) for the cathedral and, despite having a renowned architect, started to lean during its construction. The problem is the underlying soil. The lean increased about one millimeter a year and the tower is now more than 16 feet out of perpendicular. The authorities were so concerned that it would actually topple that climbing the 294 steps to the top was discontinued in 1990 and a program to stabilize the structure was begun. This has now been completed and it is hoped that the tower will eventually return to the state it was in 1990. Visitors are once again allowed to climb the tower, but only in small groups. Let's look at the other superb Romanesque-styled structures on the square. The cathedral was begun in 1064 and is distinguished for its exterior columned façade, the almost six dozen interior columns and its fine art collection. The Baptistry is about 90 years newer than the cathedral and is of special architectural interest because it is round. Since it took so many centuries to complete, it also has evidence of architectural styles other than Romanesque. The overall appearance is nothing short of brilliant, much like the acoustics beneath the lovely dome. You should complete your visit to the Campo dei Miracoli by walking through the **cemetery** on the north side of the cathedral. Although it was badly damaged during World War II, enough remains of the beautiful frescoes in the cloisters to make it worth seeing. *The tower, cathedral and baptistry are all open daily from 10 am to 7:30 pm (1-5 pm on Sunday); $ for each.*

If you plan to spend most of your shore time in Pisa, there are plenty of other attractions to fill your day. The **Opera Museum** (Museo dell'Opera del Duomo), only a couple of blocks from the Campo dei Miracoli, contains many works of art that were originally in the cathedral, baptistry and tower. *Via Arcivescovado; open daily, 9 am*

202 ● Italy's West Coast

to 7:30 pm; $. Most other sights are in an area just north of the river and include the gorgeous **Piazza dei Cavalieri,** with its many fine palaces and other structures. The **Palazzo dell'Orologio,** built in 1560, is the square's finest example of that period's architecture. Several fine churches are also in the vicinity. Finally, do try to find some time to visit Pisa's fascinating medieval section, centered along and around the **Borgo Stretto,** which runs north from the river.

Florence

Livorno is the closest cruise ship port to **Florence,** about 60 miles away (*Tourism information office: Via Cavour 1,* ☎ *055-290-832).* Because of the historical, cultural and artistic importance of Florence, it is almost always listed in the cruise brochures with Livorno. But be advised that a single day in Florence is not nearly adequate to see all of the major sites, regardless of whether you take a guided shore excursion or venture out on your own. Allowing for travel time to and from Livorno, you can probably count a maximum of nine hours in Florence. This is not meant to discourage you – a day in Florence is one that you will not soon forget. What makes Florence so special? Central Florence (**Firenze,** in Italian) has the atmosphere of a time gone by, despite the fact that this city of half a million people has a modern side. It was the home and workshop of such luminaries as Michelangelo and is, in many ways, the epitome of the Renaissance and all it stood for. The suggested itinerary is not all inclusive, but is my judgment of what you can reasonably expect to see in the time available. It follows a geographic sequence, but you may have to alter as many important sites close for several hours in mid-day! If you drive here, find a parking garage as soon as possible and walk – most of the major sights are within easy walking distance, mainly to the north of the Arno River. Although the street layout of central Florence isn't confusing, a good map will help as you navigate.

Begin your tour at the **Galleria dell'Academia,** a large art museum with many notable works. The original of Michelangelo's *David* is here, one of the most famous, most recognizable and copied statues in the history of art. *Via Ricasoli 60; open daily, 7 am to noon and 3:30-6:30 pm; $$.* Move on to the nearby **Basilica di San Lorenzo,** a stunning 15th-century church built for the Medicis. The most interesting part of the basilica is the **Laurenziana Library** (Biblioteca Laurenziana), which houses more than 10,000 manuscripts. It is reached by a Michelangelo-designed stairway. *Piazza San Lorenzo; open daily, 7 am to noon and 3:30-6:30 pm; $.* Adjacent to the basilica is the **Medici Chapel** (Capelle Medicee), one of the most ornately decorated tombs you'll ever see. There are many wonderful works of art throughout. *Piazza di Madonna degli Aldobrandiar; open daily, 8:30 am to 2 pm; $.*

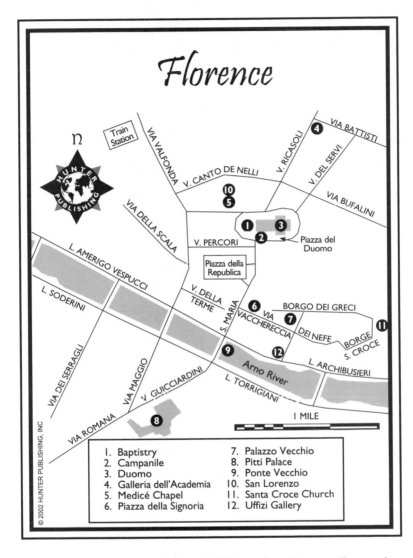

Florence

n

Train Station

VIA VALFONDA

VIA CANTO DE NELLI

V. RICASOLI

VIA BATTISTI

V. DEL SERVI

VIA BUFALINI

④

⑩
⑤

VIA DELLA SCALA

V. PERCORI

①
②
③

Piazza del Duomo

L. AMERIGO VESPUCCI

L. SODERINI

Piazza della Republica

V. DELLA TERME

S. MARIA

VIA VACCHERECCIA

BORGO DEI GRECI

⑥
⑦

DEI NEFE

BORGE S. CROCE

⑪

VIA DEI SERRAGLI

VIA MAGGIO

V. GUICCIARDINI

⑨

⑫

Arno River

L. ARCHIBUSIERI

L. TORRIGIANI

1 MILE

VIA ROMANA

⑧

© 2002 HUNTER PUBLISHING, INC

1. Baptistry	7. Palazzo Vecchio
2. Campanile	8. Pitti Palace
3. Duomo	9. Ponte Vecchio
4. Galleria dell'Academia	10. San Lorenzo
5. Medicé Chapel	11. Santa Croce Church
6. Piazza della Signoria	12. Uffizi Gallery

Next stop is the fabulous **cathedral** (*duomo*) and its equally wonderful **baptistry** and **bell tower**. This is the fourth largest cathedral in the world and its huge dome dominates Florence's skyline. The ambitious can climb a stairway that leads to the dome for a great view. The colorful exterior is also a sight to behold. The other buildings in the complex were completed at different times, but the overall design is harmonious. Be sure to see the gilded bronze doors of the baptistry with their famous decoration. *Baptistry open Monday through Saturday, 1:30 pm to 6:30 pm, Sunday, 8:30 am to*

1:30 pm; cathedral open daily, 10 am to 5 pm (from 1 pm on Sunday); $ for each. A few blocks to the south is the fabulously ornate **Piazza della Signoria**. This beautiful 13th-century plaza was the heart of Renaissance Florence. In a corner of the plaza is the **Loggia della Signoria**, with its fine covered outdoor display of monumental sculptures. The plaza is dominated by the **Palazzo Vecchio**, which served as the palace of the Medici for a time during the 16th century. Self-guiding tours of the palace include the courtyard and state apartments. *Open daily except Thursday, 9 am to 7 pm (Sunday, 8 am to 1 pm), $.* To the immediate south of the piazza is the renowned **Uffizi Gallery**. This was once another palace and it still retains a thoroughly regal aura despite the fact that it is now an art museum. And what a museum it is! It houses one of the world's foremost collections of Renaissance works with all the best Renaissance artists represented. You could spend a full day or more at the Uffizi alone, but time constraints will force you to move on. *Piazza degli Uffizi 6; open daily except Monday, 8:30 am to 10 pm (Sunday until 6:30pm); $$.* Head along the river from the south end of the Uffizi to **Ponte Vecchio**, a 14th-century bridge that may well be Florence's most famous sight. Since it was built, this unusual bridge has been the home of a number of shops and it is always crowded with tourists browsing and buying. While here, a small opening on the bridge's west-facing side offers your only view down onto the river. A little bit south of the bridge is another Medici palace, the **Palazzo Pitti**. This is the largest of all Florentine palaces. Its art works are contained within three separate museums – **Galleria Paltina**, the **Silver Museum** and the **Gallery of Modern Art**. The **royal apartments** in Pitti should not be missed. *Open daily, 8:30 am to 2 pm; $-$$ for each.* Behind the Pitti Palace are the lovely **Boboli Gardens**. You will probably only have time to make a cursory visit here, but do try to see the Venus grotto. *Open daily, 9 am until one hour before sunset; $.*

It is doubtful if you'll have any time left after this tour, but if you're a super-fast tourist and find you still have time left before you must get back to port, visit the **Church of Santa Croce**. This 14th-century masterpiece is a great example of Florentine Gothic style and many of Italy's former kings are buried here. *Piazza Santa Croce 16; Church open daily, 8 am to 6:30 pm (Sunday from 3-5 pm); Cloister and museum open daily except Wednesday, 10 am to 12:30 pm and 2:30-6:30 pm; $ for museum/cloister only.* Alternatively, you can head up to the **Piazzale Michelangelo** (bus #13 if you don't have wheels) on the south bank of the Arno, not that far from the Palazzo Pitti. From this point there's an absolutely marvelous view of all of Florence and its famous red roof-tops. It's also worth considering a quick visit to **Fort Belvedere** (Forte di Belvedere), located close to the

Piazzale Michelangelo. *Porta San Giorgio.* Today it is mainly an exhibition center.

All guided excursions to Florence pass through the pretty Tuscan countryside and one of Italy's major wine-producing areas. If this interests you, be sure your excursion includes a winery stop.

Naples/Capri

Port type: Day

Tourism information offices: Naples, Piazza del Gesù Nuovo, ☎ (081) 552-3328; Capri, Marina Grande, ☎ (081) 837-0634

The beautiful Isle of Capri is almost 20 miles offshore from the harbor at Naples. Some ships stop at Naples and some at Capri, but rare is the one that will call at both. Regardless of which one your ship pulls into, you can often explore a little of both ports. The biggest problem is choosing what you want to do, since there is no way that you can see all of the sights here in a day. Visitors to Naples are often most interested in heading out to see the famous ruins of Pompeii. The port of Naples is one of the biggest in the Mediterranean and can easily accommodate the largest of cruise liners so there is direct access to the passenger terminal. Even better is that you will find yourself right in the heart of the city in close proximity to its most important attractions. The railroad station, should you want to use the train to get to Pompeii, is about three miles from the port. Taxis are plentiful. On the other hand, the port of Capri is small and you'll have to use tender service to get to shore.

Before exploring Naples, Capri and Pompeii let's take a quick look at one other popular destination just west of Naples that includes both the Fiery Fields (Campi Flegrei) and Cumae. **Campi Flegrei** is an area of volcanic activity that reveals bubbling muddy waters and the strong aroma of sulphur. It is easy to see why the ancient Greeks and Romans thought that this area was the entrance to the underworld. Within the Fiery Fields – and of most interest to visitors – is the **Solfatara Crater.** *Open daily, 9 am to an hour before sunset; $$.* **Cumae** is the remains of a Roman resort town that now lies about 300 feet beneath the sea. It is visible via glass bottom boat tours that leave from Naples. By road it is 10 miles west of Naples. *Via Acropoli. Open daily, 9 am to an hour before sunset; $. Additional fee for boat transportation.*

Stretching for miles along the beautiful bay of the same name, Naples has one of the most dramatic settings of any major city. It is home to more than 1¼ million people. Unfortunately, the city center lacks the charm so often found in other European cities. The area is quite run-down and not attractive at all. It is also one of the poorest of Italian cities. There is more crime here than in most parts of Europe and although you probably won't have any unpleasant encounters, don't show valuables. On a more positive note, Naples does have much to see and a lot of it is within a short distance of the port. I've divided the attractions in Naples into two areas – one by the port, the other slightly to the north. If you are going to combine other area sights with touring Naples itself and won't have time to do both, I suggest the first tour outlined below.

The first tour covers a roughly circular walk that begins a few blocks west of the port. Start at the **Piazza Municipio** and its **town hall**. Taking a clockwise direction, the next attraction is the large **New Castle** (Castel Nuovo). The "new" in the name is far from true, since the entire structure dates back to the 14th century. The triumphal arch at the entrance is the most notable feature, and inside you'll find a decent museum focusing on Naples. *Piazza Municipio; open daily, 9 am to 7 pm (until 1 pm on Sunday); $$.* Across the street is the **Palazzo Reale**, set in the large square known as the **Piazza del Plebiscito**. The palace was built in the early part of the 17th century, and much has been rebuilt since the end of World War II. It was the former residence of the kings of Savoy and now contains a museum. This is one of the more elaborate palaces in southern Italy. *Open daily, 9 am to 10 pm (until 6 pm on Sunday); $$.* Next up is the cross-shaped **Galleria Umberto I**, one of the earliest enclosed shopping centers. It was built in the 1890s and, with its glass roof, resembles an even more famous center in Milan. However, if you haven't been to Milan, this one is likely to impress you. From the Gallery you should cross Via Tolddo and take the Funicular Centrale up to the top for a grand view of the area you just explored, the port and the beautiful Bay of Naples.

The second tour starts at the **National Archaeological Museum** (Museo Archaeologico Nazionale). Note: If you are combining the two tours, reach this museum from the funicular by traveling north on Via Toledo, which becomes Via Roma and finally Via Enrico Pessina. It's a little over a mile. The museum is one of the best on Greco-Roman culture in all of Italy – and that's saying a lot. Many of the original works of art found in Pompeii and Herculaneum have found their way here. *Piazza Museo; open daily except Tuesday, 9 am to 2 pm; $$.* Several blocks to the east is Naples' **cathedral**, which has seen numerous reconstructions and alterations over the centuries. It is most notable for its large size and the elaborately decorated ceiling above the main nave. *Via del Duomo; open daily, 9 am to noon and 4-7 pm; $.* Along the Via Capitelli and near the city tourist office are two interesting churches, **Chiesa di Santa Chiara** and **Chiesa di Geru Nuovo**. The first is a fine example of baroque archi-

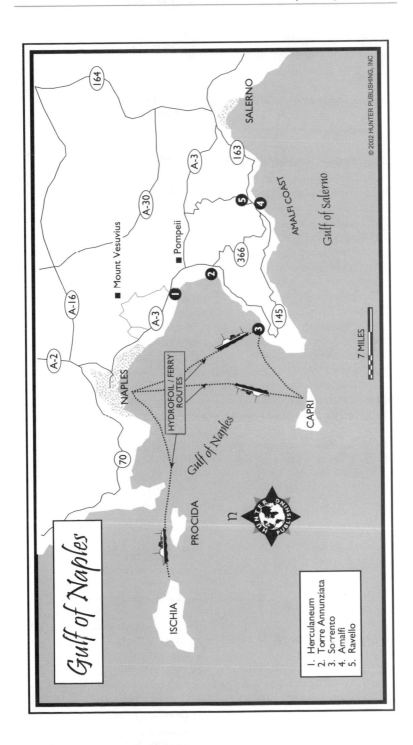

PORTS OF CALL

Gulf of Naples

164

A-2

A-16

A-30

A-3

164

A-3

SALERNO

163

AMALFI COAST

Mount Vesuvius

Pompeii

366

145

Gulf of Salerno

5
4

NAPLES

HYDROFOIL / FERRY
ROUTES

1

2

3

70

ISCHIA

PROCIDA

Gulf of Naples

CAPRI

7 MILES

N

1. Herculaneum
2. Torre Annunziata
3. Sorrento
4. Amalfi
5. Ravello

tecture as interpreted in southern Italy, while the latter has distinctive Gothic influences. Now it's time to leave the city.

The celebrated Isle of **Capri** is approximately 20 miles from Naples and less than five miles from Sorrento (if your ship also stops there, consider visiting Capri from that port). From Naples, the fastest way to reach Capri is by hydrofoil. These leave at regular intervals from the Molo Beverello, opposite the Castel Nuovo and not far from the main port. Boat rides from Sorrento take only a few minutes and depart from within steps of where you'll arrive by ship. On Capri, all boats (ship tenders and ferries from the mainland) arrive at the Marina Grande beneath the town of Capri. The view as you approach is stunning. Transportation on the island is by bus, taxi or on foot (there are no rental cars), but tiny Isola di Capri is less than four miles long and under two wide. The main areas of interest are the towns of Capri and Anacapri, along with the famous Blue Grotto and the Villa Jovis. The town of **Capri** sits high above the port and the easiest and most fun way of getting there is by the funicular railway. The town has only a few thousand people and it won't take that long to wander around its narrow streets. It is a place where time has stood still in many respects. You stop by any of the several churches here for a quick look, and also visit the **Museum of Capri** (Museo del Centro Caprese i Cerio). It has a collection of items found on Capri that date back to Neolithic times. *Piazzetia Cerio 8a.* The best sight in town is the **Gardens of Augustus**, not because the gardens are so special (although they're quite attractive), but because from this vantage point is a great view of the rocky island of Faraglioni that lies to the south. The gardens are about a quarter-mile walk from the Piazza Umberto I, the center of Capri town. *Via Matteotti. Daily from dawn to dusk.* Less than 1½ miles east of Capri is **Villa Jovis**, once the home of Emperor Tiberius. Back in Roman times there were many large villas – even then, people recognized the special qualities of Capri. Villa Jovis is the best preserved and largest of all the ancient villas on the island. However, there remains only a fraction of the original villa's many buildings. Nonetheless, it is an interesting place to visit. *Via Tiberio; open daily, 9 am to an hour before sunset, $.* **Anacapri** does not offer many sights, although there is another Roman villa here, **Villa San Michele**. Of more appeal in Anacapri is the chair lift that begins at the town's main square and rises to the peak of Monte Solaro. At 1,914 feet it is the highest point on the island and offers wonderful panoramas in any direction. The island of Capri has many sea caves (or grottoes), but none is as spectacular as the well-known **Blue Grotto** (Grotta Azzura). The Romans knew about the Blue Grotto, but it wasn't "discovered" by modern visitors until the early part of the 19th century. The only opening is nine feet high and sunlight coming through this hole is responsible for creating the unique coloring of the grotto. This is one of the most beautiful sights you could imagine and even the crowds can't spoil it. The grotto can be reached by boat from Capri or by bus from Anacapri. Either way, you'll wind up on a rowboat since motorized vessels aren't allowed into the grotto itself. *Open daily, 9:30 am until two hours before sunset; $$$.*

The most popular excursion from Naples is to **Pompeii**, 20 miles from the center of Naples. It can be reached by frequent train or bus service so, again, don't believe that you must go on an expensive excursion to see it. If you rent a car, almost all of the short ride is on a modern toll highway. Pompeii was a wealthy Roman resort town before it was buried by the volcanic eruption of nearby Mount Vesuvius in 79 AD. Although it was a great disaster, the volcanic ash and rock proved to be a wonderful preservative and excavations in this century (ongoing) have revealed a myriad of information on Roman life at that time. You don't feel you are in a dead city – given the number of visitors, it is very much alive – and it's easy to picture yourself strolling through town during the days of antiquity. In addition to the temples, baths, theaters and other public facilities that are most frequently seen in ancient sites throughout Europe, Pompeii is notable for the number of well-preserved homes. They were owned by the richest class of Roman citizens at that time. *Open daily, 9 am until an hour before sunset. $$.* Less famous than Pompeii is **Herculaneum**, closer to Naples. The ruins here are far less extensive than those at Pompeii. Since you only have a day, it would make better use of your time do only Pompeii. The one advantage of visiting Herculaneum is the view of Mt. Vesuvius it offers. *Open daily, 9 am until an hour before sunset; $$.* Excursions to **Mount Vesuvius** are also popular. You can drive up on your own, or take a bus from Pompeii or Herculaneum. The actual site is about a mile from where the bus leaves you off; you can get somewhat closer with your own car. There are many hiking trails here, but on a day shore visit you'll probably have time only for a quick look at the crater before heading back down. You must hire a guide to go into the crater itself.

If your Naples port call is the closest you'll get to either Salerno or Sorrento, be aware that it is possible to see either or both of those towns on an excursion from Naples. Each is approximately 40 miles from Naples. However, if you decide to make either trip, you'll have to forfeit Capri and much of what is within Naples itself. On the other hand, Pompeii is en route, so you could include that as part of your day on land.

Portofino

Port type: Day
Tourism information office: Via Roma 35, ☎ (0185) 269-024

Delightful Portofino is just one of many coastal communities that attracts the rich and famous, as well as the less well-heeled traveler. It is the only such town at which major cruise ships dock and it makes an ideal base from which to explore the surrounding area. The Ligurian coast is one of the more attractive in Italy (some say it rivals the better known Amalfi coast in the south). The port is as tiny as the town, but once you tender in everything is only a short walk away. Portofino sits at the end of a small promontory that juts out from the mainland into the Ligurian Sea. It is rocky and wild to the extent that the area was historically isolated from places not that far away. Take some time to walk around Portofino itself and see the markets and many villas where the glitterrati live. **San Georgio Castle** (Castello di San Georgio) isn't one of the more impressive coastal fortifications you'll encounter, but it does provide a spectacular view. *Open daily except Tuesday, 10 am to 6 pm; $.* There is also a church by the same name in the immediate vicinity. The nearby towns of **Santa Margherita** and **Rapallo** are equally fascinating. The former is primarily known for its abundance of watersports, which are offered in a sheltered bay. Rapallo is primarily another resort town. Its biggest attraction is the **Montallegro**, which attracts religious pilgrims because the Virgin Mary was said to have been seen here in 1557. It is reached by a funicular railway that passes through pleasant scenery that may even interest non-believers. There's also a 16th-century fortress within the town. Only slightly farther away are five small towns known as **Cinque Terre** – Corniglia, Manarola, Monterosso, Riomaggiore and Vernazza. These towns don't have any specific sights, but they enjoy a scenic setting and charming old-world atmosphere. The last town in this section of the coast is **La Spezia**. It is about 45 miles from Portofino and 50 from Pisa, so it can be an excursion destination from either Portofino or Livorno. La Spezia has quite a few attractions of more than casual interest. Two excellent museums are located in the vicinity of the Piazza Cavour in the western end of town. The **Art Museum** (Pinacoteca Civica Amedeo Lia) has a surprisingly large collection of European Masters, including Titian and Bellini. *Via Prione & Via del Vecchio Ospedale; open daily except Monday, 10 am to 6 pm; $$.* Nearby is the **Civic Museum** (Museo Civico). It is a regional history museum and its archaeological collection dating back to the Bronze Age is quite good. *Via Curtatone 9; open daily except Monday, 8:30 am to 1 pm and 2 -7 pm; $.* The **Naval Museum** (Museo Navale), near the port, isn't exactly a navy museum, although it does have a fine collection of ship models. Of even more interest are the *polenes*, the figureheads that were placed on ships' prows in the old days. *Across the Canale Lagora from the Piazza Domenico Chiode; open daily, 2 to 6 pm with morning hours on some days; $.*

Portofino can also be used as a jumping-off point for excursions to other interesting towns, including Genoa (under 30 miles) and Pisa (80 miles). Because the distances between Portofino and the towns mentioned isn't that great, you have a variety of options for exploring this area. A guided shore excursion will be the easy way out, but definitely not the least expensive and not necessarily the best. The train line between Genoa and La Spezia serves almost all of the towns in the area and can be used to make a reasonable day-long itinerary. A car gives you much greater flexibility, but be aware that vehicles are banned from the interior portion of many coastal towns so you'll end up doing quite a bit of walking. Car rentals are easier to obtain in Livorno than in busy little Portofino.

Rome (Civitavecchia)

Port type: Gateway/Day

Tourism information office (Rome): Stazione Termini, ☎ (06) 487-1270. There is also an office in Civitavecchia at Viale Garibaldi 42 and at the port, ☎ (0766) 25348

Unless your cruise embarks or disembarks at Civitavecchia (CHEE-vee-tah-VEK-kyah), Rome's port, you'll only be able to see a small portion of the remarkable sights of the Eternal City in a day stopover. I always subtract several merit points from any cruise that makes Rome a day port. If you could walk off the ship into the very center of Rome and had the entire day to explore, you could still only scratch the surface. In reality, however, your sightseeing time in Rome is limited even farther by the rather inconvenient location of the port. Civitavecchia is about 45 miles distant from the center of Rome and, given traffic conditions, you have to allow almost three hours for the round-trip. Because of this, consider signing up for a guided excursion that will get you quickly to many of the highlights. If you do wish to go it on your own, the best method is by train. There are frequent rail connections from near the port to Termini station in the middle of Rome. Regular bus service also connects Civitavecchia with the Via Lepanto bus station near the Vatican. (Both bus and train terminals are on subway lines, so you can easily get around Rome upon your arrival.) The cost of a taxi into town is almost prohibitive.

Before describing the major sights of Rome, it should be pointed out that there are a few things of mild interest in Civitavecchia. These include the old fortifications of Forte Michelangelo, an archaeological museum and the old Roman port. However, all of these can be bettered by attractions of the same type within Rome; use them only as "fill in" sights if you have spare time in Civitavecchia.

Highlights Tour

The most important things to see in Rome are clustered in two relatively small areas. One is ancient Rome and the other is the Vatican. These two, even briefly done, will take up your entire day. The majority of **ancient Roman** sites are clustered on and around **Palatine Hill** (Monte Palatino), one of the famous seven hills of Rome. A good starting point is the single most recognizable landmark – the **Colosseum** (*Colosseo*) on the Piazza Colosseo (Metro Line B, Colosseo station). Completed in 80 AD and capable of housing 50,000 spectators, it is almost symbolic of the Roman Empire – at least its excesses. Despite shaking from earthquakes and the subway and modern traffic, sackings by barbarians, and use of its marble by Renaissance builders, it is in remarkable shape. The grace of its many arches is evident from numerous angles throughout the surrounding area, but the true feel of history really hits as you walk inside and stand where spectators watched the games. The stadium "floor" is no longer there, so you can actually peer into the labyrinth of halls and rooms that were used as staging areas. The upper level has only recently been reopened to visitors. *Monday through Saturday, 9 am to 5 pm, Sunday until 2 pm; $$.*

On the adjacent Via di San Gregorio is the impressive **Arch of Constantine** and across from there is the entrance to the **Roman Forum** (*Foro Romano*) and the **Imperial Forums** (*Fori Imperiale*). These broad open spaces are filled with the remains of countless statues (many headless), columns and temples. Virtually all are mere shadows of their former glory but, surrounded by such pieces of history, it doesn't take much imagination to picture the whole scene as it existed about 2,000 years ago. *Forums open daily except Monday, 9 am to 7 pm.* The **Palaces of Augustus, Fiavi** and the **House of Livia** are situated on Palatine Hill itself, which overlooks the Roman Forum. All are interconnected and it is sometimes difficult to determine which one you're in without a good map. Not that it matters that much. Finally, at the northern tip of this area at the far end of the Via Dei Fori Imperiale (this street begins at the Colosseum at Via di San Gregorio) are three smaller forums: the **Forums of Caesar, Augustus** and **Trajan** (which contains Trajan's Column). Here also are well-preserved remains of what is considered to be a fine early example of indoor shopping malls.

Rome (Civitavecchia) • 213

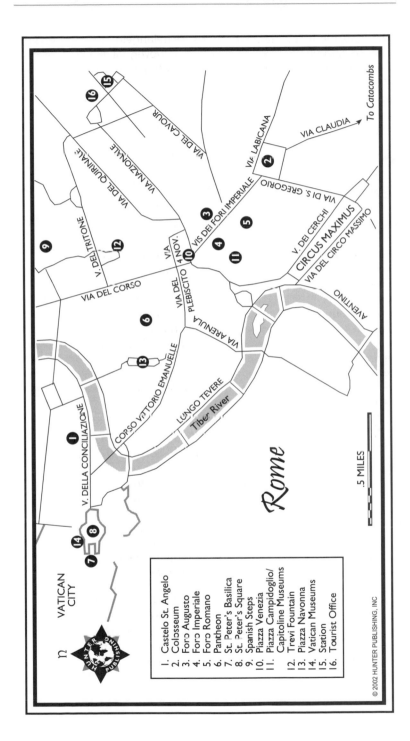

Rome

VATICAN CITY

To Catacombs

Tiber River

.5 MILES

PORTS OF CALL

© 2002 HUNTER PUBLISHING, INC

1. Castelo St. Angelo
2. Colosseum
3. Foro Augusto
4. Foro Imperiale
5. Foro Romano
6. Pantheon
7. St. Peter's Basilica
8. St. Peter's Square
9. Spanish Steps
10. Piazza Venezia
11. Piazza Campidoglio/ Capitoline Museums
12. Trevi Fountain
13. Piazza Navonna
14. Vatican Museums
15. Station
16. Tourist Office

The **Piazza Venezia** is created by the junction of Via Dei Fori Imperiale and Via Teatro di Marcello. In the middle is the huge monument to **King Victor Emanuel**. Known as the "typewriter" to its critics because of its shape, it is nonetheless a splendid piece of architecture. In front is Italy's **Tomb of the Unknown Soldier**, guarded 24 hours a day. Make your way from the forum area to the nearby **Piazza del Campidoglio**, reached by steps leading up from Via Teatro di Marcello, just south of the Victor Emanuel Monument. The plaza is the focal point for three Renaissance-era palaces in the neo-classical style. All are now museums of art that focus on classical sculpture. Each one is worth browsing through, especially the **Musei Capitolini e Pinacoteca**. *Open daily except Monday, 9 am to 9 pm; $$.* From the far end of the Piazza on Capitoline Hill there's a fine view of the ruins of the Roman and Imperial forums below.

Before moving onto the Vatican area there are four additional sights that even a day visitor to Rome should try to see – the Spanish Steps, Trevi Fountain, the Pantheon and Piazza Navona. An easy starting point is the Spagna station of Metro Line A. Turn left out of the station and go two blocks south until you reach the top of the famous **Spanish Steps**, so-called because the Spanish embassy was once located here. As you descend the steps to the **Piazza di Spagna**, you'll see why this beautiful setting is a favorite gathering place for Romans and visitors alike. Sometimes it is so crowded that it's a little difficult to see the steps! The area around the Spanish Steps is one of Rome's most fashionable shopping areas and those who have more than a day might want to browse the shops here. From the Piazza di Spagna follow Via Condotti to Via del Corso and turn left. In eight short blocks you'll come to Via della Murrate. Turn left and walk a few short blocks to the **Trevi Fountain** (*Fontana di Trevi*), Salvi's 18th-century masterpiece of flowing waters and magnificent equestrian sculptures. Celebrated in movie and song (*Three Coins in the Fountain*), this is definitely one of the more beautiful places in Rome. Head back in the opposite direction of Via della Murrate and keep going in an almost straight line (even though the street will keep changing names). It's about half a mile to the Piazza Navona, but a little more than half the way there you will come to the Piazza della Rotonda and the **Pantheon**. Built as a Roman basilica in 27 BC, this wonderfully preserved and restored structure was converted to a church. It is justly famous as one of the foremost architectural examples of Roman dome construction. The many works of art inside are also must-sees. The Pantheon houses the tomb of the artist Raphael. *Open daily, 9 am to 6:30 pm (till 1 pm on Sunday).*

Continue your journey to the **Piazza Navona**. This artistically excessive work in the Baroque style contains many fountains (the best-known is the Fountain of the Four Rivers) and statues by some of the greatest names in the history of Italian art, including Bernini. The three main fountains and their accompanying statues extend for more than 500 feet from north to south.

Anyone even remotely interested in history, architecture and the arts of painting and sculpture must go to **Vatican City**. A visit here will leave you overwhelmed not only by the beauty of the surroundings but by the historic and theological significance of this ecclesiastical enclave of Rome that covers 109 acres. Although I have put this area after the sights of ancient Rome, you may choose to do the Vatican first because large crowds come here and the later you arrive the longer the wait (assuming you're on your own). The nearest metro station is Ottaviano on Metro Line A, a little under a half-mile to the north. However, from a visual standpoint it is best to approach the Vatican on Via della Conciliazione, to the east.If you come this way you'll be greeted by **St. Peter's Square** and the magnificent colonnade that surrounds it. The square is familiar to all as the place where tens of thousands of faithful gather to hear the words of the Pope. Immediately behind the square is **St. Peter's Basilica**, easily the most recognizable religious structure in the world. No matter how many churches or cathedrals you've seen, nothing can quite prepare you for the overwhelming beauty found within the basilica. Elaborate works of art grace the massive structure. Lines on the floor act as a sort of map, showing where the naves of other cathedrals end, allowing you to further appreciate the giant size of St. Peter's. Work on the basilica was started in 1506 and completed 120 years later. You can visit the dome that was designed by Michelangelo, as well as the Vatican Crypts that document 20 centuries of church history. The famous Pietà is in one of the many side alcoves, all of which should be visited if you're to fully appreciate the remarkable museum aspects of the basilica. *Open daily, 7 am until 7 pm.*

The **Vatican Museums** (*Musei e Gallerie Pontificie*) are as superb as the basilica and take much more time to see. Although a large portion of the collection is religious art, the galleries are so vast that there is more non-religious art than is found in most fine museums. There are galleries of Egyptian, Etruscan, Greek and Roman works, among others, in addition to collections of tapestries and candelabra. Then there's the beautiful map gallery. Some galleries are largely devoted to the works of a particular artists, such as the Raphael Gallery. One of the visual highlights is certainly the two-horse Roman chariot known as the *Biga*. Of course, everyone wants to see the **Sistine Chapel** and it's no wonder. This amazing room, best known for its ceiling painting by Michelangelo, also features frescoes by at least a half-dozen other major Renaissance artists. As you wander from one gallery to the next, you will never forget that this was once a royal palace; highly ornate decoration and sumptuous architecture

PORTS OF CALL

are in constant evidence. *Open weekdays, 8:45 am to 3:45 pm; Saturday and Sunday, 8:45 am to 12:45 pm; $$.*

More Sights & Excursions

It requires a minimum of three days to do full justice to Rome. You could easily spend a week or more here and not get bored. Assuming you have time before or after your cruise (or you're on one of the relatively rare cruises that docks at Civitavecchia for more than a day), here is a quick run-through of additional sights you should concentrate on, beginning with those located inside Rome itself. Even a simple listing of Rome's many other museums and historic monuments could fill pages. Any tourist office can supply you with a brochure that summarizes the city's countless museums.

The remains of the **Baths of Caracalla** are a living museum. *Via delle Terme de Caracalla. Daily except Monday, from 9 am to 5 pm (till 1 pm on Sunday), $$.* **Hadrian's tomb** is not far from the broad avenue that leads to and from Vatican City. Today, it is better known as the **National Museum of St. Angelo's Castle** (Museo Nazionale di Castel St. Angelo) and is an art museum. While the collection isn't anything special (some of the changing exhibits are notable), it is worth a visit from an historic and architectural perspective to see the elaborate place that Hadrian had constructed for his remains. A ramp circles its way to the top of the round fortress-like structure (indeed, it was a castle for a period of time) and from there you'll get an excellent view of a good portion of Rome. *Lungotevere Castello 50; open daily except Monday, 9 am to 8 pm; $.*

Italians don't wish to glorify the memory of Mussolini, but you can't deny that he constructed a city within a city called EUR that is located south of the city center via the metro. It's a group of large and undistinguished buildings, but its **Museum of the Civilization of Rome** is excellent. The collection includes several huge and wonderful Roman sculptures as well as a beautiful scale model of Rome as it appeared at the height of the empire. *Piazza G Agnelli; open daily except Monday, 9 am to 7 pm (to 1:30pm on Sunday); $.*

A good half-day excursion (or a full day if you have the time) is to the town of **Tivoli**, home to Hadrian's Villa and the Villa d'Este. **Hadrian's Villa** (Villa Adriana) was built as a retirement home by Emperor Hadrian. During his military days he had traveled extensively and it was here that he chose to re-create many of the buildings that he had seen. The condition of various structures ranges from very poor to quite well preserved. It's a fascinating look at this period in history. Take a walk through the park-like grounds of his vast estate. *Open daily except Monday, 9 am until 90 minutes before sunset, $.* The nearby **Villa d'Este** was built as a Benedictine monastery over the site of an ancient Roman villa. It was converted into the home of Cardinal d'Este during the 16th century. Today, the home itself is of minor interest compared to the lavish grounds and wonderful fountains. In all, there are more than 500 fountains ranging from small to humongous, and from playful to extravagant. What is most striking is the overall effect, which combines natural landscaping with an incredible blend of architecture (in the form of statues and fountains) and landscaping. *Open daily except Monday, 9 am until 90 minutes before sunset; $.* Tivoli is 25 miles east of Rome via the Tivoli exit of the A-24 highway or the Via Tiburtina. Buses for Tivoli depart from the Via Gaeta near the central Termini train station.

Many visitors will want to see an example of the **catacombs**, the combination living quarters and burial grounds of the Christians during the days when they were persecuted. Many are located within a short distance of central Rome. In fact, no fewer than three are found along a one-mile stretch of the **Appia Antica**, the modern-day version of the ancient Appian Way (so well did the Romans build their roads that some of the original road bed is still in use) less than two miles south of the Coloseum. These include the **Tombo de Priscilla**, the **Catacombs of St. Sebastian** and the **Catacombs of St. Callistus**. The last of this trio is actually the middle one of the group and is probably the best example and it is certainly the most heavily visited. *Via Appia Antica 110; open daily except Wednesday, 8:30 am to noon and 2:30-5:30 pm; $.*

Finally, a worthwhile excursion can be made to **Ostia Antica**, the ancient port of Rome situated about 20 miles southwest of the city. Direct train service is available from the Termini station. While not the foremost example of Roman city ruins in Italy, the area is fairly extensive and includes commercial structures as well as apartment blocks and homes of the wealthy. I especially recommend it if you won't be getting down to Naples and, therefore, Pompeii. *Open daily, 9 am to one hour before sunset; the museum closes at 1:30 pm; $.*

Salerno/Sorrento

Port type: Day

Tourism information offices: Salerno, Piazza Vittoria Veneto, ☎ (089) 231-432; Sorrento, Via Luigi de Maio 35, ☎ (081) 807-4033

These two ports are in close proximity and your ship might call at one or the other, but almost never both. You'll probably have to tender ashore, but you'll be dropped in the heart of either town. Salerno and Sorrento are only 40 miles apart on the beautiful Amalfi Coast. You can get from one to the other by bus. However, if you plan to visit both, I recommend a shore excursion or rental car (be aware that the roads are winding and narrow). Although the best part of this region is the coastal route, we'll begin with a brief survey of the two major towns. Remember, Sorrento is close enough to Capri that you may consider a visit to the isle.

Salerno has a large port that can handle the biggest ships and is conveniently located right by the center of town. In addition, the train station is only about a mile away. Salerno may be a disappointment to some visitors. It isn't very attractive and it has only a few good points of interest. These include the elaborate **cathedral** (*duomo*) near the port, *Via Duomo; open daily 9 am to 7:30 pm*; and the **Arechi Castle**, Castello di Arechi, which stands high above the town. This old fortress offers excellent views. *Reached by steps leading off Via Resorgimento; open daily, 9 am until an hour before sunset.* A short but interesting little excursion from town is the ancient site of **Paestum**. It's not as large or spectacular as Pompeii, but it does have three well-preserved temples that are fine examples of the Doric-style of architecture. Paestum was originally a Greek colony from the 6th century BC. It came under Roman rule about 400 years later.

Almost all cruise passengers will arrive in **Sorrento** by tender. It is more of a resort town than Salerno, commercialized and almost always busier. However, it's more appealing than Salerno, and can even be described as charming. Worthwhile sights here include the **cathedral** (of course), on Sorrento's main street, Corso Italia; the lovely cloister in the **Chiesa di San Francisco**, *Via V Veneto*; and the **Palazzo Correale**. This palace, which dates from the 18th century, features an art and antique museum. The interior of the palace has some excellent murals. Outside is a pretty garden with steps that lead you down to the shore of the Gulf of Naples. *Via Correale; open Monday, Wednesday and Saturday from 9 am to 12:30 pm and 5-7 pm, and on Sunday from 9 am to 12:30 pm.* Everything that there is to see in Sorrento is within a brief walk to either the east or west of the central square, the Piazza Tasco. The square is reached from the harbor area by Via Luigi de Maio, were you'll find Sorrento's tourist office.

The road between Salerno and Sorrento often hugs the cliffs high above the Gulf of Salerno and occasionally drops down to the coast. If you've ever seen a movie where spies in sports cars race along a narrow road above the sea amid beautiful scenery (who hasn't?), this is where it was filmed! The area, known as the Amalfi Coast, is filled with natural beauty and picturesque towns that combine to make this one of the most attractive regions in the Mediterranean. Although you can see it from a bus window (either local routes or a guided shore excursion) the absolute best way to see it is to rent a car. This way, you can stop whenever you wish to take in the view.

Aside from Sorrento and Salerno, the two biggest towns along the coast road are **Positano** and **Amalfi**. Both are simply delightful – the kind of places you see on postcards. Both towns, but especially Amalfi, have their share of churches and small museums, but walking along the streets is the primary activity. One detour off the coastal road is especially worthwhile. Just east of Amalfi take the road from the shoreline that twists and climbs its way to the town of **Ravello**, which sits high above the Gulf of Salerno and offers unparalleled vistas of the coast and its towns. Take some time to see the **cathedral** and its carved lion pulpit and the crypt museum. **Villa Rudolfo** here was a temporary home for opera composer Richard Wagner, and the view from the terrace behind the house may be the best in all of Ravello. **Villa Cimbrone** has tranquil gardens that are worth a look. All of these attractions are either on or immediately off of Piazza Vescovado. Finally, Ravello has many vineyards that can often be visited. Inquire at the tourist office in the town's main square, Piazza Vescovado.

Less Visited West Coast Italian Ports

Some of the ports listed below can accommodate small vessels, but you can generally count on being tendered to and from the ship. Main towns are all within walking distance of the port.

ELBA ISLAND: This small island was originally famous because it was the place where Napoleon was exiled. Now it is overrun with more than a million visitors each year who come to relax on the beaches. The main town of **Portoferraio** has an interesting **medieval walled city** as well as the **Villa Napoleonica di San Martino**, where the banished emperor lived. *Villa open daily, 9 am to 7 pm (until 1 pm on Sunday); $.* If Elba interests you, but is not on your ship's itinerary, you can get there from Livorno by ferry (one hour) or catamaran (half-hour).

GIANNUTRI: This island sits just off the coast a bit north of Civitavecchia. It offers little more than a beach.

ISCHIA (ISH-KEY-ah): Less popular than Capri but almost as nice, Ischia is known for its beaches, thermal springs and mud baths. The **castle** (Castello d'Ischia), located on a tiny islet of its own, is the primary point of interest. Ferry service connects Ischia with Naples and Capri.

PAESTUM: Rare is the cruise ship that docks at this ancient city. Refer to page 218 (Salerno) for some details.

PALMAROLA: A beach, plain and simple. Few ships call here and those that do don't spend much time. I wouldn't bother even getting off unless you want to lie on the sand and take a dip in the sea.

PONZA: Ponza is an island group located off the coast of mainland Italy between Civitavecchia and Naples. Called Isole Ponziane in Italian, Ponza is far less popular with cruise lines than many of the other islands, which makes it more attractive to those wishing to escape from the usual tourist-beaten path. Ponza is the name of the largest island and the port town.

PORTOVENERE: Not far from Portofino, Portovenere shares many of the same attributes of the better-known Italian Riviera resort. The town itself, as well as several other surrounding towns, are all delightful villages where roaming around is the main way to spend the day. Until recently it was a rather isolated area and, even today, it is not overrun with visitors.

SAVONA: Roughly 30 miles west of Genoa, the center of Savona still retains its medieval appearance. There isn't much to do here, so I suggest a trip to Genoa (there's frequent train service) or possible travel farther west along the Italian Riviera. The one in-town sight is the **cathedral**. Make a brief visit here to see its beautiful Sistine Chapel. It's not as spectacular as the one in the Vatican, but is still an eye-pleaser.

Sicily

Fascinating Sicily covers an area of almost 10,000 square miles. It is one of the most beautiful of Mediterranean islands, as well as being the largest. The history of this Italian island goes far back – among the earliest settlers were the ancient Greeks, who established a colony at what is now Syracuse. For a time, Syracuse rivaled Athens in importance until it was finally defeated. Almost all Mediterranean cruises calling on Sicily stop at only one of the five ports detailed here. (A few more local "area" cruises might make an additional port call.) All of the cities except Palermo are located along Sicily's eastern coast and you can – on your own or via guided excursion – see two or even three localities on a full-day call. It is only 95 miles from Messina in the northeast corner to Syracuse in the southeast. Messina and Taormina are separated by only 26 miles and from there on to Catania it is another 28 miles. Palermo, on the north coast, is 140 miles from Messina and 129 miles from Catania. Palermo is connected to both of those cities via an excellent highway.

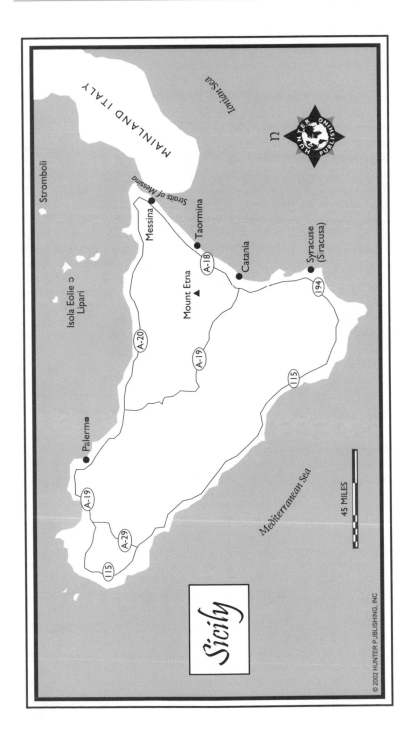

Sicily

Stromboli

MAINLAND ITALY

Ionian Sea

Isola Eolie ○ Lipari

Strait of Messina

Messina

Taormina

A-18

Mount Etna ▲

Catania

Syracuse (Siracusa)

194

A-20

A-19

115

Palermo

A-19

A-29

115

Mediterranean Sea

45 MILES

© 2002 HUNTER PUBLISHING, INC

Catania

Port type: Day
Tourism information office: Largo Paisiello 5, ☎ (095) 730-6233

Catania has more than 375,000 residents and is the second largest city in Sicily. But it wins hands down for the title of least attractive. It's industrial, grimy and run down, but an attractive side is hidden beneath this town's rough exterior. Most visitors use Catania as a jumping-off point for tours of the surrounding area (including Mt. Etna). The port of Catania can accommodate ships up to about 900 feet in length, so only the very largest mega-liners will be unable to dock. It is a little more than a quarter-mile from port to the center of town. A railroad station is about a half-mile away. In town, the central area around the **Piazza del Duomo** is the place to see. The cathedral itself is of minor interest, but the **Fontana dell'Elefante** is a rather unusual fountain that sports an Egyptian obelisk riding on the back of the animal. It is the product of the famous architect Vaccarini, whose works are on display throughout Catania, especially in this part of town. Another structure of interest because of its elaborate baroque façade is the **Palazzo del Municipo**, Catania's town hall. *On north side of Piazza del Duomo.* Closer to the port is the eerie-looking **Castello Ursino**. It's worth a brief visit. There are also some scattered Roman ruins within the center city if you're interested, but none is especially significant.

Messina

Port type: Day
Tourism information office: Piazza Cairoli 45, ☎ (090) 292-3292

Like Catania, smaller Messina (population 100,000) is not exactly the most beautiful place in Sicily. In fact, it's quite drab. Most ships that call here use it as a gateway to other nearby attractions, notably Taormina. Messina's port is right in town and there are a few things worth seeing before you head off elsewhere. Ships over 750 feet must anchor in the harbor and use tenders to bring guests ashore. The above introduction to Sicily (page 220) gives you some ideas as to possible excursions. For local trips, taxis are always available. The train station is also close by. The best part of town is centered around the **Piazza del Duomo** (does this sound a lot like Catania?), which has a lovely fountain and many interesting statues. It is also the site of the Norman-style **cathedral**, sometimes called the Norman Cathedral, originally constructed between the 12th and 15th centuries and largely rebuilt after World War II when it was almost completely destroyed. As you wander around town you'll see some small, pretty churches. The **Regional Museum** (Museo Regionale) is the local art museum. *Viale della Libertà; open daily except Sunday, 9 am to 1:30 pm, as well as 4-6:30 pm on Tuesday, Thursday and Saturday; $.*

Palermo

Port type: Day
Tourism information office: Piazza Castelnuovo 35, ☎ (091) 586-122

With almost 750,000 residents, Palermo is by far the largest city on Sicily and is the regional capital. The excellent harbor here has no fewer than nine quays to accommodate the largest of ships. The center of town is approximately a quarter-mile away and the train station is about a mile distant. Because Palermo is farther away from the quartet of possible east coast destinations, visitors to this port are more likely to spend the day in town.

From the port, stroll south on Via Vittorio Emanuele to the center of the city. At the intersection with Via Maqueda is the **Four Corners** (Quatro Canti), a good place to start your tour. The buildings surrounding this intersection all have interesting and colorful façades dating from the 17th century. In the adjacent Piazza Pretoria is the beautiful **Fontana Pretoria**, a lavish 16th-century fountain crafted by noted Florentine artists. The plaza also has the ornate **St. Catherine's Church** (Chiesa di Santa Caterina) in splendid baroque style. *Piazza Bellini; open daily, 9 am to noon and 3-6 pm.* Here you'll also find the town hall and **La Martorana**, a beautiful church best known for the Byzantine-style mosaics that grace its interior. *Piazza Bellini; open daily except Sunday, 9:30 am to 1 pm and 3:30-6:30 pm.* A little farther east from the Four Corners on Via Vittorio Emanuele will bring you to the vast Norman-style **cathedral**. *Corso Vittorio Emanuele; open daily, 7 am to noon and 4-6 pm.* Beyond that on the other side of the Piazza della Vittoria and adjacent to the Porta Nuova (New Gate) is the **Palazzo Real**. This former palace now houses the Sicilian regional government and is noted for its wonderful 12th-century Byzantine mosaics in the **Sala di Ruggero** and the impressive **Capella Palatina**, the ornate chapel. *Piazza Indipendenza; open weekdays from 9 am until noon and 3-5 pm, Saturday from 9 am to noon, and Sunday from 9 am to 10 am and noon to 1 pm.*

Syracuse

Port type: Day
Tourism information office: Via Maestranza 33, ☎ (0931) 464-255

Syracuse is home to about 125,000 people. Most of this compact city's sights are convenient to the harbor, although taxis can come in handy for some of the archaeological sites, most of which are in the **Neapolis-Parco Archaeological Zone**. *Viale Augusto; open daily, 9 am until an hour before sunset; $.* The **Archaeology Museum** (Museo Archeologico Paolo Orsi) is also nearby. It explores the Greek colonial era. *Viale Teocrito; open daily except Monday, 9 am to 1 pm; $$.* The **cathedral** (*duomo*) is built on the original site of the Temple of Athena in the attractive **Piazza del Duomo**. Also worth exploring is the medieval atmosphere on the offshore island of **Ortygia**.

Taormina

Port type: Day
Tourism information office: Palazzo Coruaja, ☎ (0942) 23243

This small town is best known for its hilltop location that affords great views of the sea and nearby **Mt. Etna**. A visit to the top of the 10,800-foot mountain and its four craters is a must. The easiest access is from Taormina (although shore excursions from Catania, Messina and Syracuse are possible as well). You can drive or hike to the top (hiking will take more time than you have available), but the cable car is the most popular way to reach the summit. Mt. Etna sometimes smokes, she was relatively inactive until the recent activity in mid-summer of 2001. The excitement didn't last long and all visitor sites were open as of press time. Even on Etna's quiet days, it's a sight that will not be quickly forgotten.

While Mt. Etna is the star of the Taormina area, there are a few other sights that make this my favorite destination in Sicily. Foremost among these is the well-preserved third-century BC **Greek Theater**. Sitting high above the sea, it is one of the most splendid ancient theater sites in all of Europe. The Romans rebuilt it in even grander proportions. It is still used for productions today. The acoustics are wonderful and the views are nothing short of spectacular. *Via Teatro Greco; open daily, 9 am until two hours before sunset; $.* Also of interest in Taormina are the **cathedral** in the Piazza del Duomo, the 15th-century **Palazzo Corvaia** (also in the plaza) and the **Trevelyan**

Gardens. The latter is in a beautiful setting overlooking the sea. Just follow the coast.

Most cruise ships that visit one or more Sicilian ports will also spend some time in scenic cruising of volcanic Stromboli and the **Aeolian Islands** (Isole Eolie). A few even call on the island of Lipari *(Tourism information office: Corso Vittorio Emanuele 202, ☎ 090 988-0095).* One of the seven volcanic Aeolians, the island of Lipari has a maze of winding streets and a medieval castle in its main town, also named Lipari. The castle is located within an archaeological park complex and has a small museum. A guided tour of the island reveals dramatic views of windswept cliffs and villages.

Italy's Adriatic Coast

Venice

Port type: Gateway/Day
Tourism information office: Piazza San Marco 71, ☎ (041) 529-8711

Few cities in the world have the magical appeal of Venice (*Venezia* in Italian), the city of water famous for its canals, gondoliers and wonderful Renaissance architecture. For sheer romanticism it rivals Paris. It is a popular destination for Mediterranean cruises, both as a day port and as a gateway. Quite a few itineraries stop overnight in Venice, giving you the better part of two days to see the sights, of which there are many. The drawback is the amount of time you spend getting to and from Venice, an entire day sailing up the Adriatic Sea and another day to get back. Keep this in mind as you select a cruise that's right for you. Venice is a splendid and worthwhile port of call, and the time you spend getting to it might be better if it includes other stops along the beautiful Adriatic coast (see Croatia for more information).

The port of Venice is large, as one would expect for a city whose very existence is based on the sea. Boat berths are in several locations, all either at or near the city center. New facilities are currently being developed so that, hopefully, all need for tendering will be eliminated within a few years. If this is a gateway city for your cruise, you will find that airport/cruise ship connections are among the most convenient and well-arranged of any port city. Public transportation is available in the form of water buses, water taxis and, of course, the famous gondolas.

We'll begin with a tour for those who have only one day here. The city's main thoroughfare is the incomparable **Grand Canal**, which winds like the letter S through Venice and is bordered by ornate palaces, beautiful churches and more. Colorful barber-shop-like poles where boats tie up line the canal. The best way to see the Grand Canal and to get from one part of the city to another is by the system of municipal passenger boats called **Vaporettos**. There are many different lines, but Vaporetto #1 is the primary Grand Canal route. **Gondola rides** are much more romantic than the crowded and somewhat noisy vaporettos, but you will pay dearly for the privilege of being serenaded by a gondolier in traditional garb. Gondolia depots are as ubiquitous in Venice as taxi stands are in most US cities. One of the most famous sights along the Grand Canal and one that you should stop at is the **Rialto Bridge**. This architectural gem is one of the city's busiest market areas and is always humming with activity. Another good place to stop is the **Galleria dell'Accadèmia**, which has a collection that includes many important pieces by Venetian artists created through the centuries. *Campo della Careta; open daily, 9 am to 10 pm (until 6 pm on Sunday); $$.* The heart of Venice is the beautiful and romantic **St. Mark's Square**, or Piazza di San Marco. This spacious plaza – usually filled with pigeons – is one of the most dramatic in Europe. Three sides of it are bordered by the brilliant architecture of the arcaded Old and New Procurias (the old administrative apparatus of the Venetian Republic) and the Library. On the west side are St. Mark's Basilica and the Palazzo Ducale (Ducal Palace). Few religious structures can match **St. Mark's Basilica**, a masterpiece of Byzantine architecture that was constructed in the 11th century. Its many domes, tile work and frescoes are wonderful beginners, but be sure to go inside the basilica museum which has, among other stunning works of art, the original bronze horses that have been copied for the main entrance. Active visitors may want to climb to the top of the bell tower, which was rebuilt at the beginning of the 20th century. Also, don't miss the **Pala d'Oro**, probably the most bejewelled altarpiece in Europe. You'll find it in the treasury behind the main altar of the basilica. *Open daily, 9:45 am to 5:30 pm (on Sunday from 2-5:30 pm); $ each for the treasury, sanctuary and bell tower.* **The Doges' Palace** was the residence of the doges who ruled the vast Venetian Republic. A busy and usually jammed self-guided tour route takes you through the main entrance and up the Giant's Staircase. Although you'll see many famous works of art in several elaborate rooms, many visitors are fascinated by the narrow and dark **Bridge of Sighs**, so called because it was where prisoners were led from the palace into the adjacent dungeons. *Open daily, 9 am to 7 pm; $$.*

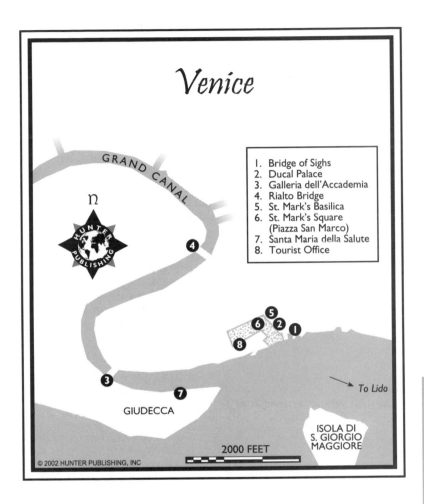

More Sights & Excursions

The first thing you'll want to do is return to St. Mark's Square to explore some of the other buildings. Also, Venice has so many beautiful historic churches that you could spend days visiting them. Some of the better ones you should consider are the **Chiesa di Santa Maria della Salute**, *near the Punta della Dogana at the entrance to the Grand Canal at Campo della Salute, $;* the **Chiesa Frari**, *Campo dei Frari, $;* and the **Chiesa del Redentore** (Redeemer), *Giudecca Island, $.* Of these three, Chiesa Frari is my choice. It contains the famous *Assumption* by Titian, whose tomb is also in the church. There are also numerous art museums and galleries to visit, including the **Peggy Guggenheim Collection**. *Calle San Cristoforo; open daily* *except Tuesday, 11 am to 6 pm; $$.* Get directions from the tourist office on the waterfront, just outside St. Mark's Square. Exploring some of the many smaller canals and backways that thread through Venice can be a lot of fun, either by gondola or by foot using the walkways that line the canals and the countless bridges. If you walk, don't stray too far from the central area as it's very easy to get lost, even if you have a good map. But perhaps that's part of the fun! Like other cities, Venice has its own unique neighborhoods. One of the more interesting is the **Jewish Ghetto**, which dates back to the early 16th century. In fact, the word "ghetto" originated here. There is a small museum about Jewish history in Venice along with a **Holocaust Memorial**. The Jewish Ghetto is located off the Grand Canal via Canale di Cannaregio. The museum and memorial are a short distance east at Campo Ghetto Nuovo.

To the east of the main group of islands which comprise Venice is the area known as the **Lido**. You can get there by a pleasant ride on Vaporettos #1, #6 and #14. The Lido is Venice's resort area and, even though its beach isn't particularly nice, it always seems to be extremely crowded. Of more interest is the island of **Murano**. There you can visit a factory where the famous Venetian glass is made. The facility has an excellent museum that displays some of the finest examples of the glassmaker's art. **Burano Island** is home to a lace factory that's open to visitors. You can reach Burano and Murano by public transportation (or through shore excursions).

Less Visited Italian Adriatic Ports

ANCONA. *Tourist information office: Via Thaon de Revel 4,* ☎ *(071) 35 8991.* Be sure to see the historic and interesting **Piazza del Plebiscito** and its **Chiesa di San Domenico**. Also of interest is the **Art Gallery** (Galleria d'Arte). *Open Monday through Saturday, 9 am to 7 pm (until 1 on Monday), and on Sunday from 3-7 pm, $.* A pretty cathedral, **Cattedrale di San Ciriaco**, is in Piazzale del Duomo. All of these attractions are located in the heart of town. Since you'll probably still have some time on your hands here, walk north from the port area to see two triumphal arches – to **Trajan** and **Clementine** – near the waterfront.

BARI. Tourist information office: Via Bozzi 45, ☎ (080) 540-4811. Of most interest is the old part of the city called **Bari Vecchia**, close to the port area. Just west of Bari Vecchia is the **Castello Svevo**, where successive rulers of this region built forts over a Roman site. Outside the castle is a nice public garden. *Piazza Federico II; open Monday from 3:30 to 7 pm, Tuesday through Saturday from 8:30 am to 1 pm and 3:30-7 pm; and on Sunday from 8:30 am to 1 pm; $.*

Croatia

Dubrovnik

Port type: Day
Tourist information office: Placa, ☎ *426 354*

This exquisite city on the Adriatic has long been a popular vacation destination among Europeans, although it wasn't well known to American travelers. The troubles in the Balkans had an adverse affect on tourism in the early 1990s when Croatia was fighting Serbia for its independence. Things are much calmer now and it has again become a place that can and should be visited. Dubrovnik's Gruz Harbor along the Gruska Obala (a street) has five berths that can accommodate all but the largest cruise ships. Port upgrades are in progress and before long the dock will be able to handle mega-liners, but for now, you'll have to use a tender to get ashore. Once there, a 15-minute bus ride will deliver you to the city center and Old Dubrovnik. I recommend that all city sightseeing be done on your own.

In addition to its historic sites, Dubrovnik and the surrounding area has many fine beaches. **Ploce Beach** is just east of the Old Town, while many others are on the **Lapid Peninsula**, closer to the harbor. Dubrovnik's many markets are delightful places to browse, especially the one in the Old Town. Dubrovnik is in a rather isolated position at the southern end of Croatia's Dalmatian coast, hemmed in by the sea, mountains and neighboring states of Bosnia and Yugoslavia (Serbia), not hot spots for visitors. Most shore excursions that do leave town just go up the coast so you're better off spending your time in Dubrovnik itself. A possible exception is a trip to **Lokrum Island**, with its gardens and monastery ruins. You could spend a bundle on a guided excursion to Lokrum, but I suggest taking the hourly ferry from just outside the Old Town for a half-day excursion.

The east end of Dubrovnik is where you'll find the walled **Old Town**. Once you pass through the **Pile Gate** you enter an entirely different world – one where time stopped several centuries ago. The main thoroughfare, the **Placa**, will bring you close to most of the major sights. In the square just beyond the gate is the pretty **Onofrio Fountain** that has occupied this spot since 1438. Pick up a map at the tourist office here. At the far end of the Placa (about a quarter-mile away) is the beautiful **Luža Square**, within which is the **Orlando Column**, which pre-dates the fountain by a couple of decades. Also here are the 16th-century **Sponza Palace** and **St. Blase's Church**, an ornate Italian baroque-style structure. A short detour a couple of blocks north will bring you to the **Dominican Monastery**. This huge building has an excellent museum. *Sveti Dominika 4; open daily, 9 am to 5 pm.* Continue south from St. Blase's on Pred Dvorom past the town hall to the Rector's Palace, which has been converted into a museum showing what life was like in 15th-century Dubrovnik. *Open daily, 9 am to noon and 3-6 pm; $.* A little farther along is the **Cathedral of the Assumption**, another baroque masterpiece. From there, head along Kneza Damjana Jude to a corner of the walled city and **Fort St. John**, now occupied by a so-so **aquarium**. *Open daily except Sunday, 10 am to 6 pm; $.* Somewhat better is the adjacent **Maritime Museum**, which chronicles the role the sea has played here. *Open daily except Monday, 9 am to 1 pm; $.* Now is a good time to visit the highlight of Dubrovnik – the 1¼-mile-long **city walls**. The walls were constructed over a period of almost 400 years beginning way back in the 13th century. They are among the most impressive you'll encounter, not only because of their excellent state of preservation, but because of their massiveness. In some places they exceed 75 feet in height. More stunning are the almost 20 different towers and bastions. The views from the top of the walls are fantastic, providing the best vistas of the city and the Adriatic Sea. *Entry to walls from the Pile Gate; open daily, 7 am to 7 pm; $.* Just outside the northeast end of the walled city via the **Ploce Gate** is an extension of the fortifications called **Fort Revelin**. The only view rivaling the one from the walls is that from **Srd Mountain**, which rises sharply from sea level to more than 1,300 feet. A winding road leads up to it and, unless you're on a guided tour, the best way to get there is by taxi. It's under two miles from the Old City.

Hvar/Korcula

Port type: Day

Tourist information offices: Hvar, Trg Sveti Stjepana (main square), ☎ 741 059; Korcula, adjacent to Hotel Korcula, at the western harbor, ☎ 715 701

Hvar and Korcula are two lovely sunny islands in the Adriatic Sea off the coast of Croatia's Dalmatia region. Internationally, these islands aren't well known, except to savvy European tourists. The Dinaric Alps on the mainland provide splendid distant views. The ports are small and transfer into town will be by tender. Once ashore you can easily explore the main towns (which have the same name as their respective islands) on foot. Korcula is the larger of the two and outside of town it offers scenic beaches and pretty winding roads. Consider a guided shore excursion if you wish to explore the countryside.

The medieval atmosphere of Hvar is its greatest attraction. Just wandering around its streets or along the attractive seafront promenade is a great way to spend a couple of hours. Highlights include the massive Gothic-style **Arsenal**, Trg Sveti Stjepana, with its 17th-century theater and two monasteries at the east and southeastern ends of town. The **Dominican monastery** has imposing ruins and a decent museum of archaeology (erratic hours). The **Franciscan monastery**, on the south side of the harbor) has an excellent collection of paintings. *Open daily, 9 am to noon and 5-7 pm.* Take some time to climb the hill to the 16th-century **Venetian Fortress** (Fortress Spanjol) that overlooks the town. Although there isn't that much to see in the fortress itself, the view from the hilltop makes the trip worthwhile. *Reached from the north town gate by proceeding through the park.*

Korcula is another fine example of a Dalmatian medieval settlement. It is believed that Marco Polo was born here, in one of the towers. In the center of town is **St. Mark's Cathedral**, an outstanding example of Gothic architecture, and the adjacent **Treasury**, located in an abbey dating from the 14th century. *Trg Sv Marka Statuta 1214; open daily, 10 am to 1 pm and 5-7 pm; treasury closed on Sunday.* Opposite the abbey is the **Gabriellis Palace** and its splendid local history museum. Also of interest in town are the remains of the city walls which you can follow along, perhaps returning by the shore.

Malta

Port type: Day

Tourism information office: 1 City Arcade (just through the main gate to the old walled city), ☎ *237 747*

The tiny nation of Malta consists of five islands. The three inhabited islands are Malta (the largest), Gozo and tiny Comino, which covers less than two square miles. The capital, main city and port of call is **Valletta**, on the island of Malta. (In the Itinerary section, you'll note that I always call the port "Malta.") This island covers some 95 square miles and has an interesting history. It has been ruled by a succession of empires and nations and traces its civilization back to 3800 BC. Its most famous time began in the 16th century when the islands were presented to the Knights of the Order of St. John of Jerusalem. Conflict with the Ottoman empire was fierce. Malta eventually passed to British control in 1814. It received its independence in 1947 after being devastated by bombing WWII. Tourism has played an important role in its current prosperity. Although there sights outside the capital and on the island of Gozo, day trippers can easily spend a day taking in the splendid sights of Valletta. If you want to venture outside the city, a guided shore excursion is recommended. If you want to travel independently, a half-hour ferry ride connects Malta and Gozo and the ferry schedules are coordinated with the bus service.

The port of Valletta was designed with tourism in mind and includes a modern terminal and five quays capable of handling big cruise ships. It is also convenient to town, which is only a quarter-mile away. Most people walk into the town center, but taxis are plentiful.

Everything of greatest interest is contained within the magnificent **walled city** that dates from the Crusader era. This is probably the best walled city in the Mediterranean – it's extensive, well preserved and filled with sights. Rhodes is the only city that can compare (see page 245). The walled city is about a mile long and a half-mile wide, so you should be able to explore it on foot on your own. The main entry point is the **City Gate**, which covers half of the peninsula between Grand Harbour and Marsamxett Harbor. It sits at the end of two streets (The Mall and Sarria Street), which provide a tree-lined parkway. The greatest of Valletta's walls face this side and consist of several major bastions as well as the **Great Ditch**. The walls continue around the peninsula and can be accessed at several points. The first attraction is the **Auberge de Castile** in Castle Square, now a government office and closed to the public. Its exterior is still worth a look. A couple of blocks east (through Castle Square and alongside the wall fronting the Great Ditch) are the pretty **Upper Barrakka Gardens**. In addition to flowers, you will be captivated by a fantastic view of the harbor from this point. Back towards the center of town are the excellent **National Museum of Archaeology** *(Republic Street; open daily, 7:45 am to 2 pm, $)* and **St. John's Co-Cathedral** on St. John Street. The latter isn't particularly impressive outside, but it does have a surprisingly lavish baroque interior. Its museum displays, among other things, a fine selection of priceless tapestries. Many of the Knights of Malta are buried here and their tombstones line the floor. A couple of blocks past the cathedral is the magnificent **Grand Master's Palace**, once the residence and offices of the Knights who ruled Malta. It still is the seat of government of Malta, now housing the Parliament. There's an extensive armory, as well as a depiction of the "Great Siege," when Malta was attacked by the Ottoman fleet in 1565. The staterooms and tapestry collection are also of great interest. *Republic Street; open weekdays, 9 am to 5 pm.* Continue towards the tip of the peninsula and you'll reach another series of walls and three more bastions surrounding **Fort St. Elmo** and the adjacent **War Museum**. If you can, walk through **Medina**, Malta's original city that dates back nearly 30 centuries.

If you have time, take in one of several multimedia theater presentations on the history of Malta. The best, called the **Malta Experience**, is located along the wall in the Mediterranean Conference Center, south of St. Lazarus Bastion. *Films start on the hour; open daily, 11 am to 4 pm (1 pm on weekends); $$.* Watersports are also a popular diversion here (best arranged on your cruise ship).

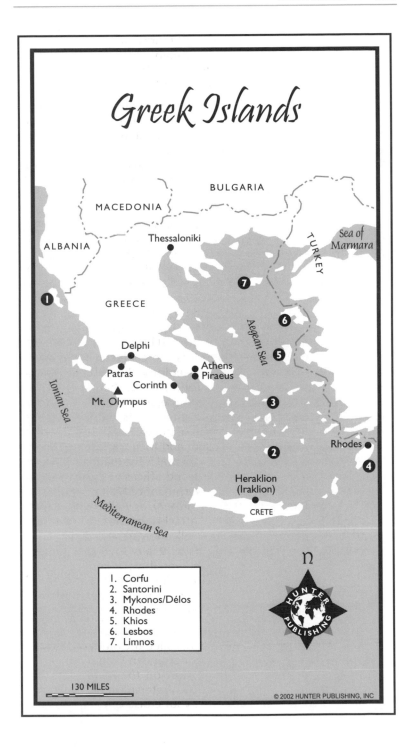

Greek Islands

BULGARIA

MACEDONIA

ALBANIA

Thessaloniki

TURKEY

Sea of Marmara

GREECE

Aegean Sea

Delphi

Patras

Corinth

Athens

Piraeus

Mt. Olympus

Ionian Sea

Rhodes

Heraklion
(Iraklion)

CRETE

Mediterranean Sea

n

1. Corfu
2. Santorini
3. Mykonos/Délos
4. Rhodes
5. Khios
6. Lesbos
7. Limnos

HUNTER PUBLISHING

130 MILES

© 2002 HUNTER PUBLISHING, INC

PORTS OF CALL

Greece & The Greek Islands

*B*ecause of the many variations in the way the Greek alphabet is transliterated into the Latin alphabet, I sometimes give more than one name for a location. This is done so as not to confuse those readers who may already be somewhat knowledgeable about Greek placenames.

Athens

Port type: Gateway/Day

Tourist information office: Amerikis 2 (near Syntagma Square),
☎ (01) 331 0561. There's also an office in the port of Piraeus,
but it is not convenient to the ship terminal.

Just as Rome evokes vivid images in the minds of people planning to visit, so too does Athens, with its famous Acropolis and other sites. It is, in many ways, the true birthplace of Western civilization. That alone would make it a desirable place to see, but modern Athens (Athíni) is also a lively and energetic city with friendly people and lots of great dining and partying. The port is located in the rather shabby industrial city of **Piraeus**. From the newly remodeled port terminal where your ship will dock, it is approximately nine miles into the heart of Athens. You can get there on your own by taxi or by walking to the train station and taking the subway. The train ride is short and inexpensive, but it is a long walk around the harbor edge to reach the station. (These options are less expensive than a guided tour.) The subway system is easy to use and takes you near most of the major sights. If you arrive by train you'll be within a short walk whatever sights you've come to see. Because of the patchwork quilt nature of street layout and the fact that many signs are in Greek only, it can be confusing to find your way around. It's a good idea to get a detailed map, preferably one of those picture maps so that you can easily spot landmarks. They're available at just about any place frequented by tourists.

Highlights Tour

Most of Athens' visitors devote much of their time to the **Acropolis**, and that's where I suggest you begin your one-day highlight tour. Most people, before they come to Greece, think that the Acropolis is the name of this particular place in Athens. In reality, Acropolis means "highest city" and it refers to any fortified area or citadel. You will encounter numerous places that are called the "acropolis" as you travel through Greece. There is little doubt, however, that the Acrop-

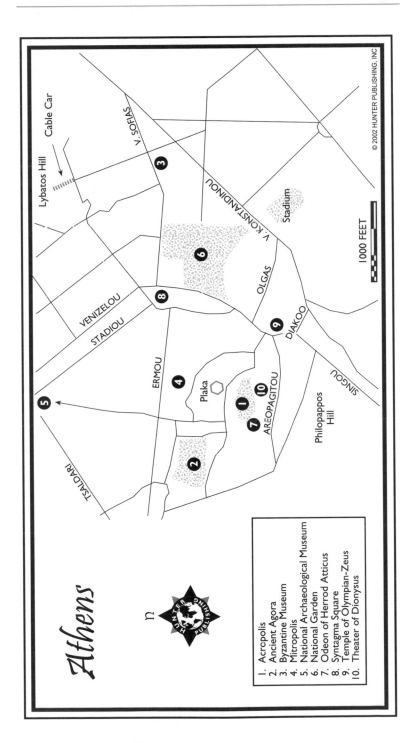

Athens

1. Acropolis
2. Ancient Agora
3. Byzantine Museum
4. Mitropolis
5. National Archaeological Museum
6. National Garden
7. Odeon of Herrod Atticus
8. Syntagma Square
9. Temple of Olympian-Zeus
10. Theater of Dionysus

© 2002 HUNTER PUBLISHING, INC

Cable Car

Lybatos Hill

V. SOFIAS

V. KONSTANDINOU

Stadium

OLGAS

DIAKOO

SINGOU

VENIZELOU

STADIOU

ERMOU

Plaka

AREOPAGITOU

Philopappos
Hill

TSALDARI

1000 FEET

PORTS OF CALL

olis of Athens is the most famous. It dominates one of Athens' biggest hills and can be seen from just about anywhere in the city. It is approached by a long winding pathway that ascends from a street called Dionyssiou Aeropagitu. Along this street beneath the Acropolis itself are two ancient theaters – the **Odeon of Herodes Atticus** and the **Theater of Dionysus**. The former is still used for concerts and is generally not open to casual visitors (but you can usually take a quick peek inside). The extensive remains of the other can be explored. *Open daily, 8:30 am until 2:30 pm; $.* Once you reach the Acropolis itself you enter through a massive entry area called the **Beule Gate** and the **Propylaia**. Then, on the top of the hill are the remains of the many temples that graced the Acropolis during the glory days of Greece. Some are in terrible disrepair, while others are quite well preserved. An ongoing restoration process means you will certainly see some scaffolding during your visit. It is easy to get a mental picture of what the Acropolis must have been like thousands of years ago. Among the more notable structures is the **Erechtheion**, with its famous columns in the form of women holding up the roof. But it's the symmetrical beauty of the **Parthenon** that is the highlight for almost everyone. Before leaving, stop by the **museum** to see the many sculptures and other artifacts that have been discovered on the Acropolis. *Open daily, 8 am until 6 pm (until 2:30 pm on weekends and holidays); $$.*

North of the Acropolis is the **Ancient Agora**, once the commercial hub of old Athens. It contains the remains of beautiful temples and many *stoas* which were, in effect, the first shopping malls. The largest has been restored to its original appearance and the interior serves as a fine museum of ancient Athens. *Open daily except Monday, 8:30 am until 2:45 pm; $.* The maze of streets immediately east of the Agora are known as **Roman Athens**. Here, interspersed with the buildings of the contemporary city, are many remains of temples, observatories and other structures that were built during the time when the Romans ruled. From Roman Athens you should continue in a generally easterly direction and you'll soon find yourself in an area known as the **Plaka**. This is the tourist capital of Athens, loaded with hotels, restaurants and shops. It is a delight to wander aimlessly here taking in the local flavors. Most of the restaurants are outdoor cafés with reasonable prices and plenty of good food. You'll likely be approached by waiter after waiter, each pushing a menu into your hands and asking you to eat at his restaurant. It's a lot of fun. At night the *tavernas* of the Plaka come alive with the sights and sounds of Greek music and dance.

The southeast edge of the Plaka is formed by the intersection of two busy streets, Dionyssiou Aeropagitpou and Amalias, one of Athens' most important thoroughfares. Cross the Amalias and go through

Hadrian's Arch into the **Temple of Olympian Zeus**. The remains of this fantastic Roman-era temple are somewhat limited today (several columns standing and a few others on their side), but the park-like setting has great views of the Acropolis and you can get a wonderful appreciation of just how massive the original temple was. *Vasilissis Olgas 1; open daily except Monday, 8:30 am until 3 pm; $.* Proceed north on Amalias past the **National Gardens**. If you think you'll have some extra time, wander in and take a break on the shade-covered benches in this mildly attractive area. Soon, Amalias reaches bustling **Syntagma Square**, the heart of commercial Athens and one of the busiest places you'll ever see! On the left is the broad square itself, and on the right is **Parliament**. Visitors aren't allowed inside the Parliament and the building itself is nothing special to look at, but on the street below is Greece's **Tomb of the Unknown Soldier**. It is constantly guarded by two soldiers in traditional military garb who march to and fro in front of the tomb. Bring your video camera! At 11 am on Sunday, a more elaborate ceremony takes places here.

At the north end of Syntagma, turn right onto Vasilissis Sofias. This is embassy row. In about 10 minutes you'll reach the **Byzantine Museum**, housed in a Florentine-style neo-classical mansion that dates from 1848. The complex has been through some modifications that allowed the galleries to sit around a pretty central courtyard. The museum has an excellent collection of Byzantine art forms (sculpture, paintings and icons, to name a few) dating from the fourth through the 19th centuries. *Vas. Sofias 22; open daily except Monday, 8:30 am until 3 pm; $.* After you've finished at the museum, walk north on Ploutarchu. This street will eventually become a series of steps as you rise towards the base station of the **cable car** that will carry you to the top of **Lykavitos Hill**, the tallest hill in Athens. At the top you'll have a superb panorama of all of Athens (assuming the weather is good and the pollution isn't too bad). If you've been quick as you tour, you still might have some time on this one-day whirlwind tour to explore some of the other sights of the hill. These include the small but lovely **St. George Church** and the **Theater of Lykavitos**. *Cable car operates from 8:30am (10:30 on Thursday) until midnight; $.*

More Sights & Excursions

You can see almost all of the major sights in Athens in just a couple of days, but there are many additional places worth your time. The first on my list is the **National Archaeological Museum**, which has a superb collection of antiquities. *28th October Street 44; Monday from 11 am until 5 pm, Tuesday through Friday from 8 am until 7 pm and weekends from 8:30 am until 3 pm; $$.* The history of modern Greece is better explored in the **National Historical Museum**, which occupies the Old Parliament building. *Stadiou at Kolokotioni; open daily except Monday, 9 am to 2 pm.* Another excellent museum is the **National Gallery of Art**. *Vas. Konstandinou 50; open daily except Tuesday, 9 am to 3 pm (10 am until 2 pm on Sunday); charge for special exhibits only.* If you can fit it into your schedule, try to spend some time in an area known as **Little Mitropolis**, northwest of the Plaka. Little Mitropolis is a bazaar shopping area. Although not like the bazaars of Turkey (which are enclosed and highly organized), browsing this open-air area is an enjoyable experience nonetheless. There's also a number of fine churches representative of the Byzantine style.

If your vessel is here overnight, you may wish to head back to the Acropolis for the nightly **Sound & Light** show, which takes place on the **Pynx Hill**. It's a popular attraction, but I don't recommend it. The narrative is boring and the illumination of the Acropolis, although a grand sight at some times during the program, is disappointing. If you do go, be sure to check the schedule to make sure you'll get the English narrative. *$$.*

If you're taking additional days here before or after a cruise, you may want to explore some of the important archaeological sites in areas away from the city. These can be done via a series of day trips from Athens or on a stay of two or three days. Guided tours are available through your cruise line or by many operators in Athens (where you can almost certainly get a better price). Or you can do it on your own via bus or rental car. Driving in Greece can be complicated by Greek road signs. To help you plan your excursions, use this mileage guide.

MILEAGE CHART	
from central Athens	
Delphi	100 miles
Sounion	40 miles
Corinth	50 miles
Nauplion	85 miles

First and foremost among the out-of-town destinations is **Delphi**. Given the distance, the reasonably good roads most of the way, and the picturesque scenery, this makes for a great day trip from Athens. It also can be reached from a number of cruise ship stops. Delphi was one of the most important of ancient Greek religious and political sites. The remains are all impressive, but especially awesome are the ruins of the round marble rotunda known as Tholos (4th century BC); the Great Altar; the treasury and stadium. The ancient Greeks believed Delphi was the center of the earth and came here to listen to the prophecies of the oracle in the magnificent natural setting between the sea and the mountains. Also relatively close to Athens is an excursion in the opposite direction (southeast) to the tip of the

Attica peninsula at **Sounion**. The natural sights are lovely here as well. Of most interest are the ruins of the **Temple of Poseidon** which, befitting Poseidon's status as God of the Sea, overlooks the Aegean. **Corinth** and the ancient city of **Mycennae** are also close (see details later under the *Less Visited Greek Ports*, below). Most people who head out to Corinth are on a lengthier exploration of the Peloponnese, including Nauplion. For some, the ultimate destination may be Olympia, but this requires an overnight stay. All of the destinations in this paragraph are described in detail under various port entries below.

Corfu

Port type: Day
Tourist information office: Rizospaston Voulefton 37, ☎ 37520

Corfu (Kérkira in Greek) is a popular resort island, although few cruise ships call here because it's located on Greece's Adriatic coast, all the way in the northwest by the Albanian border. It sits just off the Greek mainland and measures 40 miles north to south and only four east to west (except at the very north where it is widens to about 10 miles). The main town and port has the same name as the island itself. Arrival in the town of Corfu will be via tender; the port area is close to the center of town. Outside the town are some resorts and many excellent beaches. The highest point on Corfu, **Mt. Pantokratos,** measures 2,950 feet and offers splendid views. Cruise lines usually offer numerous shore excursions to the beaches, resorts and quaint towns, but you can easily explore on your own via the island's good local bus system.

Within Corfu town you can wander the crooked streets and explore the shops to pass the day. The central portion of Corfu is along the **Esplanade,** a former parade ground. The historically minded might like to visit the local **Archaeological Museum** *(Leoforos Dimokratica; open daily except Monday, 8:30 am until 3 pm; $)* and the beautiful interior of the **Church of Agios Spiridon**, west of the Esplanade off Kapodistriou. You can also take a look at the old and new **fortresses**, as well as the lovely parks and gardens. The fortresses are situated near one another along Corfu's northern edge. All of these attractions are located in a part of town known as the **Spianada**.

Crete

Port type: Day
Tourist information office: Xanthoudidou 1, ☎ (081) 228 225

It is unfortunate that more cruise ships don't make a call at **Heraklion** (Iraklion) because the island of Crete (Kríti) has many wonders and rarely disappoints visitors. (Crete sits out of the way from other Greek islands, which is the main reason few cruise itineraries include it.) Crete is 150 miles long and six to 35 miles wide. It's the largest of the Greek islands and ranks fifth largest among all Mediterranean islands. Crete was the center of the Minoan civilization, which flourished between 3000 and 1200 BC. Excavations have shown that it was on a par culturally with the civilizations of both Egypt and Mesopotamia. The main port city of Heraklion is conveniently located near the major sites of Minoan culture. It can handle several cruise ships, although there still is often a need to use tender service to reach shore. The New Harbor – where you'll touch land – is within walking distance of many of the downtown points of interest. Popular guided shore excursions from Heraklion visit traditional towns, various Minoan sites and take in the natural beauty of Crete. This includes mountains, plateaus and gorges, along with two sites that are of great importance in Greek mythology. The first is **Mount Idi**, where the great god Zeus was born. The second is **Dikteon Cave**, where the infant god Zeus was hidden from destruction by a vengeful Cronos. *Located just west of the village of Psyhro; open daily, 8 am to 4 pm; $$.* But by far the most popular excursion is to the primary Minoan site of Knossos. This is one out-of-town attraction that I suggest doing on your own; the other trips are best done by guided tour. But let's explore the city of **Heraklion** first.

About a quarter-mile from the New Harbor is the center of the city which sits to the east of a remaining section of the old city walls. The **Archaeological Museum** is just inside the walls and should be seen as a prelude to the palace at Knossos since it contains many finds from that site and the Minoan era in general. *Plateia Eleftherias; open Monday from 12:30 to 5 pm; Tuesday through Friday from 8 am until 7 pm and Saturday and Sunday from 8:30 am until 3:30 pm; $.* Not too far east from the museum in the attractive Venetian Plaza (Plateia Vinezelou) is the **Basilica of San Marco**, and the pretty **Morosini Fountain**. Immediately north of there is the stately **Venetian Lodge** (Venetian Loggia), *25 Avgoustou*. It was once a club for aristocratic gentleman and is one of many buildings from the era when Crete was ruled by the Venetian Republic. Today, it serves as the city hall. From here, head up towards the waterfront and the **Historical Museum of Crete**. This fine museum explores the history of the island from after medieval times all the way up to the present day. It's quite interesting. *Sophocleous Venizelou; open daily except Monday, 8 am until 3 pm; $.* Nearby, overlooking the Old Harbor, is the **Venetian fortress**. *Koules; open daily except Monday, 8:30 am until 3 pm; $.* This is a good place to end your city tour.

Knossos is five miles southeast of Heraklion and is the best preserved of all Minoan sites. You can reach it by taking Bus #2 from the station near the New Harbor. Departures are every 10 minutes or so. The **Palace of Knossos** is the source of the myth about the Minotaur, the part-human, part-animal beast that resided in the labyrinth beneath the palace. The ruins of Knossos were first discovered in 1900 and the reconstruction has included the palace itself along with several courtyards, royal apartments and baths. It is a wonderful place to explore, with beautiful frescoes depicting various aspects of Minoan civilization. Hours vary, so it is best to check in advance at the Archaeological Museum back in Heraklion. *$.*

The Minoan **Palace of Phaestos** predates even the one at Knossos. It isn't as large, nor has it been as well excavated. For some, that makes it more special. It's about an hour's drive into the interior and won't allow you much time for other sightseeing. If you want to visit Phaestos, consider a guided excursion.

Cyprus

Port type: Day

This island nation is the third-biggest island in the Mediterranean Sea. For some time now it has been divided between a Greek area that covers the larger part of the island and a self-declared independent Turkish state called the Turkish Republic of North Cyprus. Unfortunately, the passionate animosity that is felt between the two groups on Cyprus seems to have defied resolution and, although there has not been any fighting recently, the peace on Cyprus is sometimes fragile. Your ship may dock at **Lanarca**, but will more likely pull into **Limassol** (Lemesos). The city of most interest is nearby **Lefkosia**, the capital. Known until recently as **Nicosia**, Lefkosia is some 25 miles from Lanarca and 50 miles from Limassol (the two port cities are approximately 40 miles from one another and both are in the Greek portion of Cyprus). The port at Limassol is large enough to accommodate any ship and is about three miles from the city center. Lanarca can handle ships up to 850 feet and the dock is only 1½ miles from the town center. Taxis are available in both locations for local travel, but if you're heading to Lefkosia it's probably best to join an organized shore excursion (unless you can work out the local bus schedule with your available time). Neither port city has anything of great importance to see, but you can spend at least a short time in Limassol by strolling through the old town and visiting the 12th-century **castle** with its medieval museum. *Eirinis (near the old Fishing Harbor); open daily, 9 am to 5 pm (from 1 pm on Sunday); $.*

The sights in Lefkosia are all concentrated in the Greek portion of town. Part of the old system of walls is near the dividing line between the two sections of the city. *Tourist information office: 19 Leoforos Lemesou, in the New City,* ☎ *337-715.* The old **Venetian walls and ramparts** can be seen gracefully circling the Greek part of the old town. They aren't in the best condition, but you can get a good idea of what they were like in their heyday. Especially notable are the 11 bastions and the famous **Famagusta Gate**. I don't suggest that you wander into the United Nations-patrolled buffer zone between the two sides of the city, but do take a look at it from afar. It's enough to make you realize what the poor people of Cyprus have been going through because of ancient ethnic and national hatred. The sightseeing tour begins at Famagusta Gate. Use a good local map to negotiate the maze of streets and make your way to the **Cyprus Folk Art Museum**. Here you can see the traditional arts and crafts of the Cypriot community. *Plateia Arh Kyprianou; open Monday through Friday, 9 am to 5 pm, Saturday, 10 am to 1 pm.* Across the street is the **Byzantine Museum** and its excellent collection of religious icons. The museum complex also is home to the 17th-century **St. John's Cathedral**. Of special interest inside the cathedral are the vivid frescoes. Unfortunately, these two attractions are frequently closed to the public. Just a stone's throw to the south is the **Archbishop's Palace** which, though never open to the public, is a stately dwelling worth your time. The grounds are dominated by a huge statue of Makarios III, the national hero of Greek Cypriots. Roughly a quarter-mile to the east is the **Ledra Observatory**, a good place for a snack while you take in the best view of the city available. *Lidras & Arsinoi Streets, 11th floor; open daily, 10 am to 8:30 pm; $.* Make your final tour stop on the other side of the walls at the **Cyprus Museum**. Even if you've had your fill of Mediterranean archaeology museums, this is an excellent facility that shouldn't be missed. Well-preserved mosaics from an ancient Greek temple as well as thousands of terra cotta figures dating from the seventh century BC make this a special place. *Leoforos Mouseiou; open Monday to Saturday, 9 am to 5 pm, Sunday, 10 am to 1 pm; $.* If you have a little extra time, visit the **Municipal Gardens**, across the street from the museum, and the interesting **Faneromenis Church**. Of special note here is the beautiful mausoleum that houses the remains of heroes of the Greek War of Independence. *Faneromenis; open daily except during services.*

Katakolon

Port type: Day
There is no tourist information office.

You'll reach this small mainland port via tender. The town itself has little to offer. The reason cruise ships stop here is because of its proximity to **Olympia**, one of Greece's most important ancient sites. Since local transportation and car rentals are fairly limited, this is definitely a port where I encourage you to take one of the cruise line's guided shore excursions. Olympia is the original home of the Olympic Games. The first one (776 BC) was instituted in honor of Zeus, the principal deity of the ancient Greeks. The event grew in importance to the point where warring city states suspended their fighting when the games were on. Most of the ruins you see today date from the fifth century AD. The site is impressive (and made all the more so because of its dramatic mountain location), but this is far from the best of such sites in Greece and some of you may be disappointed (Delphi is superior to Olympia). While here you can visit the **Museum of the Olympic Games** and the **Archaeological Museum**. *Site open weekdays from 7:30 am until 7 pm and on weekends from 8:30 am until 3 pm; $ each for stadium and museum.*

Mykonos & Delos

Port type: Day
Tourist information office: No office in either location.
Inquiries in Mykonos can be made at the Tourist Police
near the ferry pier and at the museum on Delos

These two islands are less than 10 miles apart but are about as different from one another as they possibly could be. Mykonos (Mikinos) covers 35 square miles and has only 4,000 residents, while tiny Delos covers only about one square mile and consists entirely of an ancient historic site. No one (except for a caretaker) lives on Delos. At both islands your cruise ship will drop anchor just offshore and you will be taken by tender to the dock. The Mykonos dock is very close to the center of town; on Delos, the historic area is steps away from the landing. Neither location requires a guided tour. However, you may want to join a group on Myknos to visit resort areas out of town and on Delos a guide's commentary at the ruins may be beneficial. Most cruise ships stop at Mykonos, and I strongly recommend that you use this call to get over to Delos. More about that a little later.

The greatest attraction on **Mykonos** isn't a particular site but, rather, the general atmosphere of the island. In many ways, this is a typical idyllic Greek island, its town filled with white-washed buildings glistening in the splendor of the sun and the surrounding blue waters of the Aegean. The brightly painted domes (mostly blue) of local churches are about the only exceptions to the otherwise almost universal white buildings. You can get around town on foot, but taxis are available for your convenience. The town has very narrow streets filled with merchants of all kinds; gold jewelry is especially popular. Other featured items include sweaters and woven clothing. Shopping is one of the main attractions here, so learn to bargain down from the original price offering. It's easy to get a little lost in the maze of streets here and even a map doesn't offer much help. Remember, you can always work your way back to the waterfront and walk around the edge of town to the port. Within the town are several so-so museums. The **Archaeological Museum** is near the center of town and has some items from Delos as well as a series of reliefs illustrating the Trojan War. *Ayios Stefanos; daily except Monday, 8:30 am until 3 pm; $.* The **Craft and Folklore Museum** has all sorts of things representative of the local culture but, unfortunately, is open only in the evening. *Kastro; open daily, 5:30 pm (6:30 on Sunday) until 8:30 pm.* The **Maritime Museum** provides a brief look into the seafaring history of the entire Aegean. *Enoplon Dynameon; open Tuesday through Saturday, 8:30 am until 3 pm; $.* Also of interest are Mykonos' famous but defunct thatched-roof **windmills**, located near the edge of town southwest of the harbor. There are several good beaches on the island. **Megali Ammos** is the nearest to town, about a half-mile past the windmills. **St. Stephens Beach** and the far nicer **Paradise Beach** are served by taxi or buses. The latter run fairly frequently and are inexpensive, but be sure to check the schedule to make sure that you can return to your ship in time for departure.

Delos gained importance in 478 BC when the Delian League, an association of Greek city states, was founded and its headquarters placed on the island. Although the island was nominally independent for a time, it was, like the entire league, dominated by Athens. It managed to thrive under most who ruled it, including the Romans, until 88 BC when it was sacked during the Mithraditic War. It never did recover and was essentially abandoned. Excavation of the island began in the 1870's and today's site is a trip back to Delos of the second century BC. Many of the structures are in good condition, although all that is left of many structures are the floor and some partial columns. The House of Bacchus and the House of Cleopatra (both misnomers) are good examples of the homes of wealthy residents of Delos. You can also get a good idea of how the average person lived as you walk along some of the well-preserved narrow residential streets. If you have the ambition to climb to the top of

368-foot high **Mt. Kynthos**, you'll be rewarded with outstanding views of the ruins and the sea. There are also some ruins at the top. The ascent is via a combination of trail and stairs. Back down below towards the northern end of the ruins area is Delos' small but excellent museum that houses items that have been found on Delos. Among the artifacts in the museum are many of the original stone lions that once lined the Avenue of the Lions. There is a gift shop at the museum, the only shopping available on the island. The historic area will always be open when your ship calls. ☎ *(0289) 22259; $.* To get back to Delos from Mykonos, there are two options. The easiest is to take a guided shore excursion offered by the cruise line. Far less expensive, however, is to take the local ferry that runs frequently from Mykonos harbor. The trip is short. Allow about three to four hours for the round-trip excursion on your own. Thus, if time is short, you may be better off on a guided excursion, rather than taking a chance of missing your ship's departure.

Rhodes

Port type: Day

Tourist information office: Plateia Rimini (main square at north entrance to walled city), ☎ *35945*

The largest of the commonly visited Greek islands, Rhodes (Rodos) is a beautiful island that sits just a few miles from the Turkish coast. It's about 45 miles long and 22 miles across at its widest point. The Atavirus Mountain here rises to 4,000 feet above sea level. Rhodes' history is one of conflict between the Greeks and the ancient Persians, as well as the Ottomans and the modern Turkish state. Its numerous historic attractions cover more than two millennia and include ancient sites as well as many from the era of the Crusaders. The modern port of Rhodes has been serving seafarers since the beginning. Rhodes was once home to one of the seven wonders of the ancient world – the Colossus of Rhodes – a giant statue that guarded the ancient city's port until it fell victim to an earthquake. Rhodes was ceded to Greece in 1947 from Turkey.

The largest ships can generally dock right outside the city walls and the only time you'll have to use a tender is when there are too many ships to be accommodated at the dock. Rhodes City is very close to the dock, so there's absolutely no reason to take a guided tour; you can see more on your own. However, Rhodes is a fairly large island with some interesting attractions out of town. Here, too, cruise line excursions can be avoided by simply taking the cheap local bus system. Two nearby bus terminals are located just outside the walls in the heart of the New City, near the city market along Papagou Street at Rimini Square. Check at either station for schedules and routes that you might need. The most popular excursion, either by guided tour or on your own, is to Lindos on the southern coast (more about that later). Let's take a look at the wonders of Rhodes City (or **Ródhos**, as it is called in Greek).

Walking inside the walls of Rhodes is like taking a journey back in time. Even though you will encounter hundreds of merchants anxious to sell you just about anything, you can't help but feel the lure of history in almost every building. From the dock you will enter the city through **St. Catherine's Gate**, one of several old gates still in use. The sturdy walls of Rhodes are quite a sight. Most of them are surrounded by a broad moat (it never had water in it) which today is a park-like area that's good for a stroll and is made pretty by the abundantly colorful and showy flowers that grow here. The streets within the Old Town are narrow and often confusing, but you can navigate by using the walls as a guide. An important means of getting around is via the street that runs just inside the wall from St. Catherine's Gate, past the Marine Gate and on to the **New Gate** at the north side of the walls. This leads into the harbor and New Town area. Left off Sokratous, a main thoroughfare and major shopping avenue, is the historic **Avenue of the Knights**. The street once housed the various facilities of several different orders of crusader knights. Today you'll see workers sitting at their computer keyboards, but the cobblestone street looks much as it did 500 years ago. A walk along it is a must. At the end of the street is Rhodes' single most important attraction, the **Palace of the Grand Masters**. As was the case in Valletta on Malta, the palace was the seat of government under the crusader knights. The palace is sparsely furnished, yet still extremely impressive, with thick walls and vaulted ceilings. There are also excellent exhibits about Rhodes in a part of the palace. *Open Tuesday through Friday from 8:30 am until 7 pm and Saturday and Sunday from 8:30 am until 3 pm; $.* You'll see the walls of Rhodes many times during your stay, but nothing can beat a tour of the walls themselves. Unfortunately, these are given at infrequent and rather unpredictable intervals. Your best bet is to inquire at the Palace of the Grand Masters, one of the access points for tours.

Other important and worthwhile sights within the old city are museums of archaeology and decorative arts. The **Archaeological Museum**, *Museum Square (Plateia Mouseou)*, is housed in the former Hospital of the Knights. The architecture of the building makes it worth seeing, and the collection of ceramics, coins and sculpture is an interesting and educational journey through Hellenistic culture. *Plateia Mouseou; open Tuesday through Friday from 8:30 am until 7 pm and Saturday and Sunday from 8:30 am until 3 pm; $.* The **Museum of Decorative Arts** (*Plateia Argykastron; open Tuesday* *through Saturday, 8:30 am until 3 pm; $)* features items found in Rhodian houses.

Before leaving the Old City you should also take a brief look at the following items of interest at either end of Sokratous street. By the Marine Gate end is the busy square known as **Plateia Hippocrates,** which has many wonderful examples of typical Rhodian-style architecture. In the middle of the plaza is the **Castellania Fountain**. At the other end of Sokratous is the **Mosque of Suleyman**. Finally, at **Plateia Symis** (Symi Square), the **Municipal Art Gallery** has works by local artists. *Open Tuesday through Saturday, 8 am until 2 pm; $.*

Outside the old walls beyond the New Gate in the New Town you can spend some pleasant time wandering around the central market and **Mandraki Harbor**. The north entrance to the harbor is flanked by two tall columns each topped by a deer. This has become the symbol of Rhodes.

The bus ride from Rhodes City to **Lindos** is pleasant, although it's only near the end that the scenery becomes interesting. You get excellent views of the Aegean, as well as several resorts located near Lindos. The small town of Lindos isn't very important today, but it once was a major settlement during the Greek colonization period of the seventh and sixth centuries BC. The **Acropolis of Lindos** sits impressively atop of a huge 375-foot-high rock outcropping. From the bus station, walk through a narrow lane lined with shops and street vendors, part of which is covered. Simply follow the signs leading to the Acropolis. The path climbs steeply in some places (physically challenged visitors will have difficulty) and eventually becomes a staircase (292 steps) that ascends the hill to the entrance. The impressive fortress that you see on your way up was built in the 14th century. However, some notable ancient ruins lie within the fortress itself. Among the sights are a Byzantine church, a temple from the Roman period, several *stoas* (colonnaded public areas) and the magnificent architecture of the main temple *propylaia* (vestibules). In addition, you'll enjoy a magnificent view of the Aegean on one side of the fortress and the town below on the other. I highly recommend a visit to Lindos. Traveling independently, you'll need to allow a minimum of three hours, including the round-trip transportation. *Acropolis open daily except Monday, 8:30 am until 2:45 pm; $.*

PORTS OF CALL

Santorini

Port type: Day

There is no official tourist information office but you can make inquiry at the Tourist Police office in the main square in Upper Fira

The beautiful island of Santorini, called Thira by the Greeks, covers approximately 75 square miles and is home to about 12,000 people. The entire island is actually a portion of a volcano's rim. The last eruption, around 1,500 BC, is among the biggest that occurred during that period of recorded history. There are some historians who believe that the legendary civilization of Atlantis was actually on Santorini prior to the eruption. Santorini is the most stunning of the Greek islands and the sight of it is unforgettable as your ship comes into the caldera that now serves as the port area. The rocky cliffs that surround the crater rise a thousand feet above the surface of the water. From a distance you will see a narrow band of white across the top of the cliffs in several places. It almost looks like snow, but a closer look will reveal the white-washed houses so common on the Aegean islands.

Your ship will probably weigh anchor and transfer to the port of Fira will be via tender (although some smaller vessels can actually dock portside). All the cruise lines offer shore excursions to various parts of the island, but I recommend exploring independently. The town of Fira can easily be explored on foot, while inexpensive bus rides depart frequently for other parts of the island from a central terminal in the heart of Fira, near the main square of Plateia Theotokopoulou. The main street in town is 25th Maritou and it intersects the square. You'll set foot on land in the lower town and will need to ascend to the upper town, where everything to see and do is found. There are three ways to reach the upper town. The easiest is aboard the steep cable car that runs continuously throughout the day and makes the climb or descent in a couple of minutes. The view en route is gorgeous. You can also zig-zag up the winding trail via donkey. The cost for the cable car or donkey is very little. Your final option is to walk. You'll use the same route as the donkeys – and donkeys have the right of way! The hike isn't overly difficult if you're in decent shape.

Although Fira is the largest town on the island there aren't that many attractions within its narrow and often maze-like streets. Shopping for jewelry, sweaters, crafts and works of art is a popular activity. There is a small **Archaeological Museum** *(Dekigala, opposite bus station; open daily except Monday, 8 am to 2:30 pm; $)*, but the **Megaro Museum** is more interesting. It has pictures of Fira before and after a major earthquake that occurred in 1956. *Erythrou Stavrou, behind the Catholic monastery; open Monday through Sat-*

urday, 10:30 am to 1:30 pm and 5-8 pm, Sunday, 10:30 am to 4:30 pm; $.

There are two interesting excursions from Fira, one at each end of the island. To the south is **Ancient Akrotiri**, the site of an old civilization that some believe was Atlantis. Excavations are in a relatively early state so you won't see a great many large buildings, but what is there is quite fascinating. The bus to Akrotiri from Fira departs hourly and the ride takes about 40 minutes each way. En route you'll have numerous wonderful views of the port area. In fact, you'll be able to see your cruise ship anchored in the vivid blue waters from many different angles as the bus winds its way up and around the southern portion of the island. *Akrotiri site open daily except Monday, 8 am to 8 pm; $.* The second suggested excursion (which, like Ancient Akrotiri, will also always be available via guided shore excursion) goes to the most northerly part of the island and the town of **Oia**. The trip takes about half an hour each way as the way travels atop a high ridge. You'll have views of the Aegean to the left and right. Oia is a quaint little town perched at the very edge of the cliff. The view of the port areas and almost the entire island from here is the best of any on Santorini. You can pick out Fira if you have binoculars (or sharp eyes). Activities in Oia are shopping and walking around the pretty dream-like town. Some of the streets are actually steep stairs descending below the top of the cliff. Again, it is fairly easy to get lost for a short time but the whole town isn't that big and you'll eventually work your way back to familiar ground. Buses run regularly, but be sure that you allow enough time to get back to the ship.

Santorini has several wineries that are open to the public on an irregular schedule. If you like this sort of activity, sign up for a guided shore excursion to ensure the winery is open. Most island tours (and definitely those going to Akrotiri) include a winery on their half-day itinerary.

Less Visited Greek Ports

With its many inlets and numerous islands, the selection of ports in Greece seems unlimited. There are more ports available here than in any other Mediterranean country. In fact, so many are visited by just a few ships that I have room only for a brief description of each. Tenders will almost always be necessary to get to and from the ship in these ports, although some smaller vessels will be able to dock. Distances from the port to town centers are usually quite modest.

AGHIOS NIKOLAOS. *Tourist information office: located by the bridge in the port area,* ☎ *22 357.* This interesting little town sits near the eastern end of Crete. Although not nearly as popular as Heraklion, there is little doubt that Aghios Nikolaos has been "discovered" and it is becoming increasingly used by cruise ships. The town isn't old, especially by Greek standards, but it has a very pleasant setting on the Gulf of Mirabello. **Lake Voulismeni**, in the center of town, is sometimes called the Bottomless Lake, even though it is only about 200 feet deep. There is an **archaeological museum** too. *Odos Palaiolagu; open daily except Monday, 8:30 am to 3 pm; $.*

AMORGOS: One of the Cyclades Islands, Amorgos lacks any grand and famous monuments to the past, but offers many lesser ruins to explore both in and around the town. It has fine beaches, classic white-washed houses and is less crowded than most Greek island communities. The **castle** (constructed by Venetian invaders) and the Byzantine monastery of **Hozoviotissa** are the most important sites. *Both are open daily, 8 am to 1 pm and 5-7 pm.*

CEPHALONIA (Seh-Fel-low-nyeh): This Ionian island sits to the south of Corfu. It doesn't have a great deal of interest to the visitor. However, there is a pleasant beach and uncrowded resort area.

CORINTH: This city is on the Greek mainland in the Peloponnese. There is little to recommend modern Corinth although its location is picturesque. Visitors come to see **Ancient Corinth** and the neighboring **Acrocorinth**. Both are excellent archaeological sites situated about five miles from the city. *Open daily, 8:45 am until 7 pm; each $.* The **Corinth Canal** is also worth visiting while you're here.

ERMOUPOLIS: On 85-square-mile Siros Island, this town is one of the more populous and industrialized you'll find in the Cyclades. As a result, it isn't particularly attractive and there isn't much to see either.

GYTHION: Also on the Peloponnese, about 25 miles south of Sparta (although there's little at Sparta to see). Gythion, a small offshore island (no more than a few hundred feet long) has an interesting church and good beaches. The island is, according to Greek mythology, the place where Helen was held captive when kidnapped by Paris. The **Tzanetaki Tower** in town dates from around 1700.

HYDRA (IDHRA): One of the smaller Cycladic Islands, quaint Hydra is something of an artist's colony – not surprising considering its idyllic rocky setting. There are no cars on the island, so you can hike or take a donkey ride to the mountaintop **Monastery of St. Constantine**. The frescoes here are as outstanding as the views.

ITEA: This small and mostly uninteresting mainland port town's major merit is that it is very close to the famous ancient site of Delphi (see page 238 for details). The town of **Galaxidhi** is adjacent to Itea and is sometimes used by cruise ships as an alternate port, closer to

Delphi. Another such port is **Loutraki**. Whenever you see any of these in an itinerary, just think "Delphi" – that's where you'll be heading. Of course, if your ship stops here, then there is no need to arrange an excursion to Delphi from Athens.

KALAMATA (KALAMAI). *Tourist information office: Polyvriou 5,* ☎ *21-700.* On the southern coast of the Peloponnese, Kalamata's history is associated more with medieval Greece than with the ancient city states. There is a well-preserved 13th-century **fortress** (kastro) above the town. *North of Plateia Ypapantis; open Monday through Friday, 10 am to 1:30 pm.* There are also several religious structures (a monastery and churches) that are well decorated with Byzantine mosaics and colorful frescoes. Excursions can be made to ancient **Sparta** from Kalamata, but be forewarned that there is little left from that era as the Spartans did not build imposing cities.

KÉA: A small island near the Attic mainland (under 50 miles from Athens' port of Piraeus), Kéa is a quaint romantic place with fine beaches and old windmills. Of special note is the huge **lion carving** in the mountain face above the town. It dominates even the fine **Venetian-era castle** (which is generally closed to the public). Walking around the castle is a nice way to spend some time. There are also some ancient ruins to be seen at nearby **Agia Eirene**.

KHÍOS (CHIOS). *Tourist information office: Kanari 18,* ☎ *44389.* This island measures 30 miles in length and averages about 10 across. Located near the Turkish coast, Khíos is as a major production center of wine and olives. Its historic sites range from remains of some of the powerful ancient city states that flourished here through the 11th-century buildings of the Seljuk Turks. **Nea Moni** is a splendid 11th-century monastery with Byzantine mosaics. On a more somber note are the bones of some of the monks that were killed during the Turkish occupation. *Located about 10 miles west of the main town.*

MONEMVASIA: This quaint town with a pretty setting is situated on the Greek mainland at the southern end of the Peloponnese Peninsula. It's a good example of rural Greece, but you won't find many significant historic sites nearby.

NAUPLION (NAFPLIO). *Tourist information office: 25 Martiou,* ☎ *24-444.* Situated on the east coast of the Peloponnese, Nauplion (NO-plee-on) is one of the more interesting mainland ports. It's not a common cruise ship stop, but it's a pretty place with some nice sights. Two huge fortresses line the south shore of the town, the **Akronafplia Fortress** and the **Palamidi Fortress**. The former is the oldest and dates from Venetian times, while the latter sits atop a 700-foot-high rock from which there are spectacular views. There are 999 steps to the top of the rock, so you might want to take a taxi. In town there are several museums with collections on art, archaeology

PORTS OF CALL

and military history. Nauplion is also an excellent base for excursions to important nearby ancient sites such as those around Corinth (see above) and for Mycennae. ☎ *0751/76585; open daily, 8 am until 7 pm except on weekends when it closes at 3 pm; $.*

PAROS. *Tourist information is available at kiosks by the port.* Another member of the Cyclades group of islands, Paros has many small and lovely villages, as well as uncrowded beaches and resort areas. The main town has some interesting Greek churches. The best place to visit during the summer is **Petaloudes**, known as the Valley of the Butterflies because of the countless numbers of these colorful creatures that fill the area.

PATMOS: One of the Dodecanese Islands, Patmos is a hot spot for beachgoers, but those who love scenery will also find something to please them. The main sights are located, respectively, one and two miles south of the Skala Port in the town of Hora. These are the **Monasteries of St. John the Theologian** and **St. John the Apocalypse**. The first monastery includes the cave where St. John penned the Book of Revelations. The Apocalypse is of less historical significance but has a wonderful collection of ecclesiastic treasures. *Both are open from 8 am to 1 pm (to noon on Sunday) and from 4-6 pm on Tuesday, Thursday and Sunday; $.*

SAMOS: A fairly large island just off the Turkish coast opposite Kusadasi (local ferries connect the two). The largest town and the island share the same name. The known history of Samos dates back before the fifth century BC. This 300-square-mile island is dominated by the steeply rising 4,701-foot **Mt. Kerketéus**. The archaeological museum here is one of the best in the Greek islands. *Platia Dimarhiou; open daily except Monday, 8:30 am to 3 pm; $.* The old part of town, called **Ano Vathi**, is worth exploring.

SERIFOS: The main town on the Cycladic island of the same name, this is a charming and pretty place. The town is, like many in the islands, situated on top of a steep mountain and the houses are all painted white. While Santorini and Mykonos are usually regarded as typical Greek islands, Serifos can justify its own claim for that title. The advantage here, for some, is that it is still far less commercialized. Don't fret, though – you can still find places to shop.

SIFNOS: Another one of the Cyclades, Sifnos is a generally quiet island compared to many of its sister islands. It is known as a center of Greek arts and crafts and, hence, shopping is a major visitor activity. The monastery of **Hrysopigis** in the resort town of Platys Gialos is the major attraction. It has an excellent collection of beautiful icons and is located on a high point overlooking the Aegean approximately four miles from the port.

SKIATHOS: This island is part of the less-visited Sporades Islands. The majority of tourists here are European. It's basically just a good resort area.

THESSALONIKI. *Tourist information office: Plata Aristotelous 8,* ☎ *271-888.* Situated in the northern part of the Greek mainland (in the region known as Macedonia), Thessaloniki is the second-largest city in the country, with more than 750,000 residents. You can easily fill a day here by seeing several notable churches (including **Agios Dimitrios, Panagia Ahiropitos** and **Osios David**), as well as the city's most notable **Museum of Byzantine Culture** in the stunning **White Tower.** *Leoforos Stratou 12; open daily, 8:30 am to 2 pm; $.* There's also a good **archeological museum.** *Intersection of Tsimiski & Trituis septemvrion; open daily, 8 am to 7 pm (from 12:30 pm on Monday); $$.*

VOLOS. *Tourist information office: Plateia Riga Fereou,* ☎ *23 500.* Set on the northern mainland astride the pretty Gulf of Volos, this city of more than 110,000 people (one of the largest in Greece) has a few places of interest and an extensive waterfront that's great for strolls. The **Archaeological Museum** has a respectable collection. *Athanasaki 1; open Monday-Saturday, 8:30 am to 3 pm, except on Sunday when it is open from 9:30 am to 2:30 pm.* For a change of pace (and for something better), visit the **Kitsos Makris Folk Art Center.** Exhibits and demonstrations vividly portray the diverse folk art of Greece. *Kitsos Makris 38; open Monday through Friday, 8:30 am until 2 pm.* Volos is gateway to many interesting excursions too. The nearby ancient cities of **Pagasae** and **Demetrias** are a good choice, or you can opt for the more unusual trip to **Metcora,** where numerous monasteries are perched precariously atop cliffs – actually rock pillars – that tower more than a thousand feet above the sea. Although you can get to most of these "out of town" destinations by public transportation, a guided excursion would be far easier for most visitors.

Turkey
Bodrum

Port type: Day

Tourist information office: Iskele Meydani (you will see this term in many Turkish towns since it refers to the main square), ☎ *(252) 316-1091*

For many years Bodrum was a sleepy little town. It's no longer very small and about as far away from sleepy as you can get in Turkey without going to Istanbul. Bodrum is always bustling with throngs of people who come here to take in the sun and sea and to do some partying. In fact, a large number of cruise passengers come here only for the resort aspects of Bodrum. Shore excursions often visit more traditional nearby Turkish villages or take you to outlying beaches. However, there are some things to see within Bodrum itself. You might even have time to enjoy these things in addition to a shore excursion. Transportation into the port will be by tender. Once ashore, most things are pretty close at hand, including the ubiquitous shops and vendors.

Bodrum goes way back in history. In fact, the **Mausoleum** (the tomb of King Mausolus) was one of the original Seven Wonders of the Ancient World. It has been destroyed on several occasions by both natural causes (earthquakes) and by man (over-exuberant Crusaders). But you can still visit what is left. Some visitors who make this trip are disappointed, but those with a good sense of history will appreciate them. *Saray at Turgutreis Caddesi; open daily except Monday, 8 am to noon and 1-5 pm; $.* In far better shape is the former **Castle of St. Peter** that dates from 1402. Today it houses an outstanding museum devoted to underwater archaeology. The prize piece in its collection is a well-preserved shipwreck that is thousands of years old. *On promontory between the ancient harbor and Kumbahçe Bay; open daily except Monday, 8:30 am to 5 pm; $.*

Cyprus

See the entry for Cyprus on page 241.

Istanbul

Port type: Gateway
Tourist information office: At cruise ship terminal,
Karaköy Yoku Salonu, ☎ (212) 249-5776;
or in Sultanahmet at Sultanahmet Meydani, ☎ (212) 518-8754

Few cities in the world have a more colorful and exciting history than Istanbul. Strategically located between the Black and Mediterranean Seas, it has long figured in struggles for empire. As Constantinople, it was the capital of the Byzantine Empire and carried on many of the traditions of the Roman Empire long after it fell in the west. The Ottoman sultans were the successors to the splendors of Istanbul and their transformation of the city from Eastern Orthodox into an Islamic one is evident wherever you go. Although modern-day Turkey has moved the capital to Ankara, Istanbul is still the epitome of this nation and its history and culture. Here, women in mini-skirts share the same sidewalks with women covered from head to toe in traditional Islamic garments and the sounds of the call to prayer at countless mosques vie with the blaring boom boxes of equally countless street vendors. At times disconcerting, the cultural shock usually winds up being a sheer delight and valuable experience for the American visitor.

Highlights Tour

Your cruise ship will tie up in port and tenders are never required. Karakoy Marine Terminal is not far from the center of the historic city (you can clearly see it across the bustling Golden Horn with its constant boat traffic) or the commercial center of the Taksim Square area. If your ship is visiting for the day, you could walk along the waterfront and cross the Galata Bridge, then walk or take the new tram to Sultanahmet, the heart of your tour. If this is your gateway city and you have luggage to haul, it is better to take a taxi. As is the rule throughout Turkey, never accept the price that a taxi driver quotes you at the outset – always bargain to get a lower fare. Anything over $5 is too much to get to either Taksim or Sultanahmet, two likely destinations. I always try to discourage use of expensive guided tours except for those taking you to destinations farther afield from the city center. A good map is very helpful in negotiating Istanbul's streets.

The fascinating history of Istanbul comes alive in the **Sultanahmet** area, a small point of land (under two square miles) formed by the junction of three important bodies of water: the Golden Horn, the Bosporus, and the Sea of Marmara. This is the heart of the city for visitors, especially those who will have only a day or two to explore. In fact, everything except the last attraction of this suggested one-day highlight tour is within Sultanahmet and even the lone exception isn't far from it.

The tour begins with what will probably be the undisputed highlight of Sultanahmet and Istanbul, **Topkapi Palace**. This is where powerful Ottoman sultans directed their empire. Before going inside the extensive palace grounds you will see the beautiful **Ahmet III Fountain**. This is a fine example of Istanbul's fountains, which are unlike their European counterparts. Originally designed as a place to wash the hands and feet before entering a mosque (or palace), the fountain lies underneath an exquisitely decorated "dome" and dispenses water from taps around its edge. The vast Topkapi Palace complex is entered through an impressive gate and consists of many different structures (succeeding sultans each contributed their own additions). The buildings, most of which can be visited, surround several attractive park-like courtyards. The interiors range from simple to ornate and there are several collections of jewelry and other stunning possessions of the sultans. The most popular portion of the palace, however, is the **Harem**. This section can be seen only via guided tour – the demand is high so try to get there early. *Gülhane Park; open daily except Tuesday, 9:30 am to 5 pm (Harem closes a half-hour earlier); $.* Topkapi itself sits behind a wall in a large park. On the west edge of the park are the excellent **Archaeological Museums** that offer a huge collection of artifacts. Displays are housed in several different buildings and among the highlights are the sarcophagus of Alexander the Great and a complete temple to Athena. The civilizations of Sumeria, Babylonia, Assyria and the Hittite Empire are all explored. *Gülhane Park; open daily except Monday, 9:30 am to 4:30 pm (Tiled Pavilion closes at noon; Ancient & Oriental arts section is open from 1 to 5 pm); $.*

From the museum it is only a few blocks south to the **Hagia Sophia** (officially known as the **Ayasofya Museum**). Originally built as a Christian church, it was converted to a mosque before becoming a museum. The fourth-century structure isn't particularly beautiful, but it is sure to impress with its oversized architecture. The dome, for example, is more than 175 feet high. Be sure to climb the several flights of stairs to the balcony for the best view (and a true feel of just how big this place is). Don't leave the upstairs before seeing the mosaic tile art on some of the walls. *Aya Sofya Square; open daily except Monday, 9:30 am to 4:30 pm; $$.* In front of the Hagia Sophia is a pleasant park, on the east side of which is a government-owned **carpet gallery**. It is housed in the former Hurrem Sultan baths (also known as the **Baths of Roxellana**) and is also architecturally interesting. This is a good place to look at authentic Turkish carpets without being hassled to buy. And, if you do wish to purchase, the prices here are honest. *Ayasofya Meydani; open daily, 9:30 am to 5 pm.* The Imperial Sultanahmet Mosque is known to everyone as the **Blue Mosque** because of the many blue tiles found throughout the interior. If you have time to see only one active mosque while in Istanbul, this should be it. The arrangement of all mosques (both the courtyards, ablutions fountains, and the interior) is similar. This one is especially beautiful. As a sign of respect, dress modestly and avoid mosques during prayer times, especially on Fridays. *Open daily, 9 am to 5 pm.* To one side of the Blue Mosque is an open area called Sultanahmet Square, more commonly known as the **Hippodrome**. The site of a vast stadium during the days of Constantine, the park-like setting is now a good place to take a break from walking. Of interest within the Hippodrome are the **Obelisk of Theodosius** and the **Column of Constantine**.

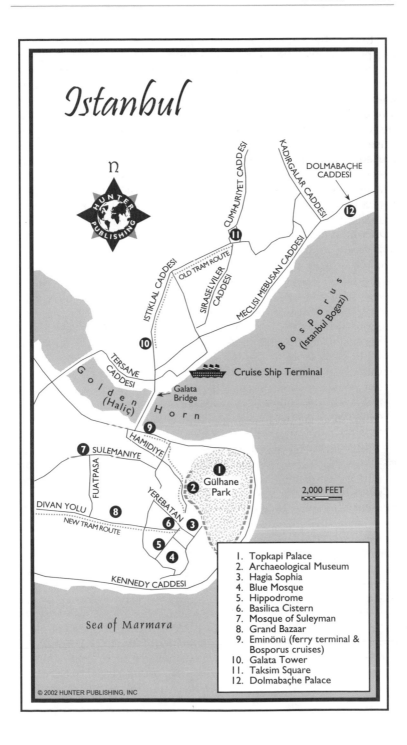

Istanbul

n

Cruise Ship Terminal

Galata Bridge

Golden Horn (Haliç)

Bosporus (Istanbul Bogazi)

Sea of Marmara

Gülhane Park

2,000 FEET

CUMHURIYET CADDESI
KADIRGALAR CADDESI
DOLMABAÇHE CADDESI
ISTIKLAL CADDESI
OLD TRAM ROUTE
SIRASELVILER CADDESI
MECLISI MEBUSAN CADDESI
TERSANE CADDESI
HAMIDIYE
SULEMANIYE
FUATPASA
DIVAN YOLU
NEW TRAM ROUTE
YEREBATAN
KENNEDY CADDESI

1. Topkapi Palace
2. Archaeological Museum
3. Hagia Sophia
4. Blue Mosque
5. Hippodrome
6. Basilica Cistern
7. Mosque of Suleyman
8. Grand Bazaar
9. Eminönü (ferry terminal & Bosporus cruises)
10. Galata Tower
11. Taksim Square
12. Dolmabaçhe Palace

© 2002 HUNTER PUBLISHING, INC

PORTS OF CALL

A block north of the Hippodrome at the intersection of Yerebatan Caddesi is the **Basilica Cistern** (Yerebatim Sarnici). More than 300 graceful columns (many elaborately decorated) support the vaulted ceiling of this former reservoir beneath the streets of Sultanahmet. The dim lights and playing of music make it kind of fun to visit, although little children might be spooked. *Yerebatim Caddesi; open daily, 9 am to 4:30 pm; $.* Even on a single day in Istanbul you must allow some time to see the **Covered Bazaar** (Karpali Çarşi). This is the largest of Istanbul's many bazaars and is more commonly known as the **Grand Bazaar**. Located in the Beyazit neighborhood, just west of Sultanahmet, you can walk here but it's quicker and easier to take the modern tram (called the New Tram) for a couple of stops from the Sultanahmet station to the Beyazit station. The Grand Bazaar is a world in itself, with more than 4,000 merchants under one roof. It is a mélange of colors and sounds, a feast for the senses. Don't mind the constant attention you get from vendors, which are no worse than those on the streets. You'll get used to it. If not interested, a polite "no thanks" will do. Keep walking. Again, prices are *never* final at the bazaar. Always haggle. After a while you might even enjoy it, but you'll always wonder if you could have done better! *Yeniceriler Caddesi; open daily except Sunday, 8:30 am to 7 pm.*

More Sights & Excursions

You could easily spend a week discovering the treasures of Istanbul. This section is for those who are lucky enough to have more than a day here. Starting again in Sultanahmet, pay a visit to the **Museum of Turkish & Islamic Art**. This fine museum is housed in the former Ibrahim Pasa Palace and is located near the Hippodrome. *Atmeydani 46; open daily except Monday, 9 am to 4 pm; $.* In Beyazit, there are a couple of large mosques that you might want to add to your inventory. These are the **Yeni Camii**, or New Mosque *(west end of Eminönü)* and the cavernous **Sülemaniye Mosque** *(Sifahane Sökak, adjacent to the University)*. Both mosques are closed to visitors at prayer times. The area between these two houses of worship is filled with a huge outdoor market, and there's another indoor market adjacent to the New Mosque. The indoor/outdoor **Spice Bazaar** is officially called the Egyptian Bazaar – you can smell it before you can see it. Although food items are the number one type of merchandise here, you can find a little of everything. *Hamidiye Caddesi; open daily except Sunday, 8 am to 7 pm.* West of Beyazit are a couple of attractions for those with significant extra time. The **Bozdoğan Aqueduct,** built by the Roman emperor Valens, allows traffic to pass beneath its arches. Farther out of the city are what is left of Istanbul's **city walls**. There are also several palace ruins along the walls.

North of the Galata Bridge is the **Taksim** area, the new Istanbul and its commercial hub. The **Tünel** is a one-stop underground railway that you can use to connect from the north end of the bridge to the so-called **Old Tram**, which clickety-clacks its way up the **Istikla Caddesi**, one of Istanbul's busiest shopping streets and now a pedestrian-only thoroughfare. Also of interest in this area is the **Galata Tower** which was built by the Genoese when this part of the city was reserved for foreigners on order of the Sultan. There are decent views from the top. *Buyuk Hendek Caddesi; open daily, 9 am to 8 pm; $.* At night the top of the tower turns into one of the city's most popular nightclubs. The old tram ends at **Taksim Square**, a major hub for buses and thousands of commuters. Busy at all times, the center of the square boasts the large **Republic Monument**. Somewhat beyond Taksim along the Bosporus waterfront are a series of palaces. The first and best is the **Dolmabahçe Palace**, which was built in a more Western style to rival the palaces of Europe. It isn't nearly as old as most of the other sights in Istanbul. The palace can be seen only by guided tour and its perfectly symmetrical interior layout contains many beautiful rooms and exquisite furnishings. *Dolmabahçe Caddesi; open daily except Monday and Thursday, 9 am to 4 pm; $$.* Not far away is the **Yildiz Palace**, which now contains the **City History Museum**. The palace also has very attractive gardens. *Ciragan Caddesi; open Wednesday through Sunday, 9 am to 4 pm; $.* Back towards Taksim and then north on the busy Cumhuriyet Caddesi is the large **Military Museum**, or Askeri Müze, which has an outstanding collection of items from all eras of Ottoman and Turkish history. If you enjoy this kind of facility, be here at 3 pm and you're in for a special treat. A Turkish military band, called the **Janissary Band**, dressed in traditional colorful garb, will entertain you with a performance of music and marching. The theater's back wall opens up so that even though you're inside the building and protected from the elements, much of the action is taking place on the outside. The performance lasts for one hour. *Vali Konoği Caddesi (north end of Cumhuriyet Caddesi; open Wednesday through Sunday, 9 am to 5 pm; $. Janissary Band performance is included in museum admission price.*

No trip to Istanbul is complete until you take a boat ride on the **Bosporus**. There are numerous options (including fancy boats with fancy prices specifically designed for the well-heeled tourist), but the best way is to go to the Eminönü dock at the south end of the Galata Bridge and take the tourist ferry. During your ride on the Bosporus (which is sometimes seen written as Bosphorus or Istanbul Boğazi in Turkish), you'll see the Golden Horn and the busy harbor, pass under modern suspension bridges and see fortresses, palaces and stately homes along both sides of this waterway that separates Europe from

Asia. This can be a trip for a full day, an afternoon or just a couple of hours. You don't have to take the boat all the way to the end or even take the boat back at all. If you're in a hurry, get off at just about any stop on the European side and hop a *dolmuş* (a shared taxi cab) back to Taksim. If you want to make a full day of it, you can get off the ferry at one or more stops to do some further exploration and re-board a later boat. The ferry leaves daily at 10:30 am and 1:30 pm for sure, but there are generally two more departures per day during the summer. *Pier 5, Eminönü; $$.*

Getting to visit other parts of Turkey before or after your cruise is a big part of the travel plans for many cruise passengers. Nearby destinations along the south and north side of the Dardanelles are the site of **Ancient Troy** and the **Gallipoli Battlefield** both possible day trips. In my opinion, there's little to see in Ancient Troy (the re-creation of the Trojan Horse is best for kids) and Gallipoli is a solemn place of monuments and museums that will thrill military historians but few others. There are far better places to go, although they're much farther away. Much of what follows is available via multi-day tours available through your cruise line, but you can get them cheaper booking independently through travel agents in the United States or in Turkey. The capital city of **Ankara** is a mostly modern metropolis, although there are some ancient ruins here as well. Of most interest are the **Archaeological Museum** and the inspiring **Atatürk Memorial**, the mausoleum of the first president of modern Turkey. If you have as much as three days to spare, the very best place you can visit is the ancient region of **Cappadocia**. This fascinating place has something for everyone – beautiful and often weird scenery in the form of eroded "fairy chimneys"; churches and even homes carved into the soft rock of these formations (especially notable is the world-class Goreme Open Air Museum); traditional Turkish towns where you can see pottery being made (Avanos pottery is among the best, and you can buy it cheap); carpet factories and much, much more.

Kusadasi (Ephesus)

Port type: Day
Tourist information office: Immediately outside of port gate at Iskele Meydani & Atatürk Bulvari, ☎ (256) 614-1103

Kusadasi (ku-shah-DAH-si) is a relatively modern city by Turkish standards and the sights of this area are well suited to a day port call. Most cruise itineraries allow between six and nine hours here. Your ship will dock near the center of town and it is rare that a tender will be needed to get to shore. The downtown waterfront has a pretty promenade along Atatürk Bulvari (Atatürk Boulevard) and there's also the remains of an old fortress on a small park-like area called Pidgeon Island. It is reached by a foot bridge and makes for a pleasant stroll. Kusadasi also has a fairly large bazaar called the **Istikial Sok**.You could shop here, but I suggest saving your money for the greater shopping wonders of Istanbul. The bazaar, located near the port just off Atatürk Bulvari, is an interesting and bustling place, full of local flavor. There are also several beaches in the area. But the reason ships call at Kusadasi is not the modern city at all; it's to allow you to visit the incredible ruins of **Ephesus**. The city of Ephesus (EF-feh-siss) was a great port in ancient times (silting has moved it several miles inland over the years) and was founded in the 11th century BC. It flourished and grew, especially under Roman rule which began in 189 BC. Most of the remains seen today are from the Roman era. Excavation of the site began in 1863 and work continues to this day. Ephesus is only a 10-minute ride from the harbor. Most cruise passengers sign up on the ship for an excursion that includes transportation to and from Ephesus and a guided tour. You can save some money by taking a taxi (car rentals aren't readily available). Bargain with the driver to get a good price or you may end up paying almost as much as for the guided excursion. The driver will drop you off at the northern gate to Ephesus and will suggest meeting him at the southern gate about an hour later. If you want more time, be prepared to pay for it (you can usually wiggle some extra time out of him for no extra charge). Ephesus can be seen thoroughly in under two hours. This is one of the best-preserved ancient cities in the world and certainly one of the most impressive. Your exploration will follow the main road through the city, which runs from north to south, although there are a few side streets that are well worth exploring too. Among the structures that have been uncovered are several important temples (most notably the **Temple of Hadrian**), the baths, apartment houses and – the most famous building of all – the **Celsus Library**. The exquisite façade of this building is a sight you will always remember. On the way out you can also see the wonderfully preserved amphitheater which can accommodate more than 24,000 people. *Open daily, 8:30 am to 7 pm; $$.*

Most of the other worthwhile sights near Ephesus are located in the town of Selçuk (remember, the use of a cedilla turns a "c" into a "ch" sound). You can get to them either by guided tour or taxi. Among the better sights are the fine **Ephesus Museum** (*open daily, 8:30 am to noon and 1-5 pm, $*) and the **Basilica of St. John** (*open daily, 8 am to 5:30 pm; $*). It is reputed that the basilica is built over the site where John is buried, but historians aren't so sure. Lots of people also want to make a pilgrimage-like trip to **Meryemana**, the modest house where the Virgin Mary is said to have lived. *Open daily, 8:30 am to* *noon and 1-5 pm, $.* Many ship itineraries don't allow long enough in port to do *both* the ruins and these other sights unless your visit is very cursory. If you have to pick one, I recommend the ancient site of Ephesus.

Marmaris

Port type: Day
Tourist information office: Iskele Meydani 39, ☎ (252) 412-1035

Sun and surf are typical daytime pleasures in Marmaris. The non-cruise set waits for after dark to loosen up and go out for a night on the town. If you think this sounds unusual for Islamic Turkey, remember that the country has a secular government. Popular resort areas are like Istanbul in this regard – almost anything goes. You should, however, behave with a greater degree of decorum if you go into less-developed surrounding areas. Guided shore excursions visit the surrounding countryside and often take short boat rides to various offshore islands. The best excursions head out on the long and narrow peninsula that juts out into the Aegean west of Marmaris. Within Marmaris itself there is little to see. The large old **castle**, set on a hill that juts into the harbor off Barbaros Caddesi, is a good way to fill up some of your shore time. *Open daily, 8 am to noon and 1-5:30 pm; $.*

Less Visited Turkish Ports

Count on using tenders in these ports if your ship is more than 500 feet long. Distances to town are usually small, but some of the better sights will require a taxi ride or a planned shore excursion.

ALANYA. *Tourist information office: Kalearkasi Caddesi, ☎ (242) 513-1240.* Once a sleepy town on Turkey's picturesque southern coast, Alanya has become a bustling resort. The city sits atop a scenic promontory overlooking the Mediterranean. Among the sights are the massive ruins of a **Seljuk fortress** *(open daily except Monday, 8 am to 7 pm, $).* This includes the so-called **Red Tower**. Both historically significant sites provide excellent views. A good way to spend some time is to take a **boat ride to the caves**, which lie beneath the promontory.

ANTALYA. *Tourist information office: Cumhuriyet Caddesi, ☎ (242) 241-1747.* A lively resort with all the usual amenities and trappings of such places, Antalya (an-TAL-ya) is known for its fine beaches. Of interest besides the scenic setting (which is almost as nice as that in

Alanya) is the old **Ottoman town** that has been nicely restored. A major activity is shopping in the town's large **bazaar**.

ÇANAKKALE (Cha-nak-kah-lay): This town has a great setting near the western end of the Dardanelles on the south shore. It's within a short distance of the ruins of ancient Troy and just about everyone who calls on this port will take an excursion there. Once believed to be a fable, the place is real enough but, unfortunately, the remains are rather meager at best. There is a re-creation of the legendary Trojan horse but, as briefly mentioned earlier, it will probably be far better received by children than those interested in archaeology or history.

DIKILI: Located on the Aegean coast about mid-way between the western end of the Dardanelles and Kusadasi, Dikili is an attractive resort with the emphasis on watersports and sunbathing, but little else. You can sign up for a day excursion, but they don't go anywhere special. The possibilities are lesser ruins, typical Turkish towns and markets, but you can see better examples of all those in other ports of call.

FETHIYE (FEH-THY-eh). *Tourist information office: Iskele Meydani,* ☎ *(252) 614-1527*. This Turquoise Coast town is situated in the extreme southwestern part of the country. It isn't well known, but it probably will be – the wonderful waters here are so blue that you can see the remains of ancient cities beneath the surface (**Caunos** is an excellent nearby example). The bay on which Fethiye is situated is filled with islands. For those who like their ruins on the land, there are plenty to be seen, starting with the **crusader fortress** that sits on a hill overlooking town. Several fascinating sites nearby date back to the empire of Lycia (before 450 BC), including hundreds of tombs built into the face of cliffs. **Ancient Telmessos** is the foremost example near Fethiye. Don't miss the rock face **Tomb of Amyntas** here. Also within easy reach (and a few of the smaller ships actually have a port call there) is the **Dalyan River**, where turtles nest on the deserted beaches. This is such a marvelous area. There's an archaeological museum in town. Depending upon how much time you have, you can explore the many nooks and crannies of the coast on a locally hired sail boat. The **12 Island Boat Tour** is the most popular but, unfortunately, you probably won't be given enough time to take the ride. Negotiate with a local boat owner for the best deal.

GÜLLÜK: South of Kusadasi, this is another of Turkey's beautiful Turquoise Coast resorts. The city is located on a body of water known as the Bay of Roses. It's a great place to just relax on the beach and walk around but history buffs can venture to nearby **Didyma** (or Didima) where the remains of an ancient Greek settlement will provide you with enough awe for the day. The **Temple of Apollo** is especially impressive.

Black Sea Ports

*T*his area is not strictly part of the Mediterranean. It is separated from the Aegean by a distance of only 120 miles via the famous water route through the Dardanelles and Bosporus. Few cruises (and none by the major cruise lines) sail entirely within the confines of the Black Sea. Instead, Black Sea ports are added to some eastern Mediterranean itineraries. Because of that, and the many beautiful sights that this area contains, the Black Sea is a part of our Mediterranean exploration.

Constanta (Romania)

Port type: Day
Tourist information office: Blvd. Tomis 46, ☎ 611-429

It's likely that few Americans other than those who have sailed to the Black Sea have ever heard of Constanta, but it is Romania's second-largest city, with a population of more than 350,000. It has a long history going back to the sixth century and there are many sites remaining from its past. Constanta and the areas to the north and south of it have beaches which range from so-so to very nice. Generally, the farther you get from the center of the city, the better the beach. The port is situated at the southern end of the central business district. It is not equipped to handle larger ships, so you'll be brought in by tender. Once ashore, just about all of the surprisingly large number of sights are within the center of the city, not far from the port, and can be done on foot.

Your walking tour can begin right near the harbor along the waterfront promenade, which offers an excellent vista of the Black Sea. On or adjacent to the promenade are Constanta's **casino** and a Genoese-built **lighthouse** dating from 1860. Also here is the **Naval History Museum** which, despite the name, covers a wide range of Romanian history. *Str Traian 53; open daily except Monday, 9 am to 8 pm; $.* Before leaving the waterfront area, take a quick look at the **Saligny Monument** and, a few blocks inland, the **Mahmudiye Mosque**. The minaret is sometimes open to the public. Its 140 steps require that you be in good shape, but the sweeping views from the top are worth the effort. *Str Muzeelor.* Once you get into the center of town you'll encounter **Victoria Park** (Parcul Victoriel), which has some remains of the **city wall** built by the Romans in the third century AD. At that time the city was known as Tomis, a name you'll still see on an important boulevard. The park also has an impressive **Victory Monument**. From here, take Tomis Boulevard to reach the **Museum of Art**. *Blvd. Tomis 84; open daily except Monday, hours vary; $.* A far better choice for art lovers is the **Folk Art Museum**, housed in a beautiful building. The exhibits here will give you a much better insight into Romanian life. *Tomis 32; open daily, 9 am to 5pm ; $.* Near the museums, also located on the Boulevard Tomis, is a 19th-century mosque called the **Geamia Hunchiar**. It was constructed with stones that once were used in a fortress built by the Ottomans. The best museum in Constanta is the large **History & Archaeological Museum**, which traces the history of Constanta from ancient times and has a remarkable collection of artifacts. The most famous item to be found among the museum's extensive displays is the **Glykon Statue**. This fearsome representation of a serpent has the muzzle of an antelope but the eyes and ears of a human. In this part of the world, the Glykon has become associated with Constanta. The attractive square on which the museum sits contains some notable antiquities. Don't miss the **Roman mosaic** that dates from the third century. It was discovered in 1959 during the construction of a train station and is remarkably well preserved. In order to keep it that way it has been placed inside a modern-looking glass enclosure. *Piata Ovidiu 12; open daily except Monday, 10 am to 6 pm; $.*

If you still have some time left you might want to hop on a bus heading to the northern part of Constanta, where you'll find the attractive **Tabacariel Park**. The park lies on the southern edge of a lake of the same name which is connected to another lake called **Siutghiol**. Among the other sights in this fashionable part of town are a **Planetarium** and the **Dolphinarium.**, which are both great for kids as well as adults. *Blvd. Mamaia 255; open daily, 9 am to 8 pm; $.* There are more activities for young ones in the nearby **Children's Park**.

Odessa (Ukraine)

Port type: Day
Tourist information office: vulitsya Derybasivska 13, ☎ 223-983

This interesting city makes a good day-long destination. The relatively modern seaport facility (Morsky Vokzal) can handle most of the ships calling at Odessa so that you don't have to use a tender to get ashore. The port is only a few blocks from the heart of the city and almost all of the worthwhile attractions are within walking distance. For those places that are farther away, buses, trams and taxis are available. Although you can easily see Odessa on your own, keep in mind that tourism and its related services aren't that well developed in the Ukraine so that you may feel more comfortable with a guided shore excursion.

An on-your-own tour begins right across the street from the ship terminal where you'll immediately encounter the famous **Potemkin Steps** (192 of them). These lead up to the attractive street known as **Prymorsky Bulvar**, where a statue of Richelieu stands (not the cardinal of France, but a duke who was once governor of Odessa). At the northwest end of Prmorsky Bulvar is **Vorontsov Palace**. This baronial mansion is quite interesting and offers excellent views of the harbor from its perch above the waterfront. *Hours are unpredictable, $.* From the palace a pedestrian bridge leads along a pathway that ends at Odessa's **Art Museum**. *Vulitsya Pushkinska 9; open daily except Wednesday, 10:30 am-6 pm; $.* Retrace your route back to Prymorsky and proceed just past the Potemkin Steps to a small square, in the middle of which sits the **Pushkin Statue**. Several of Odessa's best museums are in this vicinity. In fact, four museums are lined up in succession – the **Literature Museum** *(vulitsya Lanzheronovska 2; open daily except Sunday, 10 am to 6 pm; $)*; the **Archaeology Museum** *(vulitsya Lanzheronvska 4; open daily except Monday, 10 am to 5 pm; $)*; the **Museum of Maritime History** *(vulitsya Lanzheronvska 6; hours vary; $)*; and, a few blocks west, the **Regional History Museum** *(vulitsya Gavannaya 4; open daily except Monday, 10 am to 4:30 pm; $)*. The Literature Museum contains many interesting exhibits on such notable writers as Chekhov, Gogol, Pushkin and Tolstoy. The archaeology exhibits focus on finds from the Black Sea region, and the history museum concentrates on the story of Odessa.

There is less to see away from the city center. Some people like to visit the overcrowded and generally inferior (compared to most Black Sea resorts) beaches either side of the city center. Of greater interest are the numerous **catacombs** that have been carved into the sandstone cliff that Odessa occupies. There are more than 600 miles of tunnels. The most popular is reached by bus route 87 to **Nerubayske**. The catacombs here were used by partisans during World War II and the **Museum of Partisan Glory** is now housed inside. Because of the confusing maze of passageways it is best to secure the services of a guide to see the catacombs. Even if the guide doesn't speak English (most likely), you will find their directional assistance invaluable. *Open daily except Sunday, 9 am to 4 pm (until 2 pm on Saturday), $.*

Varna (Bulgaria)

Port type: Day
Tourist information office: Musala 3; no telephone

Varna is almost as interesting as Constanta, so don't spend too much time at the beach (which runs along the eastern edge of downtown, if you're interested). The port can accommodate most ships and is located along the waterfront boulevard known as Primorski. All of the sights covered here sit within a box-shaped parcel of a half-mile on each side that begins immediately north of the Primorski. There is no need for guided tours or transportation. Just put on a comfortable pair of walking shoes and get started.

From the port, bear to the right on Primorski and begin your tour about 500 yards later at the fine **Maritime Museum**, which documents the role that the sea has played in Varna's history. It is located in the attractive **Primorski Park** (bordered on one side by a broad boulevard of the same name and on the other side by Varna's public beach). If your port call is more than a half-day then you should have time to take in the **Aquarium** here (behind the Maritime Museum). *Museum and aquarium are open daily except Monday, from 10 am to 5 pm, as are all of Varna's other public museums; $ each.* Continue on Primorski until it ends at a large square and bear left up Slivnitsa until you reach the **Museum of History and Art**. Housed in a Renaissance-style building that used to serve as a school for girls, the museum has a large collection of beautiful religious icons. Most of the museum's exhibits are on regional archaeology. *Dimitar Blagoeu & Blvd. Slivnitsa; open daily except Monday, from 10 am to 5 pm; $.* A short walk to the west on Saborni and then left on Vladislav Varenchik will bring you to the large plaza known as the **Nezavismost**. Of brief interest here is the brightly colored **Opera House** and the imposing **Assumption Cathedral** (do step inside). On the far side of the plaza is Varna's main market. Depending upon when you arrive, it could be a hive of activity. The Nezavismost continues to the southeast. After making your way through the second part of the square, head south until you reach the **Ethnographic Museum**. This museum will give you a better insight into traditional Bulgarian life and culture through its collection of art and artifacts. *Panagyurishte 22; open daily except Monday, from 10 am to 5 pm; $.* Work your way south back to Primorski and turn left. In a few blocks you'll reach the remains of the **Roman Baths**. *ul. Han Krum 1; $.* Just north of the baths is the **City Historical Museum**. The exhibits provide a quick way of learning a lot about Varna. *8 Noemvri; open daily except Monday, from 10 am to 5 pm; $.* A couple of blocks farther north are the **Roman Thermae**, another group of baths. If you've had your fill of baths or are short of time you can skip this last stop. There is a nice Orthodox church here.

Yalta (Ukraine)

Port type: Day
There is no tourist information office but you can try the travel agency at the Hotel Yalta, ☎ 350-142

The history of this part of the Crimea goes all the way back to the ancient Greeks and it has had a succession of rulers. The Russians gained control only in 1783. The tzars immediately recognized it as a good place for summer palaces and the city became a resort. Despite its long history, most of the important buildings date only from the 19th and 20th centuries because it is only then that this city of 90,000 became a popular resort. Despite its small size, Yalta is of great historic significance. Known to millions of students because of Alfred Lord Tennyson's *The Charge of the Light Brigade* (commemorating the Battle of Balaklava in the Crimean War), Yalta took an even more important seat on the stage of world history as a host city to one of the three conferences of Allied leaders during and immediately after the Second World War.

The port can handle ships of up to 750 feet long, so you may have to tender in. However, it is only a few blocks from the city center and the attractions along the attractive waterfront promenade. There are also buses and trolleys to help you get around but limited tourism facilities (at least in the Western sense) make it just as wise to book an excursion from your cruise line.

A walking tour of downtown Yalta begins with the waterfront pedestrian-only promenade known as the **Embankment**. From here, as it sweeps around Yalta Bay, you can appreciate the beautiful setting, a verdant narrow strip of land between the mountains and the Black Sea. Turn right off the promenade at Kirova and walk to the **Alexander Nevsky Cathedral**, a golden yellow structure with the traditional onion-shaped domes of a Russian orthodox church. However, the building itself, which dates from around 1900, is in the neo-Byzantine style. *Vulitsya Sadova.* Also in the downtown area, just off Kirova as you head back towards the waterfront, is the base station of a chair lift that takes you up to **Darsan Hill**. At the top is a lookout that somewhat resembles a temple. It commands fine views of Yalta and the sea. A couple of miles inland from the waterfront are two more attractions. First is the **Chekhov House & Museum**, where the author came in the hope of alleviating his tuberculosis condition. Its collection of his memorabilia will be of interest to those who like his literary works. *Vulitsaya Kirova 112. Open Wednesday through*

Sunday, 10 am to 5pm (closed last day of the month); $. The **Polyana Skazok** is a weird place that translates into something like "Fairytale Glade." It contains numerous life-size characters from Russian and Ukrainian fairy tales and sits amid a lovely natural setting. *Two miles past the Chekhov House; open daily, 8 am to 8 pm; $.* Both attractions can be reached by bus from the city center.

The very best sights of Yalta are a short ride from town. Buses and taxis are available for those who don't wish to sign up for the guided shore excursions. Three miles to the east of town are the beautiful **Nikitsky Botanical Gardens**, which contain almost 30,000 different species from all over the world, including many tropical varieties that are supported by Crimea's warm climate and copious sunshine. The gardens cover a large area. I suggest you take the bus to the upper gate and walk down to the lower gate to re-board the bus heading back into Yalta. *Open daily, 8 am to 7 pm; $.* Opposite the lower gate is the attractive **Prymorsky Park**, which heads down to the waterfront.

There are even more attractions along a 10-mile stretch heading west from Yalta along the waterfront. Buses stop near each attraction, so you don't have to rent a car (something that isn't that easy in the Ukraine). The first stop is only a couple of miles from Yalta. **Livadia Palace** was built in 1911 for Nicholas II, the last of the Russian tsars. This is where the Yalta Conference was held. The structure, built mostly of white Crimean granite, is flanked by lovely gardens and overlooks the sea. A mile-long walking path leads through the gardens. The Italian Renaissance-style palace has an Arabic courtyard. It now houses Yalta's historical museum and an art gallery. *Open daily except Wednesday and the last day of the month, 8 am to 7:30 pm; $$.* Back on the bus, you'll soon reach the famous **Swallow's Nest**. This postcard-perfect structure (you'll recognize it featured in various media) sits rather precariously atop a sheer cliff above the sea. It was built in 1912 for a German businessman and now serves as a restaurant. You can walk around on the outside balcony without eating there, but the restaurant is a good place for a bite as well. Swallow's Nest is rather small, but certainly a unique and beautiful place. A couple of miles farther down the road is the **Ai-Petry Mount Cable Car**, which takes you to a spot offering superb views. Finally, less than two miles farther, is Alupka and the fantastic **Alupkinsky Palace**, built in 1828 for an eccentric English-educated count named Vorontsov (and thus the palace is sometimes referred to as the Vorontsov Palace). Because of his fondness for Britain, one side of the house has Scottish architecture and the other is Arabic. The wonderfully manicured grounds are graced by marble lions and magnificent gardens fill terraces both above and below the house. *Open daily except Monday, 8 am to 9 pm; $.*

Less Visited Black Sea Ports

NESSEBUR (BULGARIA): This quaint historic village is surrounded by pretty rural countryside. There really isn't much to see or do here, so if the usual meet-the-locals excursions don't appeal to you, consider heading off to relatively nearby Varna.

SOCHI (RUSSIA): Sochi is nestled snugly between the sea and the foothills of the dramatic Caucasus Mountains. Its isolated position in the far eastern end of the Black Sea makes it almost completely unknown to Western travelers. The Soviets decided that this would be a good place for a health resort – it has natural mineral springs – and began to develop it in the 1930s. Although it never reached its full potential, it's an interesting little place that's now becoming increasingly commercialized, filling up with flea markets and tacky tourist traps. However, the **Art Museum** and the **Town Historic Museum** are both worth visiting. The former is at *Kurortny Prospekt 51 and is open daily except Monday, 10 am to 1 pm and 2-5 pm. The latter, at ulitsa Ordzhonikidze 29, has the same hours.* The **Navaginskoye Fortress** is the principle historic attraction, but you may also choose to visit the **Arboretum** along Kurortny Prospekt. The best way to see this multi-leveled facility is to take the cable car to the top and work your way down on foot. *The arboretum is open daily, 8 am until 8 pm; the cable car operates from 9 am to 5 pm; $.*

A NOTE TO MIDDLE EAST VISITORS....

The highly volatile and quickly changing status of the Middle East as a tourist destination requires some warning. Potential problems are a possibility when visiting such places as Lebanon, Syria and even Israel. Lebanon and Syria are not often frequented by Americans. In fact, legal restrictions sometimes prohibit their travel here. Only a few cruise lines (all European) pay port calls in Lebanon or Syria. Americans have not been the victim of any special unwanted attention in these countries, but it is certainly advisable to check with the US Department of State to determine if there are any travel advisories or restrictions in effect *before* booking your cruise.

The situation in Israel is quite different. Tourism is extremely important here and most of the main-line cruise ship operators include Israel in their eastern Mediterranean itineraries. Again, American visitors in Israel have not been the target of attacks but the increased hostilities between Israelis and Palestinians that began in the early fall of 2000 are a cause for concern. Violence within Israel escalated in the final months of 2001, although a new "truce" just before the year's end had calmed things considerably as this book went to press. At a minimum, it could force closing of selected historic sites from time to time. While independent travel in Jerusalem and throughout Israel has always been an easy and effective way to get around, you might want to give extra consideration to the possibility of taking a supervised shore excursion. The tour operators, at least, will know about places to stay away from while you're in the area. As of press time, no cruise lines had altered their itineraries, but it is a possibility.

Lebanon & Syria
Less Visited Ports

BEIRUT (LEBANON). *Tourist information office: rue Banque du Liban & rue de Rome intersection,* ☎ *340-940.* The never-ending political problems and fighting in Lebanon keep Beirut from being frequented by cruise ships. A period of relative stability during the last decade has seen major rebuilding in the city center. The current situation in Beirut is stable enough, but many visitors will feel more comfortable on a guided shore excursion than traveling solo. No matter how you explore, try to see the following sights. In the central business district you should see the **Omari** (or Grand) **Mosque** at the intersection of rue Weygand and rue Maarad; numerous **Roman ruins**, including the baths and a small remaining part of a once grand colonnade; and the elaborate Ottoman-built **Grand Serall** marketplace. Beirut also has a large number of excellent museums, the best of which are the **National Museum**, the **Sursock Museum** and the **American University of Beirut Museum (AUBM)**. The National Museum has always been among the best museums of its type in this part of the world. It documents the long and turbulent history of Lebanon all the way back to prehistoric times. *Rue de Damas & Ave. Abdallah Yafi; open daily except Monday, 9 am to 5 pm; $.* The

Sursock is a nice art museum with a so-so art collection but a fantastic building made of lavish white Italian marble. *Rue Sursock, Achrafiye section; hours vary.* The AUBM tends to cover some of the same ground as the National Museum so, although it is an excellent facility, you don't have to do both of them if time is limited. *On the American University campus off rue Bliss; open Monday through Friday, 10 am to noon and 2-4 pm.* Also, do try to get to the western side of the city, where you can see **Pidgeon Rocks**, a group of small offshore islands. They're especially scenic before sunset.

TARTOUS (SYRIA): Because the United States and Syria don't see eye-to-eye, even fewer ships stop in Tartous. At present, only those European-owned cruise lines and those that cater to Europeans come here, and even they don't visit in large numbers. Regardless, Tartous is a pleasant place to see and the **medieval walls** that enclose the **old city** are the main sight. The tourism industry is not highly developed in this area, so I'd recommend a guided shore excursion for this port call. Excursions to Damascus are also a possibility, but I wouldn't recommend going because, allowing for travel, you won't get much time to see the city. The time would be better spent in Tartous.

Israel

*T*he Holy Land lies at the eastern end of the Mediterranean Sea and is a popular destination for adherents of both Christianity and Judaism, as well as those of the Islamic faith. Even the non-faithful will appreciate the historic nature of this region. Some logistical background is in order before we begin to explore. Cruise ships call on either Haifa or Ashdod (the latter is considered the port for Jerusalem). However, because Israel is such a small country it is possible to use *any* port as a jumping-off point to reach *any* Israeli city. The Egged Bus Cooperative provides most of Israel's urban and inter-city transportation and there is also train service between Tel Aviv and Haifa on one line and Tel Aviv and Jerusalem on another. But the greatest flexibility comes with a rented car. Whether you're in the area for just a day port call or on an extended pre- or post-cruise land tour, I recommend getting your own transportation. Independent touring in Israel is a far less expensive way to see more of the country than you will on guided shore excursions. Again, because of the Palestinian situation, you might feel more comfortable on a guided tour. The following chart will give you an idea of just how close things are to one another in Israel.

ROAD MILEAGE BETWEEN ISRAELI CITIES					
	Ashdod	Haifa	Jerusalem	Tel Aviv	Tiberias
Ashod	–	80	45	20	105
Haifa	80	–	95	55	40
Jerusalem	45	95	–	60	100
Tel Aviv	20	55	60	–	85
Tiberias (Galilee)	105	40	100	85	–

Sightseeing in the ports and cities of Israel is arranged as follows: Haifa will include both Tel Aviv and the Galilee region under its *More Sights & Excursions* sections because it is the closest city to these places. Jerusalem will be considered with Ashdod and its *More Sights & Excursions* section will also include points of interest that are located farther to the south.

Ashdod/Jerusalem

Port type: Gateway/Day

Tourist information office: Safra Square (City Hall complex), ☎ 639-5660/. There's a smaller office at the Jaffa Gate.

Ashdod is a convenient jumping-off point for trips to Jerusalem and Tel Aviv, just 25 miles to the north. It is now considered to be Jerusalem's port, and when it first opened the port in Tel Aviv lost much business. It's capable of accommodating any cruise ship and sits just a half-mile from the center of Ashdod. But most visitors don't come to Israel to see Ashdod – they quickly move on to Jerusalem. If you have some spare time in this modern planned city, you can visit what is left of the once formidable early Islamic fortress of **Fatimid**. The fortress is outside of town and can be reached by Bus #5 or taxi. Good views are available from the **Yaffa Ben-Ami Memorial Hill** which overlooks Ashdod.

Few cities in the world match **Jerusalem** in their significance to people. Holy to three of the world's major religions, the city's historic sites are worthy of the importance placed on Jerusalem by millions of people. To Jews it is the city of King David and the Temple and it pre-dates the Christian era by more than a thousand years. For Christians it is the city of Christ for this is where he was tried and crucified. And to Muslims it is the city where the prophet Mohammed ascended into heaven. It is the type of place that needs no great introduction so let's get on with what there is to see. If you have only a single day in Jerusalem, concentrate on the **Old City**. This area is contained within the **walls** that were built in the 16th century by Suleyman the Magnificent, although almost all of the important sites within the walls are much older. You can usually enter the Old City via one of seven gates. A good place to start is the **Jaffa Gate**, which separates the Old and New Cities. Be sure to ascend the walls at some point in your tour because it is a thrilling experience to see the Old City from this vantage point. The walls are only about 1½ miles around. Unfortunately, you can't make a complete circumnavigation of the roughly rectangular Old City because one section is closed due to security considerations. No matter – just go down and climb up to the ramparts once past the closed section. *Open Saturday through Thursday, 9 am to 4 pm, Friday until 2 pm; $.* Before we get beyond the Jaffa Gate area you should see the **Citadel**, also known as the **Tower of David**. The towers and minarets are splendid from an architectural standpoint, and the museum here is of similar quality, focusing on ancient Israeli history. *Open daily from 9 am to 5 pm (2 pm on Friday and Saturday). Free ($ for the evening sound and light show; inquire as to schedule).* Many of the Old City sights lie just to the east of the Jaffa Gate. First among these is the **Church of the Holy Sepulcher**, built on the ground where most scholars agree that Christ was crucified and buried, and where religious scholars say the resurrection took place. Considering the importance of this location, the church itself is not aesthetically pleasing. *Open daily, 5 am to 8 pm.* At the nearby **Lutheran Church of the Redeemer** you can climb the tower for some excellent views. *Muristan Road; open daily except Sunday, 9 am to 1 pm and 1:30-5 pm; $.* The **Wohl Archaeological Museum** is an excellent facility that will appeal to history buffs. *Hakara'im Road; open daily except Saturday, 9 am to 5 pm (till 1 pm on Friday); $.* There are many other churches in the Old City, where walking the narrow streets is a walk back in time.

In the southeast corner of the walled city is a rectangular block that is within its own walls. This is the famous **Temple Mount**, or Haram ash-Sharif. The former name is the one used by Jews and the latter is what Muslims call it. For simplicity I shall refer to the area as the Temple Mount. Of all of Jerusalem's sacred sites, Temple Mount is the most significant, especially to Muslims and Jews. Facing out from here in the southwest corner is the **Western Wall**, one of the most sacred areas to Jews. It's the only remaining piece of the Herod's great Temple. You will always encounter people (mostly men) at prayer here and proper decorum should be observed at what is, in effect, an outdoor house of worship. The same applies *at all times* inside Temple Mount. Indeed, non-Muslims have to use certain entrances and will find that small areas are off-limits altogether. Don't make a scene – just comply.

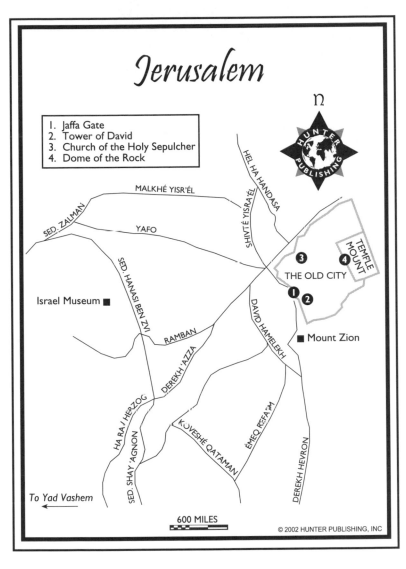

Jerusalem

1. Jaffa Gate
2. Tower of David
3. Church of the Holy Sepulcher
4. Dome of the Rock

MALKHÉ YISR'ÉL

SED. ZALMAN

YAFO

SHIVTÉ YISRA'ÉL

HEL HA HANDASA

Israel Museum ■

SED. HANASI BEN ZVI

RAMBAN

DEREKH 'AZZA

HA RA'J HERZOG

SED. SHAY 'AGNON

KOVESHÉ QATAMAN

EMEQ REFA'IM

DAVID HAMELEKH

DEREKH HEVRON

THE OLD CITY

TEMPLE MOUNT

③ ④
❶❷

■ Mount Zion

To Yad Vashem
←

600 MILES

© 2002 HUNTER PUBLISHING, INC

PORTS OF CALL

The focal point of this area is the spectacular **Dome of the Rock**. The dome, a brilliant bright gold that is easy to spot from any high point throughout Jerusalem, covers the rock where, according to religious tradition, Abraham was prepared to sacrifice his child and where Mohammed rose into heaven. You may be a little disappointed to know that the current "gold" isn't the original, nor is it even gold. The beautiful exterior façade of the structure is elaborately designed. *Open daily except Friday, 8 am to 11:30 am and 12:30-3 pm; $;*

Western Wall open at all times; no admission. Another architectural masterpiece is the **Al-Aqsa Mosque**. Its origins are somewhat obscure and there isn't even general agreement as to whether it dates from the sixth or eighth century. Either way, it is old and it is beautiful. The two structures cover only a small part of the Mount. The rest is primarily a large open area dotted with many smaller "domes" and other structures to protect items of historic but mostly religious significance. There are also many fountains. One particular interesting place is the **Stairs of Scales of Souls**. This is where, according to Islamic belief, the soul will be weighed and judged. Immediately beyond the walls to the east is the **Mount of Olives**, which affords an excellent bird's-eye view of the entire Old City. Also on the Mount are the **Garden of Gethsemane** and the **Tomb of the Virgin Mary**. *Jericho Road; open daily, 8 am until noon and 2:30-5 pm.*

More Sights & Excursions

A second day in the Jerusalem area should include additional time for strolling around the Old City. However, it's also a good time to expand your horizons to the New City and beyond Jerusalem itself. In the New City, just south of the walls, is **Mount Zion**, best known as the site of **David's Tomb**. Several attractions are located farther west, including the Israeli parliament building (the **Knesset**) and the **Israel Museum**. This ultra-modern structure contains some more traditional design elements and houses a vast collection of artifacts and exhibits chronicling thousands of years of history. *Givat Road; open daily from 10 am to 5 pm except on Tuesday (4-10 pm); Friday (10 am to 2 pm) and Saturday (10 am to 4 pm); $$.* **Yad Veshem** is Israel's Holocaust memorial and is a beautiful but solemn place of contemplation. *Off of Herzl Road; open daily except Saturday from 9 am to 4:45 pm (Friday to 1:45 pm).* A popular activity, one that is considered a pilgrimage by some, is to follow in Christ's footsteps by stopping at each of the Stations of the Cross on the way to **Calvary** via the **Via Dolorosa**.

Some important destinations are south of Jerusalem. Only a few miles away is the biblical town of **Bethlehem**. The security situation in Bethlehem is often debatable and visitors are advised to make local inquiry before setting out there. Farther away is **Masada**, which can be reached by car or Egged bus. It's about 80 miles from Jerusalem. (There are shorter routes, but they involve poor roads and going through the West Bank, which is not advisable.) Masada was first constructed about 100 BC atop a 1,200-foot cliff and was expanded about 60 years later by Herod the Great. By the time Jewish rebels took it over there were two palaces and a lavish bath, among other structures. The Jews added a synagogue and more buildings. It was at Masada where the rebels made a heroic stand against Roman legions in 73 BC. At the end, when defeat was imminent, the defenders committed suicide rather than surrendering. Although the ruins of Masada are not in a good state of preservation (excavations began in 1963), there is enough here to give a good impression of what the fortress was like during that era. Moreover, the panorama of desert, mountains and sea from the top is awesome and is almost worth the ride by itself. Ascent to the site is via cable car. *Open Daily, 8 am to 5 pm (till 4 pm on Friday); $$ plus $ for cable car.*

Haifa

Port type: Gateway/Day
Tourist information office: 48 Ben-Gurion Ave., ☎ 853-5606

Haifa is located in the northern part of the country, but Israel is small enough that you could use a day call here as a means of getting to see at least some of Jerusalem. But there's plenty to see and do in town, so don't leave immediately. Haifa has a large, modern cruise ship terminal about a quarter-mile from the heart of downtown. Taxis are plentiful, but you can also get around quite well using the local bus system. The city sits on a rounded point of land surrounded by the Mediterranean Sea and has many good beaches. Some, like **Bat Galim** and **HaShaqet Beaches**, are within a mile or so of the city center. Even nicer beaches are somewhat farther away (the **HaCarmel Beach** for example). Begin your sightseeing tour northwest of the city center in an area that begins just beyond the Bat Galim Beach. To get there, head west on Allenby Road from just south of the port area. Among the attractions here are a couple of museums, a cave and a scenic cable car ride. The **National Maritime Museum** tries to cover the entire history of Mediterranean shipping, a hard task which it only partly accomplishes. However, what is available here is still worth the price of admission. *198 Allenby Road; open Sunday through Thursday from 10 am to 4 pm (till 7 pm on Tuesday), Friday from 10 am to 1 pm, and Saturday from 10 am to 2 pm; $$.* Next door is the **Clandestine Immigration & Navy Museum**, which documents the time in the 1930s and 1940s when Zionist immigrants had to sneak through the British blockade that was being imposed at that time. *204 Allenby Road; open Sunday through Thursday, 9 am to 4 pm; $.* Close by is the **Carmelite Monastery**. A monastery has been on this site since around 1300, although the structure you see now was built in the 19th century. A church on the monastery grounds has a wonderful painted ceiling. *Stella Maris Road; open daily, 6:30 am to 1 pm and 3 to 6 pm.* From here, take the **cable car** down to **Elijah's Cave**. It is so named because it is believed to be the cave referenced in the Bible where the prophet Elijah took refuge from King Ahab and Queen Jezebel. This is a holy place to Christians, Moslems and Jews, so respect those who are praying and behave appropriately. The cave itself is not very large and not of great significance from a geological perspective. It's the cable car ride that's fun!. *Cable car leaves from 230 Allenby Road; Sunday through Thursday, 8 am to 5 pm, Friday, 8 am to 1 pm.*

Back in the city center start with the **Haifa Museum** which has exhibits on a variety of topics from art to ethnology. *26 Shabbetai Levy Street; open Sunday through Thursday from 10 am to 4 pm (till 7 pm on Tuesday), Friday from 10 am to 1 pm, and Saturday from 10 am to 2 pm; $$.* Above Allenby Road the city of Haifa rises in a series of terraced hills that are collectively known as the **Persian Gardens**. These are quite attractive and also offer a number of interesting places to explore. The best is the **Shrine of the Bab**. This is one of the two main holy places of the Baha'i faith (the other is near Chicago) and is an architectural gem that combines modern and classical forms of construction. The shrine is set amid beautiful gardens and is a memorial to the founder of the Bab faith, from which the Baha'i has been derived. *65 Sderot Hatziyonut; open daily, 9 am to noon, gardens remain open to 5 pm.* Just above the shrine is the **Gan Ha'em Park** and its many bronze sculptures. The views from both here and the shrine are impressive.

On one of the highest points in Haifa is the **Kababir** (the Muslim quarter on the hill) and its **Mahmoud Mosque**. In addition to the religious and historic significance of this site, the Kababir provides splendid views of all of Haifa and the Mediterranean Sea. You'll have to navigate a maze of streets to get here, so consider taking a taxi.

More Sights & Excursions

There are many interesting places near Haifa. If this is going to be your only Israeli port, then you'll probably spend your additional time on a Jerusalem trip. If you're staying here longer, though, a side trip to **Akko**, in the extreme north of Israel, is a very worthwhile excursion. Akko has one of the best preserved **old city** areas in Israel. Walking on the **walls** is a great way to see the sights of the old city as well as the Mediterranean Sea. Akko was important during the Crusades and the **subterranean Crusader city** is a sight that should not be missed. Nearby are the stunning **white cliffs** of Rosh Honikra, which rival the more famous ones in Dover, England. They are reached via a scenic cable car ride.

The region surrounding the Sea of Galilee is another excellent day (or overnight) destination from Haifa. The biggest city is **Tiberias** (also known as Teverya) and it has become quite a resort destination as well as a place of historic interest. As you travel here, make a stop at some of the religious sites of importance along the way, including **Nazareth** and **Mount Tabor**. At **Hammat Gader** are the splendid remains of Roman baths. Even better (but a little out of the way to the south) are the extensive ruins of the Roman-era city of **Beit She'an**. From either of those two places it's on to Tiberius. This city and the surrounding area overlooks the **Sea of Galilee** which, astonishingly, is more than 700 feet below sea level. The region is a scenic one, with waterfalls, marshlands filled with exotic bird life and numerous recreational opportunities. You can even soak in the natural hot springs here (one is adjacent to the ancient Roman baths at Hammat Gader). As you travel through this region, you'll spot the remains of many Crusader fortresses. On the north shore of the Sea of Galilee is another important biblical site – the **Mount of Beatitudes** – and nearby is another Roman city called **Capernaum**. Israeli collective farms, known as a **kibbutzim**, dot the landscape. Most welcome visitors.

Tel Aviv is another good side-trip from Haifa. *(Tourist information office: in the bus station on Levinski Street, ☎ 639-5660.)* The overall image of Tel Aviv is perhaps best seen in its modern downtown skyline of office buildings and hotels that line the broad street called the Herbert Samuel Esplanade. It separates the city from the long, wide beach along the Mediterranean. As a modern city, Tel Aviv has some excellent places that are well worth your time. The **Diaspora Museum** chronicles the lives of the Jewish population who lived in "exile." (The word Diaspora refers to all Jews who live outside of Israel; Zionism therefore considers any Jew not in Israel who wishes to be there as an "exile.") *On Klausner Street at Tel Aviv University (use Gate 2); open Sunday through Thursday from 10 am to 4 pm (till 6 pm on Wednesday), and on Friday from 9 am to 1 pm; $$.* Nearby is the **Eretz Y'Israel Museum**, actually a dozen small facilities each devoted to a specific art, such as pottery or other crafts. They complement the **Tel Qasile**, a relatively small but interesting archaeological site that is the focal point of the museum group. *2 Levanon Street; open Sunday through Thursday from 9 am to 2 pm (till 7 pm on Wednesday) and Saturday from 10 am to 2 pm; $$.* Just east of the downtown core near Rabin Square is the **Tel Aviv Museum of Art**. It has a good collection of works spanning the 19th and 20th centuries. *27 Shaul Hamelech Blvd; open Sunday through Thursday from 10 am to 6 pm (till 10 pm on Tuesday) and on Friday from 10 am to 2 pm; $$.* South of the city center near Mogen David Circle is the neighborhood of **Kerem Ha-Temanim**, also known as the Yemenite Quarter. This is the older part of the city and is filled with narrow maze-like streets and plenty of shops and markets. It makes for a pleasant stroll. Near here are the **Great Synagogue** and the **Shalom**

Tower, a shopping center on the lower floors and a good view from the 30th-floor observation deck. *Herzl Street; open Sunday through Thursday from 10 am to 6 pm, Friday from 10a m to 1:30 pm and Saturday from 11 am to 4 pm; $$.* While most of Tel Aviv is quite modern, those in search of a more traditional settlement might want to visit **Jaffa** (or Yafo). It is now part of metropolitan Tel Aviv but has a distinct character of its own and just walking its streets is a pleasant experience. It lies along the Mediterranean.

Egypt

*T*he two possible ports of call in Egypt are Port Said and Alexandria. While each has its own unique and worthwhile points of interest, most cruise passengers want to use their port time to visit **Cairo**, which is relatively nearby but, unfortunately, not near enough. So, let's look at the logistics. Some cruises stop at either Port Said or Alexandria, while others call at both ports on two successive days. In the latter case, it is sometimes possible (depending on the cruise line) to leave the ship at the first port and take an overnight land excursion through Cairo, rejoining the ship at the second port. If Cairo is something you simply must see, find an itinerary that allows you to do this. Even two days isn't really enough, but it is far better than under one day. Both Port Said and Alexandria are approximately 80 miles from Cairo. Given the relatively slow ground transportation in Egypt, a day stop to Cairo will undoubtedly leave you disappointed with your visit. If you *must* use a day port call to see Cairo, do it from Port Said since there is considerably less to see there than in Alexandria. Let's take a closer look at each of these destinations.

Alexandria

Port type: Day

Tourist information office: Midan Saad Zaghloul, ☎ 807-9885

Although it pre-dates Port Said by more than 2,000 years, Alexandria is still relatively young by Egyptian standards. It was founded in 332 BC by Alexander the Great and quickly became an important port and seat of learning. The lighthouse was one of the ancient wonders of the world and its half-million-volume library was the world's greatest for many centuries. Covering a narrow band from the Mediterranean Sea inland, contemporary Alexandria runs for more than a dozen miles parallel to the sea. Ship passengers disembark at the dock (except for a few of the largest ships that have to anchor in the harbor and transport passengers via tender). The port is just under a mile from the center of Alexandria and taxis are a good way to get into town. Alexandria's well-developed system of trams is also a good option that reaches most of the attractions. Negotiating Alexandria is a fairly easy task, so don't bother to sign up for a guided shore excursion. If you're heading to any of the several attractions away from the center, I suggest making use of the tram system.

The **Al-Corniche** is a beautiful waterfront promenade that arcs its way along Eastern Harbor. Roughly in the center is an area filled with Alexandria's finest hotels and shops. There is also an excellent beach here. The **market** (*souq*) is a few blocks inland on Faransa. Two lovely mosques are within a stone's throw of the market (**Terbana Mosque** is especially nice). Back on the waterfront, continue northwest (or take Tram 15) to **Fort Qaitbey**. This structure was built over the foundations of the ancient lighthouse by the Mamluk Sultan, for whom the fort is named. It was expanded over the years and, despite being damaged during the late 19th century, it is still quite a sight. *Hours vary; $.* The waterfront street (and the tram) goes to the point on which the fort is located and then heads south towards the **Necropolis of Antushi** at Ras At-tin in Alexandria's extreme northwest section. The Necropolis of Antushi isn't on a par with the "cities of the dead" found much farther down the Nile, but it is quite interesting. You should visit here, especially if you won't be exploring the interior of Egypt. Head back into the city center and then transfer to Tram 16 for the brief ride south to the **Catacombs of Kom ash-Shuqqafa**. Constructed in the second century AD, the site held the remains of more than two dozen wealthy Egyptians. *Open daily, 8:30 am to 4 pm; $$.* Nearby is **Pompey's Pillar** (it has nothing to do with the Roman general). Returning one more time toward the city center, a few blocks east of the tram line is the **Roman Amphitheater**, or Kom al-Dikka. Discovered less than 40 years ago, this theater is comprised of more than a dozen terraces built of white marble. It must have been stunning in the ancient sunlight because it sure still looks good to me after all these centuries. *Midan Gomhuriyya; tram 16 goes there; open daily, 9 am to 4 pm; $.* Less than a mile to the northeast is Alexandria's finest museum – the **Greco-Roman Museum**. The large collection of artifacts (almost 40,000) is nicely displayed in a series of rooms and it covers Alexandria's ancient period in fine form. Don't miss it. *5 Al-Mathaf ar-Romani; open daily from 9 am to 4 pm; $$.* From the museum continue north to the waterfront. Along the Corniche to the northeast is your final stop on this suggested tour. The **Montazah Palace** was once a royal summer retreat but is now reserved for the President of Egypt and his guests. However, the beautiful gardens are open to the public and you can get a good look at the palatial structure. It's quite a distance from the center of town so you'll want to ride a bus out here (bus route 260), or take a cab.

Cairo Side-Trip

Tourist information office: 5 Sharia Adly, ☎ 391-3454

I must emphasize that I don't see the value in visiting Cairo as a day excursion from either Egyptian port unless you have at least 10 hours off ship. Allow a minimum of four hours for transportation to and from the ship, and that gives only six hours for sightseeing, which can't even begin to do justice to Cairo's many wonders. But some people say a little is better than nothing at all. Since time is severely limited and you can't waste it trying to figure out transport, take a guided tour with the cruise line. If you're doing an overnight trip and meeting the ship at another port the following day, expect to do quite a bit more on your own. If you have only six or so hours in Cairo, be sure you see the incomparable **Egyptian Museum**. It's about three times as big as the museum in Alexandria and its highlights include the galleries of Tutankhamun and the various Mummy Rooms. *One block inland from the Corniche el-Nile (the street that parallels the Nile River), two blocks south of the 6th of October Bridge; open daily from 9 am to 4:45 pm (closed from noon to 2 pm on Friday; $$$ plus $$$ for the Mummy Rooms.* You could easily spend a day or more here alone, but limit your visit to about two hours so you'll have time to see **Giza**. This suburb of Cairo is where you'll find the great **Pyramids** and the **Sphinx**. There are many guides, both official and unofficial, so be careful who you choose if you are on your own. *Six miles from central Cairo via Al-Haram (Pyramids Road). The new subway line goes to within walking distance. Site open daily from 7 am to 7:30 pm; the pyramid chambers (which open on a rotating basis) are open only from 8:30 am to 4 pm; $$ for site plus $$ for each pyramid entered.*

More Sights & Excursions

Cairo has a modern and efficient metro system (still being expanded). It reaches to Giza, but is of limited use for getting to Cairo's most important visitor attractions. Overnight Cairo visitors can begin by allocating more time to both the Egyptian Museum and Giza. Then you should add on visits to some of the markets and mosques of **Islamic Cairo** in the area between the great bazaar or **Khan al-Khalili** on the southern end and the vast **Mosque of al-Hakim** on the north. Along the north side of the mosque are the **northern walls** and **gates** of Old Cairo. Just south of this area is the **Citadel**, which dates to the 12th century and was built by the great

Saladin. Within its walls are several mosques and museums along with nicely landscaped terraces that afford good views of Cairo; *$$*. A pleasant way to see much of Cairo is by taking an inexpensive ride on the **river bus**. You'll board the boat slightly to the north of the Egyptian Museum and run south of Giza into an area known as **Coptic Cairo**. Finally, on an island in the Nile south of the 6th of October Boulevard is **Cairo Tower**. This is a modern structure built to resemble a traditional minaret. It is a lovely sight and the views from the observation deck are outstanding on clear days. *Open daily, 9 am until at least 6 pm; $$.*

Port Said

Port type: Day
Tourist information office: 43 Sharia Palestine, ☎ 235-289

This city of more than 400,000 people didn't exist until 1859 when construction of the Suez Canal began. The canal, which is the big tourist attraction, opened 10 years later. The port is located within walking distance of the main town. Ships of less than 750 feet can dock in town, but all others require tender service. If you want to see the **Suez Canal**, take one of the guided excursions that heads south on a road that parallels the canal. Within Port Said you should take a quick look at the **Suez Canal House**, a green domed building that was, for many years, the place to go for the best canal views without going out of town. Sadly, it's now closed. Port Said does have two museums. The **National Museum** covers a broad swath of Egyptian history dating back before the pharaohs. There are better museums in Cairo and Alexandria, but you may not be getting to those ports. *North end of Sharia Palestine; open daily, 9 am to 4 pm; $.* The **Military Museum** traces important conflicts covering thousands of years with an emphasis on more recent struggles, including the two Arab-Israeli wars of 1967 and 1973. *Sharia 23 July; open Saturday through Thursday from 9 am to 2 pm and on Friday from 10 am to 1:30 pm.* You should also spend some time wandering around to admire the fine turn-of-the-century colonial architecture.

PORTS OF CALL

Tunisia

Tunis

Port type: Day
Tourist information office: Place du 7 Novembre, ☎ 341-077

Although the city sits near the location of the capital of ancient Carthage, there is little evidence of that. That's because during the Third Punic War the Romans made it their business to completely fulfill the popular jingoist expression of the day, "Carthage must be destroyed." Well, they really leveled it! Contemporary Tunis is a bustling and modern metropolis with almost two million citizens and plenty of resort facilities along with a host of places to see. The port of La Goulette can handle many ships at one time, but nothing larger than 750 feet. La Goulette is roughly six miles from downtown Tunis, but it is walking distance from the terminal to public transportation – bus, taxi or light rail. Independent travelers will find the light rail efficient and comfortable. Within Tunis itself there is also a metro system, so it's entirely possible to see Tunis on your own. However, there are cultural differences so you might feel more comfortable here with a guided shore excursion, even if you are not venturing outside the city itself.

There are many possible excursions from Tunis, including trips to the attractive suburban community of Sidi Bou Said, the resorts of the Cape Bon peninsula, the old port city of Bizerte north of Tunis, and various ruins (especially those of **Utica** and **Thuburbo Majis**). Although it's nice to get into the countryside, you only have a day and the sights within and immediately surrounding Tunis are, in my view, more worthwhile. Begin with the aforementioned site of **ancient Carthage** (on the way in from La Goulette port, about six miles from downtown via the light rail system). As mentioned at the outset, the Romans didn't leave much of the Punic city when they obliterated it in 146 BC to close out the Third Punic War. Fortunately, however, there is quite a bit to see from the era of Roman rule in the vast **Archaeological Park**, where you can admire the Roman **theater** and **baths**. The latter are among the largest Roman public baths that can still be visited in the Mediterranean. While you're here, be sure to visit the **National Museum** that sits on the top of Byrsa Hill and has an excellent view of the entire Carthage area along with informative exhibits. *Take TGM light rail to the Carthage-Hannibal Station; open daily, 8 am to 7 pm; $$ combined for ruins and museum.*

Within Tunis most places of interest are inside the old walled city (known as the **Medina**) that dates from the eighth century. Enter this area via the **Bab Bhar** (or Porte de France) on its eastern side, just under a mile from the light rail station. You could spend an entire day wandering around its maze of streets and colorful markets. The best attractions are concentrated near the center of the Medina, around the rue de la Kasbah. The two most important sites are the **Zitovna Mosque** and the **Dar Ben Abdallah Museum**. The mosque is the largest in Tunisia and dates from the eighth century. It is said to be the oldest building in Tunis still in use, and some of its columns were taken from earlier Roman structures. *Rue Jemaa Zitovna; open daily except Friday, 8 am to noon; Non-muslims can go in only as far as the courtyard.* The museum is good for learning about local history and its costume collection is outstanding. But part of the fun of visiting it is that the museum occupies a former palace. *Impasse Ben Abdallah; open Tuesday through Saturday, 9:30 am to 4:30 pm; $.* The markets (known as *souqs*) aren't as famous as the bazaars of Istanbul, but they are just as much fun. The two biggest are the **Souq el Attarine** and the **Souq des Chechias**. The former is a great place for perfume although, like all big markets, they sell a variety of goods in addition to their specialty. The Souq des Chechias is where *fezes* (traditional red hats) are made. One final attraction that you should try to find time for is the **Bardo Museum**, located two miles northwest of downtown. It can be reached by Line 4 of the metro. The museum was once a splendid palace and those surroundings will enhance your visit. The most notable items here are exquisite Roman-era mosaics that have been gathered from all over Tunisia. *Rue Mongi Slim; open daily except Monday, 9 am to 5 pm; $.*

Before we leave, it should be mentioned that a small number of cruise ships stop at the port of **Gabes** in central Tunisia. This is kind of a wasted call since there's nothing of real interest in town. However, some excursions can be made to nearby ruins, none of which are as good as you can see in the Tunis area. A better alternative if your ship comes to Gabes would be an excursion into the desert, where the scenery can be quite compelling.

Morocco

We've made it back to the western end of the Mediterranean now and will complete our exploration with a very brief discussion of the ports of the North African nation of Morocco, which mostly lies outside of the Mediterranean Sea but is an integral part of the region. Among the Atlantic ports which cruise ships regularly visit are

Agadir, Tangier, Rabat and Casablanca. All are daily ports. Regardless of which one your ship stops at, it is possible to visit one of the others (it's about 200 miles between the two farthest ports, Tangier and Casablanca).

Agadir

Port type: Day
Tourist information office: Central Market off
Avenue Sidi Mohammed, ☎ 846377

Agadir was founded by the Portuguese in the early 16th century. It sits on the Atlantic, west of the Pillars of Hercules. Much of Agadir has been rebuilt since 1960 after two devastating earthquakes, and almost as many ships seem to be visiting this port these days as other Moroccan ports, even though it has substantially less to offer. The **Kasbah** is a mostly uninspiring series of fortifications with little to see on the inside. There is a **municipal museum** with a fairly decent collection that explores local history. *Open daily except Sunday, 9:30 am to 1 pm and 2:30-6 pm; $.*

Casablanca

Port type: Day
Tourist information office: 55 rue Omar Slaoui, ☎ 271-177

Of all Moroccan ports, **Casablanca** is the most popular. While it may have many romantic connotations to Hollywood movie buffs because of the Humphrey Bogart film of the same name, Casablanca is actually the most modern and least exotic of Moroccan cities. It is also somewhat of a resort, with many fine beaches located close to the heart of the city. This bustling city of more than five million people can also be nicely divided into a modern section and a smaller and older walled city, which is called – you guessed it – the **Medina**! The Medina has several interesting mosques, the best of which is the **Al-Djemma**. *Just inside Medina gate by the clock tower at the intersection of Ave. des Forces Armeés Royales & Blvd. Houphouet Boigny.* Spend some time wandering around the Medina's crooked streets then follow the walls to its northern tip by the ocean. For here you will be met with the awe-inspiring sight of the **Hassan II Mosque**, the third-largest religious structure in the world. Although it has all of the elements of traditional mosque construction, it was completed only in 1993. Unlike most mosques, which you just visit on your own, the Hassan II offers guided tours (some in English) that are sure to enhance your appreciation of the many artistic elements throughout. Self-touring is not permitted. *Blvd. Sidi Mohammed ben Abdullah; tours daily except Friday at 9 am, 10 am, 11 am and 2 pm (sometimes 2:30 instead); $$$.*

Modern Casablanca has its share of interesting attractions too. The heart of the city (called the **ville nouvelle**) spreads out around the huge and beautifully manicured **Place Mohammed V**. This square is surrounded by some of the best architecture in North Africa. Included in this group are the **town hall, Palace of Justice** and the **Cathédral du Sacré Coeur**. Also worth a visit is the **Central Market,** just a quarter-mile away along the Boulevard Mohammed V.

Ceuta

Port type: Day
Tourist information office: Gran Vía, ☎ 509-275

Ceuta is a small enclave of Spanish territory (administratively part of Cadiz province) on a small peninsula jutting out of Morocco and I include it here following the listings for Morocco rather than with Spain because of its location on the south side of the Mediterranean. Today's city is on the site of an ancient Carthaginian settlement. Ceuta (SOO-tah) comprises seven peaks and the highest of these is thought to be Abila which, along with what is now known as Gibraltar, were the Pillars of Hercules. Today the mountain is called Jebel Musa. The cruise terminal accommodates ships up to lengths of about 700 feet. Once stepping onto dry land you're only a few hundred feet from the main part of the town. Taxis are the best way to get around if you tire of walking. Although it is small, Ceuta doesn't lack for interesting attractions, especially for those who enjoy fortresses and fortifications. Ceuta, like Gibraltar, is in a strategic location and its history is tied up with matters military.

Just a short walk south from the port is the **Foso de San Felipe**, a fortified moat begun in Moorish times. This is the best part of what remains of the city walls. From here, head east into the main part of town which sits on the narrowest portion of the peninsula and is only a few blocks wide and a half-mile long. Within these confines a short walking tour will enable you to see the **Arabian Baths** in the 13th-century Plaza de la Paz, the 10th-century **Dragon's House**, and the baroque-style **Santa Maria de la Asuncion Cathedral**. One place you should definitely spend time exploring is the **Legion Museum** (Museo de la Legíon). Exhibits document the history of the Spanish Legion (similar to the French Foreign Legion but not as well known). *Paseo de Colon; open daily except Wednesday, 10 am to 2 pm (till 1 pm on Sunday and on Saturday only from 4-6 pm).* On the north side of town along the Marina Española is the pretty **Maritime Park of the Mediterranean**. It was completed in 1995 and fronts the Mediterranean Sea. It is a tranquil place (except when the locals crowd into it on the weekends) that's not only nice to see but is good for a rest stop to break up your sightseeing activities. It has an artificial beach, pools, lakes and waterfalls, all interconnected by bridges and nicely landscaped grounds filled with sculptures. *Open daily, 11 am to 8 pm; $.*

Either road that edges the sea on the north and south sides of the town will head out toward the eastern tip of the peninsula. From here you can get some excellent views of Gibraltar and see a rock formation known as the **Monte Hacho**. Some historians feel that this (and not Abila) was the other Pillar of Hercules. By Monte Hacho is the **Fortaleza de Hacho**, first constructed in Byzantine times. Everyone who ruled has added to it over time. Also at this end of the peninsula is the **Castillo del Desnarigado**. Within the confines of the fort is the **Museo del Desnarigedo**, a small military museum. It's mildly interesting but the limited hours will make it unlikely that even military buffs will be able to stop here. Also, Museo de la Legíon (see above) is better, so don't feel cheated if you can't get here. *Open Saturday and Sunday, 10 am to 1 pm and 5-8 pm.*

Rabat

Port type: Day
Tourist information office: rue al-Abtal, ☎ 681-531

Fortunately, cruise itineraries don't visit Tangier and Rabat. Not that Rabat isn't interesting, but it is similar to Tangier and you might have a bad case of *déja vu* if you visit both. Rabat's **Medina** (smaller and not as old as the one in Tangier) is a great place to visit a **carpet market**. Rabat's **kasbah** is brilliantly constructed at the top of a bluff that overlooks the Atlantic Ocean. Not only is the locale very impressive, but the **Museum of Moroccan Arts** that now calls the palace home is an excellent facility. *Adjacent to the Bab Oudaia gate to the Kasbah; open daily, 9 am to noon and 3-5 pm; $.* Back in the Medina you should visit the Tower of Hassan (Tour Hassan). This is the minaret of what was to have been a grand mosque. It was destroyed by an earthquake before it was ever finished. Also on the site is the elaborate **Mausoleum of Mohammed V**. *Blvd. Abi Radraq; open daily, hours vary.* Finally, a visit to Rabat should include some time for the remains of the Roman city of **Sala**. *South end of Ave. Yacoub el-Mansour; open daily, 8:30 am to 6 pm; $.*

Tangier

Port type: Day
Tourist information office: 29 Blvd. Pasteur, ☎ 938-239

Tangier (or Tanger) sits like Agadir just outside of the Mediterranean beyond the Pillars of Hercules. Its port facility is capable of berthing just about any cruise ship and it's unlikely that you'll come ashore by tender. The center of Tangier is a half-mile from the dock; you can either walk or grab a taxi. The town has a wild feel to it, although as the tourism facilities mature it becomes easier for visitors to get around and see things. The city has a modern section and an old one – the walled **Medina**. The Medina is the heart of city and nowhere is there more activity than in the main square, the **Petit Socco**. Within a few blocks of the Petit Socco are the lovely **Church of the Immaculate Conception** and the **Spanish Church** on the rue as-Siaghin. Just outside the northwest end of the walls off the Grand Socco are Tangier's primary **mosque** and the **Mendoubia Gardens**. But the single biggest attraction in Tangier is just north of the Medina. The famous **Kasbah** is the hilltop location of the sultan's palace known as the **Dar el-Makzhen**. (Just as you found acropolises galore in Greece, so too will you encounter Kasbahs throughout the cities of North Africa. It is a generic name rather than one single location.) The palace was constructed in the 17th century and has now been converted into a wonderful museum of Moroccan craft arts. But the sumptuous surroundings, including the courtyards, gates and the beautiful Sultan's Gardens, will not let you forget that this was once a royal palace. *In the Kasbah; open daily except Tuesday, 9 am to 3:30 pm; $$.* On the north side of the Kasbah walls is a good vantage point that looks out over the Atlantic side of the Strait of Gibraltar.

Sunny Atlantic Isles

Many of the islands off the coast of North Africa that are provinces of Spain and Portugal are immensely popular vacation destinations, especially for sun-starved northern Europeans. Specifically, the Canary Islands, Madeira and the Azores are delightful places to visit. Although I haven't given them the full port treatment, some itineraries do include these islands among their ports of call. This brief summary is intended to provide you with enough information to determine if these are stops for you. Additional information can be requested from the national tourist offices of Spain and Portugal (see *Addendum* for contact information). You can have an enjoyable day sightseeing on each of these islands and rarely, if ever, a problem concerning time allotments.

Canary Islands

Spain's **Canary Islands** (Islas Canarias) consist of seven major islands. The most important for visitors are Tenerife, where the city of Santa Cruz de Tenerife is located, and Gran Canaria. The largest city on that island is Las Palmas de Gran Canaria and should not be confused with Palma de Mallorca. Other oft-visited islands in the group are Fuerteventura, Lanzarote and La Palma. The Canary Island chain extends over an area of almost 400 miles from east to west. Santa Cruz de Tenerife is almost in the middle and is about 690 miles southeast of Casablanca and 900 miles southeast of Cadiz. The mountainous islands are volcanic and feature many high peaks. The biggest one, Pico de Tenerife, reaches an altitude of 12,172 feet. The mountains rise abruptly form the narrow low coastal area so they often seem even more immense. The Canaries enjoy a mild and equitable climate. There is little rainfall and most of that occurs during the winter months. Resorts line the beautiful beaches and there is plenty of recreation, especially watersports. Visitors can also wander through pretty cities with lots of historic areas and take in some of the beautiful mountain scenery. The main islands offer a selection of excursions from which to choose.

Maderia

Madeira is a smaller group of islands, only two of which are of significance. The main one is called Madeira and is the location of the largest city, Funchal. A province of Portugal, Madeira is about 565 miles east of Casablanca and 750 miles southeast of Lisbon. Its climate, scenery (one mountain rises to 6,059 feet) and general orientation are much like that found in the Canaries.

Azores

Similar to both of the above island groups are the **Azores** (Açores). There are nine islands in this group, although only a couple are inhabited. The largest island is São Miguel. The Azores lie about a 1,000 miles due east of Lisbon, which makes them a less viable place to visit on a cruise unless it's part of a trans-Atlantic crossing.

Addendum

National Tourist Offices in the US

Many countries with two offices shown below may have additional office locations. Due to space considerations, I have listed only two main offices.

Bulgaria

www.mtt.govrn.bg/tour-info
Bulgarian Tourist Information Center
41 East 42nd Street, Suite 508
New York, NY 10017
☎ (212) 573-5530

Croatia

www.htz.hr
Croatian National Tourist Office
350 Fifth Avenue, Suite 4003
New York, NY 10118
☎ (800) 829-4416

Cyprus

www.cyprustourism.org
Cyprus Tourism
13 East 40th Street
New York, NY 10016
☎ (212) 683-5290

Egypt

www.egypttourism.org
Egyptian Tourist Authority
630 Fifth Avenue, Suite 1706
New York, NY 10111
☎ (212) 332-2570

Egyptian Tourist Authority
8333 Wilshire Blvd., Suite 215
Beverly Hills, CA 90211
☎ (323) 653-8815

France

www.francetourism.com

French Govt. Tourist Office
444 Madison Avenue
New York, NY 10022
☎ (212) 838-7855

French Govt. Tourist Office
9454 Wilshire Blvd., Suite 715
Beverly Hills, CA 90212
☎ (310) 276-2835

Gibraltar

www.gibraltar.gi/tourism; e-mail tourism@gibraltar.gi.
No office in the United States.

Greece

www.gnto.gr
Greek National Tourist Office
645 Fifth Avenue
New York, NY 10022
☎ (212) 421-5777

Israel

www.goisrael.com

Israel Govt. Tourist Office
800 Second Avenue
New York, NY 10017
☎ (212) 499-5650

Israel Govt. Tourist Office
6380 Wilshire Blvd., Suite 1718
Los Angeles, CA 90048
☎ (213) 658-7462

Italy

www.enit.it

Italian Govt. Travel Office
630 Fifth Ave., Suite 1565
New York, NY 10111
☎ (212) 245-5095

Italian Govt. Travel Office
12400 Wilshire Blvd., Suite 550
Los Angeles, CA 90025
☎ (310) 820-1898

Lebanon

www.arab.net/lebanon
The National Council of Tourism in Lebanon does not maintain an
office in the US. You may contact the Lebanese Embassy at:
2560 28th Street NW
Washington, DC 20008
☎ (202) 939-6300

Malta

www.visitmalta.com
Malta Government Travel Office
350 5th Avenue, Suite 4412
New York, NY 10118
☎ (800) 753-9696

Monaco

www.monacotourism.com
Monaco Tourism
565 Fifth Avenue
New York, NY 10017
☎ (212) 286-3330

Morocco

www.tourism-in-morocco.com
The Moroccan National Tourist Office has no US office. You may
contact the Moroccan Embassy at:
1601 21st Street NW
Washington, DC 20009
☎ (202) 262-7979

Portugal

www.icep.pt
ICEP-Portuguese Tourist Office
590 Fifth Avenue, 4th Floor
New York, NY 10036
☎ (212) 719-3985

Romania

Romanian Government Travel Office
14 East 38th Street
New York, NY 10016
☎ (212) 545-8484

Spain

www.okspain.org
Tourist Office of Spain
666 Fifth Avenue, 35th Floor
New York, NY 10103
☎ (212) 265-8822

Tourist Office of Spain
8383 Wilshire Blvd., Suite 960
Beverly Hills, CA 90211
☎ (323) 658-7188

ADDENDUM

Syria

www.syriatourism.org
The Syrian tourist organization does not maintain an office in the
US. For information you may contact the Syrian Embassy at:
2215 Wyoming Ave. NW
Washington, DC 20008
☎ (202) 232-6313

Tunisia

www.tourismtunisia.com
Tunisia does not have a tourist office in the US. You may contact
their embassy at:
1515 Massachusetts Avenue NW
Washington, DC 20005
☎ (202) 862-1850

Turkey

www.turkey.org
Turkish Tourist Office
821 United Nations Plaza
New York, NY 10017
☎ (212) 687-2194

Ukraine

www.ukremb.com
There is no Ukraine tourist office in the US. You may contact their
embassy at:
3350 M Street NW
Washington, DC 20007
☎ (202) 333-0606

Cruise Lines

For general cruise information, including details about the various
lines, contact:
Cruise Lines International Association
500 Fifth Avenue
New York, NY 10110
☎ (212) 921-0066
www.cruising.org

Celebrity Cruises
1050 Port Boulevard
Miami, FL 33124
☎ (800) 437-3111
www.celebritycruises.com

Crystal Cruises
2049 Century Park East
Los Angeles, CA 90067
☎ (800) 446-6620
www.crystalcruises.com

First European Cruises
95 Madison Avenue
New York, NY 10016
☎ (888) 983-8767
www.first-european.com

Holland America Line
300 Elliott Avenue West
Seattle, WA 98119
☎ (800) 426-0327
www.hollandamerica.com

Norwegian Cruise Line
7665 Corporate Center Drive
Miami, FL 33126
☎ (800) 327-7030
www.ncl.com

Princess Cruises
24305 Town Center Drive
Santa Clarita, CA 91355
☎ (800) 774-6237
www.princess.com

Royal Caribbean Int'l
1050 Caribbean Way
Miami, FL 33132
☎ (800) 327-6700
www.royalcaribbean.com
www.rccl.com

Seabourn Cruise Line
6100 Blue Lagoon Drive
Miami, FL 33126
☎ (800) 929-9391
www.seabourn.com

Costa Cruise Line
200 South Park Road
Hollywood, FL 33021-8541
☎ (800) 462-6782
www.costacruises.com

Cunard
6100 Blue Lagoon Drive
Miami, FL 33126
☎ (800) 728-6273
www.cunard.com

Fred. Olsen Cruises (Eurocruises)
33 Little W. 12th Street
New York, NY 10014
☎ (800) 688-3876
www.eurocruises.com
www.fredolsencruises.co.uk

Mediterranean Shipping Cruises
420 Fifth Avenue
New York, NY 10018
☎ (800) 666-9333
www.msccruises.com

Orient Lines
1510 SE 17th Street
Ft. Lauderdale, FL 33316
☎ (800) 333-7300
www.orientlines.com

Radisson Seven Seas Cruises
600 Corporate Drive
Ft. Lauderdale, FL 33334
☎ (800) 477-7500
www.rssc.com

Royal Olympic Cruises
805 Third Avenue
New York, NY 10022
☎ (800) 872-6400
www.royalolympiccruises.com

Silversea Cruises
110 E. Broward Blvd.
Fort Lauderdale, FL 33301
☎ (800) 722-9955
www.silversea.com

ADDENDUM

Star Clippers
4101 Salzedo Street
Coral Gables, FL 33146
☎ (800) 442-0551
www.starclippers.com

Windstar
300 Elliott Avenue West
Seattle, WA 98119
☎ (800) 258-7245
www.windstarcruises.com

Car Rental Companies

Auto Europe
☎ (888) 223-5555
www.autoeurope.com

Avis
☎ (800) 230-4898
www.avis.com

Europcar (National Car Rental)
☎ (877) 940-6900
www.europcar.com

Hertz
☎ (800) 654-3001
www.hertz.com

Kemwel
☎ (800) 576-1590
www.kemwel.com

Sixty Car Rental
☎ (800) 800-6000 (Dollar Rent-a-Car is their US travel partner)
www.e-sixt.com

International Ferry Lines

*F*ew of these ferry lines have a United States representative. The best way to secure information about their services is to browse their websites (most of which are English language). If you wish to speak with them over the phone, check their website for a number to call.

Company	Website	Area covered
Adriatica de Navigazione	www.adriatica.it	Croatia/Greece-Italy
Bland Shipping	www.blandgroup.gi	Gibraltar-Morocco
Buquebus	www.buquebus.com	Spain-Morocco
Comarit	www.comarit.com	Spain-Morocco
Compagnie Tunisienne de Navigation	www.tunisienet.com/ctn	France/Italy-Tunisia
Euroferrys	www.euroferrys.com	Spain-Morocco
Grandi Navi Velocia	www.condeminos.es	Spain-Italy
Hellenic Mediterranean	www.ferries.gr/hml	Greece-Italy
Islena de Navigacion		Spain-Morocco
Jadrolinija Line	www.jadrolinija.tel.hr	Croatia-Italy
Limadet	www.dsmaroc.com	Spain-Morocco
Losinjska Plovidba	www.island-losinj.com	Croatia-Italy
Meridiano Line		Italy-Malta
Minoan Lines	www.minoan.gr	Italy-Greece
Poseidon Lines	www.ferries.gr/poseidon	Greece-Cyprus-Israel
Salamis Lines	www.ferries.gr/salamis	Greece-Cyprus-Israel
SEM	www.sem.hr/english	Croatia-Italy
Strintzis Lines	www.strintzis.gr	Italy-Greece
Tirrenia Lines	www.tirrenia.com	Italy-Tunisia
Trasmediterranea	www.trasmediterranea.es	Spain-Morocco
Turkish Maritime Lines	www.tdi.com.tr	Turkey-Italy
UKR Ferry Shipping	www.ukrferry.com/eng	Ukraine-Bulgaria-Turkey
Virtu Ferries	www.virtuferries.com	Italy (Sicily)-Malta

Major Hotel Chains

American

Best Western
☎ (800) 528-1234
www.bestwestern.com

Choice Hotels (Comfort Inn, Quality Inn)
☎ (800) 424-6423
www.choicehotels.com

Holiday Inn
☎ (800) 465-4329
www.holiday-inn.com

Sheraton Hotels
☎ (800) 325-3535
www.sheraton.com

Foreign

ACCOR Group

This group includes numerous hotel brands. The most popular and widespread are (from least to most expensive) Ibis Hotels, www.ibishotel.com; Novotel, www.novotel.com; Mercure Hotels, www.mercure.com; Sofitel, www.sofitel.com. ☎ (800) 221-4542 for all Accor properties.

Golden Tulip Hotels
☎ (800) 344-1212
www.goldentulip.com

Minotel
No US office
www.minotel.com

Hotel Booking Services

There are countless on-line reservation services booking European hotels. I have found that the best approach is to search the Web for "Hotels + country name." Try **www.hotelbook.com**, which represents a number of major chain properties throughout Europe, as well as scores of independent places. **Utell** is another good one, www.utell.com, ☎ 800-448-8355.

Index